American diplomacy and the
narcotics traffic, 1900-1939

Arnold H. Taylor

American diplomacy and the narcotics traffic, 1900-1939

*A study in international
humanitarian reform*

Durham, N. C.

Duke University Press

1 9 6 9

*Printed in the United States of
America by Heritage Printers, Inc.*

To the memory of my mother and father

Preface

International efforts to control the traffic in narcotic drugs reflect a dualistic interplay of humanitarian and political influences in international relations. It was within the political context of the Opium War that the misuse of opium first attracted widespread attention in the Western world near the middle of the nineteenth century. Opium consumption was regarded then, however, as a problem peculiar to the East, especially China. It was to help China rid itself of this problem and thus take its place in the international community as a stable and prosperous nation capable of carrying on mutually profitable trade relations with the West that the United States inaugurated the international antidrug campaign in the first decade of the twentieth century.

Up to the outbreak of World War I China's welfare was the chief consideration underlying American promotion of the movement. At the same time, however, it was discovered that Western nations, and particularly the United States, had a substantial drug problem of their own. After the war, therefore, the United States paid increasing attention to its own drug situation, and China's difficulties were relegated to a secondary though still very important place.

Though morally inspired and promoted by the United States with missionary vigor, the antidrug campaign was carried on within a highly political context. Many nations, because of economic and social conditions in their territories, were reluctant to take drastic steps to suppress the traffic in and consumption of narcotic substances. From the standpoint of the United States, the movement was conceived within the framework of a broad interpretation of the Open Door policy in regard to China. It was complicated and sometimes retarded by the American attitude toward the League of Nations, Japanese designs on China, and recognition of the Soviet regime in Russia.

Despite the intrusion of political considerations, a highly complex (and imperfect) system of international control of the drug traffic based largely on principles advocated by the United States had been put into effect by the outbreak of the Second World War. Nevertheless, the problem of drug addiction remained acute in the United States and other nations as well. Efforts to ameliorate the situation were continued in the postwar period under the auspices of the United Nations.

The literature on the narcotic drug traffic and the efforts to curb it is voluminous. That the United States has played a prominent role in these efforts is generally known, but the role has not heretofore been given adequate, organized historical coverage. This study is thus an attempt to fill a gap in the existing literature on the subject by discussing in detail, within the context of the principles, motivations, and objectives of American foreign policy, the nature and extent of the activities of the United States in promoting consideration and solution of the problem. As such, it is a study in international relations and humanitarian reform.

My debt to others for assistance is large. The labor of research was eased considerably by the assistance given me by the personnel of the Foreign Affairs Section of the National Archives, particularly by Mrs. Patricia G. Dowling and Mr. Albert Blair, and of the Manuscript Division of the Library of Congress when I was working on this study as a doctoral dissertation at the Catholic University of America. For permission to consult the records of the State Department later than 1930 I am indebted to the late Dr. E. Taylor Parks of the Historical Division of that Department. As my advisor, the late Dr. John T. Farrell gave me considerable help, inspiration, and encouragement, for which I am deeply appreciative. I also wish to thank Sister Marie Carolyn, O.P., Ph.D., and Dr. John K. Zeender for reading the manuscript and offering many helpful suggestions. In revising the manuscript for publication, I am grateful for the encouragement of my wife Joyce, who, among other things, kept little Bradford occupied, and to the Faculty Research Committee of North Carolina College, which awarded a grant for photocopying the manuscript. The discussion in Chapter II on the opium problem in the Philippines was published in revised form as an article in the *Pacific Historical Review*, August 1967.

Arnold H. Taylor

Durham, North Carolina
March 1969

Contents

American diplomacy and the
narcotics traffic, 1900-1939

Chapter one

The United States and the opium problem
in the nineteenth century

The misuse of narcotic drugs is a problem that touches most areas of the world and goes back many centuries. The recognition of the universality of the problem is, however, a rather recent development, and a concerted effort to deal with it on an international level did not begin until the opening of the twentieth century. Not until near the middle of the nineteenth century did the Western world become publicly aware of the problem, and then it was regarded as restricted to the consumption of opium in its several forms by the people of the Far East, especially the Chinese. That more and more Western people were becoming addicted to narcotic drugs was little realized.

A significant development in the twentieth century was the discovery that there were two phases of the traffic in narcotic drugs—a Western as well as an Eastern phase.[1] The degree to which the two problems were interrelated varied from time to time. In general, the Western problem was the extensive use of opium and coca leaf derivatives and the need to suppress illicit traffic in these drugs. The problem stemmed from the manufacture and use of morphine, heroin, cocaine, and other derivatives of raw opium and the coca leaf in quantities greatly in excess of legitimate needs. The traffic in and use of marihuana, a product of *Cannabis sativa*, or Indian hemp, was also a matter of concern. The traffic in the raw materials constituted a menace in the West only in the sense that surplus supplies resulted in an excess of the manufactured products derived from them. The principal sources of these raw materials included not only the Far East, where opium production was prominent, but also Turkey, Persia, and Eastern Europe for opium and Bolivia and Peru for the coca leaf. The Eastern

---

1. The relationship between these two phases of the drug traffic is admirably explained in a memorandum in the Division of Far Eastern Affairs of the State Department, Oct. 16, 1922, Decimal File 511.4A1/1728, Records of the Department of State, National Archives, Record Group 59. Records in this group are indicated below by the symbol SDR followed by the decimal file number.

source of the coca leaf was confined to Java in the Dutch East Indies.

Opium produced in the Far East and prepared for smoking, the principal method of consumption there, played only a minor part in the domestic problem of the United States and other Western countries. The use of prepared opium was mainly confined to resident Chinese and a small number of other habitual opium smokers. Paradoxically, this form of use was the one most publicized in the United States in the first decade of the twentieth century, and it was the investigation of this aspect of the problem that led to the revelation that there was also widespread addiction to manufactured drugs.

The Eastern problem involved the areas where the poppy plant was cultivated for the production of raw opium and where the principal methods of consumption were opium smoking and eating. The main areas of this kind were Turkey and Persia in the Middle East, and China and India in the Far East. Adjacent areas, especially in the Far East, were drawn within the orbit of the traffic. Although opium was consumed in the Middle East, the chief focus of attention was on the Far East, where opium was eaten, smoked, and drunk. In China and among Chinese abroad, opium smoking was the main habit. In India, opium was eaten and also consumed in the form of a beverage. In the early twentieth century the use of manufactured derivatives of opium, prepared in Japan and in the West, began to rival the traditional methods of consumption. Thus, contrary to contemporary popular opinion, the Far East was less a source of the opium problem in the West than it was a victim of participation by Westerners in the Far Eastern opium trade and of the production of opiates in Western nations for consumption in the Far East.

During most of the period of the international campaign to control the traffic in dangerous drugs covered by this study, the traffic in opium in the Far East bore little direct relation to the drug question in the United States. Yet in the public mind in this country, the term "opium traffic" has Oriental connotations, for the earliest concern and involvement of the United States in the narcotic drug trade dealt with the Eastern phase of the problem. For example, the extent of the American involvement in the opium trade was first popularly revealed by the events leading to the so-called Opium War between China and England from 1839 to 1842. In addition, among the main efforts of the United States in the twentieth century to promote China's general prosperity and well-being was the movement which the United States initiated on an international scale to help China rid herself of the opium vice. A proper understanding of this movement necessitates a review of the conditions out of which it grew: the opium problem in the Far East, especially in China, in the nineteenth century and the nature and extent of the American involvement in that problem.

By the beginning of the nineteenth century opium had been known in China, and in the Far East generally, for at least a thousand years. Supposedly the Arabs introduced it to that area. The Middle East and India were the two principal sources of supply for the early Far Eastern trade. On establishing themselves in India in the sixteenth century the Portuguese captured the major share of that trade from the Indians and the Arabs and exported the drug mainly to China. They were later rivaled, especially in the eighteenth century, by the Dutch and the English. The islands of the East Indies became the chief markets for the Dutch opium trade, while the English competed with and soon outdistanced the Portuguese for the China market. In the nineteenth century the China market was dominated by the English. From the latter part of the eighteenth century through the first decade and a half of the twentieth century, China's foreign opium supply came primarily from India under the auspices of an opium monopoly held first by the British East India Company and later by the British crown.[2]

Throughout most of the nineteenth century the importation of Indian opium into China was on the increase. Prior to the beginning of the Opium War in 1839 the average annual importation of Indian opium increased from some 4,500 chests in the decade 1811–1821 to nearly 25,500 chests in the decade 1829–1839.[3] This steady increase continued after the war, reaching a high point in the decade 1875–1885, when the average annual importation was 82,000 chests;[4] thus opium constituted the largest single commodity imported into China.[5] During the same period the importation of Persian opium also grew, but it

---

2. The literature on the Indian-Chinese opium trade is extensive. Representative works used in this study are Wie T. Dunn, *Opium in Its International Aspects* (New York: Columbia University Press, 1920); David E. Owen, *British Opium Policy in China and India* (New Haven, Conn.: Yale University Press, 1934); and Wen-tsao Wu, *The Chinese Opium Question in British Opinion and Action* (New York: The Academy Press, 1928).

3. Owen, *op. cit.*, p. 80 n.

4. The annual averages for the following decades are estimated as follows: 1840–1849, over 37,000 chests; 1850–1859, about 68,000 chests; 1865–1875, some 77,000 chests; and 1875–1885, some 82,000 chests. *Ibid.*, pp. 209, 265 n.

5. *Ibid.*, p. 260.

never constituted more than 10 percent of the Indian import in any one year. Therefore it had no appreciable effect on the China market for the Indian drug.[6] The net importation of foreign opium into China reached its zenith in 1879, when 82,927 piculs (133⅓ pounds to a picul) were imported.[7] After the 1880's there was a gradual decline in China's foreign opium imports to the extent that by 1894 opium constituted only about 14 percent of China's total imports.[8]

The chief reason for the decline in the importation of foreign opium into China was the increasing cultivation of the poppy for the production of opium in China itself. This increase in domestic production, like the importation of foreign opium, was also a characteristic feature of the Chinese opium situation in the nineteenth century. Any accurate determination of the extent of this production is impossible, and estimates vary. David Owen concludes that by 1885 a conservative estimate would put China's opium production at twice her opium imports.[9]

Naturally accompanying the growing importation of opium and the increase in domestic production was a rise in the consumption of the drug by the Chinese. On one estimate, the number of consumers in 1835 exceeded 2,000,000.[10] By 1906, it is estimated, the number of opium smokers was nearly 13,460,000 out of a population of 400,000,-000—i.e., 3⅓ percent of the total population and 27 percent of the adult males.[11]

The Chinese government made repeated but ineffective efforts to stem the opium trade and the production and consumption of the product in China. Beginning with the imperial edict of 1729 which prohibited the importation and sale of opium for smoking, numerous edicts and regulations designed to stamp out the drug habit were promulgated, up to the legalization of the trade in 1858.[12] Even after 1858 there were nominal efforts to suppress the cultivation of the poppy and the practice of opium smoking. As is widely known, it was the efforts of Commissioner Lin in 1839 to enforce some of the existing regulations against

---

6. *Ibid.*, pp. 286–288.

7. *Report of the International Opium Commission, Shanghai, China, Feb. 1 to Feb. 26, 1909*, Vol. II: *Reports of the Delegates* (Shanghai: North-China Daily News and Herald, Ltd., 1909), p. 48. Cited below as *Report of Shanghai Opium Commission* followed by the volume number.

8. Owen, *op. cit.*, p. 331.   9. *Ibid.*, pp. 234–238, 266–267.

10. Wen-Tsao Wu, *op. cit.*, p. 27.

11. *Report of the Shanghai Opium Commission*, II, 66.

12. Owen, *op. cit.*, pp. 17, 51, 64, 65.

the importation of foreign opium that precipitated the crisis resulting in the Opium War.

In summary, the opium situation in China in the nineteenth century was characterized by increasing importation of the drug, primarily from India and under British auspices, up through the 1880's, followed by a decline largely attributable to the increase in domestic production from the 1830's on. Accompanying these developments was the considerable spread of the drug habit among the Chinese people. The efforts of the Chinese government to deal with all three aspects of the situation were a complete failure. The opium trade with China in the nineteenth century was a large-scale smuggling operation in which the British were chiefly involved. Other foreigners, including Americans,[13] were also implicated.

The first notable participation of Americans in the China opium trade was as conveyors of Turkish opium, in whose transportation to the Far East after 1805 they held a virtual monopoly. The Americans owed their monopoly to the policy of the British East India Company, which barred its ships from carrying opium and at the same time shut out private English shipping from the trade between Europe and China. For a brief period during 1817 and 1818 Americans also carried Persian opium to China; together, their Turkish and Persian cargoes contributed substantially to the flooding of the Chinese opium market. The American carrying trade in the Turkish and Persian commodity was never large, although for the seasons of 1816, 1817, and 1818, estimates of the quantity transported vary from a minimum of 6 percent of the total American trade with China to a maximum of over half. It has been contended that if silver dollars are excluded, even the minimum estimate would make opium account for 20 to 30 percent of the value of American shipments to China at that time. Between 1824 and 1830 the Americans carried to Canton between 1000 and 1500 chests of Turkish

13. The ensuing discussion of the participation of Americans in the China opium trade is based largely on the following studies: Tyler Dennett, *Americans in Eastern Asia: A Critical Study of the Policy of the United States with Reference to China, Japan and Korea in the Nineteenth Century* (New York: Barnes and Noble, 1941) and Charles C. Stelle, "Americans and the China Opium Trade in the Nineteenth Century" (unpublished Ph.D. dissertation, Department of History, University of Chicago, 1938); a portion of this work is published under the title *American Trade in Opium to China in the Nineteenth Century* (Chicago: The University of Chicago Libraries, 1941). The unpublished dissertation is relied upon here, however.

opium.[14] Small or large, the American trade with China in Turkish opium was sufficient to cause the Chinese commissioner at Canton in 1839 to think that Turkey was an American possession.[15]

The ending of the monopoly of the East India Company over the China trade in 1834 changed the character of the American participation in the opium trade. Since private English vessels could now engage in the carrying trade from Europe to China, the American monopoly of the Turkish opium trade ended, and the American carrying trade in the drug declined. To offset this decline the Americans participated increasingly in traffic between India and China.[16] The nature of that participation prior to 1839 had been shaped by the fact that Americans were barred from the carrying trade in opium between India and China. The East India Company maintained control over most of the drug produced in India, and although it forbade its own vessels to engage in the trade, it licensed "country ships," principally private English and Indian vessels, to carry the drug to China. As a result the American participation took primarily two forms: through the consignment business American firms at Canton sought to underbid British merchants in China for the opium produced in India, especially that of individual producers and merchants not under the control of the East India Company; and in imitation of the British, American firms established receiving ships or storeships which were anchored in waters around the islands near the Chinese mainland to receive the drug from carriers from India, Persia, and Turkey for subsequent smuggling into China.[17]

In comparison with the English and Portuguese, the Americans played a minor role in the Indian drug trade prior to 1839. Not over one-tenth of the total importation into China was carried on American vessels or received on consignment by American firms. This amount in turn rarely accounted for more than one-tenth of the total American trade to China in any one year.[18] The opium trade in general, however, benefited American traders far beyond their direct participation in it. Opium and furs had early been used by Americans to supplement Spanish dollars as a medium of exchange for the teas, silks, and other goods of China.[19] For a considerable period prior to 1839 silver for the purchase of Chinese commodities had constituted the largest single

14. Stelle, *op. cit.*, pp. 32–33, 51.
15. Dennett, *op. cit.*, p. 116.
16. Stelle, *op. cit.*, pp. 57–59.
17. *Ibid.*, pp. 54–57.
18. Dennett, *op. cit.*, p. 117.
19. *Ibid.*, p. 20.

item of American exports to China. The opium trade enabled Americans to substitute for specie the bills of exchange on London which the Chinese needed to purchase Indian opium. These bills of exchange were obtained by American traders through the sale of American products to England and the sale by Americans of Chinese goods in Europe. Consequently, the quantity of American specie brought to China decreased in 1826 from over $5,000,000 to less than $2,000,000.[20] In the decade 1831–1840 the importation of specie from America was reduced by 80 percent over the preceding decade.[21]

By 1839, then, the position of Americans in the Chinese opium trade was this:

American vessels carried the Turkey drug; an American receiving ship was stationed in the outer waters; and an American firm, Russell & Company, ranked as the third largest agency for Indian opium in China. But, on the other hand, Americans had lost their strategic position in the Turkish drug; American capital no longer played a dominant role in the provision of opium for American consignment; and American vessels were still barred from the carrying trade in opium between India and China.[22]

The efforts of the Chinese to bring the illegal trade in opium to a halt in 1839, which brought on the Anglo-Chinese War, caused a temporary withdrawal of the Americans from the trade. The American merchants at Canton, including those who had been engaged in the traffic, signed a voluntary pledge to refrain from transactions in opium in the future. They then addressed a memorial to Congress expressing on moral, humanitarian, and economic grounds their desire not to see the trade revived. The principal determinant of the attitude of the merchants seems to have been the fact that opium did not constitute a major part of their trade; this circumstance was coupled with the belief that the opium traffic was really an encumbrance on their legitimate business. They believed that it restricted their business by reducing the desire and purchasing power of the Chinese for their legitimate products and by jeopardizing harmonious relations with the Chinese government.[23]

American abstention from the trade was short-lived, however. By 1841 American traders had resumed their operations. Commodore Lawrence Kearny, who was dispatched to the Far East in 1842 with

---

20. Stelle, *op. cit.*, pp. 51–52.   21. Dennett, *op. cit.*, p. 73.
22. Stelle, *op. cit.*, p. 59.
23. *Ibid.*, pp. 75–76; Dennett, *op. cit.*, pp. 119–123.

orders to take action against American ships engaged in the trade, and various other naval officers sent under similar orders, were powerless to prevent such activity, since there was no American law under which opium smugglers could be punished.[24] Furthermore, as the Sino-American Treaty of Wanghia of 1844 merely withdrew the protection of the United States from Americans engaged in the trade, the participants had to worry only about eluding Chinese punishment, a fear of slight substance, for after their defeat by the British in 1842, the Chinese interfered very little with the trade and it flourished more than ever.[25]

The decades of the 1840's and 1850's saw American traders and shippers fully competing in all aspects of the opium traffic between India and China. They carried the drug from India to China, maintained receiving ships, and marketed the drug in the ports of China. While some small companies and individual merchants did participate, the American drug trade was dominated by two large firms, Russell & Company, which had also been active in the 1830's, and Augustine Heard & Company. American ships carried from 3,000 to 5,000 chests annually from India to China, and Americans in China handled about $2,000,000 worth of the drug per year.[26]

In 1858 the importation of opium into China was legalized. Paradoxically, this contributed to a decline in the American participation in the trade. American firms had been able to compete effectively in the business through the maintenance of storeships, by charging shippers less for storage than the British, even on occasion remitting the storage costs, and through preferential agreements with Parsi shippers. Legalization of the trade relieved opium of its special character as contraband and thus ended the necessity for receiving ships. The result was that small shippers could more easily engage in the trade. Because of this situation, coupled with the general decline in American shipping during and after the Civil War, American participation in the drug traffic had already dwindled to an insignificant level by the time of the signing in 1880 of the Sino-American treaty prohibiting such activity by Americans.[27]

Americans had been engaged in the Far Eastern opium trade for over a quarter of a century before the American government took

24. Stelle, *op. cit.*, pp. 86, 87; Dennett, *op. cit.*, pp. 124–126.
25. Owen, *op. cit.*, pp. 192–197.
26. Stelle, *op. cit.*, pp. 107, 141–144.   27. *Ibid.*, pp. 135–138.

official cognizance of the fact. The attention of the government was focused on the trade for the first time when the Treaty of Amity and Commerce of 1833 with Siam was negotiated by Edmund Roberts. Roberts had tried to open the trade in opium with Siam to Americans, but instead he was forced to agree to the stipulation in Article II of the treaty that opium was contraband and that Americans were forbidden to import it.[28] This prohibition was rescinded, however, by Article VII of the treaty of 1856 which Townshend Harris negotiated with Siam, whereby opium was permitted to be imported free of duty, but could be sold only to the opium farmer or his agents, who held a monopoly of the business.[29] In the commercial treaty with Japan of the same year, however, at the suggestion of Harris, the importation of opium into Japan by Americans was prohibited, and the vessels of those guilty of violating this prohibition were made subject to seizure by Japanese authorities.[30]

The opium clauses in the above treaties excited little interest among Americans, for the opium traffic itself aroused little comment except in relation to China. Even in the case of China the American public and the government exhibited no interest prior to the crisis at Canton in 1839. Then American public opinion, shaped largely by missionaries who had been in China for about a decade and by commercial interests who believed that American commerce would benefit from the abolition of the trade, decidedly supported the Chinese side of the question.[31] The British were roundly denounced for forcing the trade on China, and this denunciation remained the theme of the public's opposition to the trade well into the twentieth century. The American antipathy to the trade was expressed officially in Article 33 of the Treaty of Wanghia, which stipulated:

> Citizens of the United States, who shall attempt to trade clandestinely with such ports of China as are not open to foreign commerce, or who shall trade in opium or any other contraband articles of merchandise, shall be subject to be dealt with by the Chinese Government without being entitled to any countenance or protection from the United States; and the United States will take measures to prevent their flag from being abused by the

28. William M. Malloy (compiler), *Treaties, Conventions, International Acts, Protocols and Agreements Between the United States of America and Other Powers, 1776–1937* (4 vols.; Washington, D.C.: Government Printing Office, 1910–38), II, 1627.

29. *Ibid.*, p. 1631.

30. *Ibid.*, p. 1003; Dennett, *op. cit.*, p. 357.

31. Dennett, *op. cit.*, pp. 102, 105–106.

subjects of other nations as a cover for the violation of the laws of the Empire.[32]

The treaty provision was almost a dead letter from the start, for Americans continued to engage in the trade in the next decade to a greater extent than ever before and as freely as did the British. As Tyler Dennett points out, "the only difference between the policy of the United States and that of England, in practice, was in the extent of participation in the smuggling."[33]

The treaty provision, though unenforced, nevertheless put on record America's official disapproval of the traffic. There was no variance from this policy thereafter, although a different approach to the problem was followed for the period 1858 to 1880. This approach took the form of the legalization of the trade, in which William B. Reed, the American minister sent to Tientsin in 1858 to seek a revision of the Treaty of Wanghia, played a prominent part. In his instructions to Reed, Secretary of State Cass emphatically condemned the traffic. Reed's "particular attention" was called to "the effort of the Chinese Government to prevent the importation and consumption of opium. . . ." He was directed to "make known to the Chinese officials . . . that the Government of the United States does not seek for their citizens the legal establishment of the opium trade, nor will it uphold them in any attempt to violate the laws of China by the introduction of that article into the country."[34] The American draft of the proposed treaty contained a provision specifically listing opium as contraband, and Reed informed the Chinese commissioners that the United States would support Chinese efforts to suppress the traffic.[35]

Despite his clear-cut instructions and his initial efforts to carry them out, Reed subsequently embarked upon a different course. First he deleted the clause in the American draft treaty designating opium as contraband. He explained this action on the grounds that having observed Americans freely and openly participating in the trade, he felt that a repetition of the prohibition contained in the Treaty of Wanghia would merely make the activities of the Americans more disgraceful. Furthermore, Lord Elgin, his British counterpart, requested that the word opium be omitted in the American and Russian treaties

---

32. David Hunter Miller (ed.), *Treaties and Other International Acts of the United States of America* (7 vols.; Washington, D.C.: Government Printing Office, 1931–1941), IV, 570.

33. *Op. cit.*, p. 168.

34. Miller, *op. cit.*, III, 858.   35. *Ibid*, p. 73.

and promised in return to disregard his instructions and not attempt to secure legalization of the trade.[36] Thus both the American and British treaties of Tientsin were silent on the question of opium, and the situation remained as it was defined by the British Treaty of Nanking of 1842 and the Treaty of Wanghia.

In the supplementary treaties regulating tariffs and trade, however, opium was made a legitimate article of commerce. Reed was largely responsible for this development. In a letter to Elgin in September 1858, Reed vigorously denounced the opium traffic and the role played by both the British and Americans in it. He characterized it as "a great smuggling transaction" conducted openly and defiantly. He suggested that it be dealt with in one of two ways: that the Chinese be urged to undertake thorough suppression of it by seizure and confiscation, and that as the British government would soon be taking over the privileges and responsibilities of the East India Company in India, that it use the occasion to end the production of opium in India and its export to China; or alternatively, since it was unlikely that the Chinese would undertake effective prohibition, that they should be urged to "put such high duties on the drug as will restrain the supply, regulate the import and yet not stimulate some other form of smuggling. . . ."[37] Elgin concurred in the latter recommendation on the grounds that it would be impossible to suppress the traffic because of the ease with which opium was produced and transported as well as the great demand for it, and so legalization was the "only available remedy."[38]

In order to avoid having the United States appear to the Chinese as desiring the relaxation of their laws of contraband, Reed took no part in the negotiations on the revision of the Chinese tariff schedule. However, he accepted unreservedly the draft of the tariff agreement which Elgin sent him, in which the opium trade was legalized, and indicated his willingness to sign such a supplementary treaty on behalf of the United States. In forwarding the treaty to the State Department he defended his position as the most practicable in securing the limitation of the trade.[39] The legalization was effected in the supplementary tariff treaties to the Treaties of Tientsin by the stipulation that the import duty on opium should be 30 taels (about $44) per picul (133⅓ pounds) and that it should be sold by the importer only at the port of import, and after the sale it could be carried into the interior only by Chinese

36. *Ibid.*, p. 898.
37. *Ibid.*, pp. 73–76.

38. *Ibid.*, p. 77.
39. *Ibid.*, pp. 79–81.

as Chinese property and subject to such transit duties as the Chinese government saw fit to levy.[40]

Reed's conduct, which became fully known to the American public in 1860 when the treaties were ratified, aroused no adverse comment.[41] As a matter of fact many American merchants, diplomatic officials, and missionaries supported his view that legalization was the best method of controlling the opium traffic.[42] Indeed, one unforeseen result of this development, as already pointed out, was the relatively swift diminution of American participation in the trade. Although in suggesting legalization of the trade Reed acted in direct contravention to his instructions, he was inspired by the highest of motives.[43] This is why his course was tacitly assented to by the State Department and the American people, for in reality it did not represent a departure from the American policy of disapproval of the trade. It was a new approach, but the end desired—the control and eventual abolition of what was considered to be a harmful and unedifying commercial practice—remained the same.

The American diplomats in the field heartily endorsed and supported their government's expostulations against the opium trade. Virtually all of them believed it to be largely responsible for the degeneration of China, regarding it also as a barrier to China's adoption of Western methods as well as a hindrance to Western trade. This view was succinctly expressed by S. Wells Williams, a former missionary, in a dispatch to the State Department in 1869. He blamed the traffic for the deterioration of the resources, energy, and efficiency of both the government and people of China and cited it as a major reason why the Chinese were slow to adopt some of the improvements Western powers urged upon them.[44]

A similar view of the effects of the traffic came in 1871 from Frederick T. Low, the American minister at Peking. Among the various factors responsible for the decline and decay of China which he

40. *Ibid.*, p. 31.   41. Dennett, *op. cit.*, p. 326.
42. Miller, *op. cit.*, III, 79, 80.
43. See John Bassett Moore, *The Collected Papers of John Bassett Moore* (7 vols.; New Haven, Conn.: Yale University Press, 1944), VI, 418–419, for the defense of Reed's action against the severe strictures of H. M. Morse.
44. U.S. Department of State, *Diplomatic Correspondence and Papers Relating to the Foreign Relations of the United States*, 1869, Part I (Washington, D.C.: Government Printing Office, 1869 and continuing), pp. 511–513. This series is referred to below simply as *Foreign Relations*.

listed—"profligate expenditures of Chinese rulers" and "chronic rebellions and foreign wars"—he cited the increase in the consumption of opium as "more potent, probably than all the other causes combined." In support of this contention he echoed the statement of Williams as to the effect of the vice upon the energies and productive powers of the Chinese people, as a consumer of their earnings, and as a cause of the impoverishment of the Chinese government. In pointing out that the effects of the traffic were not limited to China, he repeated the views expressed by the American memorialists in 1839 as to the bearing of opium on trade in general. He contended that the entrance into China of 85,000 chests of foreign opium in 1869 and the native growth of an additional 75,000 chests in the same year, amounting together to $68,000,000, equaled 75 percent of the value of the tea and silk imported into foreign countries from China. This, he concluded, was a sad commentary on foreign trade.[45]

Even though Americans were free to engage in the traffic from 1858 to 1880, American diplomatic officials in China were careful to avoid giving it any encouragement. In 1876, while in the process of negotiating the Chefoo Convention revising the Treaty of Tientsin, the British minister, Sir Thomas Wade, tried to get the support of the American minister, George F. Seward, for his scheme to have the Chinese mark out a district within each treaty port in which no likin taxes would be levied on foreign goods. Outside the zones the Chinese would be free to levy taxes on any goods not in transit under transit passes. For this supposed concession the Chinese would be asked to open up a considerable number of new ports to foreign trade.[46] This proposal arose out of the repeated protests of British and other foreign merchants against the establishment by the Chinese of likin collectorates within the foreign concessions, almost at the doors of foreign warehouses, where the tax was collected on opium and other goods bound for the interior. They contended that the uneven rates assessed on the drug and the surveillance and sometimes arrest of Chinese purchasers were injurious to their business.[47]

Seward initially rejected Wade's proposal on the grounds that the Tientsin treaties gave the Chinese government the right to deal with opium as it chose after the import duty of 30 taels had been paid on

45. *Ibid.,* 1871, pp. 82–84. 46. *Ibid.,* 1870, p. 73.
47. Owen, *op. cit.,* pp. 240–241, 251–252.

it and after it had passed into Chinese hands. Wade's scheme, he charged, would have the effect of making the drug duty free at each port within a given area, a situation which neither he nor the American government would regard with favor. Upon receiving subsequent assurance from the British minister that the American interpretation of the Tientsin treaties would not be contradicted by the proposed plan, Seward gave his endorsement to the scheme.[48]

By 1880, despite the assent to legalization in 1858, the official opposition of the United States to the opium trade was so firmly established that the American commissioners negotiating the immigration treaty of that year welcomed the Chinese proposition that Americans be prohibited from further participation in the traffic.[49] Thus in Article 2 of the commercial treaty negotiated concurrently with the immigration treaty and signed the same day, the United States and China mutually forbade their subjects to import opium into each other's ports, and Americans were prohibited from trafficking in it within China.[50] It was upon this article that in the first decades of the twentieth century the United States was to base its pretensions to a superior moral position in regard to the trade, a position which, it felt, partly justified its efforts to get other nations, particularly Great Britain, to make a similar agreement with China. As a matter of fact, the Chinese skillfully used the occasion of the treaty negotiations to get a stringent provision against the trade so as to place the British in the untenable position of being the only Christian nation "forcing" the odious traffic on China.[51] In pursuit of this objective the Chinese secured a prohibition similar to that in the American treaty in treaties with Brazil and Russia,[52] although the nationals of neither of these countries were engaged to any significant degree in the trade.

The prohibition in the commercial treaty of 1880 was repeated in the first treaty between the United States and Korea in 1882.[53] Li Hung Chang, the Chinese statesman with whom the treaty was negotiated, wanted the first treaty between Korea and the Western powers to be with the United States rather than the British, for he feared that in

---

48. *Foreign Relations*, 1876, pp. 74–75.   49. *Ibid.*, 1880, p. 200.
50. Malloy, *op. cit.*, I, 239–240.
51. See the statement of James B. Angell, president of the American commission which negotiated the treaties, quoted in Dennett, *op. cit.*, p. 543.
52. *American Journal of International Law*, Supplement, III (Oct., 1909), 269, 328; abbreviated *AJIL* below.
53. Malloy, *op. cit.*, I, 1003.

any treaty with the latter the traffic in opium would be legalized.[54] He was particularly happy with the prohibition in the treaty of 1880, not because of its effect upon the minuscule American trade, but because of the impetus he hoped it would give to the antiopium efforts of the Chinese government and to the general campaign against the traffic in both China and England. He was emboldened to assume that Great Britain might now be more amenable to suggestions for the modification of the Indian-Chinese trade. He confided these hopes to the sympathetic American minister, John Russell Young, to whom he also expressed his indebtedness to the United States for the moral effect of the provision in the American treaty. Through Young, Li continuously besought the active cooperation of the United States in inducing Great Britain to agree upon a policy for the gradual abolition of the trade. He even went so far as to suggest that either Young or the American government put forth a plan to achieve this. He contended that if the Indian trade were ended China would immediately suppress the domestic cultivation of the poppy.[55]

In response to the entreaties of Li Hung Chang, Young expressed what remained American policy to 1906. He declared that while the United States had no material interest in the drug traffic, it did look with sympathetic interest upon efforts to suppress it. Nevertheless, he maintained, the problem was one between China and the government of India, the solution of which lay in a new source of revenue to replace the $50,000,000 annual revenue which India derived from opium. He felt that the problem could best be solved by "persistent agitation" and an appeal to public opinion such as had been effective in inducing England to abolish slavery in the West Indies at a great financial sacrifice and of the kind that had achieved similar results in the United States.[56] It is significant to note here that during the course of the international antiopium movement in the twentieth century a prominent feature of the pleas by Americans for swift and effective action without regard to financial considerations was the comparison of the opium problem to that of slavery. Li Hung Chang, however, felt that the opium trade was a greater evil than slavery.[57]

Over six years elapsed between the signature of the treaty of 1880 and the passage of enforcement legislation by Congress. In the interval,

---

54. Dennett, *op. cit.*, p. 461.
55. *Foreign Relations*, 1883, pp. 123–129, 181–187.
56. *Ibid.*   57. *Ibid.*, p. 125.

though American participation in the trade was slight, American merchants and shippers occasionally breached the treaty stipulations.[58] In the absence of legislation, the American legation in China was forced to rely on its moral influence to prevent such activity. Charles Denby, the American minister from 1885 to 1898, interpreted the treaty provision strictly, even to the extent of holding that Russell & Company violated the treaty by allowing an Englishman in their employ to store opium in their warehouse upon which they received a commission. The State Department upheld his conclusion.[59]

Congress finally passed the necessary legislation on February 23, 1887. Chinese violating the treaty provision were subject to a $50 to $500 fine or from thirty days' to six months' imprisonment or both. Because of an error in printing, the bill as reported from committee stipulated that Americans violating the treaty provision were subject only to the money penalty. Consular and district courts were given jurisdiction, and the opium involved in illegal transactions in China was to be seized and made forfeit by the consular courts to the United States "for the benefit of the Emperor of China."[60]

The Chinese government, fearful of interference by foreign powers with its local laws, objected to the provision calling for the confiscation of contraband opium by American consuls as contrary to Article 14 of the treaty of 1858 which recognized China's right to enforce her own laws against contraband. They contended that in ordinary cases where only forfeitures were made, coupled with a fine by the Chinese customs officials, but no imprisonment, there was no need for consular interference.[61] Their objections were met by an agreement that American consuls in China would prosecute and punish Americans engaged in the trade, while Chinese customs authorities would have the right to confiscate the opium. In case of dispute a joint investigation would be held.

If many Americans had still been actively engaged in the opium trade, it is highly unlikely that this legislation would have been sufficient to deter them. Considering the profits that had once been derived from the traffic, the money penalty was mild, and no other form of punishment, except confiscation of the opium, could be levied on the Americans. Thus the benefits of continued participation, even in viola-

58. *Ibid.*, 1881, pp. 216–217; 1887, p. 183.   59. *Ibid.*, 1887, pp. 174–175, 186.
60. *AJIL*, III, Supplement (July, 1909), 254–255 n.
61. *Foreign Relations*, 1887, pp. 211–212, 225–227.

tion of the treaty and the law, might well have far outweighed the risks involved. Therefore it was indeed fortunate that by 1880 American participation in the trade had practically ceased. The treaty of 1880 and the Act of 1887 merely provided for its official interment.

For the remainder of the century the United States contented itself with merely watching sympathetically the antiopium agitation in England and China. Believing that having cleared itself of all complicity in the traffic, it had no further material interest in it, the American government confined itself to expressions of humanitarian concern for the Chinese people. Regarding the traffic as essentially a Sino-British problem, the United States did not feel that it could justifiably interfere. This was the government's response not only to the appeals for help from Chinese statesmen but also to the supplications of American missionaries in China, who in themselves constituted an antiopium society. These missionaries worked zealously to arouse public opinion in the United States and elsewhere against the trade. They succeeded in branding Great Britain with the guilt of fostering a degenerative vice on the Chinese simply for financial profit.

Thus by the close of the century the pattern of opposition to the opium trade had been set. Not only American missionaries but the American government, American diplomats in the field, and some American commercial interests as well were denouncing the trade on moral, humanitarian, and economic grounds. In the meantime developments in the international situation in the Far East were conspiring to give the United States once again a concrete interest in seeing the traffic stopped. In addition, there were other developments in the general field of international relations, especially in regard to international cooperation in the solution of technical and humanitarian problems, which foreshadowed similar cooperative action in regard to opium and the narcotics problem in general. As a result, efforts to solve this problem were to constitute a significant aspect of American diplomacy in the twentieth century.

Chapter two

The genesis of the international
movement

The nineteenth-century setting out of which the international movement to control the traffic in narcotics arose was not confined to the specific question of opium. A major characteristic of that century was the tendency toward increasing cooperation in the international sphere on a variety of subjects. The Congress of Vienna, the Concert of Europe, the Hague and various other multilateral conferences, and the public international unions consisting of agencies concerned with multifarious problems in fields considered nonpolitical were all examples of this cooperative spirit. Most significant for this study was the extension of international consideration to nonpolitical questions. This represented an expansion of the subject matter of international relations and was marked by new types of participants in international affairs. Experts and specialists in technical and professional fields, government officials outside the foreign offices, and representatives of private interest groups and humanitarian organizations vied with the traditional diplomats in international negotiations, and sometimes replaced them.[1] Among the problems which might be designated nonpolitical which were the subjects of such negotiations in the nineteenth and early twentieth centuries were the slave trade and the traffic in women, obscene literature, liquor, and dangerous drugs. These matters were humanitarian; yet insofar as they required political activity for their ultimate solution, they were also political. Since the drug problem affected the interests of the particular states involved to a greater degree than most of the other questions, it was in that sense the more political. Its political character was enhanced by the fact that it was often entwined with other more definitely political issues.

The immediate sources to which the international antidrug campaign can be traced, however, were involved primarily with opium and kin-

1. Inis L. Claude, Jr., *Swords into Plowshares: The Problems and Progress of International Organization* (New York: Random House, 1956), pp. 14–42.

dred matters. Principal among these were the reform movement in China in the late nineteenth and early twentieth centuries; the anti-opium agitation in England; the concern of reformers in the United States with the prevalence of liquor, opium, and kindred vices among peoples in so-called pagan lands which were viewed as largely the results of the spread of Western civilization to those areas; and the discovery by the United States of an opium problem in the recently acquired Philippine Islands.

The reform movement in China began about 1898 as an effort to strengthen and modernize that nation so as to enable it to cope with both its internal and external problems. Three main factors inspired and gave impetus to the movement: the defeat of China by Japan in 1895, the continuing incursions of the Western powers, and the Boxer Rebellion which served to convince the court officials of the Empress Dowager of the necessity of reforms along Western lines in order to resist these powers and hold the loyalty of the Chinese masses. Among the major improvements undertaken were the revision of the educational system, the strengthening and modernization of the armed forces, constitutional reform through the gradual introduction of elective institutions on the Western model, and the reform of the imperial finances.[2] By far the most intensive of the reforms undertaken, and the most successful, was the movement to end the trade in opium and to suppress its production and consumption domestically.[3]

Since early in the eighteenth century the Chinese government had maintained a posture of opposition to the traffic in opium and its use. Even after the legalization of the Indian-Chinese trade in 1858, the Chinese government continued to assert its moral objections to the trade and made several representations to the British government to bring it to an end. The first decade of the twentieth century witnessed a considerable strengthening of the government's position by the development of public sentiment in China against the vice. American missionaries, by their ceaseless campaign against the use of the drug, played a major role in creating this sentiment. In 1906, for example, in a meeting with the Chinese foreign office arranged by the American minister on orders from the State Department, the Reverend Hampden

2. Meribeth E. Cameron, *The Reform Movement in China, 1898–1912* (Stanford University, Calif.: Stanford University Press, 1931), pp. 29–30, 56–58, 65–135.
3. Numerous treatises on China cover the opium reform movement there. The following discussion, however, unless otherwise indicated, is based on Cameron's work (cited above), pp. 136–159.

C. Du Bose, an American missionary in China, was instrumental in getting an antiopium campaign started.[4] Sentiment against the traffic in and consumption of the drug spread through all classes of the population. Contributing to its growth was the report of the American Philippine Opium Committee in 1904 which was translated and circulated throughout the Empire. Also furthering the movement was the agitation in England against the traffic between India and China.

The Empress Dowager launched the antiopium campaign in 1906 when in May of that year a consolidated tax on opium cultivation previously in use in seven provinces and designed to be prohibitory was extended to all of China. This was followed in September by an imperial proclamation setting forth a plan for the gradual suppression of the cultivation and use of opium within ten years. This was supplemented a month later by regulations to put the policy into effect. The government then turned its attention to the Indian-Chinese traffic.

In January 1907, the Chinese government submitted six proposals to the British government. These called for the reduction by one-tenth annually of the amount of Indian opium imported into China so that by 1916 both the Indian trade and domestic cultivation should come to an end; the stationing of a Chinese official at Calcutta to watch the trade; a doubling of the duty on the opium exported from India; the suppression of smuggling from Hong Kong to China; and the suppression of opium dens and of the sale of morphine instruments in the foreign concessions in the same manner as they were suppressed in the rest of China. The British, who as early as 1905 had already intimated through officials of the government of India that they would be receptive to proposals to reduce the Indian export, met the Chinese more than halfway. The agreement signed in 1907 between the two powers provided essentially what China had requested. Using the period 1901–1905 as a base, the two powers agreed to the annual reduction over a period of ten years of the quantity of opium *exported* from India by 10 percent of the average annual Indian export (5100 chests); the stationing of a Chinese official at Calcutta for observation but not interference with the trade; the prohibition of the import and export of prepared opium between Hong Kong and the mainland; and the suppression of smuggling. In addition, China expressed satisfaction at the orders issued to

4. *Foreign Relations*, 1906, I, 352.

British consuls to take measures against opium dens in the British concessions. The agreement was to undergo a trial period of three years, after which if it were established that China's campaign against domestic production was being effectively pursued, it should be renewed for the remaining seven years.[5]

When the Ten Year Agreement came up for renewal in the latter part of 1910 negotiations were complicated by the question of what to do with the 1800 chests of opium in bond which had accumulated by virtue of the fact that although the amount of opium exported from India had been reduced by one-tenth annually, the amount imported into China had actually increased, having been attracted thither by higher prices resulting from the decline in domestic production. As a matter of fact, 570 more piculs of opium were imported into China in 1909 than in 1908. The British wanted another three-year probationary period, but the Chinese demurred. The resulting accord of 1911 provided for the continuation of the agreement to 1917, during which time the reduction of production of opium in China was to proceed *pari passu* with the reduction of the export from India. The export from India was to cease before 1917 if China completely suppressed poppy cultivation before that time. In addition, any province would be released from the obligation of accepting Indian opium when it could prove that it had thoroughly eliminated the cultivation of the poppy and the importation of native opium. British officials were to be allowed to travel throughout China to observe the progress of suppression. Other terms provided that China would be permitted to tax Indian opium at 350 taels per chest, that chests designed for China be covered by export permits, and that responsibility for the surplus opium in bond be assumed by Great Britain and that its entrance into China be charged against the amount exported from India to China over a three-year period.[6] It is significant that in 1913 the British announced that they were ceasing to export opium from India to China, an announcement which was based on evidence that only a nominal amount of poppy cultivation still existed in China.[7] This was a tribute to the great success of the antiopium campaign which had been launched a scant seven years earlier.

5. For the text of the agreement see John V. A. MacMurray (compiler and editor) *Treaties and Agreements With and Concerning China, 1894–1919* (2 vols.; New York: Oxford University Press, 1921), I, 865–866.

6. *Ibid.*, pp. 861–864.   7. Owen, *op. cit.*, p. 348.

Meanwhile, China had given attention to another aspect of the narcotics problem. As the antiopium campaign progressed, the use of morphine in the form of antiopium pills or through subcutaneous injections in the place of opium had become of increasing concern. In the commercial treaties with Great Britain and the United States in 1902 and 1903, respectively, there were included provisions against the importation of this type of drug and the instruments for its injection.[8] In January 1909, after obtaining the consent of the other treaty powers, China put into effect the prohibition of the importation and manufacture of the drug. Through this action, coupled with the successful campaign against domestic opium production and the Indian-Chinese traffic, China had by 1911 thoroughly proved the sincerity of its determination to end the opium menace. This demonstration of singleness of purpose against tremendous odds helped to create a favorable climate for international consideration of the problem. The British argument, used in years past, that China merely wanted to end the Indian-Chinese trade in order to increase domestic production lost all force. China's progress in combating the vice was watched closely by the Western powers, particularly by Great Britain and the United States, and public opinion in both countries encouraged and applauded her efforts.

Ever since the Opium War in 1839 sentiment in England against the opium traffic, fostered by reports of missionaries, literature on the subject, and debates in Parliament, had steadily grown.[9] With the formation of the Anti-Opium Society in 1874, renewed impetus was given to the agitation. Primary emphasis was placed on Great Britain's role in fostering the vice on China. The agitation reached its threshold in 1893 when a royal commission was appointed to investigate the opium situation in India as to the feasibility of curbing the growth, manufacture, and trade of the drug. The commission's report in 1895 whitewashed and rubber-stamped the existing situation.[10] It had the effect of vindicating the Indian government and of quieting the agitation in Parliament against the trade for ten years. It constituted a definite check on the antiopium movement in England, although expressions against the trade did not entirely cease.

8. MacMurray, *op. cit.*, pp. 351, 431.
9. For the antiopium agitation in Great Britain, principal reliance has been placed on Wen-tsao Wu, *op. cit., passim,* and on Owen, *op. cit.*, pp. 311–328, 333–335.
10. Wen-tsao Wu, *op. cit.*, pp. 133–134; Owen, *op. cit.*, pp. 318–319.

The revival of the antiopium movement in England came contemporaneously with and partly as a result of the stirrings in China and the increasing attention given by the United States to the problem, especially in the Philippines. The Philippine Opium Committee, which traveled throughout the Far East in 1903–1904, presented a report whose conclusions were almost exactly the opposite of those of the Royal Commission of 1895. The Philippine Committee was very critical of the way the British handled the opium question in their Far Eastern possessions. A softening of the official British policy was foreshadowed in 1905, however, when, as previously mentioned, officials of the Government of India let it be known that the question of the Indian-Chinese trade was open for negotiation with China. Prospects in this regard were considerably brightened by the Parliamentary elections of 1906 whereby 250 candidates pledged to support the antiopium cause were elected to the House of Commons. Thus on May 30, 1906, the following resolution was moved in that body: "That this House reaffirms its conviction that the Indo-Chinese opium trade is morally indefensible, and requests His Majesty's government to take such steps as may be necessary for bringing it to a speedy close."[11] In the ensuing debate much attention was given to the report of the Philippine Opium Committee, which was contrasted favorably to that of the Royal Commission. The resolution was passed unanimously. The change in the attitude of the British government did not escape the notice of the United States and was a factor in the American decision to initiate an international investigation of the opium problem.

The relations between Great Britain and China on the opium question formed an essential aspect of the international campaign against the drug traffic initiated by the United States in 1906. As a matter of fact, the improvement in those relations as contributed to and evidenced by the Chinese reform movement and the antiopium agitation in Great Britain supplied the necessary favorable atmosphere in which the successful launching of the campaign was assured. Without this favorable setting, the American proposal for international consideration of the drug question would most likely have been ignored or rejected. The American decision, however, had its roots in several factors, not all directly confined to opium, in which Americans evinced a special interest. Among these factors were the concern of Americans—

11. Quoted in Wen-tsao Wu, *op. cit.*, p. 150.

missionaries and their associates particularly—with the moral aspects of liquor and opium not only in China but among so-called pagan peoples in general; the desire on the part of the American government to see a strong, independent and prosperous China as a factor of stability and trade opportunity in the Far East; and the rather sudden realization that in the Philippines the United States had a Far Eastern drug problem of its own.

The United States has often been chided for conducting its foreign relations on a moralistic rather than a realistic political basis, giving to matters of secondary importance the character of vital interests and thus suffering adverse effects in the long run. Many cite aspects of our twentieth-century China policy as an example. Nevertheless, it should be pointed out that some good often comes from America's moral excursions into politics. The fact is that many of the problems of international relations are intrinsically moral in themselves and must be dealt with accordingly. Some are extensions of domestic conditions that can only be ultimately solved through international action. Many of the humanitarian problems already mentioned are examples of these conditions. Another circumstance gave a moral flavor to many of the problems cited—the fact that the nineteenth and early twentieth centuries constituted a period of great missionary activity in so-called pagan lands. This period was also an age of imperialism, in which the Western nations carried the many facets of their civilization, including their vices, to these pagan lands. Consequently, the missionaries found themselves not only concerned with civilizing and Christianizing their charges but sometimes, as a matter of self-defense, with protecting these people against the vices of their own civilization. Thus they pressured their respective governments to take action to control and prohibit the activities of their less morally inclined and more commercial-minded compatriots.

Of particular concern to the missionaries, and viewed in the same light as opium, was the liquor traffic. Their opposition to the corruption of the natives by alcoholic beverages received the hearty support of prohibition and temperance advocates at home. Consequently, in the 1890's and the early 1900's several multilateral treaties were concluded which prohibited the sale of such beverages to certain of the peoples of Africa. The United States became a party to these conventions. It adhered to the Congo Treaty of 1890 which established a liquor-free zone in the Congo,[12] and to the Brussels Treaty of 1899, which sought to increase the tax and price on liquor to a level that would be prohibitory for all the natives of Africa.[13] Although these treaties contained no reference to opium, primarily because the drug was not a problem in the areas involved, the missionaries and other reformers considered the opium traffic to be within the same general category as the liquor traffic but more harmful. Thus, in the first decade of the twentieth century the United States, in response to the importunings of these reformers, urged the inclusion of prohibitive measures against the sale of opium in the antiliquor treaties. After 1900 the matter was continuously before both Congress and the State Department.

On January 4, 1901, the Senate adopted a resolution submitted by Henry Cabot Lodge:

That in the opinion of this body the time has come when the principle, twice affirmed in international treaties for Central Africa, that native races should be protected against the destructive traffic in intoxicants should be extended to all uncivilized peoples by the enactment of such laws and the making of such treaties as will effectively prohibit the sale by the signatory powers to aboriginal tribes and uncivilized races of opium and intoxicating beverages.[14]

This resolution was supported by a petition signed by numerous individuals, reform societies, and missionary groups addressed to all the governments which had signed the treaties of 1890 and 1899. Accompanying the petition was a letter from former President Benjamin Harrison supporting the principle of the appeal and including a paragraph from his opening address at the Ecumenical Missionary Conference held in New York City in April 1900, in which he bemoaned the fact that the missionary effort in foreign lands had been hampered by those who carried "rum and other corrupting agencies . . . with our boasted civilization" to those lands. Indicative of the growing interest in the kindred problems of liquor and opium was the great demand for copies of the resolution.[15]

12. U.S. Congress, Senate, *Compilation of Treaties and Laws for the Protection of Native Races Against Intoxicants*, 56th Cong., 2nd Sess., 1901, Senate Doc. 200.

13. *Ibid.*

14. U.S. Congress, Senate, *Resolution, Adopted by the Senate January 4, 1901, Relative to the Protection of Uncivilized Peoples Against the Destructive Traffic in Intoxicants*, 56th Cong., 2nd Sess., 1901, Senate Doc. 159.

15. For the deliberations on this resolution in the Senate see U.S., *Congressional Record*, 56th Cong., 2nd Sess., 1901, XXXIII, Part 1, 526, 528; Part 2, 2291.

Without awaiting action by other nations, Congress passed a bill in 1902 forbidding Americans to sell firearms, opium, and intoxicating liquors to the inhabitants of Pacific islands having no civilized government.[16] In the meantime Secretary of State John Hay, in response to the Lodge resolution and the importunings of a group of reformers referred to as the Native Races Deputation, had proposed to the British government that it join with the United States in submitting a treaty to the other powers prohibiting the sale of intoxicants and opium to all uncivilized races. Great Britain made no reply to this proposal, presumably because of her involvement in the Boer War.[17] The United States did not drop the matter, however. In October 1906, on the occasion of the Brussels Conference for the revision of the rules relating to the liquor traffic in Africa, the United States again raised the question. President Roosevelt sent a message to the conferees urging the adoption of measures "for the universal prevention of [the] liquor and opium traffic with all uncivilized tribes and races."[18] Supplementing Roosevelt's message, the State Department sent to the American minister at Brussels for transmission to the conference copies of the Senate resolution of 1901 and Hay's endorsement of it, along with the petition of the Native Races Deputation and various other publications, so as to show the "wide interest of the American people" in the matters mentioned.[19] Thus by the end of 1906 the American government and people, on strictly humanitarian grounds, had committed themselves through treaties, legislation, and a resolution of Congress, and by representations to foreign governments, to the principle of international action to control the traffic in the twin intoxicants of alcohol and opium for the benefit of unprotected peoples. Meanwhile pressure for similar action was coming from another direction, where the principal motivation was concern for the people of China.

It is impossible to gauge how far America's interest in China's opium problem constituted a part of the general American concern for the well-being of China. The United States desired a strong, stable, and prosperous China able to resist the incursions of foreign powers and

16. *Ibid.*, 57th Cong., 1st Sess., 1902, XXXV, Part 2, 1202.

17. U.S. Congress, Senate, *Report of the Hearing at the American State Department on Petitions to the President to Use His Good Offices for the Release of China from Treaty Compulsion to Tolerate the Opium Traffic, with Additional Papers*, 58th Cong., 3rd Sess., 1905, Senate Doc. 135, pp. 1, 29.

18. *Foreign Relations*, 1906, I, 53.   19. *Ibid.*, pp. 53–55.

providing opportunities for mutually profitable trade relations. This was the essence of the Open Door policy. As already pointed out, American diplomatic officials in China in the nineteenth century had contended that opium was a formidable barrier to the fulfillment of this desire. They made much of the fact that the opium problem was sapping the economic strength of China to the detriment of foreign trade and that its suppression was a *sine qua non* for the regeneration of China, not only economically but politically and socially as well. American business interests in both the United States and China followed this line of thought, and American missionaries and other reformers hammered the point home again and again. And during the course of the international movement against the traffic the State Department toyed briefly with the idea of promoting the release of China from stifling treaty obligations which compromised China's independence and freedom of action through the medium of the fight against opium.

It was the American missionaries in the Far East, however, who played the greatest part in inducing the United States to take the lead in the movement against the traffic. So great was their role, evoking the inauguration of the movement, and in promoting the early work once the movement had been started, that in its early stages the international campaign might quite appropriately be referred to as a missionary movement—or better still, as missionary diplomacy. In China missionaries had perhaps more influence on American policy than anywhere else in the world, both as objects of American interest in the area and as shapers of American public and official opinion in behalf of China and the Chinese people. Through their reports to their churches and sponsors in America, through personal correspondence with friends, and through missionary and religious journals they stimulated public opinion favorable to the Chinese and highly sympathetic to their problems. By frequent contact with American diplomatic and consular officials in China, consultation on their visits to America with State Department officials, and letters and cables to the President, the State Department, and members of Congress, they also often helped shape American official policy in regard to China.[20]

On no issue did the missionaries exercise greater influence in both

20. John W. Masland, "Missionary Influence upon American Far Eastern Policy," *Pacific Historical Review*, X (Sept., 1941), 279–296. See also Dennett, *op. cit.*, pp. 555–577.

public opinion and official policy than on the opium question. The
literature indicating their concern is extensive. They, along with other
foreign missionaries in China, presented petitions, memorials, addresses,
and articles and reports to the press on the problem. As a group they
constituted themselves as an antiopium society. They established hospitals and clinics for the curing of addicts, and excluded from membership in their organizations and in the native churches the cultivators,
manufacturers, sellers, and consumers of opium. They took the
lead in establishing antiopium societies—for example, the Anti-Opium
League, whose first president, the Reverend H. C. Du Bose, was an
American missionary.[21] Unlike the British missionaries, the Americans
had no opposing vested interests competing for the support of the government and people at home. Therefore they were listened to. Besides,
they had a material stake in the solution of the problem. Hostile Chinese
delighted to point out the contradiction between their Christianizing
efforts and preachments and the fostering of the opium trade by their
countrymen. Furthermore, because the opium trade and missionary
activity were both protected by foreign force, they were associated
together as similar evils.[22] Occasionally, however, some recognition was
given to the missionaries for their work in opposing the traffic and
habit. On a visit to America in 1896 Li Hung Chang praised the American missionaries for their struggle against the vice.[23]

At the beginning of the twentieth century the missionary effort to
get the United States officially involved in the campaign against opium
was redoubled. The petition that the Native Races Deputation had
presented to Secretary Hay in 1900 had been prepared by two former
missionaries who had hoped that at the conclusion of the Boxer Rebellion, when international questions concerning China would be
opened, an opportune occasion would arise to bring international pressure on Great Britain to end the Indian-Chinese traffic. In September
1904 the International Reform Bureau, an organization interested in

21. The role of the missionaries in antiopium activity is well covered in James S.
Dennis, *Christian Missions and Social Progress: A Sociological Study of Foreign Missions* (3 vols.; New York: Fleming H. Revell Co., 1898–1906), II, 125–134; Kenneth
Scott Latourette, *A History of Christian Missions in China* (New York: The Macmillan Company, 1929), pp. 426–463 *et passim*, and *The History of Early Relations Between the United States and China, 1784–1844* (New Haven, Conn.: Yale University
Press, 1917), pp. 125, 126.

22. H. M. Morse and H. F. MacNair, *Far Eastern International Relations* (New
York: Houghton Mifflin Company, 1931), p. 273.

23. Dennis, *op. cit.*, p. 129.

various social reforms, with headquarters in Washington, D.C. and headed by the Reverend Wilbur F. Crafts, thought that a similar opportunity would be presented at the close of the Russo-Japanese War. Therefore the old petition, supplemented by additional signatures not only from religious and reform organizations but from business interests as well, was again presented to Secretary Hay on November 10 by a delegation of reformers who appeared before him. They stressed the moral evil of the traffic, but placed special emphasis on the detrimental effect which opium had upon trade, declaring that "the development of China means the development of commerce with China; the decay of China, the decay of commerce with China."[24] The reformers obviously thought that the appeal to the pocketbook would make a greater impression than the mere denunciation of the trade on humanitarian grounds. This emphasis on the effect of opium on commerce was to remain a characteristic feature of the remonstrances against the trade.

Secretary Hay was deeply impressed with the speakers who appeared before him and with the petition they presented. He promised to take their views into consideration, but expressed the opinion that "much more was to be hoped from an aroused public opinion" than from official action.[25] The opinion of which Hay spoke was already building up—in the United States, Great Britain, and China. The opportunity for official action came when the United States discovered that it had more than just a moral concern in China's plight, that in the Philippines there also was an opium problem the solution of which depended in large measure upon the solution of the problem in China.

When the United States acquired the Philippines in 1898, the farming out or contract system of opium regulation which the Spanish had established in 1843 was in effect. Under this system the right to sell opium was sold to a wholesale dealer who purchased the right at public auction. The opium was then retailed by his agents to the people. Its sale to and use by the Filipinos, however, except for medical purposes, were strictly prohibited. Licensed opium-smoking dens could be maintained for the patronage of Chinese only. The object of the system was twofold: to raise revenue and to prevent addiction among the Filipinos. Total prohibition involving the Chinese population was believed un-

24. Senate Doc. 135, p. 12.
25. "Memoirs in Morocco, 1904–1905," Library of Congress (cited below as L.C.), John Hay Papers, V, 315.

attainable. Under the system, Spain received annually about $600,000 silver, while the burden of preventing smuggling was placed on the contractor, thus relieving the government of the necessity of maintaining an expensive revenue service. The system was well enforced and the use of opium by the Filipinos was negligible.[26]

When the United States took possession of the islands the Spanish system was discontinued. The only substitute was the placing of a tax on the drug and the requirement that all towns forbid the establishment of opium dives. The result was a marked increase in opium consumption, especially among the Filipinos. In 1903 there were 190 opium shops in Manila alone.[27]

As early as 1899 the American missionary, the Reverend Hampden C. Du Bose of Soochow, China, called the attention of the American government to the opium situation in the islands. Declaring that the United States had a great responsibility in the matter, he set forth the principle which was to become the basic tenet of American policy throughout the international movement, that "there can be no judicious use of opium save as administered by a physician. . . ."[28] Du Bose's letter made the rounds of those organs of the executive branch of the government concerned with the Philippines—the President, the State Department, the War Department, and the Treasury Department—and finally ended up with the Collector of Customs for the Philippines. This official recommended the reestablishment of the farming-out system. He contended that as the use of opium was confined mainly to the Chinese and was impossible to stop, a high tariff on the drug as

26. Philippine Commission, Opium Investigation Committee, *Use of Opium and Traffic Therein. Message from the President of the United States, Transmitting the Report of the Committee Appointed by the Philippine Commission to Investigate the Use of Opium and the Traffic Therein.* . . . , 59th Cong., 1st Sess., Senate Doc. 265 (Washington, D.C.: Government Printing Office, 1906), pp. 3–4, 49. Referred to below as *Report of the Philippine Opium Committee.*

27. *Ibid.*, pp. 3–4. See also "Memorandum Showing the Results Obtained in Enforcement of Laws Aimed at the Total Suppression of the Opium Habit in the Philippine Islands." Records of United States Participation in International Conferences, Commissions, and Expositions, National Archives, Record Group 43, Entry 33. Because the material used in this study is State Department material, it will be cited below by the symbol SDR followed by Record Group (RG) and Entry (E) numbers.

28. Extract from a letter of Reverend H. C. Du Bose transmitted to the President by Senator McLaurin, enclosed in Frederic Amory (Chief, Bureau of Foreign Commerce) to John C. Scofield (Chief Clerk, War Department), Sept. 22, 1899, file 1023–1, 2, 3. Records of the Bureau of Insular Affairs of the War Department, RG 126. Records in this group are cited below by symbol BIA followed by file number with a dash separating the specific item from the series number.

suggested by some, which would be designed to raise its price beyond the reach of the poorer Chinese, would merely cause smuggling, an art at which the Chinese were adept and which would be facilitated by the extent and peculiarities of the Philippine coastline. His conclusion was that "as a business proposition I should say that more net revenue would accrue to the Government from the contract system than from any other that can be devised, and it will entirely relieve the Government from the necessity of maintaining an expensive Secret Service Department to prevent the smuggling of opium."[29] But there was more than just "a business proposition" involved. The views of the Collector of Customs were proscribed by the Secretary of the Treasury on the ground that the contract or farming-out system was "foreign to our administration of the revenue." He therefore recommended that no change be made in the existing practice by which opium was admitted as a legitimate article of commerce on payment of the duties imposed by the tariff act of 1897.[30] The War Department endorsed the Secretary's views. Furthermore, by the Philippines Customs Administrative Act of February 6, 1902, which removed the prohibition, so far as the Philippines were concerned, imposed by the Sino-American treaty of 1880, Chinese were permitted to import opium into the islands.[31]

By early 1903, however, the Philippine Commission, the civil government of the islands, had decided that the contract system would be best for the islands after all. The prevailing system of regulating the sale of opium by taxation and the issuance of licenses to those who were engaged in selling it, somewhat analogous to the manner in which liquor was regulated, was now deemed insufficient. The justifications for the proposed reinstitution of the contract system were the same as those given by the Collector of Customs in 1899. In the words of H. C. Ide, the Secretary of Finance and Justice, the purpose of the bill then drafted "is not to increase or diminish the sale of opium but to regulate it in such a manner that the whole operation of the system can be known to the Government and to secure a large revenue from a source not now available."[32]

29. The Collector of Customs, Philippine Islands to the Secretary of War, Dec. 21, 1899, BIA 1023–1,2,3.
    30. Secretary of the Treasury to the Secretary of War, April 2, 1900, SDR 1023–3.
    31. Customs Administrative Circular No. 129, Addressed to the Collectors of Customs by W. Morgan Schuster, Collector of Customs for the Philippine Archipelago, Dec. 13, 1902, BIA 1023–7.
    32. Memorandum by H. C. Ide, enclosed in Secretary of War Root to Secretary of State Hay, May 16, 1903, BIA 1023–7.

The bill to reestablish the contract system, as introduced in the Philippine Commission, restricted all transactions in opium from importation to consumption (except medicinal opium prescribed by a physician) to full-blooded adult Chinese. The monopoly concession for the importation, preparation, and sale of the drug was to be awarded triennially to the highest bidder, who was required to give a bond of $50,000, and importation and preparation of opium was confined exclusively to Manila. Only licensed agents of the concessionary could engage in retail transactions, and records of all transactions had to be kept by them and the concessionary. Pharmacists and druggists, however, could import opium for medical purposes and put up preparations containing it and sell them on the prescription of a physician. Revenue derived by the government from these transactions (except for the license fees of opium dealers, which were to go to the municipality in which the dealer did business) was to be used as an educational fund to pay the expenses of Filipino students sent to study in the United States by the insular government, to pay the salaries of the Filipino teachers who were paid out of the insular treasury, and to finance the construction of school buildings.[33]

The bill almost immediately aroused a chorus of protests from various residents of the Philippines, and these protests were soon echoed in America. As a new imperial power, the United States, for both domestic and international reasons, wished to avoid the charge of copying the example of the "perfidious British" in fastening the opium habit on a dependent people. Therefore, the first group of protests to reach Washington caused Secretary of War Root to cable to Taft, the Civil Governor of the Philippines, warning him that American public opinion would not sanction a bill regulating the opium traffic which could be interpreted as promoting that traffic.[34]

As the bill moved rapidly toward passage by the Philippine Commission, appeals were made directly to President Roosevelt. Two weeks before the "third reading" of the bill, Bishop Homer C. Stuntz, the Methodist presiding elder in Manila, sent a cablegram to Crafts of the International Reform Bureau urging him to approach the President immediately in the matter.[35] Crafts sent several communications to

33. Copy of the "Proposed Law," BIA 1023–13. See also *Report of Philippine Opium Committee*, p. 3.

34. Root to Taft, June 5, 1903, BIA 1023–10.

35. Legislative Committee, International Reform Bureau to President Roosevelt, June 5, 1903, BIA 1023–16.

President Roosevelt and then set out to organize what became a highly effective protest movement. On June 11, with only four days remaining before the bill was due for final passage, the International Reform Bureau had two thousand petitions printed on telegraphic blanks. These were sent to influential persons throughout the country, who signed and mailed them to the President.[36] By this time Roosevelt had already responded to Crafts's remonstrances. Disturbed by the import of the proposed law, he demanded a full report on the matter from the War Department.[37] Root thereupon ordered the postponement of final passage of the bill pending receipt and study of a report from the Philippine Commission, not only on the situation in the Islands but also on how the subject was treated in Japan and Burma.[38]

The postponement of the passage of the bill gave the opposition in both the United States and the Islands time to crystallize. The President and the State Department were inundated with petitions and other forms of protest from ministers, churches, missionaries and missionary societies, businessmen, congressmen, educational institutions, temperance and prohibition societies, and other various and sundry individuals from all over the country.[39] Their remonstrances included assertions that the proposed monopoly would increase the traffic in and consumption of opium because the monopolist would try to increase sales in order to increase profits; that to prohibit the use of opium by Filipinos while allowing the Chinese to use it would be both ridiculous and immoral; that the United States would be following the bad example of England and would be thus departing from its traditional policy in regard to the traffic; and that in general the bill was simply bad morals and bad policy. The petitioners favored instead the adoption of a system of prohibition similar to that which then prevailed in Japan.

The protests eventually reached such volume that in order to dispel any notion that the government in Washington approved the bill, the War Department, with the endorsement of President Roosevelt and

36. For Crafts's activities see *ibid*. Also Wilbur F. Crafts, "Diplomacy and Agitation," Speech Before the U.K. Branch of the International Reform Bureau's British Council, n.d., SDR, RG 43, E 36.
37. Roosevelt to the Secretary of War, June 6, 1903, BIA 1023–14.
38. Colonel Edwards, Chief of Bureau of Insular Affairs to Taft, June 9, 1903, BIA 1023–25.
39. Root to Roosevelt, July 18, 1903; Root to Taft, July 22, 1903, BIA 1023–49; B. F. Barnes, Acting Secretary to the President to Root, July 20, 1903, BIA 1023–50; Taft to Root, July 23, 1903, BIA 1023–51.

Governor Taft, considered publishing the correspondence between
the Department and Taft on the issue. Roosevelt and Root had expressed reservations about the bill from the beginning.[40] On June 17,
Root again informed Taft of the vigorous opposition in America to
the bill. He suggested that the Philippine Commission consider the
feasibility of absolute or qualified prohibition of the importation of
opium into the islands, a step which he believed Congress would be
inclined to make possible by the removal of any barrier in the customs
law to such action.[41] About three weeks later he came out fully against
the proposed monopoly bill, citing essentially the same arguments
against it as those made by the protesters. He recommended instead that
a law be passed prohibiting all importation of the drug, except for
medical purposes, and confining all retail transactions to sales between
druggists and to persons specifically licensed to purchase the drug. Importers and druggists should be required to keep a record of all their
transactions.[42]

While the government in Washington was attempting to clarify its
position, the Philippine Commission was holding hearings to ascertain
the opinion of the islands' residents. Four main groups were concerned
with the monopoly bill: the Filipinos, the Chinese, the missionaries,
and the Commission itself. In general the Filipinos did not object to the
proposal, since it constituted essentially a restoration of the Spanish
system, which had been effective in preventing the spread of the habit
among them. Taft claimed that "not a single Filipino or Spanish paper
. . . opposed the bill."[43]

The Chinese in general opposed the proposed legislation. Their opposition stemmed from mixed motives. In fact, the first protest to reach
Washington came from the Chinese consul-general in Manila on behalf
of Chinese dealers in the drug, who naturally opposed the establishment
of a monopoly of transactions in the drug, because this arrangement
would put them out of business.[44] A later petition from Chinese merchants argued against the proposed monopoly system on the grounds
that the monopoly would raise the price of opium to the detriment of
poor Chinese, who would either die or try to secure money illegally

---

40. See above, pp. 34–35.
41. Root to Taft, June 17, 1903, BIA 1023–25.
42. Root to Taft, July 10, 1903, *ibid*.
43. Taft to the Secretary of War, July 13, 1903, BIA 1023–46.
44. Copy of Memorandum of the Chinese Legation, Washington to the Secretary
of State, April 22, 1903, BIA 1023–6.

in order to purchase the drug. It was further contended that the monopolist's desire for profit would lead him to sell opium to Americans and Filipinos, and that his agents would falsely accuse others of smuggling, and under the guise of examining a person's goods for suspected opium, would rob innocent people of their possessions.[45] Still another petition, containing 561 signatures, many of them fictitious, argued against the bill on moral grounds, contending that the contract system would increase the use of opium, debauch their countrymen, and encourage the consumption of the drug among young men by giving it an air of respectability.[46]

To fight the bill more effectively, Chinese merchants hired an American, Major W. H. Bishop, as counsel. He was given 6,000 pesos with which to conduct the campaign. Bishop circulated petitions drawn up by the Chinese merchants among the Chinese; to many of these papers fictitious names were attached. He also paid for telegrams sent to Washington by the three American newspapers in Manila and by other individuals protesting on moral grounds against the bill. In testimony before the Philippine Commission he admitted that his clients really wanted the licensing of opium dens, but that they would prefer prohibition to the contract system because prohibition could be more easily evaded.[47] It is therefore clear that Chinese opposition to the bill was not based primarily on humanitarian considerations but on the fear by the consumers of a rise in the price of opium and the fear on the part of merchants and opium dealers of being put out of business.

The leading and most effective opposition to the proposed monopoly bill came from the American missionaries in the islands. Their protestations were led by the Methodist presiding elder, Bishop Homer C. Stuntz, and by the Episcopal bishop of the Philippines, Charles H. Brent. Listened to perhaps with the greatest respect was Bishop Brent, who had accompanied Taft and several other members of the Philippine Commission on their journey to the islands in 1902. As his views were typical of those of the missionary body, some extended consideration of them is justified.

Bishop Brent regarded the opium question as essentially a moral question and transactions in the drug as a "social vice . . . a crime." He

45. Acting Chinese Consul General to A. W. Ferguson, Executive Secretary, May 19, 1903, BIA 1023–86.
46. See "Petition B," BIA 1023–95. Two hundred and eight of these signatures were written by the same hand. Twenty were not names at all.
47. Taft to the Secretary of War, July 13, 1903, BIA 1023–46.

believed that the monopoly system would cause an increase in the consumption of opium, from both legitimate and illicit sources. He also objected to the system on the ground that the government would be deriving revenue from a "polluted source" whose use for educational purposes would be a case of destroying character to build up character. He urged the American government to take advantage of the opportunity "to create a new era in opium legislation in the East" by having the Philippine Commission go to the limits of its authority in suppressing the traffic in and consumption of the drug.[48]

Taft and the Philippine Commission favored the bill and were prepared to enact it into law. They regarded the bill as a forward step in preventing the spread of the drug habit among the Filipinos. As the system had been successful in this regard under the Spanish, they contended that to make the drug permissive to the Chinese, who constituted only about 2 percent of the population and of whom they claimed nearly half were already addicted, was a small price to pay for the achievement of what they deemed to be the greater goal. They defended themselves against the charge of wanting to follow the example of the "perfidious British" by pointing out that the Anglo-Indian system was maintained solely for revenue, while the motive behind the system advocated by them was solely restrictive, revenue being only incidental to the enforcement of the system. As they saw the matter, the only "practicable" restraint on the use of opium would be an increase in its price beyond the purchasing power of the bulk of the consumers, a result which they believed the monopoly system would effect. They reiterated the argument made as early as 1899 that because of the personal motive and knowledge of the monopolist, smuggling would be a minor problem. They criticized the opponents of the bill, in the case of the missionaries who were prohibitionists on principle, as lacking a proper understanding of the Far Eastern opium situation, and in the case of the Chinese dealers and consumers, as being motivated by ulterior considerations.[49]

The members of the Philippine Commission opposed a policy of prohibition for the islands. Their objection to such a policy was based on the contentions that it would lead to the corruption of the police

48. Brent to James F. Smith, Commissioner of Education of the Philippines, Manila, July 6, 1903, BIA 1023–68. Copy also in L.C., Bishop Charles H. Brent Papers, Box 6.

49. The views of Taft and the Commission were set forth in a long despatch from Taft to Root, July 13, 1903, BIA 1023–25, 46.

and customs service which were already subjected to great temptations owing to Oriental conditions, and to the blackmail and persecution of Chinese by Filipino municipal authorities. In addition it would induce smuggling which would be almost impossible to suppress, and by confining the sale of opium to druggists, it would spread the habit among the Filipinos, since most of the druggists were Filipinos whose stores, like the country stores in the United States, were gathering places for the people. They argued further that most of the Chinese used opium moderately as a sedative and that "the effects are probably not worse than those of liquor among Americans."[50]

The arguments on both sides of the question merely foreshadowed the positions taken by the contending sides during the international campaign. In the case of the Philippines, these views were sincerely held. Taft and the Commission, however, realized that the American public regarded opium smoking in a somewhat different light from the way they regarded the liquor habit. They were conscious, too, not only that the fate of the proposed bill depended on American public opinion, but that the American people were watching, many critically, how the United States conducted its first experiment in colonial rule. They therefore did not wish to discredit this experiment by insisting on a system of opium control which was regarded by most Americans as both "bad morals and bad policy" and contradictory to the blessings which many had claimed would come to the inhabitants of the islands from the imposition of American civilization on them. The administration in Washington, which had played so great a role in the acquisition of the islands, also wished to avoid any action that would possibly discredit America's imperialist venture.

As a result of these considerations, the Philippine Commission, though refusing to yield to the clamor for prohibition, nevertheless suggested an alternative to the proposed contract system. They recommended a plan whereby a high license would be imposed on wholesale and retail dealers and the sale of opium to Filipinos would be prohibited. They felt that such a high license system would, by raising the price of the drug beyond the reach of the poorer consumers, bring about a decrease in its traffic and consumption. Fearful, however, that because of a lack of understanding of the Far Eastern situation the American public would not even accept this compromise, they suggested that

50. *Ibid.*

before the government adopted what they regarded as the unwise prohibition system, a commission be sent to other Far Eastern territories to investigate the operations of systems in those areas.[51] Root and Roosevelt approved both the proposition of a high license system and the idea of a commission of inquiry.[52] Pending the conclusion of the investigatory commission's work the proposed monopoly bill was tabled.

The Opium Committee appointed by Taft to investigate the opium situation in other Far Eastern territories consisted of two physicians, Major Edward C. Carter, Commissioner of Public Health of the Philippines, and Dr. José Albert, a prominent Filipino physician, and Bishop Brent. They were instructed to gather information on the laws governing the importation, sale, and use of opium and the effect of these measures in either limiting or encouraging the use of the drug and to ascertain the number of consumers and their proportion to the total population, the amount of opium consumed, the manner in which it was consumed, its price, the effect of its use on different races, the amount smuggled, and the annual value of the monopoly concessions where they existed.[53]

The itinerary of the committee included Japan, Formosa, Shanghai, Singapore, Burma, and Java, thus touching the possessions of Great Britain, France, and the Netherlands as well as China and Japan.[54] Their investigation lasted five months—from August 17, 1903, to January 15, 1904. Two of these months were spent in Japan and Formosa, the areas to which they gave the fullest attention.[55]

As a result of its labors the committee concluded that the opium situation was one of the gravest, if not the gravest, of problems in the Far East, with possible solutions to be affected by the fact that it was "a prolific source of revenue." They were most commendatory of the Japanese system of control, in both Japan and Formosa, and most condemnatory of the British. Their attitude toward the British system was expressed thus:

The laws in the English colonies visited, Burma excepted, accomplish the purpose for which they were drafted. The drift of the report of the royal commission represents the official mind of Great Britain in the Orient,

51. *Ibid.*
52. Root to Taft, July 14, 1903, BIA 1023–25.
53. *Report of the Philippine Opium Committee*, p. 59.
54. *Ibid.*, pp. 11–17.   55. *Ibid.*, p. 19.

and it is to the effect that (1) the use of opium is not necessarily injurious to orientals, in some cases possibly being beneficial; (2) when it obtains as a fixed habit it is useless to try to extirpate it; and (3) as it affords a means of revenue, the government may as well as not seize the opportunity it gives of swelling its credit. As carefully drawn laws protecting trade interests they are above criticism. . . . They do not pretend to be laws for the protection of the people against a vice, but rather commercial regulations guarding a branch of commerce.[56]

The committee spent so much time examining the Japanese system of regulation because this was the system which the missionaries and other reformers were urging for the Philippines. In Japan the importation, manufacture, and distribution of opium and opium preparations were under strict government control and were restricted to medical purposes only. The government designated the private manufacturers who could make the opium preparations. These could then be purchased by government-appointed wholesalers, who had to be druggists or pharmacists. Druggists and physicians could purchase the drug from the wholesalers only by certificate, and it could be dispensed only on a physician's prescription.[57] Because of the rigid enforcement of this system, backed by public opinion, there was no opium problem in Japan, not even among the 8,000 Chinese residents. The committee was quite impressed with this system and with the fact that Japan was the only area they visited in which the opium question was viewed "solely as a moral problem" whose control was unencumbered by "commercial considerations."[58]

In Formosa the situation was different. There the Japanese were confronted with a population the bulk of which was Chinese and among whom opium addiction was widespread. Indeed, the habit had reputedly spread from Formosa to mainland China. There the Japanese were endeavoring to stamp out the use of the drug through a system of progressive prohibition of which the features were a government monopoly, the licensing and registration of users, and an antiopium propaganda campaign conducted especially in the public schools.[59] This was the system which the committee recommended for the Philippines. As to the other methods of regulation which they had observed, they rejected the high-tariff or high-license system on the grounds that it merely enhanced the price, promoted smuggling, and gave the gov-

56. *Ibid.*, p. 49.
57. *Ibid.*, pp. 215–220.

58. *Ibid.*, pp. 21–24.
59. *Ibid.*, pp. 24–28.

ernment an interest in the revenue aspects of the trade. They denounced the local option system as "not suitable in any way to the opium traffic." Against the farming or contract system they directed the traditional arguments relative to the increased use of opium, the encouragement of smuggling, and the tying of the government to the opium revenue.[60]

The committee's observations on the effects of a system of immediate prohibition were partly based on experience in Hawaii, where the attention of the government had been drawn to the opium situation as early as 1892. It was then reported that the opium traffic was widespread and that it was being promoted with the connivance of police and customs officials.[61] In 1897 the importation, sale, and use of opium were prohibited except for medicinal uses. According to the High Sheriff of the Hawaiian Islands, while this system was in force, the blackmailing of opium addicts was extensive. The law was repealed as of April 1, 1903, after which there was no restriction on the use of the drug. The result was an increase in consumption but not to the extent anticipated. The High Sheriff concluded that Hawaii was probably better off without the law.[62] The committee concluded that immediate prohibition was impracticable for areas where the habit was already entrenched, since it would cause intense suffering among the existing addicts and make them victims of blackmail.[63]

For the Philippine situation, therefore, which the committee maintained was not as "grave a social calamity . . . as . . . in neighboring territories," a system of progressive prohibition and government monopoly modeled on the Japanese system in Formosa was recommended. This would embody, as already stated, an exclusive government monopoly of the importation and wholesale and retail transactions of the drug. After three years, strict prohibition, except for medical purposes, would be put into effect. During the three-year period of progressive prohibition, the drug, except for medical purposes, would be dispensed in limited quantities and only by salaried officials of the government solely to chronic adult male workers who would be registered with and licensed by the government. Free treatment would

---

60. *Ibid.*, p. 52.
61. Hawaiian Islands, Legislature, Special Committee on Opium, *Report of Special Committee on Opium to the Legislature of 1892, Acting Under Resolution of Honorable J. H. Waipulani* [Honolulu, 1892].
62. *Report of the Philippine Opium Committee*, p. 282.
63. *Ibid.*, p. 52.

be given to those desiring it, while "incorrigible offenders" would be punished or expelled from the islands. The young would be discouraged from using the drug by an educational campaign against it and by prohibitive legislation.[64]

An informal copy of the report of the Opium Committee was made available for the use of Congress in considering a revision of duties on opium and other commodities imported into the Philippines. The result was the passage of a law by Congress on March 3, 1905, providing that the total prohibition of the importation, sale, and use of opium, except by the government and for medical use only, should go into effect after March 1, 1908. The Philippine Commission was empowered in the meantime to prohibit entirely or adopt whatever other measures it deemed feasible relative to transactions in and use of the drug. The sale of opium to Filipinos, however, except for medicinal uses, was forbidden.[65]

For the three-year period prior to the going into effect of strict prohibition, the Philippine Commission, with the approval of President Roosevelt and the War Department, decided to institute the high-license system.[66] They thus rejected the recommendation by the Opium Committee of a system of government monopoly, which, as had been earlier pointed out, was foreign to the American tradition. With the suggestions and under the prodding of Taft, now Secretary of War, the High License Act was enacted on March 8, 1906, to go into effect three weeks later. Only the clergymen, who desired prohibition, and Bishop Brent, who desired a government monopoly, opposed the bill, but in view of the short time remaining before total prohibition was to go into effect, the objections were not strenuous.[67]

The Act in question repeated the Congressional prohibition of the sale of opium to Filipinos, confining its use to adult male Chinese, who were required to take out a "habitual user's certificate" costing 5 pesos. Heavy annual license fees of 1,000 pesos for wholesalers and 200 pesos for retailers were imposed. In addition, wholesalers were required to pay a specific tax of 2½ pesos per kilo on crude opium and 7½ pesos on prepared opium. Strict government scrutiny of imports as well as

64. *Ibid.*, pp. 53–55.   65. *Ibid.*, p. 54.
66. Luke Wright, Governor General of the Philippines, to Secretary of War Taft, Jan. 8, 1905; Taft to Wright, Jan. 8, 1905, BIA 1023–11.
67. Colonel Edwards to Governor General Henry C. Ide, Jan. 25, 1906, BIA 1023–136; Taft to Ide, Feb. 28, 1906, and Ide to Taft, Feb. 24, 1906, BIA 1023–139; Ide to Taft, March 1, 1906, BIA 1023–141.

of wholesale and retail transactions was provided. Revenue derived from the license fees and specific taxes was to constitute a special fund for an antiopium educational campaign, hospital treatment of addicts, payment of informers, financing of the education of Filipino students in the United States, payment of the salaries of insular school teachers, and construction of school buildings.[68]

This Act was followed by another in October 1907 which was designed to ease the transition to total prohibition. Provisions were made for the establishment of official dispensaries under the joint supervision of an opium dealer and an internal revenue officer to supply opium in decreasing quantities monthly to users whose licenses were increased in price monthly. Although there was some opposition to the measures from merchants, shipping firms, and opium-dive keepers, public opinion strongly backed the acts.[69]

About 12,700 user's certificates were issued under the Act of 1906, although a conservative estimate of the number of Chinese smokers alone was in excess of 20,000. It was claimed that by March 1908, about 40 percent of the users had given up the habit and that many others had become moderate users.[70] Prohibition, however, by no means brought an end to the opium problem in the islands. The traffic went underground, and the efforts to suppress smuggling and illicit opium dens were only moderately successful. Authorities claimed that effective enforcement was often frustrated by the lenient sentences imposed on violators by the courts, the average fine being about 269 pesos and the average term of imprisonment about four months. Much progress was made, however. In 1911 the number of Chinese addicts was estimated at 5,000 while the number of Filipino users was set at less than 5 percent of the estimated 4,000 users in 1906.[71] Thus total suppression had not been achieved, and the likelihood of it being achieved in the near future was slight. Daily arrests and convictions continued, and old addicts returned to the vice.[72]

Because prohibition forced the traffic in and consumption of the drug underground, it is impossible to determine with accuracy the extent of the problem in the Philippines after 1908. During the next three decades, Philippine officials contended the problem was not a

---

68. "Memorandum Showing Results obtained in the Enforcement of Laws Aimed at the Total Suppression of the Opium Habit in the Philippine Islands," SDR RG 43, E 36.
69. *Ibid.*
70. *Ibid.*
71. *Ibid.*
72. *Ibid.*

serious one.[73] The islands, however, remained in the international lime-light. During the course of the international movement to control the drug traffic, the Philippines stood as the concrete expression of the American attitude and policy toward the trade in the Far East. It was the only area in the Orient where a Western nation had adopted pro-hibition, a system which the other Western powers deemed neither practicable nor desirable for their Far Eastern possessions, and which they were anxious to discredit.[74] Furthermore, the Philippines revived America's material interest in the whole Far Eastern drug situation. As long as opium consumption and the traffic were allowed and even fostered in surrounding areas, the Philippines could never hope to be entirely free of the vice. Smuggling of opium into the islands from other Far Eastern territories, particularly from the British possessions of Hongkong, Singapore, and North Borneo, which themselves were largely supplied with the drug from India, constituted a continuous problem.

A recapitulation of the influence of the report of the Philippine Opium Committee on Chinese and British opinion is feasible here. The contrast between the committee's report and the report of the Royal Commission in 1895 is representative of the difference in the official American and British views. Whereas the British report held that the use of opium was not necessarily injurious to Orientals, the American account contended that its use constituted "one of the gravest prob-lems in the Far East." The futility of trying to suppress a long-standing social habit was stressed in the British document, whereas the necessity for immediate action to end the practice was emphasized by the Ameri-cans. The British placed revenue considerations in the way of ending the traffic, whereas the Americans held that no amount of revenue could justify the continued degradation of a people for which the traffic was responsible. In short, the Royal Commission's report white-washed the traffic, while the Philippine Opium Committee's report condemned it unreservedly.

The conclusions of the Philippine Opium Committee corresponded

73. See, for example, Francis Burton Harrison, Governor General, to Hamilton Wright, May 28, 1914, SDR 43, E 36; Frank R. McCoy to Mrs. Wright, May 4, 1926, BIA 1023–270; Frank McIntyre, Chief of the Insular Bureau, to Governor General Leonard Wood, April 15, 1926, BIA 1023–268; Wood to McIntyre May 27, 1926, BIA 1023–271.

74. See for example Arthur Woods, Assessor on the Opium Advisory Committee of the League of Nations, to Secretary of War Dwight F. Davis, July 2, 1927, BIA 1023–280.

very closely to those uttered by Henry J. Wilson, a member of the Royal Commission, who had filed a minority report to that of the commission. He requested a copy of the Opium Committee's report for use in the pending debate in the House of Commons on the question in 1906.[75] As already pointed out, parts of the report were quoted several times to buttress sentiment for ending the Indian-Chinese traffic. In China the report was translated by a missionary and circulated throughout the empire.[76]

That the influence of the work of the Opium Committee would extend beyond the confines of the Philippines was foreseen by Bishop Brent. Even before the committee was formed he had urged that the United States set an example in legislation in the Far East on the opium question.[77] And during the course of the committee's itinerary he wrote: "The opium traffic is admitted to be the gravest moral question in the East, and I only hope that the result of our work will have something beyond local value, as people seem to think it will."[78] The language and spirit of the committee's report bears very strongly Brent's imprint. To him must go the credit for seeing that their work would indeed be of more than local value. He was cognizant of the varied but convergent influences—in China, Great Britain, the United States, and on the international level—which were creating an environment in which the idea of international consideration of the opium question might be favorably received. He was discerning enough to realize that through the injection of the Philippine problem as an added component into the general opium situation in the Far East, the material basis for such international consideration might be established.

75. Henry J. Wilson, M.P., to the Chief of the Bureau of Insular Affairs, April 10, 1906, BIA 1023–143.

76. See above, p. 22. See also Brent to F. C. Shattuck, Manila, May 27, 1907, Brent Papers, Box 6.

77. See above, p. 38.

78. Brent to Bishop Hall, Manila, Nov. 13, 1903, Brent Papers, Box 6.

Chapter three

The Shanghai Opium Commission

Down to 1939 two major considerations constituted the motive force behind American participation in the international campaign against the drug traffic. To the close of World War I the United States was primarily concerned with helping China rid itself of the vice. During the 1920's America's own problems of dope addiction came to the fore, and these were only remotely related to the situation in the Orient. In the thirties China's problem gradually regained a prominent place in American considerations as China became more and more the victim of a Japanese-sponsored drug traffic and also a source of illicit traffic to the United States. Throughout the movement, however, China held a leading place in American deliberations. It was to help China that the United States initiated the international movement. The problem in the Philippines was of importance in the American decision only in giving the United States justification for interfering in a matter in which it had previously expressed merely a moral interest.

On July 24, 1906, Bishop Brent addressed a letter to President Roosevelt suggesting the initiation by the United States of an international investigation of the Far Eastern opium question in which England, France, Holland, China, and Japan should participate. He cited America's responsibility in the Philippines as ample justification for the move, and the recent antiopium agitation in England as creating the proper climate for successful action. "The sole hope of the Chinese," he declared, "is concerted action." He believed that such a movement in pursuit of a common goal would tend to unify and promote peace among the Oriental nations and Western nations with Far Eastern possessions and dependencies.[1] Roosevelt heartily approved of the suggestion as one that might "do far-reaching good" and proceeded to take the matter up with Root and Taft.[2] Taft expressed some skepticism as to British cooperation in such a movement, in view of that gov-

1. *Foreign Relations*, 1906, I, 361–362; also Brent Papers, Box 6.
2. Roosevelt to Brent, Washington, D.C., Aug. 28, 1906, Brent Papers, Box 6.

ernment's dependence on the revenue derived from opium in its Far Eastern possessions. Nevertheless, he suggested that the time was ripe for approaching Great Britain, in view of the change to a Liberal government in the recent parliamentary elections. He agreed with Brent that "the opium question in China is one of the most important in the improvement of Chinese and Oriental Civilization."[3]

The State Department, taking note of the influences likely to make the movement successful—the antiopium agitation in Great Britain, the consistent interest of the United States in China's problem, now fortified by America's concrete interest in the Philippines, and the impetus it would give to antiopium sentiment in China—also heartily approved of the suggestion. Another factor given consideration was the gratitude China would be likely to feel toward the United States for broaching the subject. The Department realized, however, that the acceptance of the proposition by the other powers would be dependent on the Chinese Empire's sincerity in seeking to suppress native production; therefore, it was suggested that a distinct pledge in this regard be obtained in advance from China.[4]

It was soon discovered that a pledge from China was unnecessary. Independent of importunings from the United States, the Chinese authorities had decided to embark on a campaign against opium. The United States watched this movement with great interest and lent its moral encouragement. As mentioned above, two weeks before Brent's letter to Roosevelt, the State Department had instructed its minister in China to arrange a meeting between the Reverend Hampden C. Du Bose and the Chinese foreign office for a discussion, at Du Bose's request, of a movement to suppress the opium traffic in China. Minister Rockhill was further instructed to report on the opium situation in China and to advise the Department on the position of the United States should take in regard to it.[5] Rockhill's reports, while reflecting skepticism about China's ability to carry out her reforms, nevertheless confirmed the sincerity of the government's efforts and urged the United States to give all possible support to the antiopium agitation in China which was being led by the Anti-Opium League.[6] By the end of 1906 the United States was convinced that China was serious and

3. Taft to Roosevelt, Sept. 1, 1906, SDR 774/1.
4. Memorandum, Charles Denby to Robert Bacon, Sept. 7, 1906, SDR 774/1–2; Alvey A. Adee to Ambassador Whitelaw Reid (London), Sept. 27, 1906, SDR 774/3.
5. *Foreign Relations*, 1906, I, 352.
6. *Ibid.*, p. 353; *Foreign Relations*, 1907, I, 147–148, 151.

communicated that conviction to the other powers. So sure was the United States that China would participate in an international movement that China was among the last of the nations approached in regard to the matter.

While American officials were approving with some alacrity Brent's suggestion, Brent himself was interceding with British religious leaders and was successful in getting such of them as the Bishop of China and the Archbishop of Canterbury to approach the British government.[7] Great Britain, of course, held the key to the fate of the launching of the movement. Therefore the first powers invited were Great Britain, because of its great stake in the opium trade, and Japan, because of its influential position in the Far East and its propinquity to the Philippines. They were queried on the feasibility of holding an international conference on the Far Eastern opium situation. The British Foreign Office immediately concurred on condition that the other powers invited would also agree, and that the proposed conference also consider the growth and trade in opium in China as well as in India.[8] The Japanese likewise responded favorably to the idea on condition that assurances of China's sincerity in coping with her own domestic situation could be obtained.[9] Later, the interested powers agreed to the British suggestion that a commission investigate the facts of the opium situation in order to arrive at intelligent conclusions, lest an international conference form an agreement which would not be based on a proper understanding of the matter.

In addition to the powers mentioned in Brent's letter, the United States initially approached Germany and Siam as well. By July of 1907 all of them but China had agreed to the investigative commission. The recalcitrance of China caught the State Department by surprise. In its notes to the various powers the Department had stated that the cooperation of China was assured as evidenced by her efforts to suppress domestic production and consumption of opium as well as the traffic in the drug.[10] Particularly emphasized was the point that the discussion would include an inquiry into the importation of opium into China. Thus when the Department finally got around to making a definite and formal inquiry of China as to whether it would partici-

---

7. *Foreign Relations*, 1906, I, 352; Brent to the Archbishop of York, Manila, July 30, 1906, Brent Papers, Box 6.
8. *Foreign Relations*, 1906, I, 365.
9. *Ibid.*, p. 364.   10. *Foreign Relations*, 1907, I, 144.

pate in the proposed commission, it was taken aback by the discovery that China looked upon the proposal with something less than enthusiasm. China's refusal to participate would naturally kill any hope of international consideration of the question as well as cast serious doubt upon the sincerity of that nation's antiopium professions and activities.

China's procrastination was due to a misunderstanding of the nature and function of the proposed commission. The Chinese foreign office believed that the commission would travel throughout China investigating opium production and consumption. It feared that the commission might be exposed to physical attack in the remoter sections of the country, thus giving an excuse for a repetition of the military intervention of foreign powers which had become somewhat of a pattern in the past, the most recent and vivid experience being the Boxer incidents. Another consideration was the fear that the commission would inquire into China's financial methods and would make recommendations that would infringe on Chinese sovereignty.[11] This would manifestly be a serious matter in the light of the current efforts of the Manchus to strengthen China against the Western powers so as to maintain the respect of the Chinese people and to repair their own shaken position. On being assured by Rockhill that each country would conduct the investigation of its own domestic situation and that commissions only made recommendations to the home governments, which were free to accept or reject them, the Wai-wu pu finally accepted in principle the idea of a joint commission.[12] Thus by the end of August all the powers originally approached had agreed to a commission, and by December they were inquiring as to the time and place of the meeting.

It was not only the official representations of the United States that contributed to the favorable response of the nations invited. Again the missionaries entered the movement. Bishop Brent had marshaled the support of his counterparts in China and other parts of the Far East and in Great Britain. Fortuitously, the foreign missionaries in China held their periodic conference in April and May of 1907 at Shanghai. Bishop Brent attended their meeting for the specific purpose of getting their support for the proposed joint commission. In this he was successful, for the conference adopted essentially what he recommended. It presented a memorial condemning the Indian-Chinese opium trade and the production and use of the drug in general and commending China

11. *Ibid.*, pp. 159, 164–165.   12. *Ibid.*, p. 165.

and Great Britain for their new attitude toward the problem as indicated by the Chinese efforts at repression and the British agreement to reduce gradually the export of Indian opium to China. For the change in public attitude toward the question the memorial credited the Philippine Opium Committee, the practice of Japan, and the experience of employers of Chinese laborers. It declared that no government or people would be justified in imposing the drug on China, regardless of whether China fulfilled her promises of reform or not.

The Missionary Conference adopted resolutions reaffirming the opposition to the opium trade taken by the Missionary Conference in 1877 and 1890; expressing gratification with China's present effort to deal with the problem and at the cooperation given by Great Britain through the Anglo-Chinese Ten Year Agreement; and taking note of the movement for an international commission, declaring it to be both timely and necessary. In addition, the conference urged that the opium question be brought before the approaching peace conference at The Hague and that all civilized governments prohibit the sale of opium and intoxicants among "non-Christian races in the mission fields."[13] This action of the Missionary Conference served to focus public opinion on the American suggestion and was another example of missionary interest in the problem and the part it played in building up antiopium sentiment.

Besides the powers on the original list of those invited by the United States to participate, five more powers were invited to join the commission. At the suggestion of Bishop Brent and Hamilton Wright, members of the American delegation to the commission, Turkey and Persia, as two of the largest producers of opium, and Russia, because of her Far Eastern territorial possessions and large Chinese population, were invited to attend. Italy and Austria-Hungary asked to be invited, and the United States reluctantly extended an invitation to them after ascertaining that the other powers had no objections. Thus what was intended to be a gathering of countries with Far Eastern interests developed into a conference of nations whose interest in the drug problem extended beyond the Orient.

13. *China Centenary Missionary Conference Records, Report of the Great Conference Held at Shanghai, April 5th to May 8th, 1907* (New York: American Tract Society, 1907), pp. 387–392, 754, 750–760. For Brent's influence on this Conference see Brent to the Archbishop of Canterbury, Manila, Feb. 28, 1907; Brent to John W. Wood, Manila, May 20, 1907; Brent Papers, Box 6.

Although the invited powers agreed to participate in the commission, they were by no means united in their enthusiasm for it. Western powers with Far Eastern possessions in which opium played an important part in revenue only reluctantly consented. They were not prepared to enter into any binding agreement calling for any disturbance of that revenue. This was especially true of France,[14] the Netherlands,[15] and Great Britain. The British had to take into consideration the uncompromising attitude of India—the government and most of the people, English and native—to any participation in an international movement that threatened India's valuable opium trade.[16] Persia and Turkey were the only powers invited that did not have possessions in the Orient, but they played a great role in the cultivation of the poppy and the preparation of opium, much of which found a market in that area. Turkey flatly refused to send a representative to the commission. Persia agreed to be represented only after much urging by the American minister there, for the Persian government wanted no restriction on that country's opium trade. The American minister finally persuaded the government to send a representative by pointing out that the commission would meet anyway, even without Persia, that its decisions would merely be reported to the interested governments to act on as they saw fit, and that in any case Persia should be represented in order to make her views known.[17]

The time and place of the meeting were set for January 1909 at Shanghai. The United States suggested that each country invited should come to the International Opium Commission prepared

(1) to devise means to limit the use of opium in the Possessions of that country;

(2) to ascertain the best means of suppressing the opium traffic, if such now exists, among their nationals in the Far East;

(3) to be in a position, when the various Commissions meet in Shanghai, to cooperate and offer jointly or severally definite suggestions of measures which their respective Governments may adopt for the gradual suppression of opium cultivation, traffic, and use within

14. Ambassador Henry White (Paris) to the Secretary of State, Aug. 16, 1908, SDR 774/306–307.

15. Minister Arthur M. Beaupre (The Hague) to the Secretary of State, Nov. 6, 1908, SDR 774/402–403.

16. Consul General William H. Michaels (Calcutta) to the Assistant Secretary of State, Oct. 22, 1908, Brent Papers, Box 8.

17. Minister John B. Jackson (Teheran) to the Secretary of State, Dec. 25, 1908, SDR 774/534.

their Eastern possessions and thus to assist China in her purpose of eradicating the evil from the Empire.[18]

In order to make sure that China would be properly prepared for the Commission, supplemental suggestions were later made to the interested powers to the effect that a full study should be made of the importation, manufacture, and consumption of all forms of opium and its derivatives, licit or illicit; the possibilities and extent of poppy cultivation; and the laws, national and local, dealing with the importation and use of opium and its derivatives.[19]

To prepare the United States for the Commission and to represent the government at Shanghai, an American opium commission was named consisting of Bishop Brent, Dr. Hamilton Wright, and Charles C. Tenney. As the careers and personal interests of each of these men reflected the American orientation toward the anti-narcotic-drug movement, a brief description of their backgrounds is in place.

Charles Tenney's role in the antiopium movement was short, though not uninfluential. A native of Boston and a graduate of Dartmouth College, he went to China in 1878 as a missionary, having just completed a four-year divinity course at Oberlin Theological Seminary. In 1886 he gave up missionary work and became tutor to the sons of the Chinese statesman Li Hung Chang. In the same year he established a school in Tientsin for Chinese students and served as its principal until 1895. In this year he was appointed as the first president of the Imperial Chinese University at Tientsin, holding that position until 1906. Among other positions in the field of education which he held were those of superintendent of high and middle schools in the province of Chihli (1902–1906), director of Chinese government students in America (1906–1908), and lecturer on Chinese history at Harvard (1907–1908). He was long associated with the American foreign service in China. From 1894 to 1896 he served as vice-consul and interpreter to the American consulate at Tientsin. At the time of his appointment to the American opium delegation he held the position of Chinese secretary to the American legation at Peking. He was considered so valuable a man to that legation that Minister Rockhill objected to releasing him for the opium work. He later served as

18. Ambassador Reid to Sir Edward Grey, May 8, 1909, enclosed in Reid to the Secretary of State, Aug. 25, 1908, SDR 774/310–313.

19. Acting Secretary of State Adee to American Embassy (London), July 11, 1908, SDR 774/245 B.

American consul at Nanking, again as Chinese secretary to the American legation, and in various other positions with the legation. In 1921 he retired from diplomatic service.[20] He was sincerely pro-Chinese and passionately "antiopium," being very critical of the British for their part in creating China's opium problem. The Chinese trusted him, and in preparing for the Shanghai Commission they consulted him frequently.

Prior to World War I the most energetic American participant in the antidrug campaign was Hamilton Wright. He was born in Cleveland, Ohio, in 1867 and divided the later years of his life between Washington, D.C., and Livermore Falls, Maine. He received his elementary and high school education in the public schools of Boston, and thereafter entered McGill University in Montreal to study medicine. In 1895 he graduated sixth in a class of sixty-seven and was soon after appointed registrar and neuropathologist at the Royal Victoria Hospital in Montreal. In 1895–1896 he visited the Far East to observe such tropical diseases as beriberi, the plague, and malaria, spending most of his time in China and Japan. Three years later, after having worked in clinical laboratories in Germany and England, he returned to the Far East under the auspices of the British government to organize a laboratory system and to investigate beriberi and malaria in the Federated Malay States and the Straits Settlement. He returned to the United States in 1903 and became engaged in research at The Johns Hopkins University, being made an honorary fellow of that university for the academic year 1903–1904. From 1904 until his appointment to the American opium commission in June 1908 he continued his research in both America and Europe. He wrote numerous articles on neuropathology and tropical diseases. It was because of his work on tropical diseases that he was recommended to serve on the American commission, an appointment which came to him unsolicited.

Wright's appointment to the American opium commission marked a turning point in his career. Virtually all the remainder of his life was devoted to the antinarcotics campaign. Up to the outbreak of the First World War he was almost continuously in charge of the State Department's antiopium work. He developed a rather possessive attitude toward American drug policy and practice. Not only was he largely entrusted with the framing and carrying out of American foreign

20. *Dictionary of American Biography*, XVIII, 371–373. For Rockhill's objection to releasing Tenney, see Rockhill to State Department, Jan. 3, 1909, SDR, RG 43, E 33.

policy in regard to the traffic in narcotics, he was also given the tedious task of drafting the domestic legislation dealing with the problem. Outspoken and dedicated, his colleagues in the State Department sometimes found his enthusiasm irritating, and because of this he did not always receive proper appreciation for his work or adequate financial compensation. It was because of personal differences with Secretary of State William Jennings Bryan that he was kept from attending the international conference on narcotic drugs which was held just before the First World War interrupted the movement. In a sense he himself became a casualty of the war; while engaged in civilian relief work in France in 1915 he was severely injured in an automobile accident and never fully recovered. He died of pneumonia in Washington on January 7, 1917.[21] After the war the work in which he played so prominent a part was continued by his wife with the same dedication and zeal that he had shown. To him, more than to any other single individual, must go the greatest share of the credit for the success of American efforts in the antiopium drive in the first two decades of the twentieth century, for he built the groundwork of policy and practice upon which the international and domestic actions of the United States were based throughout the period covered by this study.

Bishop Brent was not originally considered for appointment to the American opium commission, but when Judge Thomas Burke of Seattle declined the appointment, it was realized that Brent, to whose inspiration the international movement owed its origin, would be the ideal man to head the American delegation.[22] Brent was born in the town of Newcastle, Ontario, in April 1862. After graduating from Trinity College of the University of Toronto in 1884, he studied independently for the Anglican priesthood for two years while teaching school. He was ordained a deacon in 1886. The following year he was ordained priest. From 1886 to 1901 he was engaged in religious work, first in Buffalo, New York, and later in Boston as first curate and later assistant minister of a church there. In 1901 he was elected Episcopal Bishop of the Philippine Islands, the first to hold such a position. Before leaving for his post he went to Washington and met President Roosevelt, Cabinet officers concerned with the Philippines, and William Howard Taft, the civil governor of the islands. Roosevelt told him

21. *DAB*, XX, 552–553.
22. Bacon to Brent, Washington, D.C., July 8, 1908, Brent Papers, Box 7. Also in SDR 774/233.

to feel free to communicate directly with him whenever he wished, a privilege which Brent was subsequently to make good use of. He sailed for the Philippines in May 1902 in the company of Governor Taft. This contact was to be invaluable to him and to his work in the islands. Taft and others respected his views.

Brent's appointment as senior American commissioner to the Shanghai meeting was fortunate for the antiopium movement as a whole. A man of great moral conviction tempered by an ability to analyze issues realistically, he gave the international movement against drug abuse the character of a moral crusade. On speaking terms with political leaders in both England and the United States, he was able to exert considerable influence upon the course of the movement. His personal prestige was bolstered by the support he received from his and other religious denominations. He was a world religious leader, greatly admired and respected. He gave up his position in the Philippines in the latter part of 1917, and after serving with American troops in Europe in 1917–1918, he entered upon his duties in 1919 as Bishop of Western New York, a position which he held until 1929. During the 1920's he led a movement for Christian unity among the churches of the world. From 1926 to 1928 he was in charge of the Protestant Episcopal churches in Europe. Because religious work was his primary field of activity, he did not devote as much time to the drug traffic as did Wright. But because of his personal contact with people all over the world he was more widely known and could therefore exercise through these contacts an immeasurable influence on the antiopium movement as a whole. He and Wright made an ideal team, the one the strict moralist but patient realist and soother of ruffled feelings; the other an outspoken, impatient, and energetic master of details. Unlike Wright, Brent did not continuously participate in the antidrug campaign. Like Wright, however, he maintained a keen interest in the work until almost the day he died. One of his last major acts was in the interests of the movement. Two weeks before his death at Lausanne, Switzerland, on March 27, 1929, he sent a letter to President Hoover urging the continued leadership of the United States in the campaign.[23]

The American opium commissioners were instructed to make a general study of the opium situation in the Far East from both the

23. Alexander C. Zabriskie, *Bishop Brent, Crusader for Christian Unity* (Philadelphia: Westminster Press, 1948), pp. 19–23, 44. For Brent's opium work, see chap. vii.

foreign and American points of view, giving due consideration to the commercial, medical, and humanitarian aspects. A full study of the problem in the United States and the Philippines was also ordered.[24] The commissioners entered upon their duties in early July, 1908. Tenney confined himself to an investigation of conditions in China with particular attention to practical means by which China might be helped to suppress the vice. In pursuit of this objective he talked with Chinese officials, translated the imperial edicts and other official notifications and proclamations, read Chinese newspapers, and corresponded with American missionaries in all parts of China. In the course of his investigation he discovered the widespread sale and use of so-called antiopium remedies which themselves contained opium and morphine, and which he arranged to have collected and analyzed. He reported the results to the Chinese authorities, who conducted an investigation of their own, the results of which they placed in their report to the Shanghai Commission. Tenney prepared no report of his own on the Chinese situation, believing this to be the duty of the Chinese government, but as a result of his studies he was able to confirm the general accuracy of the Chinese report to the Commission, especially with reference to the statistics on the importation of foreign opium, the estimates of opium production and consumption in China, the danger of antiopium remedies, and the sincerity and extent of antiopium sentiment on the part of the government and people of China.[25]

Bishop Brent's major preparation consisted of a survey of the data in the State Department on the opium problem and a study, with the help of the Philippine Commission and other interested officials, of the situation in the Philippines. In December he and Wright toured the southern islands, visiting the principal ports and surveying local conditions. Their investigation confirmed in their minds the wisdom of the prohibitive system. They discovered that smuggling was the chief obstacle to the effective enforcement of the system.[26]

Hamilton Wright performed by far the greater part of the work in preparation for the Shanghai meeting. Before reporting to the State Department on July 1, he collected and mastered various documents,

24. Root to Wright, June 20, 1908, SDR 774/227a; also in Brent Papers, Box 7.

25. "Report to the Department of State by the American Delegation to the International Opium Commission at Shanghai," Confidential, March 1, 1909, SDR 774/606, pp. 32–38, Brent Papers, Box 37. Hereafter cited as Confidential Report of American Opium Commission.

26. *Ibid.*, pp. 25–26.

laws, international agreements, and other pertinent literature on the drug question. At the State Department he was given the diplomatic correspondence leading up to the calling of the Commission and also the correspondence on the Philippine opium problem. He then conducted a thorough inquiry into the nature and extent of the opium problem within the United States. Through correspondence and personal interviews with police officials, state health and pharmaceutical boards, drug manufacturers and their organizations, firms dealing in the various forms of opium, and members of the medical profession, he discovered that the United States had a considerable drug problem of its own.[27] His work made him the best prepared of the American delegation on all aspects of both the international and domestic situation.

The revelation that the United States had a substantial domestic opium problem came as a surprise to most Americans, who had long viewed the consumption of the drug as a habit peculiar to the Orient. The problem in America stemmed from two main sources: the excessive importation of crude opium from Turkey for manufacture into morphine and other medicinal preparations, and the importation of smoking opium from the Far East, principally from Portuguese Macao, to supply Chinese and other habitual opium smokers in the United States. It was estimated that the maximum annual needs of the American people for opium for medicinal use were 100,000 pounds, whereas the actual annual importation of opium for this purpose was over 500,000 pounds. From 70 to 80 percent of the crude opium imported was used to manufacture morphine, and it was estimated that from 50 to 70 percent of such morphine was used for improper purposes. The remainder of the crude opium was used in medicinal preparations such as laudanum and other extracts which were themselves subject to misuse.[28]

There was no legitimate use for smoking opium; yet its importation had been legal since 1840, either under the tariff schedule or on the free list. Prior to that time opium had not been separately taxed, but had been admitted under the title of "drugs, chemical, *et cetera*." Since 1900 the average annual quantity of smoking opium legally imported was 151,944 pounds. In addition a great deal had been smuggled in,

27. *Ibid.*, pp. 27–31.
28. *Report of Shanghai Opium Commission*, II, 7, 8, 19. See also Hamilton Wright, "The International Opium Commission," *AJIL*, III (July, 1909), 652–653.

much from Canada, where Chinese firms manufactured it; and some had been surreptitiously manufactured in the United States. Wright estimated that there were in the United States about 52,000 Chinese smokers—about 40 percent of our total Chinese population—and from 100,000 to 150,000 non-Chinese smokers in the American population.[29] He further estimated that of the 650,000 pounds of opium in all forms, imported legally into the United States, 550,000 pounds were used for illegitimate purposes.[30] The revenue derived from the tariff duties on such opium averaged nearly a million and a half dollars annually, constituting one-fifth of 1 percent of America's total revenue.[31]

This discovery of an extensive internal drug problem served to strengthen the hands of the American representatives at Shanghai; it established a material interest in the international problem beyond the Philippines. In another sense, however, such a situation, if allowed to go unchecked, could very well vitiate American influence at the conference. Other powers could point to the extensive use of the drug in the United States, unencumbered by prohibitory federal legislation, as evidence of the insincerity or lack of seriousness about the problem on the part of the United States. The State Department realized that this might well be the case. In a memorandum dated August 13, 1907, William Phillips, second secretary of the American legation at Peking, pointed out that the importation of both crude and prepared opium into the United States had been steadily increasing, and that the transportation of opium from China on American vessels for subsequent sale to the Chinese in America was perfectly legal. To assume the initiative in helping China, he contended, the United States must first end the supply of opium to the Chinese in America and cease deriving revenue therefrom.[32]

Aside from the tariff laws, the Act of 1887, and the Excise Act of 1890 placing a tax of $10 a pound on smoking opium manufactured in the United States and restricting its manufacture to American citizens, the only other federal law regulating the sale of narcotics in the United States prior to 1909 was the Pure Food and Drugs Act of 1906. This

---

29. *Report of the Shanghai Commission*, II, 7–8, 19–20. Subsequent, more systematic investigations (see p. 125 below) indicate that Wright greatly exaggerated the extent of opium consumption in the United States. His figures are important, however, in that they provided the conceptual basis for remedial legislation regarding the problem in the first two decades of the twentieth century.

30. *Ibid.*, p. 19.

31. *Ibid.*, p. 20.

32. SDR 774/146–147.

act, in addition to prohibiting the movement in interstate commerce of adulterated and misbranded food and drugs, required that the quantity or proportion of morphine, opium, heroin, or their derivatives and preparations in the substances within the package be stated on the label. To improve America's regulatory system relative to the drugs, the State Department, in cooperation with the Department of Agriculture, set about drafting a bill to regulate the importation and sale of opium and its derivatives in the United States and its dependencies. Some felt that the amendment of the Food and Drugs Act would accomplish the desired object. But as the date of the convening of the International Commission neared, it was decided to restrict the bill merely to the prohibition of the importation and manufacture of smoking opium, a prohibition which the importers and manufacturers of opium unanimously favored. A bill touching all aspects of the opium traffic—from importation to consumption—would manifestly be too complicated and controversial for hurried consideration by Congress. The object was to get a law passed before the convening of the Shanghai Commission. Thus Senator Henry Cabot Lodge introduced in the Senate a very simple bill, drafted by the State Department, prohibiting the importation into the United States of opium except for medicinal purposes. To the joy of the American commissioners, the bill was finally passed on February 9, 1909, just a little over a week after the Joint Commission assembled.[33] Thus the American representatives were able to point to this legislative manifestation of the American attitude toward the opium problem as a worthy example for the other nations to follow.

In the Far East also, the drive toward international consideration of the opium situation was productive of beneficent results even before the Commission convened. When China announced its intention to abolish the use of opium within ten years, most foreigners in China, and even many Chinese, doubted the sincerity of this profession. Those who accepted China's sincerity doubted the government's ability to achieve its goal. The Chinese government, however, encouraged by the United States, took stern measures to carry out its program. By 1909 most impartial observers admitted the genuineness of the cam-

33. For the drafting and discussion of the bill in the State Department see Wright to Root, enroute to China aboard S.S. *Siberia*, Oct. 30, 1908, Brent Papers, Box 8; H. W. Wiley (Department of Agriculture) to Bacon, Jan. 2, 1908, SDR 774/146–147; Root to Senator Lodge, Jan. 6, 1909, SDR 774/521. For the consideration and passage of the bill by Congress, see *Congressional Record*, 60th Cong., 2nd Sess., 1909, XLIII, Part 1, 449; Part 2, 1396–1400, 1681–1684, 2098.

paign undertaken and were no longer inclined to discount the possibility of its success. The United States had a considerable stake in the movement, for it realized that without concrete proof of China's sincerity the pending international deliberations would accomplish little. Therefore the American government threw its influence, moral and other, behind China's efforts.

Of particular concern to China was the growing morphine problem. The provisions of the commercial treaties of 1902 and 1903 with Great Britain and the United States, respectively, in which it had been agreed that China might prohibit the importation of the drug and the instruments for its injection, could go into effect only when the other treaty powers similarly consented to such a step.[34] China requested that the United States waive the right of most-favored-nation treatment and allow the prohibition to go into effect for Americans. This request was refused on the ground that unilateral action on the part of the United States and without concurrent action by China to suppress the domestic manufacture and use of the drug would be of no effect.[35] The United States also initially refused to intercede on China's behalf with the other treaty powers on the matter, holding that China herself should approach them.[36] By July 1908 all the powers but Japan had agreed to the prohibition. Rockhill reported on July 30 that the Wai-wu pu had approached Japan six times on the matter, but had received no reply.[37] He had, in the meantime, continually urged the Chinese to carry out their own obligations under the provisions of the treaties by framing and putting into effect the regulations needed relative to domestic production and use. Since the calling of the International Commission, Rockhill had redoubled his representations so that China would avoid creating an unfavorable impression in regard to the matter when the Commission met. But the Wai-wu pu was hamstrung by Japan's delay. Rockhill believed that because much of the morphine smuggled into China came from Japanese ports, and many of the instruments for its injection were manufactured in Japan, that nation wanted some *quid pro quo* for stopping the traffic. He himself had already approached the Japanese chargé d'affaires on the matter.[38]

Meanwhile several pressures were combining to force Japan to act.

34. See above, p. 24.
35. *Foreign Relations*, 1907, I, 140–144, 149.
36. Root to H. C. Du Bose, June 19, 1907, SDR 774/65.
37. Rockhill to the Secretary of State, July 30, 1908, SDR 774/323.
38. *Ibid.*

First, she was placed in an unfavorable light by being the only treaty power which had not consented to the prohibition. Secondly, she would occupy an untenable position at the International Opium Commission, where the question would most certainly be raised, charged with refusing to aid China in a matter to which all the other nations had acceded. And thirdly, in response to repeated prodding by Rockhill,[39] the State Department finally decided to approach Japan on the problem, despite the fear by some in the Department that Japan might resent such intrusion as undue interference with her material interests.[40]

The first approach by the State Department to Japan on July 10 through the Japanese ambassador in Washington brought no response.[41] After a second approach on September 22, the Japanese embassy informed the Department a few days later that Japan had agreed to the prohibition and would soon so inform China.[42] On September 29 Rockhill reported that the Wai-wu pu had informed him that all the treaty powers had now consented to the morphine prohibition and that it would go into effect on January 1, 1909.[43]

In response to China's request, the United States also threw its influence behind China's efforts to have her regulations against the sale and use of opium enforced in the foreign settlements. The State Department ordered its consuls to give strong support to endeavors to suppress the use of the drug in the international settlements.[44] One result of these actions was the decision by the international settlement at Shanghai to decrease by one-fourth, effective July 1, 1908, the number of opium house licenses to be issued.[45]

Perhaps the greatest influence that the prospective meeting at Shanghai had on the opium situation was its contribution to the framing and signing of the Anglo-Chinese Ten Year Agreement. The sensitivity of the British to the possibility that the Indian-Chinese opium trade might bear the brunt of denunciations at the forthcoming conference will be discussed more fully later.[46] It is sufficient to point out here that although the British would probably have eventually signed such an

39. *Ibid.*, Rockhill to the Secretary of State, July 15, 1908, SDR 774/246.
40. Memorandum by William Phillips to Bacon, July 15, 1908, SDR 774/323, Sept. 25, 1908, SDR 774/246.
41. Bacon to Rockhill, July 16, 1908, SDR 774/246.
42. Adee to Rockhill, Sept. 24, 1908, SDR 774/323; Sept. 25, 1908, SDR 774/246.
43. Rockhill to the Secretary of State, Sept. 29, 1908, SDR 774/350.
44. *Foreign Relations*, 1907, I, 140–144.
45. Root to the American Consul (Shanghai), March 13, 1908, SDR 774/167; Consul Cloud to Secretary of State, March 20, 1908, SDR 774/168.
46. See below, pp. 64–65.

agreement, even if there had been no call for international consideration of the opium question, the ease and speed with which an accord was reached was largely a result of the fact that the announced primary purpose of the forthcoming international deliberations was consideration of the Indian-Chinese traffic with a view to its abolition.

When the International Opium Commission began its discussions at Shanghai on February 1, 1908, the groundwork had been carefully laid by the United States. The American commission, consisting of a missionary, a physician, and a diplomat, all quite familiar with the Far East and well versed in the opium problem, was quite prepared to exercise leadership in the deliberations. At the suggestion of the British Foreign Secretary, Sir Edward Grey, the other powers had agreed that Bishop Brent should serve as permanent president of the Commission. Twelve other nations were represented at the meeting: Austria-Hungary, China, France, Germany, Great Britain, Japan, Italy, the Netherlands, Persia, Portugal, Russia, and Siam. Only Turkey refused to attend. It was the second commission of its kind to meet since the formulation of the Hague rules of 1899 as to the functions of such commissions. The Commission therefore adhered to the rules formulated by the First Hague Conference relative to the nature and functions of such gatherings and operated under the rules of procedure of the Second Hague Conference.

In order that deliberations might be held in an atmosphere of equanimity, devoid of agitation and emotion, the American representatives decided to use the term "moral" as little as possible, to avoid "needless historical references" to the opium problem, and to urge no conclusion that could not be carried unanimously or by an overwhelming majority. They wished to avoid majority and minority reports.[47] Therefore, in his opening speech as chairman of the Commission, Bishop Brent, while pointing out the difficulty and complexity of the opium problem and urging that the Commission face it with thoroughness and sincerity, stressed the view that the preliminary stage of agitation and emotion had passed and that the time for the consideration of "facts and solutions" had arrived. He urged the delegates that since they would not be committing their governments to the views expressed and the conclusions reached, they should give thorough consideration to all the questions presented and state their opinions frankly.[48]

47. Wright, "International Opium Commission," *op. cit.*, pp. 853–855.
48. *Report of the Shanghai Opium Commission*, Vol. I: *Report of the Proceedings*, pp. 11–16.

The American delegation's hope for a frank and full discussion of the opium question devoid of emotion was not to be realized. In the first place some of the delegations came unprepared for a full discussion.[49] Despite the correspondence between the American government and other governments prior to the meeting, many of the delegations thought that the inquiry was to be restricted to the Orient, and they had therefore neglected to investigate conditions in their homelands. They obtained some information, however, during the course of the Commission's proceedings. In marked contrast were the American preparations, which in addition to a study of the situation in the United States and its possessions and in the Far East included information gathered by American diplomatic and consular officials on the nature, extent, and measures for the control of the traffic in the countries represented at the Commission and in other countries as well. Indicative of the initial confusion was the fact that the Japanese came prepared to discuss the scientific aspects of the problem by including two physicians in their delegation, while the French had instructions to consider only the trade and commercial side of the question. Thus a full and frank discussion was precluded from the start.

The principal barrier to a thorough consideration of the questions before the Commission was the determination of the British delegation that the Ten Year Agreement on the Indian-Chinese trade should not be discussed. While the commissioners were gathered in Shanghai, but shortly before the Commission convened, the British minister in China, Sir John Jordan, elicited an expression of satisfaction with the agreement from the Chinese foreign office. The American delegation got wind of this and cabled the State Department to find out if, as claimed by the British delegation, the Chinese had assured the British minister that the Agreement would remain binding and would not be discussed by the Chinese at the joint Commission. If this was true, they held, it would defeat the aims of the International Commission and tie the hands of the Chinese.[50] The State Department immediately cabled Ambassador Reid in London to find out if the British delegation's claim was correct, and to assure the British government that while the United States had no intention of interfering with the Ten Year Agreement or of questioning its binding character, it believed that the British gov-

49. Confidential Report of the American Opium Commission, pp. 8–9.
50. Brent to the Secretary of State, Shanghai, Jan. 27, 1909, SDR 774/606; RG 43, E 36; Brent Papers, Box 37.

ernment was quite willing that all aspects and facts of the opium trade and habit be fully and frankly discussed in the coming conference.[51] The British Foreign Office confirmed the fact that the Chinese had expressed their satisfaction with the Agreement, but that they had not said that the subject was withdrawn from discussion.[52] Throughout the deliberations of the Commission, however, the British delegation insisted that the matter was not a proper one for discussion as the Chinese had expressed satisfaction with it. For the sake of harmony the American delegation refrained from disclosing to the Commission the specific statement of the British Foreign Office that the question was not closed to discussion.

Before the Commission convened, the American and Chinese delegations met to plan strategy. The Chinese confidentially informed the Americans that at first they had had no specific instructions, but that later the Wai-wu pu had instructed them not to initiate proposals, but to wait and see what the other delegations proposed. Tuan Fang, viceroy of Nanking, and the other Chinese commissioners had objected to this and had requested permission to advocate a government monopoly and a reduction in the time prescribed in the Ten Year Agreement for the prohibition of the importation of Indian opium. After consulting the Board of Revenue, the Wai-wu pu vetoed the first proposition but gave permission for the consideration of the latter. At the urging of Tenney, Tuan Fang had also suggested an imperial edict prohibiting poppy cultivation after 1909. This would have put pressure on the British relative to the Indian trade. The Board of Revenue and the Wai-wu pu advised against this idea, however, for fear that it would result in increased imports from India. Tenney later telegraphed Rockhill to request the Wai-wu pu to give the Chinese delegation the freedom to demand a change in the Anglo-Chinese Agreement, but Rockhill refused on the grounds that this would be improper interference on his part.[53]

In order to avoid embarrassing the British and causing ill feeling, Wright and Tenney carefully reviewed the speech the viceroy had prepared for delivery at the opening of the conference and deleted all "historical references and disputatious points." Their efforts were

---

51. Bacon to the American Embassy (London) Jan. 27, 1909, SDR 774/545.
52. Reid to the Secretary of State, Jan. 28, 1909; Bacon to Brent, Jan. 28, 1909, SDR 774/547; Brent Papers, Box 8. Reid to the Secretary of State, Feb. 17, 1909, SDR 774/547.
53. Confidential Report of American Opium Commission, pp. 10, 35–37.

nullified, however, when the chairman of the British delegation, Sir Cecil Clementi Smith, sent an emissary to Tuan Fang informing him that he should not refer to the Ten Year Agreement before the Commission as the Wai-wu pu had told Sir John Jordan that they were satisfied with it and therefore would not permit the Chinese delegation to bring it before the international gathering. This enraged the viceroy. He destroyed the draft revised by the Americans and prepared a new speech in which he included all the controversial matter that had been deleted.[54] Thus, when the Commission convened, the British representatives were quite surprised and chagrined at Tuan Fang's statement. He reviewed the progress that China had made in suppressing opium production and consumption since the issuance of the imperial edict of 1906, and stated that there were great hopes that the consumption of the drug could be eliminated entirely before the end of the ten-year period. Repeatedly emphasizing the matter of treaties which hampered China in her fight against opium, especially its importation and consumption, he expressed the hope that the Commission would go thoroughly into the matter of such treaties. He concluded by thanking the United States for initiating the movement to aid China, and expressed appreciation for the steps taken thus far by the British in helping China in her antiopium campaign.[55]

The deliberations of the Commission took the form of a discussion of the reports and resolutions of the various delegations. Of these reports and resolutions the American, British, and Chinese were the most prominent. After discussion of the various reports the Commission settled down to the task of arriving at recommendations which the delegations could submit to their governments. As its program for the conference, the American commission submitted eight resolutions, which were the first ones considered. They embraced the following proposals:

1. That a uniform effort be made by the countries represented to restrict the use in their territories of the various forms of opium and their derivatives to what each country considered to be legitimate medical practice.

2. That no government should depend upon the production of the various forms of opium and their derivatives for an essential part of its revenue, and that such dependence should be discontinued as

54. Wright to the First Assistant Secretary of State, Feb. 10, 1909, SDR 774/604.
55. *Report of the Shanghai Opium Commission*, I, 9–10.

soon as possible so that the use of opium might be confined to legitimate medical practice.

3. That the manufacture, distribution, and use of prepared opium should be prohibited as soon as possible.

4. That countries which produced the various forms of opium should prevent at the ports of departure the shipment of such forms of opium to countries which prohibited their entry.

5. That as the use of morphine and its salts and derivatives constituted a part of the abusive use of opium, strict international agreements were needed to control the traffic in and use of these products.

6. That since no government could by its own national laws solve its own domestic opium problem without the assistance of all the governments concerned in the production and manufacture of the various opium products, a concerted effort should be made by each government to aid other governments in the solution of their internal opium problems.

7. That an international conference should be held to provide for international cooperation in the solution of the opium problem.

8. That "every nation which effectively prohibits the production of opium and its derivatives in that country, except for medical purposes, should be free to prohibit the importation into its territories of opium or its derivatives, except for medical purposes."[56]

The principle which ran throughout the American resolutions was that medical purposes constituted the only legitimate use of opium and its derivatives, and that the production, distribution, and use of opium for any other purpose, regardless of the problems involved, should be prohibited. The Americans asserted that private and governmental considerations of revenue constituted the main if not the only barrier to a proper solution of the problem. They felt that the problem was akin to that of the once vexatious slavery controversy in its economic and moral aspects. Therefore they urged that the governments concerned follow Great Britain's example in regard to that controversy by sacrificing finance in the interest of the physical and moral well-being of the peoples affected.[57]

The ensuing discussion of the American resolutions revealed that not all governments—particularly not those concerned with the revenue aspects of the opium problem—shared the American view of the legitimate use of opium and the necessity for the suppression of other uses

56. *Ibid.*, pp. 44–48.   57. *Ibid.*, pp. 43–44.

of the drug. Sir Cecil Clementi Smith, the senior British delegate, objected to the first American resolution on the ground that on the basis of the experience in India, his government could not accept the view that opium should be confined to strictly medical uses or that its use for other than medical purposes should be proscribed. He declared that in India the people relied upon the drug as a common household remedy which the British government would not be justified in withholding from them. He maintained that the declared policy in India of *regulation* rather than *prohibition* was quite the wiser one. A policy of prohibition in India in the near future would be both impracticable and futile, for the use of opium was a national habit whose evil effects were minor and against which there was no strong Indian public opinion. Such a policy, he declared, could be effected only by the maintenance of a huge preventive force to guard the long inland frontier, a long period of preparation in which the consumption of opium could be gradually reduced, and adequate time in which a strong public opinion could be built up against the use of the drug. He admitted that financial considerations also constituted a barrier to a policy of prohibition, but only to the extent that sacrifices of revenue should not be contemplated until ordinary taxation had grown to the point where it could replace the revenue derived from opium transactions. Furthermore, in objecting to the second American resolution, he was careful to point out that without minimizing the financial difficulties involved, this aspect of the problem might not be as prominent as the other issues. A growing revenue derived from opium, instead of being the result of the widespread use of the drug, might well be due to the most efficient system for its regulation whereby more revenue is collected. In support of this point and in reference to the United States, he observed that even in countries where the drug was not extensively used a large revenue was acquired from an excise on it.[58]

As a result of the objections voiced by Sir Clementi Smith the American delegation withdrew its second resolution and agreed to confer with the British on the first. A compromise proposal was subsequently adopted which constituted Resolution 3 of those finally adopted by the joint Commission.[59] The third, fourth, and fifth American proposals occasioned no great objections.[60] The delegation agreed to a

58. *Ibid.*, pp. 48–51.   59. See below, p. 76.
60. *Report of the Shanghai Opium Commission*, I, 51–52.

modification of their third resolution so as to embody the principle expressed by the British and Japanese delegations of the *gradual* suppression of the traffic in and use of prepared opium. Except for a minor revision in terminology suggested by the British, the fourth resolution was approved essentially as it was presented. The Americans withdrew their fifth resolution in favor of a similar British resolution on the same subject. The American proposal had called for strict international agreements to control the traffic in and use of morphine, whereas the British resolution proposed that the responsibility for this control be assumed by the governments concerned within their own territories and possessions.

The remaining three American resolutions were vigorously opposed by the British. Sir Clementi Smith asserted that the principle of the sixth resolution calling on governments to assist one another in the solution of their internal opium problem constituted "a direct interference with the internal administration of a country and was thus beyond the scope of the Commission's power."[61] He pointed to the Opium Exclusion Act of 1909 as indicative of the ability of the United States to handle its own domestic situation. Wright replied that only with the assistance of other powers would the United States be able to make this and other laws effective, an assistance which the government thought it should get. Nevertheless, he agreed to withdraw the resolution with the understanding that it was the sense of the Commission that the principle was covered by the fourth American resolution which had been already adopted.[62] It was obvious that the British objection to the controversial item stemmed from the desire to avoid accepting any obligation to aid the Chinese in the liquidation of their internal problem.

The seventh American resolution, calling for an international conference on the opium problem, was withdrawn after Sir Clementi Smith objected to it on the ground that he would not like to approach his government telling it what to do.[63] Although raised again later, it was finally withdrawn in such a manner as to leave the American delegation with the impression that the other conferees understood that the United States would eventually issue a call for such a conference.[64]

The eighth American resolution was the occasion for one of the most

61. *Ibid.*, p. 52. 62. *Ibid.*, pp. 52–53.
63. *Ibid.*, p. 53.
64. Wright, "International Opium Commission," pp. 866–867.

bitter and impassioned exchanges of the conference. This resolution had been drawn up by Tenney, and it was he who led the discussion on it. At first the American commissioners had considered drawing up a resolution urging the treaty powers to give China immediately and unconditionally full freedom to prohibit the importation of opium. Faced with the certainty that the British would vehemently oppose such a proposition, they formulated instead a resolution expressing the duty of the treaty powers to notify the Chinese government that they would consent to the total prohibition of the importation of opium and its derivatives when China had suppressed the growth of the poppy. Proof of such suppression should result in the abrogation of any treaty provision or agreement limiting China's freedom in this regard. Strong British objections to this phraseology led to the revision of the resolution so as to express merely the right of any nation which had effectively prohibited the production of opium to be free to prohibit the importation of the drug.[65] The resolution was aimed squarely at the Anglo-Chinese Ten Year Agreement, which the British were determined should not be discussed by the Commission. In leading the discussions on the proposal, Tenney made a strong plea for the powers to deal fairly with China and to grant her a free hand to handle her opium problem. He castigated as a disgrace to modern civilization the paradox by which China, as the worst sufferer from the drug habit, was the only nation which was deprived by existing treaties of the freedom that a sovereign nation should have to protect its own people. He therefore demanded that Great Britain and the other treaty powers, without demanding the usual *quid pro quo*, allow China to help herself by exercising her rights as a sovereign nation.[66]

T'ang Kuo-an, the head of the Chinese commission, supported Tenney's resolution, but stated that he intended to introduce a similar one. This evoked an inquiry from the chairman of the British delegation as to whether T'ang was speaking with the approval of his government, which had already expressed satisfaction with the Ten Year Agreement. T'ang refused to answer this question on the ground that it was improper to put such a query to a representative of a sovereign state. However, he proceeded to assert that while China intended to adhere to all its treaties, the Ten Year Agreement included, and while it was satisfied with that agreement when it was signed, it looked upon

65. Confidential Report of American Opium Commission, pp. 9–11.
66. *Report of the Shanghai Opium Commission*, I, 53–54.

the accord as merely a tentative step which did not preclude China's right to bring it up for discussion. Furthermore, in view of the progress which China had already made in suppressing opium production and consumption, his delegation felt that it was fully justified in seeking sympathetic consideration from the British as well as from the other delegations in shortening the period prescribed for the importation of the drug.[67]

The British, however, firmly resisted consideration of the question. Despite Tenney's plea that to refuse to grant China the right to prohibit importation whenever proof had been furnished that domestic production had been suppressed was "grossly unjust," they remained adamant. In this they were supported by the French and Japanese delegations. The latter delegation maintained that the question of treaties between Great Britain and China was a diplomatic matter and thus the Commission was not a proper place in which to discuss it. This contention was sustained by a vote of 8 to 3. The American, Chinese, and German delegations voted for the inclusion of the resolution within the compass of the Commission. Siam abstained.[68] The effort of the Chinese delegation to reopen the discussion on the question in the presentation of their own resolutions was similarly thwarted.[69]

The refusal of the British to permit the discussion of the Ten Year Agreement served, more than any other development at the conference, to strengthen the American prejudice against them and to foster the belief that on the opium question the British could not be trusted. The Americans felt that the British delegation had acted in bad faith in eliciting first an expression of satisfaction from the Chinese government in regard to the treaty on the eve of the conference, and then in insisting that the Indian-Chinese traffic, which was the major factor in the Far Eastern drug situation, be excluded from the scope of the Commission's work. While they recognized the right of the British to refrain from discussing the matter, they contended that this did not justify depriving the Chinese of the right to discuss it. Certainly, they held, China had as much right as a sovereign nation to bring the matter before the Commission as the British had in refraining from so doing. The expression of satisfaction by the Wai-wu pu did not make the issue a closed question. They pointed out that in the correspondence leading up to the conference the United States had made it clear that

67. *Ibid.*, pp. 55–56.
69. *Ibid.*, pp. 71–72.

68. *Ibid.*, pp. 56–57.

all aspects of the opium question would be considered. The British had made no reservations to this. Therefore their contention that the matter concerned only Great Britain and China and that its discussion threatened the sanctity of international treaties was untenable. Furthermore, as the power of the Commission was limited to study and recommendation, it could not directly affect the agreements mentioned. Thus in the mind of the American delegation the British refusal to permit discussion of the Ten Year Agreement was "*prima facie* evidence" that it was "too weak to stand criticism."[70]

The American delegation withdrew from final discussion its first, second, third, sixth, and seventh resolutions, either because they had been modified or merged with other proposals or had been completely rejected by the conferees. The remainder of the work in the Commission was devoted to the propositions of the British and Chinese representatives. The British resolution giving unqualified recognition to the sincerity of the Chinese government in its efforts to root out the opium vice was unanimously and heartily endorsed.[71] Also adopted with only slight modification was the British proposal that since the Commission was not competent to investigate the scientific aspects of the various forms of opium, their derivatives, and the so-called antiopium remedies, the individual delegations should recommend to their respective governments the undertaking of such investigations. This resolution arose out of discussions at the sixth and eighth sessions of the Commission when first Wright and later T'ang Kuo-an suggested the appointment of a committee to study the medical aspects of the opium question, including an investigation of the antiopium remedies.[72] As China was then being flooded by these so-called antiopium pills which themselves contained opium, this was a most important matter. Moreover, an American, Charles C. Towns, who had come to China with letters from both the State and War Departments plus the endorsement of the government of the Philippines to try out his treatment for opium addiction and who reportedly had achieved striking success, had placed his formula before the Commission for consideration.[73]

70. Confidential Report of American Opium Commission, pp. 9–14, 35–38.
71. *Report of the Shanghai Opium Commission*, I, 58–61, covers discussion of British Resolutions.
72. *Ibid.*, pp. 31–38.
73. Confidential Report of American Opium Commission, pp. 22–23.

Three of the delegations—the American, Japanese, and Chinese—were staffed with medical or scientific men. However, the British insisted that the Commission did not have a sufficient number of members of scientific training to investigate the medical aspect of the question. To this, Wright gave the cryptic reply that if the Royal Commission of 1895 had only one medical member and this was deemed sufficient, surely three members of the present Commission should be sufficient. The Chinese delegate also pointed out that the Commission could readily obtain competent men from the outside. But again the British remained adamant, and their proposal that each delegation recommend to its respective government the study of this aspect of the problem was adopted by a 7 to 6 vote. Voting for the resolution were Great Britain, France, the Netherlands, Persia, Portugal, Russia, and Siam. Voting in the negative were Austria-Hungary, China, Germany, Italy, Japan, and the United States.[74]

The real and obvious reason for the British opposition to a scientific study of the opium problem by the Commission was their objection to the view that the use of opium for other than strictly medical purposes was both physically and morally harmful—a vice. As most of the opium produced and used in their Far Eastern possessions and exported to China and other territories was used for other than strictly medical purposes, the British could not allow the Commission to place on record the conclusion that such use was injurious. The other nations which voted with her were similarly affected by the traffic in and use of the drug in the Far East. In spite of the refusal of the Commission to consider this aspect of the question, Town's formula was placed at the disposal of the delegations, and in their report the American delegation presented it to the American government with the endorsement that "the treatment . . . is the most successful on record for the use of the victims of the opium habit in any of its forms."[75]

As the British government had made their acceptance of the idea of an international investigation of the opium question dependent on thorough consideration of the matter of production in China, their representatives at Shanghai manifested keen interest in the Chinese report on the progress made. They expressed extreme skepticism about the accuracy of the statistics presented by the Chinese which showed

74. *Report of Shanghai Opium Commission*, I, 37–39, 58–59.
75. Confidential Report of American Opium Commission, pp. 23–24. Brent to Towns, March 9, 1909, Brent Papers, Box 8.

a substantial reduction in the production and consumption of the drug.[76] They therefore proposed that the Commission recommend that the interested governments enter into negotiations with China with the view to getting China to initiate more systematic methods of dealing with production. The Japanese delegation objected to this with the observation that the Commission, composed as it was of delegations from different countries with different traditions, forms of administration, and degrees of accuracy in taking statistics, should not pass judgment on the statistics presented by China.[77] The Japanese point was well taken, for the statistics of no government in attendance at the Commission, including those of the British, gave a full and accurate picture of all aspects of the opium problem. The resolution was withdrawn. On this matter at least, the Japanese stood with the Chinese in refusing to admit the superiority of Western methods.

As a replacement for the first and second American resolutions an Anglo-American compromise recommendation was adopted which urged upon the governments concerned the desirability of reexamining their systems of regulation in the light of the general consensus that the nonmedical use of opium should be prohibited or carefully regulated. The American delegation went on record, however, as still adhering to the principle of total prohibition except for legitimate medical purposes.[78]

Next to the American proposals, the Chinese resolutions were the most controversial. In his statement introductory to the presentation of these resolutions, T'ang Kuo-an stressed what he claimed to be the devastating economic effect of the opium traffic on China and on foreign trade. He estimated that the cultivation and importation of opium cost China 400,000,000 taels[79] annually and resulted in an annual loss in the earning power of the Chinese people of 456,000,000 taels. All together, this constituted an annual loss to China of 856,000,000 taels. He pointed out that the leading commercial nations shared in this loss in that China's trade with them was adversely affected. For example, fifty years earlier, China's demand for foreign goods was confined

76. *Report of Shanghai Opium Commission*, I, 27–30.
77. *Ibid.*, p. 62.   78. *Ibid.*, p. 62.
79. The basis on which these estimates were made was as follows: cost of opium imported into China—300,000,000 taels; and value of a crop like wheat which would replace opium cultivation—150,000,000 taels. *Ibid.*, pp. 67–68.

principally to opium and silver. Now, he observed, it increasingly embraced such products as cotton goods, kerosene, flour, and matches. Moreover, whereas in 1867 opium formed 46 percent of China's imports and there was therefore a plausible reason for protecting the trade, it now accounted for only 7½ percent of China's imports. He concluded therefore, that "no greater commercial folly can be imagined than that of fostering what is at present 7½ percent of China's foreign trade at the expense of the almost infinite expansion of that trade. . . . The opium traffic is economically as well as morally indefensible."[80] T'ang sought to show that in addition to making "commerce a curse" and thus causing "misunderstanding and prejudice," the opium traffic's international significance was further magnified in that the traffic served as a barrier to the achievement of other reforms in China whereby international relations would be improved and China would be able to participate more fully in international affairs on a modern basis.[81]

As already mentioned, the first Chinese resolution urging the interested governments to promise their cooperation in reducing the importation of opium into China *pari passu* with the curtailment of poppy cultivation in China was opposed by the British and Japanese delegations and was therefore withdrawn. Their second proposal, aimed at the French, called on the foreign governments to close the opium shops and divans in their concessions and settlements in China. As the Chinese themselves had not closed the shops in the areas under their control, the French suggestion that the words *opium shops* be deleted from the resolution was accepted. The French effort to weaken the proposal further by the insertion of the words *as soon as they may deem it advisable* in relation to the closing of the divans, was finally rejected when the amended resolution substituting the word *possible* for *advisable* was unanimously adopted.[82]

The third Chinese resolution urged the governments concerned to prohibit the sale of antiopium medicines containing opium or morphine or their derivatives, except on qualified medical advice, in their concessions and settlements. The French and Japanese objected to this proposal on the ground that this was a matter to be regulated by diplomatic negotiations between China and the powers concerned. The

80. *Ibid.*, p. 68.
81. *Ibid.*, p. 69. 82. *Ibid.*, pp. 72–74.

suggestion made by Hamilton Wright that the Commission should recommend such negotiations was offered as an amendment by the French and adopted.[83]

The fourth resolution offered by the Chinese called for the enactment of laws prohibiting the sale, except to medical practitioners, of morphine, its salts, and instruments for its injection by foreign nationals in China, and for the adequate punishment of violators of such laws. In consultation with Wright and Dr. Rossler of the German delegation, the Chinese revised their resolution to read "that . . . each Delegation move its Government to apply its pharmacy laws to its subjects in the consular districts, concessions and settlements in China."[84] As amended the resolution was unanimously adopted.

The only other proposals of note were those presented by the Dutch delegation. These called for a government monopoly of the opium trade and listed specific measures for the systematic regulation of all opium transactions. These resolutions were placed in the record as expressing the views of the government of the Netherlands, and the feasibility of their adoption was left to the discretion of the governments concerned.[85]

The International Opium Commission finally adopted unanimously nine resolutions.

In Resolution 1 the Commission gave warm and emphatic recognition to the sincerity of the Chinese government and people in their anti-opium campaign and to the progress which they had already made.

Resolution 2 called on each government concerned to take measures "for the gradual suppression of the practice of opium smoking in its own territories and possessions, with due regard to the varying circumstances of each country concerned."

Resolution 3 expressed the desirability of each of the participating government's re-examining its system of regulation in light of the near unanimous agreement that the use of opium for other than medical purposes should be prohibited or carefully regulated.

Resolution 4 stressed the duty of each country to prevent the export of opium and its various products to countries which prohibit their entry.

Resolution 5 called for drastic measures by all governments in their territories and possessions to control the manufacture, sale, and dis-

83. *Ibid.*, pp. 74–77.
84. *Ibid.*, p. 77.   85. *Ibid.*, pp. 64–65.

tribution of morphine and other opium derivatives so as to curtail the grave and growing danger caused by these products.

Resolution 6 expressed the desirability of each government's conducting an investigation of the scientific aspects of antiopium remedies and of "the properties and effects of opium and its products."

Resolution 7 called on governments which had not done so to take steps to close as soon as possible the opium divans in their concessions and settlements in China.

Resolution 8 recommended negotiations between China and the governments concerned for the adoption of "effective and prompt measures" for the prohibition of the trade in and manufacture of antiopium remedies in the foreign concessions and settlements in China.

The final resolution urged the governments concerned to apply their pharmacy laws to their subjects in the consular districts, concessions, and settlements in China.[86]

In general, these resolutions represented a position midway between the views of the Americans and Chinese on the one hand and those of the British and other Western powers with Far Eastern possessions on the other. The unanimity with which they were adopted is indicative of their compromise nature. Resolutions 4 and 9 were American proposals adopted without substantial modification, although Resolution 9 was an American substitute for a Chinese resolution of the same general import. Resolutions 2, 3, and 6 were the results of compromises between the proposals of the American and those of the British delegations, while Resolutions 1 and 5 were British offerings slightly modified at the suggestion of the Americans. Thus only one of the resolutions originally offered by the American delegation—Resolution 4—was adopted substantially as it was presented to the Commission. However, it was this one resolution which the American delegation regarded as the most important of all those adopted.[87] Expressing as the sense of the Commission that it was the duty of countries to prevent the export of opium to countries which prohibited its entry, the resolution was particularly applicable to the problem of both China and the United States.

In the case of China, Resolution 4 came up squarely against the Anglo-Chinese treaties which by the application of the most-favored-nation principle gave other nations as well as Great Britain the right,

86. *Ibid.*, p. 84.
87. Wright, "International Opium Commission," p. 864.

if they had not renounced it, of exporting opium to China. Technically, therefore, the resolution did not touch the Indian-Chinese trade, as China was barred from prohibiting the entry of Indian opium by the Ten Year Agreement. The principle of the resolution, however, constituted an indirect attack on that trade. In view of British touchiness on the issue of the discussion of that traffic in the Commission, it is somewhat surprising that their delegation accepted the resolution.

Resolution 4 also bore directly on the main problem for the United States. As the importation of opium into the Philippines and the continental United States for other than medical purposes was strictly forbidden, the delegates in adopting the resolution put their countries under the moral obligation of helping the United States enforce this prohibition. The resolution soon bore fruit as several of Great Britain's Far Eastern possessions took tentative steps to prevent the shipment of opium from their territories to the Philippines.[88]

Being merely declarations and recommendations, the resolutions were not binding on any country; whatever force they had was moral in nature. Moreover, they represented a rather cautious approach to the problem with which they dealt. The vested interest of the British and other Western nations in the opium traffic was responsible for this. They would not accept the view that the use of the drug was an unmixed evil, and they dismissed specific suggestions for its suppression as unwise and impractical.

The work of the Commission, however, was significant in several respects. First, what had been previously regarded as essentially an Anglo-Chinese question was now clearly a subject of international concern. The realization that the drug problem was not confined to the Orient, but was a growing menace in Western countries as well, underscored the need for cooperative action in combatting the evil. Secondly, the deliberations of the Commission contributed to a deeper and more comprehensive understanding of all aspects of the problem. The difficulties involved in effecting a solution were more clearly perceived, especially by the Americans, who were accustomed to regard the issue in rigid terms of right and wrong. Their appreciation of the difficulties did not cause them to modify their basic demands for immediate action to deal with the situation, however. Thirdly, in spite of the carefully phrased language of Resolution 3, there was general

88. See below, p. 92.

support for the principle that the consumption of opium for medical purposes was the only justifiable use of the drug, and that any other use constituted an abuse and should be prohibited.

In other respects too, in matters not confined to the specific problem of opium, the Shanghai deliberations were of consequence. The government and people of China were highly appreciative of the role played by the United States in this effort to help China.[89] It was another demonstration, in addition to the Open Door policy and the remission of the Boxer indemnity, of American concern for the welfare of that nation. In the matter of the drug problem the two countries became virtual allies, and despite recurrent difficulties between them, they maintained this posture of cooperation to the end of the Second World War. Of equal importance was the fact that the Shanghai Commission constituted the first conference of foreign powers dealing with Chinese problems in which China was granted a status equal to that of the other powers and uncompromised by threats. In the words of a Chinese statesman, it was the first international gathering in China which "had not gone off with either a province or an indemnity."[90]

The public reaction in Europe and America to the work of the Commission was mixed. Much of the criticism of the lack of more substantial achievements and the failure to formulate stronger measures stemmed from a misunderstanding of the nature and purpose of the Commission—that its function was merely to investigate the opium situation and make recommendations, not to formulate binding agreements.[91] Those who commended the Commission's performance regarded its achievements as only the beginning of more formal and effective action.[92]

In the United States the overall impression created was that the successes of the Commission were due to the efforts of the American

89. Wright, "International Opium Commission," pp. 867–868. See also "Delegates for China on the International Opium Commission to the Chief Commissioner of the United States Delegation," Shanghai, Feb. 27, 1909, Brent Papers, Box 8.

90. Hamilton Wright, "Report on the Opium Conference at Shanghai," *Proceedings of the American Society of International Law* (April, 1909), p. 94.

91. Representative of the criticism of the Commission is "The Fight Against Opium," *The Nation*, LXXXIX (July 29, 1909), 92–93. The misunderstanding on which such criticism was based is explained in Brent to Leonard Wood, May 28, 1909; Brent to Whitelaw Reid, June 10, 1909, Brent Papers, Box 66.

92. "A Conference of Poisons," *The Outlook*, XCII (June, 1909), 422; "The International Opium Commission," *Missionary Review of the World*, XXII (May, 1909), 323; R. P. Chiles, "The Passing of the Opium Traffic," *The Forum*, XLVI (July, 1911), 22–39.

delegation supported by the Chinese, while the failure to adopt stronger recommendations was due to the attitude and conduct of the British. The published report of the American delegation fostered this view. Because of this the British were moved to protest and correct point by point what they termed the "loose popular phrases" and exaggerations in the American report. For a brief period it appeared that the report would imperil further international action on the opium problem.[93] The American representatives were even more critical of the British in their confidential report and private correspondence. The British were bitterly assailed for their refusal to permit a discussion of the treaties that deprived China of its freedom to deal as it chose with the opium traffic and for their opposition to a scientific study of the medical aspects of the drug. The Americans thought that by adopting a role of "passive resistance" rather than "constructive leadership," the British passed up a splendid opportunity to clear their country's name of the odium attached to it by their fostering of the opium traffic.[94]

The British deserved much of the criticism directed at them. Perhaps they were somewhat shortsighted in taking an adamant position on the Indian-Chinese traffic, a traffic which they were already committed to bringing to an end. The criticisms, however, tended to obscure the genuine efforts the British government was making to meet the problem of that traffic. Unlike the United States, they were caught between two conflicting currents of opinion. On the one hand public opinion in Great Britain, the United States, and China was calling for an abrupt end to the traffic. On the other hand the opium merchants in India and China, the opium producers in India, and the Indian government wanted the trade to continue indefinitely. Thus the British government had justifiable reasons for approaching the problem with a great deal of caution. This cautious approach, however, was responsible for an enduring distrust of British motives on the part of Americans throughout the period of this study.

Although the Shanghai Opium Commission was credited with only limited achievements, the State Department was satisfied with the re-

---

93. State Department memorandum, Jan. 12, 1911, SDR, RG 43, E 38; Ambassador Reid to the Secretary of State, Dec. 27, 1910, SDR 511.4A1/956.

94. Confidential Report of the American Opium Commission, pp. 11–14, 37–38; Brent to Bishop Laurence, Manila, May 7, 1909; Brent to Leonard Wood, Manila, May 28, 1909; Brent to Mrs. Reid, Manila, June 10, 1909, Brent Papers, Box 8.

sults. In fact, more was accomplished than the Department had expected. Elihu Root, for example, had expected that bickerings and mutual recriminations would cause the Commission to break up.[95] The fact that this did not happen facilitated the efforts of the American delegation to persuade the Department to take action to insure that the work of the Commission would result in more than what one critic had characterized as "pious words." The outcome was the issuance of a call by the United States for a conference to incorporate the Commission's declarations and recommendations in a treaty and thereby make them concrete and binding.

95. Wright to Brent, May 14, 1909, SDR, RG 43, E 51.

Chapter four

The Hague opium conferences

At the Shanghai meeting the Americans withdrew their resolution proposing an international conference on the opium problem when the British objected to it. The idea remained alive with the members of the American delegation, however, and they were determined that it should eventually be acted upon. Therefore, in their confidential report to the State Department, they made a strong plea for the calling of such a conference by the United States.[1] Brent and Wright followed up this proposal with individual entreaties to the Department. They contended that to give binding effect to the resolutions of the Shanghai Commission and to control the opium traffic in general, a conference was needed to adopt measures that would prevent the smuggling of opium from producing countries to the consuming countries which prohibited its entry; would block other producing and manufacturing countries from succeeding to India's position as the supplier of foreign opium to China and other Far Eastern territories, as well as prevent the smuggling of opium from the Native States of India to China; would regulate the manufacture and distribution of morphine, cocaine, and Indian hemp so as to control the growing traffic in these drugs from Western countries to China, India, and other parts of the Orient; and would suppress completely the traffic in certain drug articles by declaring them contraband in both land and sea traffic and by declaring vehicles transporting them open to search.[2] They also laid heavy emphasis on the need to discuss treaty obligations and agreements hampering China's freedom of action in dealing with the opium trade with a view to their possible amendment.[3]

1. Confidential Report of the American Opium Commission, p. 8.
2. Memorandum by Hamilton Wright to William Phillips, May 18, 1909, SDR 774/633; also Wright to Brent, June 9, 1909, Brent Papers, Box 8. The proposal of mutual right of search of carriers of contraband opium calls to mind the fact that prior to 1862 the United States consistently rejected repeated overtures from the British government for a treaty embodying this principle with reference to the slave trade. The old issue of impressment and the influence of the South were responsible for this recalcitrance. See Samuel Fagg Bemis, *A Diplomatic History of the United States* (3rd ed. revised; New York: Henry Holt and Co., 1950), pp. 330–333.
3. Brent to the Department of State, July 2, 1909, SDR, RG 43, E 36.

Despite divided opinion in the State Department, the proposal was rather quickly approved.[4] Wright, who had been retained in the employ of the State Department to investigate the cocaine problem by means of the surplus funds remaining from the appropriation for the Shanghai Commission, was instrumental in getting the hearty endorsement of Secretary Knox.[5] The British indicated informally that they would not oppose the calling of such a conference by the United States, and the Netherlands suggested The Hague as the meeting place. This offer of the Dutch was particularly welcome and indeed had been informally solicited by the United States, for the holding of the conference at The Hague would serve to emphasize the international character and worldwide aspects of the drug problem rather than just the Far Eastern situation.

The circular letter, drafted by Wright, inviting the powers who had participated in the International Opium Commission at Shanghai to meet again in a conference at The Hague, was sent out on September 1, 1909, just eight months after the conclusion of the Shanghai meeting. As justification for issuing the invitation, the State Department stressed America's own drug problem. It pointed out that because of a large Chinese population, trade relations with the Orient, and the hitherto unrestricted importation of opium and the manufacture of morphine, the United States had a substantial opium problem in both the Philippines and within its own continental borders. The letter declared that the United States could not handle its own problem alone; in order for its laws to be effective, international cooperation was needed to control the shipment of opium to this country and its possessions.[6]

As a tentative program for the conference the State Department suggested the following items:

> Control of the production, manufacture and distribution of opium and its products through uniform national laws and regulations;
> Restriction of the number of ports through which opium producing countries might ship the drug;

4. Huntington Wilson, the Assistant Secretary of State, had little faith in the idea and only reluctantly cooperated in its effectuation once it had been adopted. See Huntington Wilson to Secretary of State Knox, April 29, 1909, SDR, RG 43, E 36; also Wright to Brent, Washington, D.C., Nov. 12, 1909, Brent Papers, Box 8.
5. Wright to Brent, Washington, D.C., Nov. 12, 1909, Brent Papers, Box 8.
6. Acting Secretary of State Adee to the Diplomatic Officers of the United States Accredited to the Governments Which Were Represented in the Shanghai International Opium Commission, Sept. 1, 1909, SDR, RG 43, E 46. Also in Brent Papers, Box 9.

Prevention at the port of departure of the shipment of opium and its products to countries prohibiting their entry;

Reciprocal notification of the quantity of various forms of opium shipped from one country to another;

Regulation by the Universal Postal Union of the transmission of opium and its derivatives and preparations through the mails;

Restriction and control of the growing of the poppy so that countries not currently producing would not become producers, and thereby replace the reduction made in India and China;

Application of the pharmacy laws of governments to their subjects in the consular districts, concessions, and settlements in China;

Restudy of the treaties and international agreements under which the traffic was being conducted;

Uniform penal law provisions for violation of agreements that the powers might make concerning opium production and distribution;

Uniform marks of identification for packages in international transit containing opium;

Granting of permits to opium exporters;

Reciprocal right of search of vessels suspected of carrying contraband opium;

Measures to prevent the unlawful use of a flag by vessels engaged in the opium traffic;

An international commission to carry out the international convention concluded.[7]

Two of the items, because of the reasoning which lay behind them, deserve extended consideration.[8] The call for a restudy of the agreements dealing with opium was aimed at the various treaties with China which touched upon the drug and which limited China's freedom of action in regard to it.[9] The treaties involved were not only those be-

---

7. *Ibid.* The first, third, and seventh items were expressive of Resolutions 5, 4, and 9 of the Shanghai Commission. The second, fourth, tenth, eleventh, and thirteenth items were presumably suggestions of measures to give effect to Resolution 4 of the Commission, which was repeated in the third item. The eighth item, however, because of the opposition of the British, had been specifically rejected at Shanghai. The remaining proposals were new but could be interpreted as coming in a general way within the spirit and purpose of the Shanghai resolutions.

8. For the reasoning which lay behind the various items in the tentative program see "Bases," SDR, RG 43, E 37.

9. *Ibid.,* "Bases" X.

tween China and Great Britain, but those between China and other Western powers as well. In regard to opium they hampered China in several ways. For example, one of the methods by which the United States initially hoped that China might more effectively control the traffic in opium was through the establishment of a government monopoly of the manufacture and distribution of opium and its products. The monopoly articles in the Treaty of Wanghia (1844) with the United States, the Treaty of Nanking (1842) with the British, and the Treaty of Tientsin (1858) with the French, and extended to the other treaty powers by the most-favored-nation principle, by which the Chinese commercial monopoly through the Hong merchants was abolished and such monopolies afterwards forbidden, could presumably block the establishment of such a system. It was also thought that by limiting the number of ports through which opium could be imported, China could more effectively control the importation of foreign opium and thus suppress smuggling. The various treaties with the Western powers which opened the treaty ports to foreign trade served as a possible barrier to this step. Furthermore, the United States took the view that China should have the right to prohibit the importation, except for medical purposes, of all opium as soon as domestic cultivation had been suppressed. The State Department suggested to China that it insist upon the discussion of all three of these proposals at the forthcoming conference.[10]

The State Department also gave a great deal of consideration to the possibility of coupling the opium problem with other desired reforms in China. At the Shanghai deliberations, T'ang Kuo-an, the head of the Chinese delegation, had tried to get the support of the American delegation for a resolution which he had been instructed to introduce after first sounding out the Americans. The proposed resolution provided that in order to replace the loss of revenue incident upon the suppression of opium in China, the delegates should recommend to their governments a revision of the Tientsin treaties in order to allow China to place an import duty of 30 percent ad valorem on petroleum, spirits, and tobacco, to be accompanied by an equivalent internal tax on these articles produced in China. Wright had opposed the proposed resolution on several grounds. His chief objection was that the Shang-

10. Huntington Wilson to Minister William J. Calhoun (Peking), June 30, 1910, SDR 774/761a.

hai Commission was called to consider only the question of opium. He therefore advised the Chinese delegates that financial matters related to that question might better be considered in a subsequent international conference after the foundation for favorable international consideration of such matters had been laid by the achievement of unanimity in the Commission. T'ang Kuo-an reluctantly agreed not to introduce the resolution, but to advise the Wai-wu pu to hold the matter over for the probable conference.[11] Wright thus felt that as a result of this conversation the United States was morally obligated to support the Chinese not only in bringing the matter up in the pending conference, but also in giving support to the proposal. He also regarded it as a splendid opportunity to induce China, as a *quid pro quo*, to carry out the reforms relative to internal taxes, mining, trademarks, patents, copyright, and coinage which it had promised to do in the commercial treaty with the United States in 1903.[12] The State Department was particularly concerned with currency reform in China. In the course of the deliberations leading up to the conference, Wright and Professor Jeremiah Jenks, the international monetary expert who had already devised a system of monetary reform for China, held several conversations as to the feasibility of tying such reform to the opium question.[13] Finally, it was hoped that all the treaties and agreements between China and the treaty powers in regard to opium and its various products would be incorporated for the sake of uniformity into a general act of the opium conference.

The second item deserving consideration was the proposal for an international commission to supervise the carrying out of any agreement made. What was contemplated in this proposal was a body with a minimum membership of eight persons, each representing an interested power, which would serve as a collector and clearinghouse of information regarding the drug trade. Specifically, it would serve as the centralizing agency for all information, statistics, laws, and regulations relating to opium which the conference might provide for, and as adviser to the interested governments on all aspects of the drug situation. Its expenses were to be shared equally among the interested

11. Memorandum by Wright to the Secretary of State, March 29, 1910, SDR 774/715; also Memorandum by Wright to Baker, May 10, 1909, SDR 774/623 1/2.
12. *Ibid.*
13. Wright to Jenks, March 18, 1910, SDR, RG 43, E 36.

powers.[14] As it turned out, this suggestion was made some ten years too soon.

In the circular letter the powers were informed that the American suggestions were not intended to be exhaustive, and comments and additional suggestions were requested. Coca leaves, cocaine, and Indian hemp were deliberately left unmentioned in order to avoid creating the impression that the United States intended to prescribe the scope and dominate the activities of the proposed conference. The State Department was confident that other countries would suggest the consideration of these items.

The governments of the invited nations were slow in replying to the American invitation. It soon became obvious that except for the United States and China, no government really wanted an early conference and that some wanted no conference at all. Wright had anticipated that the conference would convene in May 1910. By the end of that month, however, neither Great Britain nor France nor Austria-Hungary nor Turkey had assented to the American proposal. Most of the other powers had agreed to the conference in principle only, and some with rather pronounced reservations. Portugal, for example, made it quite plain that though accepting the conference in principle and this only to please the United States, it was bound to protect the opium trade of Macao and would not take into consideration any decisions of the conference unless they were adopted unanimously by all the countries present and were applicable to all countries, including those not in attendance at the conference.[15]

Russia also agreed in principle to the idea of a conference, but with a reservation to the proposal that poppy cultivation be restricted and confined to the existing producers on the ground that as the poppy was grown in Russia for purposes other than opium, there was little opium production there; therefore the restriction of poppy cultivation would be unnecessary and also damaging to one branch of Russian agriculture.[16] Italy assented to the conference only after its request was agreed to that the trade in Indian hemp and hashish, for which Italian territory served as a collection and storage center for smuggling

14. "Bases" LXXI, SDR, RG 43, E 37.
15. George Lorillard, American Chargé d'Affaires ad interim (Lisbon), to the Secretary of State, May 18, 1910, SDR 774/735, 745; May 31, 1910, SDR 774/751.
16. Minister Rockhill (St. Petersburg) to the Secretary of State, Jan. 29, 1910, SDR 774/693a.

into other territories, be considered, and after receiving assurances that the proposed international commission would not have executive powers which would enable it to interfere in the internal administration of a country.[17]

Even the Chinese, who were heartily in favor of the conference, had significant reservations. They opposed the advocacy of uniform national laws on the ground that there should be no interference with the sovereign rights of any country. They also declared that there was no need for an international commission. On the same ground they stipulated that offenses against treaty provisions be punished by each country according to its own penal laws, and that the right of search be restricted to vessels within a country's own territorial waters.[18] Thus the Chinese were opposed to any measures that would give other powers the right or opportunity to interfere in Chinese affairs or infringe on Chinese sovereignty.

Germany, Holland, Japan, Persia, and Siam assented in principle to the conference pending more thorough consideration of the American program. Austria-Hungary and Turkey eventually reported that they would not be represented at the conference.[19] The French, while agreeing to the conference, took exception to several of the items in the tentative program. They contended that the subject of uniform national laws and regulations to control the various drug operations should not be brought up, nor should the matter of uniform penal laws covering the violation of treaties, as this would require the modification of French penal laws, a matter of such grave import that the French government would not be prepared to bring the question before the legislature. France also objected to the suggestion that the powers apply their pharmacy laws to their subjects in China on the ground that this proposal was not likely to be accomplished, for it would place

17. Baryon Mayor, Italian Ambassador (Washington), to the Secretary of State, Feb. 12, 1910, SDR 774/697; Secretary Knox to the Italian Embassy, March 2, 1910, NA 774/694; The Italian Undersecretary of State, P. Di Scalea, to the American Ambassador, John G. A. Leishman, April 8, 1910, SDR 774/722. The above are also in RG 43, E 38.

18. Huntington Wilson to William J. Calhoun (Peking), June 30, 1910, SDR 774/761a. Also in RG 43, E 38.

19. Secretary of State Knox to Ambassador Reid (London), May 24, 1910, SDR 774/682. Also in RG 43, E 38. The Acting Secretary of State to Messrs. Charles H. Brent, Hamilton Wright, and Henry J. Finger, Delegates of the United States to the International Opium Conference, Washington, D.C., Oct. 18, 1911, Brent Papers, Box 9.

in Chinese hands or those of nationals of other countries not signatory to a convention the practice of pharmacy in the foreign concessions and settlements. On the subject of reciprocal right of search the French declared that French public opinion was sensitive on this matter and that therefore the government would not renounce its principle on the issue just to prevent the traffic in contraband opium. They reserved their opinion on the proposal for a supervisory commission.[20]

A year elapsed before the British, without whom no meaningful conference could be held, replied to the American invitation. Then they assented conditionally to the conference. The British government explained the delay as being due to the necessity of consulting the government of India and other interested departments of the home government and to the desire to examine fully the report of the Shanghai Commission.[21] In reality, the British and Indian governments thought that the call for the conference was quite premature and that the American program went considerably beyond and was inconsistent with the Shanghai resolutions. They objected to the proposals calling for the mutual right of search and measures to prevent the unlawful use of a flag by carriers of opium. They also opposed the idea of a supervisory commission. They were particularly averse to the inclusion of matters affecting any treaty arrangements between Great Britain and China or the domestic opium situation in India and other British possessions within the scope of the conference. They finally consented to participate in the conference on condition that the other invited powers first agree to a thorough consideration by the conference of the question of restricting the manufacture, sale, and distribution of morphine and cocaine. The other powers should also agree to undertake studies, preliminary to the conference, of these aspects of the subject in their own territories and give an indication of their readiness to impose severe restrictions on the manufacture and trade in these drugs.[22] The spread of the morphine and cocaine traffic and habit in India had recently received prominent attention in England, and the State De-

---

20. *Ibid.*

21. Ambassador Reid to the Secretary of State, Nov. 29, 1909, NA 774/682. Great Britain, House of Commons, Sessional Papers, Vol. LXVIII (*Accounts and Papers*, Miscellaneous No. 3, 1913) Cd. 6605, "Instructions to the British Delegates to the International Opium Conference Held at The Hague, December, 1911–January, 1912," p. 2.

22. Reid to the Secretary of State, Sept. 19, 1910, SDR 511.4A1/594; see also *Accounts and Papers*, Miscellaneous No. 3, 1913, Cd. 6605, pp. 2–3.

partment had suggested that the British take the initiative in raising the question of these drugs.[23] The United States thus readily assented to the British conditions, and desperate for British cooperation, also agreed to the British reservations, specifically disclaiming any desire to discuss the Anglo-Chinese agreements at the conference.[24]

Even after assenting to the conference, the British were opposed to its early convocation, and several of their actions, whether designed to do so or not, succeeded in delaying it. Their stipulation that each government conduct preliminary studies of morphine and cocaine manufacture and traffic provided the principal means of procrastination, as such studies obviously took some time. To carry out their own study they found it necessary to require that declarations be made in regard to the amount and value of imports and exports of morphine and cocaine so that the necessary information and statistics might be collected to enable the government to determine the extent of the manufacture and traffic in these drugs in the United Kingdom. This, they declared, would take several months.[25] Then the British found fault with Wright's report on the deliberations of the Shanghai Commission. One of the delegates from India, James B. Brunyate, who sat with the British at the Commission, took vigorous exception to many aspects of the report. In general his comments amounted to the contention that Wright had misrepresented the British position at the Commission, had assigned too much credit to the American delegation for the Commission's achievements, and had exaggerated the sense and conclusions of the Commission relative to the condemnation of the traffic in and use of opium. This criticism disturbed Brent and Ambassador Reid to the point that they feared the holding of the conference might be jeopardized. Reid sent the criticisms to the State Department, and Brent wrote Wright suggesting that he withdraw from the opium work for the good of the movement. Fortunately, both the State Department and Wright disregarded Brunyate's remarks.[26]

The crux of the British desire for delay was the Anglo-Chinese Ten Year Agreement. Even more so than at the time of the Shanghai

---

23. Huntington Wilson to Reid, Aug. 5, 1910, SDR 511.4A1/789.
24. Adee to Reid, Sept. 24, 1910, SDR 511.4A1/794.
25. Reid to the Secretary of State, Dec. 2, 1910, SDR 511.4A1/927.
26. For Brunyate's comments and the discussion of them, see Reid to the Secretary of State, Dec. 27, 1910, SDR 511.4A1/956; State Department Memorandum, Jan. 12, 1911, RG 43, E 38; Brent to Wright, Jan. 24, 1911, RG 43, E 51; Brent to Mrs. Reid, Manila, Dec. 24, 1910, Jan. 26, 1911, and March 23, 1911, Brent Papers, Box 66; Ambassador Reid to Brent, London, April 11, 1911, Brent Papers, Box 9.

gathering the British felt that it was vital that no international discussion of this accord be permitted.[27] The Agreement was due to come up for reconsideration in the latter part of 1910, and the British wanted no exertion of outside influences on the negotiations. Thus they desired to have the matter settled before the conference met. The United States repeatedly assured the British that in spite of the subject being an item in the tentative program, it was disinclined to bring the matter up in the conference.[28] And during the course of the negotiation of the revised agreement, the American minister in China turned down repeated requests from the Chinese for advice.[29] Yet some American influence was informally exerted on the matter. Bishop Brent, while in England in the summer of 1910, had several conversations with Sir Edward Grey, the Foreign Secretary, and other British officials. Acting in his private capacity he urged the British to get together with the Chinese before the conference and modify the Ten Year Agreement so as to bring to a close the Indian traffic as soon as China had suppressed domestic production. Though Brent was not authorized to speak officially for the United States, the British knew that this was the view of the State Department.[30]

As already mentioned, the British and Chinese signed in May 1911 a revised agreement providing for the ending of the Indian-Chinese traffic not later than 1917, but earlier if the Chinese in the meantime had suppressed domestic cultivation. Just what effect the American attitude had on this agreement cannot be determined. Wright claimed, however, that the British were persuaded to sign the treaty by "a bit of informal diplomacy" exerted by the State Department.[31] Whether this "bit of informal diplomacy" was as great a factor as Wright claimed is doubtful. Both the British and Indian Governments had already decided that the traffic should be brought to an end. The details of a working agreement and the desire to hold China to its domestic anti-opium campaign were the main factors causing delay.[32] There can be no doubt, however, that the pressure being exerted for international

27. Wright to Brent, Washington, D.C., May 17, 1910, Brent Papers, Box 9; SDR, RG 43, E 51. Brent to Wright, July 8, 1910, SDR, RG 43, E 51; Brent to Knox, July 8, 1910, SDR 774/765. Also in RG 43, E 38.
28. *Ibid.*
29. William J. Calhoun to the Secretary of State, May 15, 1911, SDR 774/761a. Also in RG 43, E 38.
30. Wright to the Archbishop of Canterbury, July 25, 1910, SDR, RG 43, E 36. Brent to Mrs. Reid, Jan. 26, 1911, Brent Papers, Box 66.
31. Wright to Henry J. Finger, May 18, 1911, SDR, RG 43, E 36.
32. Owen, *British Opium Policy in China and India*, p. 353.

consideration of the Agreement was an element in inducing the British to consent to a rapid settlement of the matter. The Chinese were quite prepared to carry the terms of their demands for a revision of the Agreement before the proposed conference if these demands were not met by the British beforehand.[33] As the British wanted to participate in the pending conference from a stronger moral position than they had enjoyed at Shanghai, they agreed essentially to the terms which the Chinese requested.

Contributing also to the strengthening of this moral position were the steps the British took to carry out Resolution 4 of the Shanghai Commission. In the spring and summer of 1910 Brent met with British colonial officials in the Far East and with officials of the Foreign Office in London in an effort to secure measures to stop the smuggling of opium from such British possessions as Hong Kong, British North Borneo, the Straits Settlements, and India to the Philippines.[34] The result was that several months prior to the conference Hong Kong and India prohibited the export of opium to countries prohibiting its entry.[35]

The British were not alone in their opposition to an early convocation of the conference. To the Americans there appeared to be a conspiracy afoot to block the meeting. The United States had first suggested September 15 in 1910 as the tentative date for the conference. The proposed date was later changed to October 15. As the conference was to meet at The Hague, the Netherlands government assumed the obligation of arranging for its actual meeting. By the time of the first suggested date Great Britain and several other powers had not even indicated whether they were prepared to participate in the conference. The British reply of September 17 making their participation conditional on a study of the morphine and cocaine question naturally precluded the October 15 date. The Netherlands government then suggested May 30, later changed to July 1, 1911, as the date for the proposed conference.[36] As this date approached, however, the British announced that they could not participate, since several powers—

33. Calhoun to the Secretary of State, Jan. 26, 1911, SDR 774/761a.

34. Sir Frederic D. Lugard, Governor of Hong Kong, to Brent, April 1, 1910; Brent to Lugard, April 9, 1910; Brent to Secretary of State Knox, April 12, 1910; Brent to Wright, April 12, 1910; Knox to Brent, June 18, 1910, Brent Papers, Box 9; also Brent to Knox, June 1, 1910, SDR 774/753.

35. Huntington Wilson to Brent, May 25, 1910, SDR 774/734. Copy of Wright to Cameron Forbes, Governor General of the Philippines, May 31, 1911, Brent Papers, Box 9.

36. Jonkheer Loudon, Minister of the Netherlands (Washington) to the Secretary of State, March 10, 1911, SDR 511.4A1/989.

France, Germany, Japan, and Portugal—had not completed their studies of the morphine and cocaine situation.[37] The State Department replied that it would urge the governments to try to meet the British conditions by the July 1 date, but that as the governments had agreed in principle to those conditions the United States hoped that Britain would not insist on their extreme letter.[38] Sir Edward Grey replied that the conference should not assemble before it was ready to do its work, for the result would be a decline of public interest in the drug problem as well as in future conferences in general.[39] As a result, and in spite of the fact that France had indicated that it was ready for a July 1 conference, the Dutch postponed the conference *sine die*.[40] The United States then suggested the date of October 16, 1911, after having received assurances from the four powers that they would be ready by October 1.[41] In spite of the statement of the four powers by August that they would be ready to meet in October, the Dutch refused to endorse the October 16 date and suggested the postponement of the conference until the spring of 1912.[42] When the United States pushed the matter, the Dutch declared that they would not call the conference until they received direct intimations from the four powers and Great Britain that they were ready for the conference.[43] Thus Huntington Wilson's prediction in 1909 that it would take two years for the United States to get a conference was borne out.

The State Department's suspicion that there was complicity to delay the conference was based on information from several different sources. It appeared that the main culprits were Great Britain, Germany, and the Netherlands. As early as May 1911 the American minister at The Hague, Arthur Beaupre, confided his suspicions to the State Department that neither the British nor the Dutch wanted an early conference.[44] He supported his contention in regard to the Dutch by enclosing correspondence between the United States and the Nether-

37. Ambassador Reid to Knox, May 5, 1911, SDR 511.4A1/1055. Also RG 43, E 38.
38. Knox to Reid, May 10, 1911, SDR 511.4A1/1092a. Also RG 43, E 38.
39. Reid to Knox, May 11, 1911, SDR 511.4A1/1083. Also RG 43, E 38.
40. Beaupre to the Secretary of State, May 10, 1911, SDR 511.4A1/1094. Also RG 43, E 38.
41. Knox to Reid, Aug. 2, 1911, SDR 511.4A1/1166b; Knox to the American Legation (The Hague), Aug. 2, 1911, 511.4A1/1166a. Also RG 43, E 38.
42. Beaupre to the Secretary of State, Aug. 11, 1911, SDR 511.4A1/1199. Also RG 43, E 38.
43. Beaupre to the Secretary of State, Aug. 25, 1911, SDR 511.4A1/1186. Also RG 43, E 38.
44. Beaupre to the Secretary of State, May 13, 1911, SDR 511.4A1/1138. Also RG 43, E 38.

lands in 1908 which revealed the reluctance of the Dutch to participate in the Shanghai Opium Commission if the decisions of that commission was later to be incorporated in a convention. The State Department agreed with the minister's analysis of the situation. In July the State Department then received information from its embassy in Germany that Germany, influenced by the large chemical manufacturing interests, who wanted no interference with the manufacture of and traffic in morphine and cocaine, was opposed to a conference before the end of the year.[45]

That Britain and Germany were using their influence to delay the conference was confirmed in private and confidential conversations that Beaupre had with officials of the Dutch foreign office and with the French minister to The Hague, M. Marcellin Pellet. On August 25 the Dutch foreign minister, Van Swinderen, in rejecting the plea for convening the conference before the end of the year, informed Beaupre confidentially that Great Britain did not want an early conference.[46] Then in early September, Pellet confidentially informed Beaupre of the substance of the former's conversation with Count van Limburg Stirum of the Dutch foreign office in charge of the conference arrangements. Van Limburg Stirum had told Pellet that the reason for the delay of the conference was the fact that only the United States and China desired the conference at an early date, and that Germany, influenced by her large chemical manufacturers, had been opposed from the beginning to the holding of the conference; and that thus hostile German influence was partly responsible for the delay. This view was confirmed in Pellet's mind by the attitude of the German minister with whom he had conversations on the matter.[47] Thus long before the suggested October date the State Department knew that it was working for the conference against both the active and passive hostility of several of the major powers.

Overcoming the prevailing sentiment against the conference on the part of some and the inertia on the part of others was a difficult and tedious task. Bishop Brent, in his private capacity, and Wright, in his official position of being charged with the conduct of the negotiations

45. Irvin Laughlin, Chargé d'Affaires ad interim, American Embassy (Berlin) to the Secretary of State, July 14, 1911, SDR 511.4A1/1160. Also RG 43, E 38.

46. Beaupre to the Secretary of State, Aug. 25, 1911, SDR 511.4A1/1186. Also RG 43, E 38.

47. Beaupre to the Secretary of State, Sept. 7, 1911, SDR 511.4A1/1195. Also RG 43, E 38.

under the Solicitor of the Department, James Brown Scott, bore the brunt of the work. They had succeeded, after some initial lukewarmness on the part of the State Department, in getting President Taft and Secretary Knox squarely behind the movement for the conference.[48] Thereafter the State Department applied increasing pressure on the powers. In addition to addressing repeated notes to the powers concerned, the Department pressured the Dutch, German, and British ambassadors to the United States to move their governments to act.

On the same day (August 11) that the State Department was informed that the Dutch opposed the October 16 date and suggested instead the postponement of the conference until the spring of 1912, but prior to receiving the message, Wright, armed with a letter signed by Knox expressing the personal interest of President Taft in the conference and the desire that there be no further delay, went to Maine to discuss the matter with Jonkheer Loudon, the Dutch minister to the United States. Wright intimated to Loudon that if the Netherlands did not call the conference, the United States might convene it in Washington. Loudon promised to push the matter with his government and suggested that the United States urge the four powers and Great Britain to inform his government directly that they were prepared for the October date.[49] This was done.

About three weeks before the Wright-Loudon conference the State Department had decided to send Wright to Berlin to persuade the Germans to give their approval to the October meeting. On the day he was supposed to leave, the Department was informed by the German ambassador that Germany agreed to the October 1 date.[50]

Although the State Department had ample evidence that neither Germany nor the Netherlands wanted an early conference, many in the Department thought that the attitude of Great Britain constituted the chief obstacle. In response to the American request of August 19, 1911, urging the British government to inform the Netherlands directly of its readiness for an October meeting, the British reply was that the Netherlands had informed them that the October date was too early.

48. Brent to the Secretary of State, Manila, Dec. 29, 1909; Brent to President Taft, Manila, Dec. 29, 1909, Brent Papers, Box 8; Taft to Brent, Feb. 8, 1910; Wright to Brent, Feb. 10, 1910, Brent Papers, Box 9. Also in SDR, RG 43, E 51.
49. Knox to Loudon, Aug. 11, 1911, SDR 511.4A1/11772a; Wright to Knox, Aug. 15, 1911, SDR 511.4A1/1171. Also RG 43, E 38.
50. J. Bernstorff to the Secretary of State, July 26, 1911, SDR 511.4A1/1162. Also RG 43, E 38.

Wright was thereupon sent to Maine to confer with the British ambassador, James Bryce. After being shown Beaupre's cables accusing the Dutch, the British, and the Germans of complicity in delaying the conference, Bryce agreed on September 6 to send a cable to London urging that Britain inform The Hague that it was satisfied with the assurances of the four governments.[51] The British, however, after much pressure from the United States, had already informed the Netherlands on September 5 that they were prepared for the conference if the other governments were also ready.[52] On September 20 the Dutch foreign minister informed Beaupre that owing to the changing attitude of Great Britain the conference might be called for December 1.[53]

When the International Opium Conference convened at The Hague on December 1, 1911, the American tentative program had been considerably modified—restricted in some aspects and broadened in others. As already indicated, several of the suggested subjects had been objected to by one or more of the powers, and as a result were presumably barred from discussion. On the other hand, the scope of the conference had been broadened to include the consideration of Indian hemp drugs as suggested by the Italians and of morphine and cocaine as suggested by the British. The powers which offered no objections or suggestions accepted the American program as a basis for discussion pending the expression of their views at the conference.

When the conference met there was therefore no definitive single program before it. Instead of drawing up such a program based on the suggestions and views of the invited powers as promised, the United States decided merely to collate and prepare for circulation the proposals and reservations of the powers and leave the drawing up of a program based on them to the conference itself. This was all that could reasonably be done as most of the powers failed to send the American government any definitive views on the suggested tentative program. Of the fourteen powers invited, twelve attended. Austria-Hungary and Turkey declined the invitation, and the Italian delegation met with the conference only once.

The American delegation consisted of Brent as chief delegate,

51. Wright to Huntington Wilson, Sept. 6, 1911, SDR 511.4A1/1189, Sept. 8, 1911, SDR 511.4A1/1198. Also RG 43, E 38.

52. Reid to the Secretary of State, Sept. 8, 1911, SDR 511.4A1/1193. Also RG 43, E 38.

53. Beaupre to the Secretary of State, Sept. 8, 1911, SDR 511.4A1/1200. Also RG 43, E 38.

Wright, and Henry J. Finger, a physician who had been active in the fight against the opium menace in California as a member of the California State Board of Pharmacy. Frederic Huidekoper and Wallace J. Young of the State Department accompanied the delegation as secretary, and assistant secretary and disbursing officer, respectively. In their instructions the American delegation was advised to keep in mind the fact that while the United States had a material interest in the problem it had "no revenue of moment at stake, and that primarily the international movement for the suppression of the opium evil was initiated by this government with the object of assisting China in her recent and energetic effort to suppress the opium evil."[54] Another matter on which the delegation was instructed had occasioned considerable controversy in the State Department. As already mentioned, Wright had wanted the conference to consider the matters of financial reform in China and the revision of treaties with that nation to allow her to raise her tariffs in order to replace revenue lost as a result of the opium-suppression movement. Others in the Department, like Huntington Wilson and R. S. Miller, thought that such matters were outside the scope of the conference and would cause complications that would jeopardize its success. Furthermore, it would mean consideration by the conference of tariff provisions of American treaties with China, something which, paradoxically, the Department did not favor.[55] The result was a compromise suggested by the Acting Secretary Alvey A. Adee, which was incorporated in the delegation's instructions. They were thus advised:

If in the course of the deliberations the point be raised in any quarter that economic disturbances have resulted from the Anti-opium movement in China and Siam, with their bearing on treaties now in force between these countries and the treaty powers, you should not oppose its consideration, inasmuch as it is a matter in which any interested Power may legitimately express its views. Where the United States is not an interested party in this regard, it would not wish to participate in a discussion of the conventional rights and interests of other Powers. These economic disturbances have not yet been clearly defined. However, as Dr. Hamilton Wright has made a close study of them, much dependence must necessarily be placed by you upon his good judgment and discretion in the event of the interested Governments bringing them forward for discussion; but

54. The Acting Secretary of State to the Delegates of the United States to the International Opium Conference, Oct. 18, 1911, pp. 5–9, Brent Papers, Box 9.
55. *Ibid.*, p. 9.

any commitment of this Government in respect to the revision of its convential tariff with China would not be considered germane to the scope of the Opium Conference.[56]

Thus the effective participation of the American delegation in discussions which might arise in regard to the treaty relations of other powers with China was precluded by the unwillingness of the United States to have certain of its agreements with China bearing on the same matter considered by the conference.

Bishop Brent was chosen president of the conference. In his opening statement he defined the scope of the conference as being the conventionalization of the Shanghai resolutions and the consideration of such other matters as Indian hemp and cocaine. As in the Shanghai Commission, the work of the conference consisted of the consideration of the reports and resolutions of the various delegations. After the tremendous effort required to bring about the convening of the conference, its work, to the American delegation at least, must have seemed anticlimactic.

Unlike the discussion at the Shanghai Commission, the greatest controversy at The Hague was not based on the merits and demerits of the Far Eastern opium trade. This question was indeed given much attention. But thanks to the settlement by the Chinese and the British, prior to the conference, of their major differences over the Indian-Chinese trade, much of the heat that would otherwise have accompanied this phase of the drug problem did not arise. As a result of the settlement of the Indian-Chinese situation, China was in a much better position to demand concessions from the other powers. The British delegation was again headed by Sir Cecil Clementi Smith and consisted of Sir William Meyer, chief secretary of the government of Madras, William G. Max Müller, counselor of the embassy, and Sir William Collins, deputy lieutenant of the county of London and an antidrug advocate. This time the British proposed very progressive measures, which formed the basis of Chapters I and III of the Convention that was finally adopted. The Germans now replaced them in bearing the odium of being the major recalcitrant delegation.

The deliberations in which the provisions of the Convention were finally hammered out were characterized by both controversy and compromise. Chapter I of the Convention dealt with raw opium and

56. *Ibid.*, p. 10.

consisted of five articles regulating the domestic and international traffic in it.[57] Under Articles 1, 2, 4, and 5 the powers pledged to control the production and distribution of raw opium by passing effective laws and regulations limiting the number of ports, cities, and places through which it might be imported or exported; providing for the marking of packages containing over five kilograms of the drug; and restricting to duly authorized persons the right to import and export it. The most controversial and most important provision of this chapter was Article 3, by which Resolution 4 of the Shanghai Commission was to be conventionalized. Under Article 3 the powers pledged to take measures to prevent the exportation of raw opium to countries which prohibited its import and to control exportation to countries which regulated its import. The Portuguese delegation had attempted to weaken this British proposal through an amendment specifying that *by special agreement or otherwise* the powers would take measures to carry out the provision of the article.[58] Obviously the Portuguese objective was to leave the problem of the trade in raw opium, especially the importation of opium into China from Macao, to the meanderings of bilateral diplomacy between the countries concerned. Their amendment would either permit them to claim most-favored-nation treatment on the basis of the Anglo-Chinese Agreement or confine the problem of the opium trade between China and Macao to negotiations between China and Portugal, thereby stalling or preventing China from prohibiting such trade.

Eight delegations initially voted for the Portuguese-amended British resolution, while the United States, China, and Persia reserved their votes. When the matter was brought up again for final consideration, the United States supported the Chinese objection to the Portuguese amendment on the ground that it weakened the entire article. Wright aptly pointed out that the conference was being held to "conventionalize something, not to provide that special conventions might be made."[59] On the basis of the assurance which the Chinese delegation gave to the British delegation that the existing agreements between China and other powers would not be affected, a Chinese amendment that the words "by special convention or otherwise" be deleted was

---

57. International Opium Conference, The Hague, Dec. 1, 1911–Jan. 23, 1912, *Summary of the Minutes* (*Unofficial*) (The Hague: National Printing Office, 1912), pp. 19–24. Cited below as First Hague Opium Conference, *Minutes.*
58. *Ibid.,* p. 19.   59. *Ibid.,* p. 126.

carried by an 8-to-3 vote, with France, Russia, and Portugal in the negative.[60] A Persian amendment, similar to that of the Portuguese, calling for the insertion of the words "by special convention or through diplomatic channels" was likewise rejected by a 7-to-2 vote, Persia and Portugal voting in the negative and France and Germany abstaining.[61] Portugal subsequently withdrew its vote against deletion of the words and urged Persia to do likewise.[62] Another Persian amendment to insert the words "as soon as possible" was rejected 7 to 3, with one abstention.[63]

The conventionalization of the principle embodied in Article 3 was a most important development and its meaning was not lost on the powers. It established a new principle of international commercial law which might later be applied through other conventions to other commodities considered undesirable and prohibited by a country. Chapter I, as a whole, was a commendable achievement. Its weakness, which was subsequently to become very apparent, lay in the fact that while it called for the regulation and restriction of the traffic in raw opium, no specific mention was made of the suppression or reduction of the cultivation of the poppy from which raw opium was derived. As a result, limiting the quantity of drugs available by limiting production at the source was to remain a constant but unattainable goal throughout the period of this study.

Chapter II of the Hague Opium Convention dealt with the traffic in prepared opium and was based on resolutions submitted by the American delegation. In the three articles (6, 7 and 8) which constituted this chapter, the powers pledged to adopt measures for the control and gradual and effective suppression of the domestic traffic in opium prepared for smoking and its manufacture and use. Their promise to prohibit immediately the external trade in the drug was modified, however, by the stipulation that a power not ready to prohibit the export of prepared opium would limit the number of places through which it was exported, prohibit its export to countries prohibiting its entry, control its export to countries restricting its import, and require a special mark of identification on packages exported as well as restrict export transactions to authorized persons.[64]

While Chapter II was aimed at the traffic in prepared opium and its

---

60. *Ibid.*, pp. 130–31.
61. *Ibid.*, p. 131.
62. *Ibid.*, p. 143.

63. *Ibid.*, pp. 144–145.
64. *Ibid.*, pp. 30–31, 33–35.

extensive use in China and the Far Eastern possessions of Japan and the European powers, it was also of concrete significance to the United States. Portuguese Macao was the center of the export trade in prepared opium, and from it the colony derived a substantial revenue. From Macao opium was smuggled directly or indirectly into the Philippines and the continental United States. Much that came into the United States was imported first into Canada and Mexico and then smuggled overland.

Chapter II aroused very little controversy, for the American delegation acquiesced in weakening it for the sake of harmony. Its defect lay in the fact that in calling for the gradual and effective suppression of prepared opium it set no time limit for the achievement of this objective. This defect was to be a major weakness of the Hague Opium Convention as a whole and was to constitute a divisive element in the relations of the United States with the other powers having possessions in the Far East.

The most controversial of the substantive chapters of the Hague Convention was Chapter III, which was based on resolutions introduced by the British delegation.[65] This chapter dealt with the domestic and international traffic in cocaine and the derivatives of opium—medicinal opium, morphine, and heroin. It will be recalled that the British, alarmed at the flooding of their Far Eastern possessions with morphine and cocaine, had insisted upon an investigation of the manufacture and traffic in these drugs as a *sine qua non* of their participation in the conference. The British delegation therefore came armed with strong proposals to deal with the problem. The measures finally adopted, however, constituted the weakest articles of the Convention. By Articles 9, 11, and 12 respectively, the powers pledged to enact pharmacy laws and regulations to confine the manufacture, sale, and use of morphine, cocaine, and their salts to medicinal and legitimate uses; to prohibit in their domestic trade the transfer of these products to unauthorized persons; and to confine their import to authorized persons.

In Chapter III the weak articles were Articles 10, 13, and 15. In Article 10 the powers promised to "use their best efforts to control or cause to be controlled" persons and buildings engaged in the manufacture, distribution, and sale of morphine and cocaine and their salts, and suggested specific measures by which this was to be effected.

65. For the discussions on this Chapter, see *ibid.*, pp. 36–38, 44–46, 48–51, 76–78, 118–121.

Under Article 13 the powers undertook the obligation to "use their best efforts to adopt, or cause to be adopted, measures" to prevent the shipment of morphine, cocaine, and their salts from areas under their jurisdiction to persons unauthorized by the importing country and the areas under its jurisdiction to receive them. Finally in Article 15 the powers promised to apply their laws and regulations in regard to the manufacture, sale, importation, and exportation of morphine, cocaine, and their salts to medicinal opium; to preparations containing more than certain percentages of morphine, cocaine, and heroin; to heroin; and to new forms of the drugs which might prove to be harmful. The weakness of the above articles obviously lay in the fact that no definite pledge was undertaken to perform certain acts but merely a promise to "use their best endeavors to take" certain measures. The exemption of preparations containing certain minimum percentages of the drugs in question and of codeine from regulation and control constituted another major weakness. This defect was partly offset, however, by the provision made to bring new drugs discovered to be injurious under control.

The delegation most responsible for the watering down of the British resolutions regarding the manufactured drugs was the German. The German chemical industry had put much pressure on the German government not to attend the conference. Germany was a major manufacturer of opium derivatives and had almost a monopoly of cocaine production. The German delegation therefore was out to scuttle any strong measures that might jeopardize the favored position of their manufacturers. They argued that to be effective any convention for the control of these drugs would have to be adhered to by all the nations of the world; otherwise, Germany and the other powers participating in the conference would be merely sacrificing their industry and trade for the benefit of the industry and trade of other countries nonadherent to the convention. They further contended that Germany already had an effective system of domestic control and therefore other countries should similarly protect themselves through effective police and customs systems. They pointed to constitutional difficulties blocking acceptance of the British resolution: the Convention, if ratified by the Reichstag, would become a part of German law, and as the cocaine and morphine articles dealt with matters within the sphere of the individual states and not within that of the imperial government, as drawn up, the Convention was not likely to be ratified, for the articles mentioned would infringe on state autonomy. Upon its return to The Hague after the Christmas recess, the German delegation was even more adamant in its opposition to the British measures.[66] Obviously its government had instructed it not to yield.

Faced with the fact that the German delegation would not acquiesce in the British proposals and that without German approval the proposals would not be effective even if adopted because of the prominent place Germany occupied in the production and trade in the manufactured drugs, the British yielded, after a week's deadlock, to the compromise propositions of the Germans by agreeing to the insertion of the phrase "the contracting parties shall use their best endeavors to take" the measures indicated. It was on German insistence also that codeine was exempted from the drugs to be controlled on the grounds of lack of evidence that the drug would produce habituation. Because of American and Chinese opposition to this deletion, Germany lost by a vote of 8 to 2 (Russia supporting Germany) on the original vote. The amendment was later carried, however, for the sake of harmony and unanimity when Germany still insisted. Even in their weakened form, the articles of Chapter III still did not satisfy the German delegation, and that dissatisfaction was primarily responsible for the novelty of the clauses outlining the procedure for putting the Convention into effect.

The resolutions of the Chinese delegation (T'ang Kuo-an was again a member) constituted the basis of Chapter IV of the Convention, which suggested measures to be taken by China and the treaty powers for the control of the drug traffic in China.[67] Under Article 15 China and the treaty powers pledged to adopt measures to prevent the smuggling of the various drugs covered by the Convention into each other's territories or areas under their jurisdiction. Under Article 16 China was to adopt pharmacy laws for its subjects which, on communication to the treaty powers for examination and if found by them to be acceptable, were to be applied to the nationals of those powers residing in China. By this article China attempted to get around the barrier of

66. For a convenient summary of the attitude of the Germans at the Conference as well as the activities of the Conference as a whole, see *Report of the British Delegates to the International Opium Conference Held at The Hague, December 1911–January 1912*, Great Britain, House of Commons, Sessional Papers, Vol. LXVIII (*Accounts and Papers*, Miscellaneous No. 11, 1912) Cd. 6448, pp. 16–20.

67. For the discussion of the measures constituting Chapter II, see First Hague Opium Conference, *Minutes*, pp. 64–68.

extraterritoriality in dealing with the foreigners in China engaged in the drug traffic. In Articles 17 and 18 the treaty powers placed themselves under the obligation of adopting measures to restrict and control the consumption of smoking opium in areas under their jurisdiction in China, to close *pari passu* with the Chinese government opium divans and similar establishments, to reduce gradually *pari passu* with the Chinese government the number of opium shops, and to restrict and control the retail trade in opium in these areas. Under Article 19 the powers having post offices in China promised to adopt measures to prevent their use for illegal transmission into and within China of the drugs covered by the Convention.

In Chapter IV China obtained the confirmation of principles for which she had long been contending and was thereby able to block the other treaty powers from taking advantage of the revised Anglo-Chinese Ten Year Agreement through the application of the most-favored-nation principle and continuing to export opium to China. That this was a definite danger had been made clear early in the conference when the Portuguese insisted that because China was pledged to receive Indian opium for six years, she was not permitted to prohibit the importation of foreign opium from other sources except by special agreement with the other powers. T'ang Kuo-an held that special conditions applicable to the Indian-Chinese opium trade would not exist in regard to other trade; therefore Portugal and other nations should not insist on similar privileges.[68] The adoption of Chapter IV as well as Article 3 of Chapter I was a victory for the Chinese.

To assure that the victory should not be tarnished, Wright backed the Chinese in opposing the suggestion of Sir William Collins that the Chinese resolution be embodied in a separate convention. This proposition stemmed from the fact that Persia and Siam, not being treaty powers, felt that they should refrain from taking a position on the resolutions, as these resolutions did not apply to them. Therefore it was suggested that in order to get unanimity on questions in which all were concerned, Chapter IV should constitute a separate convention. Wright took vigorous exception to this proposal on the ground that it "would distinguish China invidiously from the rest of the sovereign Powers here represented," and that China's participation in the conference represented "a new era—an era of greater comity between

68. *Ibid.*, pp. 19–21.

China and the Western Powers which should not be diminished."[69] His countersuggestion that all the powers should sign a general convention with Persia and Siam attaching a note excepting them from articles not applying to them was the procedure finally followed.

Chapter V consisted of only two articles. Article 20 called for the consideration of the possibility of enacting domestic legislation providing penalties for the illegal possession of the drugs covered by the Convention. This was implicit acceptance, but only after some opposition, of the American view embodied in the Opium Exclusion Act of 1909, that illegal possession should be regarded as evidence for conviction. Article 21 was based on an American proposal. Under it the powers agreed to exchange through the medium of the Netherlands government the texts of laws and regulations and statistical data regarding the drug traffic.[70]

Several resolutions of substantive content which were considered by the conference and either withdrawn or rejected deserve brief mention here. Early in the conference, Wright announced his intention of introducing a resolution providing for the outlawing of the drug products of opium-producing countries which failed to adhere to the Convention within two years after its adoption.[71] There is, however, no record that the resolution was ever presented or considered. Undoubtedly it would have failed of passage. Wright withdrew his resolution calling upon the powers to forbid their citizens and subjects to supply opium, morphine, and cocaine and their various products to the unprotected natives of the Pacific islands when the other delegations pointed out that they could accept it only *ad referendum*, as they had no instructions on the matter.[72] The proposal was similar to the American law of 1902. The American delegation objected to a proposal of the Netherlands delegation that the purchase of raw opium and wholesale transactions in it should be made a government monopoly, on the grounds that such a system was so adverse to American principles in regard to any article of commerce that Congress would be unlikely to consider it.[73] This was surprising in the light of the fact that the United States had proposed such a system for China. A proposal from a member of the French delegation, who claimed that there was increased consumption of alcohol in Indochina as a result of the decrease in the

69. *Ibid.*, pp. 90–91.
70. *Ibid.*, pp. 75, 141.
71. *Ibid.*, pp. 44, 47.

72. *Ibid.*, p. 88.
73. *Ibid.*, pp. 41, 45.

consumption of opium, that the conference express the desire that governments mutually aid each other and take measures equal to those in regard to opium to suppress the evils of alcohol, was objected to by Wright and Sir Clementi Smith on the grounds that the opium question and parallel matters should be kept separate.[74]

Even more controversial than the substantive articles of the Convention were the proposals for putting it into force.[75] The German delegation, supported by the French, had insisted throughout the conference that in order for the measures adopted to be effective, they would have to be adopted by the powers not represented at the conference, for the matters dealt with were of worldwide concern and many of the powers not represented at the conference occupied a very important position in these matters, especially Turkey in regard to raw opium, Bolivia and Peru in regard to cocaine, and Switzerland in regard to manufactured drugs. They therefore insisted that the adherence of the outside powers should be obtained before ratification of the Convention took place. Many of the other delegations, desirous of putting the Convention into effect as soon as possible, objected to the delay that would be caused by the necessity of getting the adherence of thirty-four powers.

The crux of the difficulty was Chapter III relating to morphine and cocaine drugs. The German delegates were adamantly opposed to having their government make any pledges in regard to the control and restriction of the traffic in these drugs while other powers might remain free to do as they like. Furthermore, they cast doubt upon American sincerity in the matter by putting to the American delegation the following rather impertinent questions: (1) "What guarantee can they [the American Delegation] give to the other delegations that the United States Government, after having signed and ratified the treaty . . . will pass the necessary legislation to put the stipulations of the treaty into force?" (2) "What guarantee can the American Delegation give that the stipulations of the convention, after having been put into force, will not be invalidated by subsequent laws not in harmony with the convention?"[76] The questions were embarrassing to the

---

74. *Ibid.*, p. 59.   75. *Ibid.*, pp. 74 ff.

76. *Ibid.*, p. 105. Wright regarded these questions as part of a deliberate plan to embarrass and defeat the objectives of the United States. See Hamilton Wright, "A Recent Deployment of the Latin Americas in Support of a Diplomatic and Humanitarian Policy Initiated by the American Government," *AJIL*, X (Jan., 1916), 127–128.

American delegation not only because of their rudeness, but also because, in spite of Wright's efforts to get the Congress to pass drug-control legislation before the conference met in order to strengthen the American position at the conference, Congress had not responded. The result was that the American delegation entered the conference, which the United States had called, lagging behind all the Western nations and Japan in legislation to control the domestic traffic in the drugs under consideration. Wright's reply was to the effect that "the good faith of the United States was a sufficient guarantee that Congress would pass the necessary legislation to enforce the Convention if Germany would sign and ratify it."[77]

To meet the dilemma presented by the German attitude, and to provide for the normal procedure for ratification and adhesion, Wright proposed that the Convention be divided into two parts. Chapters I, II, and IV relating to raw and prepared opium, on which there had been no substantial disagreement, should constitute a separate convention from Chapter III, on which there was major discord, in order that the former might not be pulled down to the level of the latter and thus make difficult the adhesion to and ratification and effectuation of the whole work of the conference. The British, French, and Siamese delegations objected to this resolution on the grounds that it was contrary to the agreement with Great Britain preliminary to the conference stipulating that the morphine and cocaine question would be considered on the same level as opium. They maintained that the morphine and cocaine problem was as important as the opium problem, and that it should not be relegated to second place. Wright's motion that his proposal be discussed was defeated, with only Germany and China supporting it.[78]

A compromise scheme was drawn up by the drafting committee which, amended along lines suggested by the British delegation, formed the basis for Articles 22 and 24. Article 22 provided for the adherence of nonsignatory powers through a special Protocol. Article 23 provided for the ratification of the Convention and the supplementary Protocol after all the powers had signed the Convention or the Protocol. If this were done by December 31, 1912, the Netherlands government was to invite all the signatory powers to another conference at The Hague to consider the possibility of fixing a date for the depositing of ratifica-

77. *Ibid.*
78. First Hague Opium Conference, *Minutes*, pp. 132–136.

tions. Article 24 stipulated that the Convention should go into effect three months after the Netherlands government had given notification of its ratification by all the signatory powers. Not later than six months after the Convention went into effect the powers were to have drawn up measures called for in the Convention and recommended their enactment to their respective legislatures. Article 25 provided for the denunciation of the Convention and stipulated that questions arising in regard to the ratification and effectuation of the Convention or in regard to its substantive measures might be settled in a subsequent conference of the signatory powers at The Hague.[79]

The provisions embodied in Articles 22–24 were quite new in that they represented a radical departure from similar provisions in other international conventions. Though novel, they were necessary, for without them unanimous adoption of the Convention and the Protocol of Cloture would have been impossible. The Protocol of Cloture contained two main provisions. The part based on an American proposal requested the International Postal Union to take steps to prevent the transmission of drugs through the mails. The other called for a scientific and statistical study of Indian hemp looking toward its domestic and international regulation.[80] The Convention and Protocol were unanimously adopted by the participating powers, and the conference came to a close on January 23, 1912.

It was generally agreed that the Hague Convention was a distinct advance in the antiopium movement, that it represented a new standard of international morality in that the participating powers agreed to help each other in the solution of a problem that was beyond the control of any individual state, and that it firmly established the principle of the necessity of such international cooperation.[81] In addition to con-

79. For the text of the Convention see International Opium Conference, The Hague, 1911–1912, *The International Opium Convention* . . . (London: H.M. Stationery Office, 1912).

80. *Ibid.*

81. For some representative appraisals of the Convention, see "Report of the British Delegates to the International Opium Conference," pp. 26–27; Confidential Report of the American Delegation to the International Conference at The Hague, Dec. 1, 1911, to Jan. 23, 1912, enclosed in Brent, Wright and Finger to the Secretary of State, Feb. 12, 1912, SDR 511.4A1/1283; U.S. Dept. of State, *The Opium Evil: Message from the President of the United States Transmitting Communication of the Secretary of State Covering the Report of the American Delegation to the International Opium Conference Held at The Hague from December 1, 1911 to January 23, 1912*, 62nd Cong. 2nd Sess., 1912, Senate Doc. 733 (Washington: Government Printing Office, 1912), p. 27. (Cited below as Senate Document 733). For some unofficial views see Elbert

ventionalizing the Shanghai resolutions, which were concerned primarily with the opium problem in the Far East, the Convention contained measures designed to deal with what was rapidly being recognized as truly a worldwide problem. It marked the beginning of sincere British cooperation in at least one aspect of the antidrug campaign—that of the manufactured drugs. For China it was another step forward in her relations with the West after the Shanghai Commission, in that for the first time she participated in an international conference and signed a treaty on terms of equality with other states.

Despite the fact that it stood as a landmark in the drug movement, in international comity, and in the foreign relations of China, the Hague Convention was an imperfect instrument. It was, as is usual in international conventions, necessarily a compromise: a compromise between the powers whose governments or citizens had an economic interest in the drug traffic and the powers who would subordinate or even disregard all economic considerations in favor of the humanitarian goal of eliminating the misuse of these drugs. The strongest provisions of the Convention were in Chapters I and IV. Chapter II was weak in that the powers were not pledged to suppress the use of prepared opium within a specific period of time, but only promised to take steps to suppress gradually the traffic and use. Chapter III was the weakest. No distinct pledges were made to control and restrict the traffic in and manufacture of morphine and cocaine and their products; it contained merely the hollow promises of endeavoring to take certain measures. In addition, one of the Convention's greatest defects was the lack of an organ of administration to supervise the carrying out of the provisions of the Convention. Fear by the powers of an international body that would infringe on their sovereignty prevented even the consideration of this step at the conference.

Nevertheless, the Convention was probably the best that could be obtained at the time and under the circumstances. It fell short of the goals set for it, and probably no participating power was totally satisfied with it. In the United States there was initially a great deal of disappointment and suspicion, official and unofficial, at the results

---

F. Baldwin, "The Background of the Opium Conference at The Hague," *American Review of Reviews*, XLV (Feb., 1912), 214–218; William J. Collins, "Work of the International Opium Conference at the Hague," *Contemporary Review*, CI (March, 1912), 317–327; Foreign Policy Association, *International Control of the Traffic in Opium: Summary of the Opium Conferences Held at Geneva, November, 1924 to February, 1925* . . . (New York: Foreign Policy Association, 1925), pp. 3–4.

achieved. Closer examination, however, led the President and the State Department to conclude that a significant advance had been made.[82] This view was shared by the American delegation, which though cognizant of the outstanding shortcomings of the Convention, nevertheless found much in it to applaud.[83] They regarded the conventionalization of the American principle, first raised at Shanghai and strenuously opposed there by the British because of the Indian-Chinese trade, that the export of opium to countries prohibiting or regulating its entry should be similarly prohibited or regulated, as a most significant step forward and capable of application to other products and other situations. This principle was embodied in Articles 3, 7, 8, and 13 of the Convention. The British were the first to apply it in relation to the export of opium from Hong Kong, the Straits Settlement, India, and Canada. Equally significant in their view, was the recognition in Chapter II of the Convention of the principles of the Opium Exclusion Act of 1909 and of the opium legislation in the Philippines to the effect that the use of opium for other than medical purposes was unjustified and should be suppressed. Despite American disappointment with the Convention, it was to remain until 1931 the only foundation on which the United States was willing to base its international drug policy.

By Articles 22 and 23 of the Convention the government of the Netherlands was entrusted with the task of securing the signatures of the states not represented at the conference and of receiving the deposits of ratification of all the states. As informally prearranged with the American delegation, the Dutch requested the aid of the United States in obtaining the signatures of the Latin American countries. To this end the State Department addressed a long and urgent appeal to these states for their cooperation.[84] The Latin American nations responded heartily to the request, and by the end of 1912 all of them except Peru had notified the United States that they had signed or would do so. Peru hesitated because of her deep economic involvement in the cultivation of the coca leaf and (with her large Chinese population) her revenue interest in the opium trade.[85] Despite serious differences

82. Wright to Lloyd Bryce, April 8, 1912, SDR, RG 43, E 36.
83. Confidential Report of American Delegation to the First Hague Conference, SDR 511.4A1/1283.
84. Circular Instruction Addressed to Diplomatic Officers of the United States Accredited to the Governments of Latin America, April 15, 1912, SDR, RG 43, E 40.
85. H. Clay Howard, American Legation (Lima) to the Secretary of State, Nov. 9, 1912; Secretary of State Bryan to the American Legation (Lima), July 7, 1913, SDR,

on other matters, this response of the Latin American States was typical of their relations with the United States on the drug problem throughout the international movement, a situation about which the United States was most appreciative.

As the signatures of all the powers were not obtained by December 31, 1912, the Dutch, pursuant to Article 23 of the Hague Opium Convention, called on the signatory powers to meet in a second conference at The Hague on July 1, 1913, in order to examine the possibility of nevertheless depositing ratifications. When the conference convened, thirty-four powers had signed the Convention and twenty-four of these, as compared to the twelve present at the First Conference, were represented at the conference. Twelve powers had not signed the Convention, and of these, four—Austria-Hungary, Bulgaria, Norway, and Uruguay—had indicated that they would sign, four—Montenegro, Peru, Serbia and Sweden—had not replied, one—Rumania—was still considering the question, and three—Greece, Turkey and Switzerland —had said they would not sign. Greece had given no specific reasons for refusing to sign; Turkey merely stated that it would not sign for economic reasons; and Switzerland claimed that her cooperation would be valueless as she neither produced nor exported opium and already had effective domestic legislation on the matters in question.[86] In face of the above situation the prevailing attitude among diplomats and others at the opening of the Second Conference was one of pessimism. Most thought that the work of the conference would be marked by much talk and little or no action.[87]

The American delegation was this time headed by Hamilton Wright, who was accompanied by Lloyd Bryce, the American minister at The Hague, and Gerrit John Kollen, president emeritus of Hope College. After ascertaining the somewhat hopeless attitude prevailing in the

---

RG 43, E 40. See also U.S. Department of State, *Second International Opium Conference. Message from the President of the United States Transmitting a Communication from the Secretary of State, Accompanied by a Report Prepared by Hamilton Wright, on Behalf of the American Delegates to the Second International Opium Conference Which Met at The Hague . . . July, 1913 . . .* 63rd Cong., 1st Sess., 1913, Senate Doc. 157 (Washington: Government Printing Office, 1913), pp. 8–11, cited below as *Report of American Delegation to the Second Hague Opium Conference.*

86. Second International Opium Conference, The Hague, 1–9 July 1913, *Summary of the Minutes* (The Hague: National Printing Office, 1913), pp. 1–3. Cited below as Second Hague Opium Conference, *Minutes.*

87. Lloyd Bryce to the Secretary of State, July 14, 1913, SDR 511.4A1/1408. Also in RG 43, E 40.

first session of the conference the American delegation obtained a twenty-four hour adjournment in order that informal conversations on various aspects of the Convention might take place. Private discussions were held among the British, French, German, Dutch, Russian, and American delegations for the formulation of measures to give effect to a British proposal that a combined effort be made by the signatory powers to secure the signatures of the states which had not signed, including those which had expressed their intention not to do so. Out of these discussions came a resolution calling upon the governments of the Netherlands to clear up the misunderstandings which many of the recalcitrant powers seemed to have as to both the purpose and the provisions of the Convention, and at the same time to urge these states to sign immediately and agree to ratify the Convention. The supplications of the Dutch government were to be supported at the capitals of the nonsignatory countries by the diplomatic representatives of the states which had signed the Convention. After only minor objections, this proposal was unanimously adopted and embodied in the Protocol of Cloture, which was signed by the representatives of the members of the conference on July 9.[88] Before the conference adjourned, Uruguay and Peru, after urgent appeals from the United States, agreed to sign the Convention. The Protocol was thus directed at only ten powers.

The adoption of the above resolution constituted the major work of the Second Conference. During the course of discussion on the proposal, the Chinese delegate had suggested that representations be made to the nonsignatory powers at once, and that pending the receipt of replies, the conference should adjourn and then reassemble when the results had been ascertained. Hamilton Wright endorsed this proposal, but a majority of the other delegations rejected it on the ground that as several of the nonsignatories were at war (the Balkan States), the replies might be slow in forthcoming. Moreover, they contended, the conference had already discharged its duty by examining the possibility of ratification as specified in Article 23 of the Hague Opium Convention.[89]

Some difficulty arose over the question of whether the powers had

88. Second Hague Opium Conference, *Minutes*, pp. 18–20.
89. Great Britain, Foreign Office, *Correspondence Respecting the Second International Conference Held at The Hague, July 1913*, Miscellaneous No. 2 (1914), Cd. 7276 (London: H.M. Stationery Office, 1914), p. 10.

to meet again to deposit ratifications after the nonsignatory powers had been heard from. Early in the conference several delegations had declared that their governments were not ready to ratify the Convention. France declared its readiness to ratify for France proper, but not for Indochina, because of the smuggling on that territory's frontier with China. On the other hand, Portugal and Russia expressed their unwillingness to deposit their ratifications until certain other powers had signed the Convention. The crucial attitudes were those of the British and the Germans. The Germans reiterated their First Conference argument that the efforts of a limited number of powers to regulate the narcotic drug trade would be futile so long as other powers, not bound by the Convention, were free to engage in the manufacture of and trade in these products. Germany therefore would not ratify the Convention until all the powers had signed. The British delegation took a similar position. The nonadherence of Austria-Hungary, Switzerland, and Norway, they declared, would make ineffective the proposals for preventing the exportation of morphine and cocaine, while the nonadherence of Peru alone would render the articles relative to the coca leaf worthless.[90] Thus the process of ratification was delayed by the unwillingness of several of the major powers involved in the drug traffic to sacrifice their commercial interests for fear that other countries might profit at their expense and at the same time render ineffective the provisions of the Convention. It was finally decided that powers which were prepared to do so might deposit their ratifications according to Article 23 of the Hague Convention.[91] Embodied in the Final Protocol of the Second Conference was the stipulation that a third conference should be held if the signatures of all the powers were not obtained by December 31, 1913, to consider the possibility of putting the Convention into effect.[92]

The Second Conference had no spectacular achievements to its credit. Its accomplishments were merely procedural. Nevertheless some impetus was given to the antidrug movement. At the close of the conference, thirty-six nations had signed or indicated that they were ready to sign the Convention, and several were ready to ratify.[93] Only a small, though powerful, minority delayed ratification, which was no longer dependent on universal adherence to the Convention. The con-

90. Second Hague Opium Conference, *Minutes*, pp. 10–14.
91. *Ibid.*, pp. 22–23.   92. *Ibid.*, p. 32.
93. Report of American Delegation to Second Hague Opium Conference, pp. 21–22.

ference itself attracted little public attention, since it was overshadowed by the several international crises in Europe.

The United States deposited its ratification of the Hague Opium Convention on December 10, 1913. But by December 31, 1913, several powers still had not subscribed to the Convention. Thus the Dutch called for a third conference to meet at The Hague in May 1914 in order to consider the possibility of putting the Convention into effect even though it had not been signed by all the states. Meanwhile, the United States sought to put its own house in order. The change in administrations in Washington in 1913 had occasioned no slowing down of the campaign in the United States. President Wilson and Secretary of State Bryan gave their hearty support to the work.[94] A report by Wright to the Secretary of State on the opium question was submitted without change to Congress on April 21, 1913, as President Wilson's first special message.[95] The State Department hoped that before the third conference met, Congress would pass all the proposed narcotic legislation pending before it. It was also hoped that in order for the United States to have Mexico's support at the conference, relations with that country might be cleared up. Therefore, at America's request, the conference was postponed until June 15, 1914.[96]

When the Third Conference convened, forty-three powers had signed or had declared their intentions of signing the Convention. Austria-Hungary had not signed for constitutional reasons, but had finally declared that she would adhere to the Convention. Greece was prepared to adhere for Greece proper, but with a reservation exempting her newly acquired territory from the provisions of the Convention. This reservation was later withdrawn, however. Thus only two recalcitrant powers remained. Serbia still pleaded lack of sufficient time to give consideration to the question as its reason for not subscribing. On the other hand, Turkey had categorically refused to sign, citing economic reasons. Only eight powers had ratified the document.[97]

94. Memorandum by Hamilton Wright, April 28, 1913, SDR, RG 43, E 41.
95. *Ibid.* This was Wright's report on the Second Hague Opium Conference.
96. Hamilton Wright to J. Butler Wright, American Ambassador (Rio de Janeiro, Brazil), May 4, 1914, SDR, RG 43, E 36.
97. Henry Van Dyke and Charles Denby, American Delegates to the Third International Opium Conference to the Secretary of State, June 26, 1914, SDR 511.4A1/1489. Also in RG 43, E 36. Cited below as Report of the American Delegation to the Third Hague Opium Conference.

For the first time Hamilton Wright did not represent the United States in an international gathering on the drug traffic. As a result of financial difficulties with the State Department concerning claims of back salary due him and a resultant petty dispute with Secretary of State Bryan, Wright was unceremoniously dropped from the American delegation.[98] The United States was represented at the conference by Henry Van Dyke, the American minister at The Hague, and Charles Denby, the American consul general at Vienna. The British were again represented by William Max Müller and Sir William Collins; the French by Marcellin Pellet, French minister to the Netherlands; the Germans by Felix von Müller, the German minister to the Netherlands; and the Chinese by Yen Hui-ch'ung and T'ang Tsai-fou, the Chinese ministers to Germany and the Netherlands, respectively. Altogether envoys of thirty powers were in attendance.[99]

The question which the Third Conference had to consider was essentially whether the Convention should come into force without the signature of two powers, Turkey and Serbia. The American position was summed up by Van Dyke both at the beginning and at the end of the Conference to embrace the following points:

1. An earnest desire to make the Anti-Opium Convention of 1912 effective soon.

2. A sincere wish that all nations shall join.

3. A willingness to put it into force between a limited number of Powers under proper conditions.

4. A definite intention to do this only in *such a form as will not foster or* [will] *prevent a profitable monopoly in opium for the abstaining Powers.*[100]

In support of the American position and as proof of the absolute sincerity of the United States, Charles Denby reviewed the legislation and other measures taken by the United States to make the Convention effective.[101] As a result of the passage of several measures by Congress shortly before the conference convened, the American representatives

98. See Bryan to President Wilson, March 21, 1914; Wilson to Bryan, March 23, 1914; Wright to Wilson, June 7, 1914; and Bryan to Wright, June 10, 1914, SDR, RG 43, E 46.

99. For the members of the respective delegations, see Great Britain, Foreign Office, *Correspondence Respecting the Third International Opium Conference, Held at The Hague, June 1914*, Miscellaneous No. 4 (1915) Cd. 7813 (London: H.M. Stationery Office, 1915), pp. 13–14.

100. Report of the American Delegation to the Third Hague Opium Conference, pp. 4–6. Italics added.

101. *Ibid.*, p. 3. Denby's speech attached. For the legislation discussed see below, pp. 128–129.

could point with pride to the fact that their country was once again in the vanguard of the antidrug campaign.

In their preliminary statements the French and German delegates reiterated the arguments they had made in the Second Conference. Marcellin Pellet took the position that to put the Convention into effect without the adhesion of all the powers would result in the creation of a very lucrative commercial monopoly for the nonadhering states, while Felix von Müller pointed to the absence of Turkey and Serbia, to the reservations accompanying the signatures of Sweden, Montenegro, and Greece, and to the "unsatisfactory declaration" of Austria-Hungary as the reasons why Germany had not ratified the Convention and could not agree to put it into effect.[102]

The British delegates had reversed their attitude of the previous conference. Sir Edward Grey had instructed them to work for the signature and ratification of the Convention by as many states as possible, even if this meant the support of proposals for signatures with reservations by those powers who would not otherwise adhere. As a result of the expressed intentions of Greece, and more especially of Austria-Hungary, to sign, and the reversal of technical obstacles to signature and ratification on the part of Britain's dominions and possessions, Great Britain, he declared, was ready to ratify. He therefore advised them that if the conference decided that the Convention could go into force without the signature and ratification of all the powers, they should direct their principal attention to the date of its going into force.[103] The British delegates therefore maintained that as forty-three out of the forty-six states had signed, nine had ratified, and others were ready to do so, the putting of the Convention into force should not be thwarted by two or three powers whose abstention might well "be neutralized" by certain measures. Furthermore, the decision of the Second Conference that ratification should not remain dependent on universal adherence to the document implied that its effectuation should similarly not be blocked by the failure of a few powers to subscribe to it.[104]

The views of the American and British delegates were strongly supported by Van Deventer of the Netherlands. He emphasized the

---

102. Great Britain, Foreign Office, *Correspondence Respecting the Third International Opium Conference*, pp. 4–6.

103. *Ibid.*, pp. 1–3.   104. *Ibid.*, pp. 4–5.

success of the two previous conferences in securing the signatures of thirty-two of the thirty-four nonsignatory powers, an achievement which he felt should not be allowed to go to waste. Giving voice to those measures which the British had implied might be adopted to bring the recalcitrant powers into line, he pointed out that if all the powers but Turkey and Serbia put the Convention into effect, the unregulated production and traffic in opium and other drugs would be confined to the abstainers' own territories, and they would thus be forced to come into the Convention.[105] The Russian delegate took his position with the French and Germans. While expressing the readiness of his government to ratify the Convention, he stated that Russia's willingness to put it into force depended largely on the preparedness of Germany, Austria-Hungary, and Switzerland to do likewise.[106]

At the first session of the conference Van Dyke had offered a resolution which "resolved, that the Signatory Powers pledge themselves to ratify as soon as possible the Convention of 1912, and to put it into effect from the first of December, 1914."[107] This resolution was referred to the Redaction Committee which was instructed to draft a formula providing either for the coming into force of the Convention on a fixed date as suggested by Van Dyke or after ratification by a certain number of powers. The plan brought forth specified that the Convention might be put into force without the signatures of all the powers; its coming into force among all the signatory powers should take place as soon as they had ratified it; and the date of its coming into force should be either three months after all the signatories had ratified as stipulated in paragraph one of Article 24 of the Convention, or on December 1, 1914, whichever was earlier. Twenty-five powers voted for the first proposition while one, Luxembourg, abstained. Sixteen favored the second proposal, while eleven, including the United States, abstained. Only Germany and Portugal opposed both recommendations. The third proposal was referred again to the Redaction Committee when an amendment, suggested by the Chinese, calling for the putting into force of the Convention on December 1, 1914, for the powers which had deposited their ratification and on the date of the deposit of their ratifications for powers which had delayed ratifica-

105. *Ibid.*, p. 6. 106. *Ibid.*
107. Report of the American Delegation to the Third Hague Opium Conference, p. 3.

tion for constitutional reasons, was objected to by several powers as an improper inquiry into the reasons for nonratification.[108]

The United States was hopeful that the conference would unanimously agree to the coming into force of the Convention among all the signatory powers. When it became obvious that Turkey could not be induced to sign the document, the State Department, at Van Dyke's request, tried to persuade Germany to ratify the Convention nevertheless and agree to put it into force.[109] But Germany remained adamant in its insistence on the "unconditional adhesion of all the powers" as a preliminary to its confirmation of the Convention.[110]

Realizing that Germany's intransigence would affect the willingness of other powers, including Great Britain, to put the Convention into effect, the American delegation therefore requested permission of the State Department to agree to put the Convention into force even among a limited number of powers, that is, among those who would agree to do so. The Department suggested instead a three weeks' adjournment of the conference so that the United States and the Netherlands might exert pressure on Turkey, Greece, and Serbia. Fearing that an adjournment might cause the dissipation of sentiment among the powers which were then prepared to act, the American delegation advised against such a step. They maintained that in order to avoid losing the advance already made in the international movement, the United States should consent to putting the Convention into force even among a limited number of states.[111]

Meanwhile the Redaction Committee had come forward with a formula which was acceptable in most of its aspects to all the delegations and which was embodied in the Protocol of Cloture. It included the two proposals already approved which provided that the Convention might be put into effect despite the failure of some powers to sign, and that it should come into force among all the signatory powers three

---

108. Great Britain, Foreign Office, *Correspondence Respecting the Third International Opium Conference*, pp. 7–9.

109. Report of the American Delegation to the Third Hague Opium Conference, p. 4. See also Van Dyke to the Secretary of State, June 17, 1914; Secretary of State Bryan to J. H. von Bernstorff, the German Ambassador, June 18, 1914; Bryan to the American Embassy (Berlin), June 18, 1914, SDR 511.4A1/1477. Also RG 43, E 43.

110. Bernstorff to the Secretary of State, June 24, 1914, SDR 511.4A1/1487. Also RG 43, E 43.

111. Van Dyke to the Secretary of State, June 29, 1914; Bryan to the legation (The Hague), June 22, 1914, SDR 511.4A1/1480; Van Dyke to the Secretary of State, June 23, 1914, SDR 511.4A1/1481. Also RG 43, E 43.

months after they had ratified it. The additional provisions specified that if by December 31, 1914, all the signatory powers had not deposited ratifications, the signatory powers which had done so might put the Convention into force; that accession to the Convention remained open to the states which had not yet signed it; and that a protocol should be opened at The Hague whereby the signatory powers which had not ratified might declare their intention of putting the Convention into effect. Also embodied in the Protocol was an Anglo-American resolution requesting the Dutch government to urge the signatory powers to ratify the Convention as soon as possible so that it might go into effect at an early date.[112] On June 25, at the last session of the conference, it was announced that Greece had signed the Convention without reservation. The Protocol of the Conference was also signed by all the delegates without reservation. Portugal had in the meantime withdrawn its opposition to the putting into force of the Convention without its being signed by Turkey and Serbia. Although the German delegation signed the Protocol, it was obvious that their government would neither ratify nor put the Convention into force.

At the close of the conference forty-four out of forty-six governments had signed the Convention or had expressed their firm intention of doing so; eleven had ratified it—the United States, Belgium, China, Denmark, Guatemala, Italy, Portugal, Siam, Sweden, Venezuela, and Honduras; four were ready to ratify—Great Britain, Japan, the Netherlands, and Persia; ten were ready to ratify as soon as legislative approval could be obtained; eighteen signatories had not announced their intention of ratifying; and two—Turkey and Serbia—had not signed nor announced their intentions of doing so.[113]

This was the third and final conference on the drug question at The Hague. These conferences had resulted in a widening of the sphere of attention from the Far Eastern drug traffic to the universal aspects of the problem, with increasing emphasis on the situation in the West. A concomitant development was the extension of the realm of responsibility or blame for the traffic. At Shanghai the British were regarded as the principal villains, in American eyes at least. At The Hague the Germans were similarly regarded. Germany's intransigence slowed the movement, particularly on the part of Great Britain, France, and

112. Great Britain, Foreign Office, *Correspondence Respecting the Third International Opium Conference*, pp. 10–11.
113. *Ibid.*, pp. 11–12.

Russia, toward the ratification and execution of the Convention, which in turn lightened the pressure on other powers which otherwise might have been induced to take decisive action. In defense of Germany, however, it may be pointed out that subsequent developments were to support her contention that as long as any single great producer remained outside international control, no effective check on the drug traffic was possible. Turkey was adamant in refusing to cooperate. No amount of pressure could induce her to change her policy. In fact, it was not until 1932, after virtually all other nations had adhered, that Turkey agreed to put the Convention into force. Furthermore, as war enveloped Europe in 1914, very little progress in carrying out the international aspects of the Convention was possible anyway. The failure of the powers to put the Convention into effect during the war years was thus not a significant drawback to the movement.

Yet, by providing for the execution of the Convention even among a limited number of powers, the Third Hague Conference represented a step forward. Enough powers did take sufficient action to keep the issue alive. Since not all the signatory powers had ratified the Convention by the end of 1914 (as everyone knew would be the case), the United States, China, and the Netherlands put the Convention into effect among themselves by signing the Protocol on February 11, 1915.[114] They were joined later the same year by Honduras and Norway. By the fall of the year sixteen powers, including Great Britain, had deposited their ratifications.[115] The preoccupation of the powers with World War I hampered further action. By the time of the Paris Peace Conference in 1919 only two other nations, Belgium and Luxembourg (on May 14, 1919), had put the Convention into effect.

Aside from administrative agreements and bilateral smuggling and extradition treaties, the Hague Opium Convention remained the sole international arrangement down to 1933 on which the United States was willing to base its international drug policy. Yet, some fourteen years after it had put the Convention into effect, the question arose in the State Department whether the United States was legally a party to it. The matter became of concern in connection with investigations of the history of the Harrison Narcotics Act, the basic federal statute controlling the narcotics traffic in the United States, in relation to the

114. Van Dyke to the Secretary of State, Feb. 11, 1915, SDR 511.4A1/1502.
115. Van Dyke to the Secretary of State, Sept. 28, 1915, SDR 511.4A1/1514.

status of the Convention. Congressman Stephen G. Porter wanted this information for use in preparing another narcotics bill. The question of the validity of the Convention had been brought up in 1926 before the Supreme Court in *Alston* v. *the United States*,[116] but the Court had ignored the question and merely ruled on the constitutionality of the Harrison Act, which it upheld. The crux of the matter was that the Final Protocol of the Third Hague Opium Conference providing for the bringing of the Convention into force, though signed by the United States, was never submitted to the Senate for ratification. The government, however, had proceeded to act as if it had Senate approval and put the Convention into effect. If it were held that the failure to submit the Protocol to the Senate meant that the United States had not legally ratified and put the Convention into force, then acts of the United States to carry it out might be ruled invalid. It would also mean that the United States was not legally a party to the Convention, and this would furnish ammunition to foreign critics who resented the part played by the country in the antidrug movement.

The Treaty Division of the State Department maintained that the question of the validity of the ratification and the putting into effect of the Convention revolved around the issue of whether the Final Protocol added something of substance to what had previously been approved by the Senate—the Hague Opium Convention and the final protocols of the First and Second Conferences. If nothing of substance was added, then the action of the government was valid. It was finally decided by the Solicitor, the Treaty Division, and the Division of Far Eastern Affairs to let matters lie and accept the Convention as validly ratified and in effect and not to submit the question to the Attorney General for a ruling. Cited in support of this decision was the argument of the current Attorney General before the Supreme Court in 1926 when, as Solicitor General, he maintained that the United States had legally become a party to the Convention, an argument to which the Court had not expressed any views to the contrary in its opinion.[117] Furthermore, they maintained, the government of the United States had regarded the Convention as being in force since 1915, and Congress had sanctioned that view by several acts and resolu-

116. 247 U.S. 289 (1926).   117. *Ibid.*

tions. In addition, the United States had long acquiesced in general, they noted, in the Convention. Thus the question was buried, but not without some trepidation that it was not permanently settled and might give future trouble.[118] There is no evidence, however, that the issue was ever given further consideration.

118. The following memoranda cover the discussion of the question in the State Department: Conversation between Caldwell and Tennyson, May 14, 1929; Caldwell to the Solicitor, May 16, 1929; Caldwell to Dr. McClure, Treaty Division, May 20, 1929; Treaty Division memorandum, May 20, 1929; Caldwell to the Solicitor, May 23, 1929, SDR 511.4A1/2118. The Solicitor to Caldwell, June 18, 1929; Caldwell to Johnson, June 19, 1929, SDR 511.4A1/2117. Caldwell to Johnson, June 24, 1929, SDR 511.4A1/2119. Caldwell to Porter, July 5, 1929, SDR 511.4A1/2119a.

Chapter five

Opium as a domestic
and international issue,
1914-1924

After the meetings at The Hague the next international conference on the narcotics drugs problem was held at Geneva in 1924–1925 under the auspices of the League of Nations. In the interim the United States gave its attention in varying degrees to three aspects of that problem: her own domestic predicament, the situation in China, and the question of whether and to what extent the United States should cooperate with the League of Nations in the solution of the problem. Because the drug problem transcended national boundaries, these aspects of the problem were closely interrelated.

Paradoxically, just as the United States began to ascertain the full dimensions of her internal problem, claims were made that the problem, in numbers of people involved, was already contracting in scope. Although there could be no accurate statistics on the extent of drug addiction in the United States, the best estimates submitted at different periods indicated that more people in total numbers and in proportion to the total population suffered from drug addiction prior to 1908, when the situation was first brought into general focus, than after that period. Estimates of the number of drug addicts in the United States between 1900 and 1924 ranged from a low of about 100,000 to an obviously inaccurate and extreme figure of 4,000,000. The American commission to the Shanghai conference also overestimated the problem. In his report on the Shanghai Opium Commission, Hamilton Wright estimated that 150,000 Americans, excluding Chinese, were habitual opium smokers, and that of the medicinal opium imported, 75 percent was manufactured into morphine, of which 80 percent went to habitual users.[1]

1. U.S. Department of State, *Opium Problem. Message from the President of the United States Transmitting from the Secretary of State A Report on the International*

In 1918 the Secretary of the Treasury appointed a special narcotics committee to investigate the drug problem in the United States and to recommend remedial measures and administrative changes in the narcotic laws. Their report confirmed previous statements that there was a very serious narcotics problem in the United States. Their findings were very largely based on information received from police officials, physicians, and local and state public health officials. They reported that between 1910 and 1915 at least 75 percent of the opium and coca leaves and their derivatives imported legally and consumed in the United States was used for other than medical purposes, and that there was consumed in the United States ten times as much opium per capita than in the largest consuming country in Europe. They maintained further that the smuggled supply was just as great as the legitimate. They estimated the number of addicts at about 1,000,000. The committee found that addiction was acquired primarily in two ways: by association with drug addicts, in which case the principal drugs used were heroin and cocaine, and through physicians' prescriptions, in which case the principal drugs used were morphine and opium preparations. Drugs used by addicts, in order of their frequency, were morphine, heroin, the various forms of opium, and cocaine. Codeine, laudanum, and paregoric were used in equal amounts. Addiction cut across all racial, social, and economic barriers and was discovered to be equally prevalent among both sexes.[2]

An interesting feature of the report was the prominence given to liquor prohibition as a cause of drug addiction. In the responses from police officials, prohibition stood third behind physicians' prescriptions and association with other addicts as a cause of drug addiction. In reports of state and local health officials it stood third in order of frequency behind physicians' prescriptions and use of drugs for chronic diseases. The prohibition referred to was that on the state and local level, since nationwide prohibition had not yet come into effect. Without committing themselves on the matter, the committee held that the increased sales of narcotics and patent medicines containing opiates in the Southern states, where liquor prohibition had been long in effect,

Opium Problem . . . Senate Doc. 377. 61st Cong., 2nd Sess., 1910, pp. 44–45. Hereafter cited as Senate Doc. 377. For the reliability of these estimates, see above, Chapter III, note 29.

2. U.S. Special Narcotic Committee, *Traffic in Narcotic Drugs. Report of Special Committee of Investigation Appointed March 25, 1918 by the Secretary of the Treasury, June, 1919* (Washington, D.C.: Government Printing Office, 1919), pp. 8–9, 19–27.

supported the consensus of opinion that nationwide prohibition would result in an increase of drug addiction.[3] This was an argument that the "wets" could well use, and they did. Paradoxically, missionaries and other reformers were claiming at the same time that American liquor interests were seeking to foster the drink evil in China to replace the opium vice which was then being suppressed.

In its recommendations the Committee urged (1) the enactment of legislation on the national, state, and local levels providing care and treatment of addicts; (2) that the State Department urge the signatories of the Hague Opium Convention to enact enforcement measures; (3) that the cooperation of Mexico and Canada be secured to suppress smuggling; (4) that an educational campaign against the drug traffic be initiated throughout the country; (5) that research be undertaken by both public and private medical organizations into the nature of drug addiction and the means of treatment; and (6) that there be absolute prohibition of the use of heroin and the traffic in it, as its evil effects far outweighed its medical benefits.[4]

The next and by far the most scientific and comprehensive study of the extent of the drug evil in the United States was that completed by two officials of the United States Public Health Service, Lawrence Kolb and A. G. Du Mez, in 1924.[5] They based their conclusions on analyses of a number of surveys made on the state and national level after 1914, on reports of agents of the Bureau of Internal Revenue and others, on various reports of narcotic clinics in existence from 1919 to 1921 in the United States, on personal interviews with physicians, and on statistics on the dose of addiction, the world production of narcotics, and quantities of narcotics imported into the United States. They concluded that on the basis of narcotic surveys, reports from clinics, and other sources, there could have been about 215,000 addicts in 1915 and about 110,000 in about 1922. They maintained that if the entire quantity of opiates imported had been used solely for addiction, it would have supplied at no time over 246,000 addicts, a development which would have occurred in the period from 1890 to 1909. They estimated that on the basis of imports of the coca leaf and its derivatives the highest possible number of cocaine addicts would be 18,000, and

3. *Ibid.*, pp. 14, 18, 22.   4. *Ibid.*, pp. 28–29.
5. Kolb and Du Mez, *The Prevalance and Trends of Drug Addiction in the United States and the Factors Influencing It* (Treasury Department, United States Public Health Service; Washington, D.C.: Government Printing Office, 1924).

thus the highest possible number of drug addicts at any one time would have been 264,000. Taking into account both legitimate and illicit imports of opium and coca leaves and their derivatives for the years 1920 to 1923, they declared that between 120,000 and 140,000 addicts could have been supplied. Their final conclusion was that at the time of the completion of their report the maximum estimate would place the number of addicts at 150,000. Their estimate of the probable number was 110,000.[6] They further noted that by 1924 the character of drug addiction had changed. Prior to the enactment of federal legislation regulating the drug traffic, smoking opium, gum or crude opium, and laudanum were the principal drugs used by addicts. By 1924 the alkaloids and derivatives of opium and cocaine were almost solely responsible for addiction. Taking note of the steady decrease since 1900 in the number of addicts, they ended their report with the optimistic conclusion that in the not too distant future the only users of opium would be psycopathic delinquents and persons suffering from incurable disease.[7]

On the basis of the foregoing questionable estimates, the equally questionable claim was made that an increase in the general population had been accompanied by a decline in the number of addicts. In 1915 there was perhaps about 1 addict in every 460 persons; the claim for 1924 was 1 in every 1,000 of the general population.

It was presumed that the major factor in this assumed decline was the passage of both state and federal, but particularly federal, legislation regulating and restricting the traffic in and use of these drugs. As stated earlier, prior to the Opium Exclusion Act of 1909 the only federal legislation controlling such traffic and use were the Internal Revenue Act of 1890, which placed a tax of $10 per pound on smoking opium manufactured in the United States and restricted such manufacture to American citizens, and the Food and Drug Act of 1906, which required that the label on the package specify the quantity or proportion of morphine, heroin, opium, and their products contained in the substances in the package, and prohibited the movement of misbranded drugs in interstate and foreign commerce. None of the federal laws controlled the importation and use of narcotic drugs in the United States. The

6. *Ibid.,* pp. 24–25.
7. *Ibid.,* p. 25. It should be observed that all of the estimates suffered from miscalculations, some grievously so. There was a tendency to exaggerate the number of addicts for the pre-World War I period and to underestimate the number for the years thereafter. See Alfred R. Lindesmith, *The Addict and the Law* (Bloomington, Ind.: Indiana University Press, 1965), pp. 104–122.

Opium Exclusion Act, however, dealt with only one aspect of the drug problem, that of smoking opium. It did not touch the great excess of medicinal opium imported which was used illicitly, nor did it affect the interstate traffic in the various forms of such opium. The cocaine traffic likewise remained uncontrolled. The situation was compounded by the weakness of many state laws. In some states, habit-forming drugs could be bought without a prescription, some such as laudanum and paregoric and preparations containing opiates being sold in grocery stores. The laws of many states requiring the sale of drugs by prescription only were easily evaded, as illegal possession was not considered evidence for conviction, and illegal sale was therefore often hard to prove. Furthermore, in the absence of federal legislation controlling the interstate traffic in narcotics, even the states with stringent laws could not effectively deal with the problem.[8] Thus, even after 1909 there was a pressing need for federal action to meet the domestic situation and also to carry out the country's international obligations, both moral and legal, which it had had so great a part in formulating through the Shanghai Opium Commission and the Hague Opium Convention.

In his report on the Opium Commission submitted by the President to Congress in 1910, Hamilton Wright urged the passage of legislation so as to confine the opium problem in the United States to a "triangle." The Opium Exclusion Act of 1909 would constitute one side of the triangle. A bill taxing and regulating the production, manufacture, and distribution of the various narcotic drugs would constitute another side. The third side would consist of a prohibitive internal revenue tax on the manufacture of smoking opium which Wright feared would take place because of the rise in price of smoking opium as a result of the Opium Exclusion Act, from $13 to $60 per pound. As smoking opium could not legally be manufactured from imported medicinal opium, Wright believed that poppy cultivation for the purpose of producing smoking opium might be resorted to in the United States in the states which did not prohibit it. In addition to these measures he proposed that a bill regulating the practice of pharmacy and the sale of poisons in the consular districts of the United States in China should be enacted to carry out our moral obligations to that nation. Drafts of the proposed legislation were contained in the same report.[9]

The responsibility for drafting and garnering public and con-

8. For discussion of this situation, see Senate Doc. 377, pp. 18–19, 54–60.
9. *Ibid.*, pp. 59–60, 75–79.

gressional support for the proposed legislation was placed largely in Wright's hands. This was a difficult, exasperating, and complex task, especially in view of Wright's desire to see such legislation passed or at least well on its way to passage by the time of the First Hague Conference. In this he was unsuccessful. The only measure of significance enacted by that time was a law which became effective on January 1, 1910, empowering the Postmaster General to prohibit the transportation of cocaine and other drugs through the mail. Thus the United States went into both the First and the Second Hague Opium Conferences with narcotics legislation in many respects considerably inferior to that of a number of European powers, as well as inferior to that of China and Japan. Because of objections by the drug interests to many features of the proposed legislation and the preoccupation of Congress with other matters, the desired legislation was not passed until 1914, in spite of the general sentiment in favor of the measures and the support given them by such leading congressional figures as Henry Cabot Lodge, John Sharp Williams, Elihu Root, and Furnifold M. Simmons and by both the Taft and Wilson administrations.

In January 1911 the Secretary of State recommended to Congress enactment of the desired legislative program in the form of the following measures: (1) amendments to the Opium Exclusion Act of 1909 so as to prohibit vessels trading between the United States and its possessions and foreign ports and places from carrying smoking opium, and to prohibit the exportation from the United States and areas under its jurisdiction of opium and cocaine and their products to countries regulating or prohibiting their entry unless the exporter conformed to the regulations of the importing country; (2) amendment of the Internal Revenue Act of 1890 so as to prevent the manufacture of smoking opium from opium that might be produced in the United States by the imposition of a prohibitory tax on the opium manufactured, and requirement of a prohibitory bond on the part of the manufacturer; and (3) the enactment of legislation to control the importation, manufacture, and distribution in interstate commerce of opium, morphine, cocaine, and other habit-forming drugs.[10] Much of the proposed legislation was already before Congress.

The first two acts made their way through Congress with little or no

10. U.S. Department of State, *The Opium Traffic. Message from the President of the United States Transmitting Report of the Secretary of State Relative to the Control of the Opium Traffic*, Senate Doc. 736. 61st Cong., 3rd Sess., 1911, p. 6.

controversy and were passed in their final versions by the Senate on December 20, 1913, and by the House on January 12, 1914, and signed by the President on January 17, thus becoming law before the Third Hague Conference. The Opium Exclusion Act was amended substantially as recommended, while the Internal Revenue Act of 1890 was revised by raising the tax on manufactured opium to $300 per pound and by increasing the manufacturer's bond from $600 to $100,000 and also including the use of the residue from smoked opium (yenshee) for the further production of smoking opium in the term manufacture,[11] a use which the Supreme Court had earlier held did not constitute manufacture under the act of 1890.[12]

Much more difficult to pass was the bill designed to control the domestic manufacture of and traffic in narcotics, primarily because this affected directly American dealers in the drugs. The drug interests in question did not object to the principle of the bill, which was to control the drug traffic so as to restrict consumption to medicinal uses. They objected to the details of the bill, especially the administrative features requiring the keeping of numerous records of transactions by wholesalers, retailers, and manufacturers, as imposing an intolerable burden. Some of the drug interests suggested that the control measures be confined to opium, morphine, and cocaine and their various products since the production of other narcotics such as eucaine, chloral, and cannabis (Indian hemp) was so small as not to justify restrictive measures. On the other hand, those in favor of the administrative measures defended their onerousness as the means of effecting the desired restriction of the traffic.[13]

The congressional committees gave the bill their warm endorsement, the Senate Finance Committee adopting the report of the House Ways and Means Committee as its own except for minor amendments. They maintained that such legislation was necessitated, even if the United States had no problem of its own, by the role of the United States in the international drug movement and by the obligations resulting from

11. *Congressional Record*, 63rd Cong., 2nd Sess., 1914, LI, Part 2, 12881 1543; Part 3, 2329. A convenient collection of American opium legislation down to 1955 is Elmer Lewis (compiler), *Opium and Narcotic Laws* (Washington, D.C.: Government Printing Office, 1955). For the text of these laws see pp. 2–3, 5.

12. *United States* v. *Alfred Shelly*, 229 U.S. 239 (1913).

13. For the conflicting views on the measure see U.S. Cong., House, Committee on Ways and Means, *Hearings on H.R. 25240, H.R. 25241, H.R. 25242, and H.R. 28911, Importation and Use of Opium*, 61st Cong., 3rd Sess., 1911, pp. 49–96.

the International Opium Commission and the Hague Opium Convention.[14] But the complex details of the bill delayed passage. Hearings in the committees took up considerable time. The House-passed version of the bill was not reported from the Senate Finance Committee until February 18, 1914. Discussion of amendments recommended by that committee delayed Senate passage until August 15. The most controversial issue was Section 6 of the House bill, which exempted preparations containing not more than two grains of opium, one-fourth grain of morphine, one-fourth grain of heroin, and one grain of cocaine to the fluid ounce from the bill's regulations. Senator Harry Lane of Oregon claimed that preparations containing less than these quantities of opiates were responsible for the deaths of 10,000 children under a year of age annually. Nevertheless, the provision was not deleted by the Senate. The Senate did throw out, however, a proviso in the House-passed bill requiring physicians to keep a record of the drugs they dispensed. This deletion was a principal reason for the refusal of the House to accept the bill as amended by the Senate. Whereas physicians had pushed for the Senate deletion, druggists opposed such action on the grounds that it would prevent the restriction of the sale of the drugs as intended and would give the physicians special privileges which were denied to druggists. It was not until mid-October that the two bodies were able to resolve their differences. The compromise formula provided that only physicians personally attending patients to whom they administered drugs were exempted from keeping a record of the drugs dispensed.[15]

The bill as finally passed on December 17, 1914, and popularly referred to as the Harrison Narcotics Act, was the most comprehensive relevant federal legislation passed up to that time. It required the registration of all persons engaged in drug transactions, from production to dispensation, with the collector of internal revenue in their districts. The sale or exchange of drugs in any way—except by a physician, surgeon, dentist, or veterinarian in personal attendance upon a patient, or by a pharmacist to a consumer on the prescription of a physician—could be made only in pursuance of a written order of the purchaser

14. U.S. Cong., Senate, Committee on Finance, *Registration of Persons Dealing in Opium*, 63rd Cong., 2nd Sess., 1914, S. Rept. 258 to Accompany H.R. 6282, p. 3.

15. For the progress of the bill through Congress after being reported out by the Senate Finance Committee see *Congressional Record*, 63rd Cong., 2nd Sess., LI, Part 4, 3591; Part 6, 5670–71; Part 7, 6786–6788; Part 10, 9936–38.

or receiver on forms issued by the Commissioner of Internal Revenue. The transportation of the drugs, except by common carriers and on physicians' prescriptions, was restricted to persons registered under the Act, and possession of the drugs by unauthorized persons was to be regarded as presumptive evidence of violation of the Act. Preparations and remedies containing so small a proportion of narcotics as to make them insufficient to cause addiction were exempted from the provisions of the Act. The maximum penalty for violation of the Act was set at a $2,000 fine or five years imprisonment or both.[16]

The Harrison Narcotics Act constitutes the basic narcotics law of the United States although it has been amended and supplemented by other legislation several times. It was first amended in 1919. And although after considerable congressional debate, a provision was included in the Act permitting physicians to prescribe and dispense drugs for *legitimate medical use* to patients they personally attended, the determination of what is *legitimate medical use* has been made in the final analysis by federal enforcement officials, who through administrative regulations and enforcement practices have made the Act a prohibition measure. Thus as administered, the Act is representative of the attitude and establishes the policy toward narcotics in the United States that still prevails today.

The prevailing attitude, which was fully developed during the period under study, regards the use of narcotics as morally wrong, physically and morally debilitating to the human body and personality, contagious in its growth, and a menace, both physically and morally to society. The policy that stems from this attitude, and as represented in the enforcement of narcotics legislation, both federal and state, views the use of narcotics not only as morally wrong but as a criminal activity. Thus possession of the drug is regarded as presumptive evidence of illegal traffic or use. The only effective way to deal with the problem, it is held, is to make transactions in and use of such drugs for nonmedical and nonscientific purposes illegal. The only way to stop illicit use is to cut off the source of illicit supply, which can only be accomplished by limiting world production, manufacture, and traffic to quantities needed for medical and scientific uses. Today, both the attitude and the policy are being increasingly challenged in the United States. As in the period under study, controversy rages on all aspects

16. Lewis, *op. cit.,* pp. 6–11, 12–15.

of the narcotics situation— from cause, development and treatment to methods of control. The whole issue is beclouded by uncertainties, and opposing authoritative opinions render synthesis impossible.[17]

The next major legislation on narcotics was passed in 1922. This was the Narcotic Drugs Import and Export Act which replaced the Opium Exclusion Act of 1909 as amended. The Act restricted the importation of crude opium and coca leaves to quantities which the Federal Narcotics Control Board, established under the Act and consisting of the Secretaries of State, Treasury, and Commerce, deemed to be required for medicinal and legitimate needs; prohibited the importation of all derivatives of these drugs; and repeated the prohibition on the importation and exportation of smoking opium. Manufactured drugs were to be exported only on an import certificate from the importing country. In 1924 the Act was amended to prohibit the importation of opium for the manufacture of heroin.[18] Thus by 1924 the basic narcotics legislation of the United States had been enacted. Other legislation to follow included an act of Congress approved on January 19, 1929, providing for the establishment of two Public Health Service hospitals for the treatment of narcotics addicts; an act of Congress approved on July 3, 1930, establishing a Bureau of Narcotics headed by a Commissioner of Narcotics under the Treasury Department and replacing the Federal Narcotics Control Board; the Marihuana Tax Act of August 2, 1937, which brought the traffic in marihuana under regulations similar to those of the Harrison Narcotic Act; an act of Congress in 1939 as amended in 1950 which made illegal the transportation of contraband drugs upon or by means of any vehicle, vessel, or aircraft; and the Opium Poppy Control Act of 1942, which in effect prohibited the growth of the opium poppy in the United States.[19] Subsequent legislation has been passed to tighten up the system through penalties for violations and to bring new drugs under control.[20]

17. For the principles on which the traditional American attitude and policy on narcotic drug addiction are based and some of the myths underlying those principles, see William B. Eldridge, *Narcotics and the Law: A Critique of the American Experiment in Narcotic Drug Control* (New York: The American Bar Foundation, 1962), pp. 9–34. Among other representative criticisms of American drug policy are Alfred R. Lindesmith, *The Addict and the Law* and Edwin M. Schur, *Narcotics Addiction in Britain and America: The Impact of Public Policy* (Bloomington, Ind.: Indiana University Press, 1962).

18. Lewis, *op. cit.*, pp. 16–18, 25.

19. For the text of these laws in the order listed see *ibid.*, pp. 29–33, 34–36, 47–53, 71–73, 74–78.

20. *Ibid.*, pp. 37, 43, 54.

The United States considered its legislation as enacted by the end of 1924 to be a model for other countries to follow. The American drug interests, put at a disadvantage by the legislation in competing in the world drug market, pressured the government to urge other powers to adopt similarly stringent measures. Thus, from a position behind several European nations as well as China and Japan up to 1914, the United States had again forged ahead to leadership rank in meeting both its international obligations and domestic needs. From this position it was able to appeal to other powers to take similar steps and thereby meet their international obligations, and at the same time help to make the American legislation more effective. So comprehensive was this legislation that the United States saw no need to enact additional measures to carry out subsequent international conventions which were formulated in the 1920's and 1930's, and the government even refused to adhere to some of these conventions on the grounds that they were several steps behind the existing regulations of the United States.

Having instituted the international movement to control the drug traffic in order to help China, the United States was naturally interested in the progress China was making in solving her internal problem. To an extent the American position on control of the traffic—that prohibition was the best if not the only effective method—was being tested in China. China's success or failure would strengthen or weaken the validity of the American concept. By 1913 China was making such progress in suppressing opium cultivation that in May of that year the Indian government declared that if such progress continued it would cease the shipment of opium to China.[21] Thus for all practical purposes the opium trade between India and China came to an end in 1913.

China's remarkable achievement was applauded in the United States. Problems remained, however. Aside from the task of complete suppression of the native drug there was the problem of excess stocks of Indian opium held by merchants in China who could find no market for the drug. They owed their plight to the new revolutionary government in China, which declared all trade in the drug illegal, while provincial officials barred the entrance of the foreign drug into the provinces of China, including those which had not completely ended native cultivation. The action of the provincial officials was contrary to the Anglo-Chinese agreement of 1911. Nevertheless, by 1915 the

21. Owen, *op. cit.*, p. 348.

British government had ceased to insist on the entrance of this opium, and it was left up to an opium combine of merchants in India and China to secure an outlet for their stocks of opium held at Hong Kong and Shanghai. This they did in an agreement with the government at Peking on May 1, 1915, whereby they were to be permitted to sell their stocks of opium in the provinces of Kiangsu, Kiangsi, and Kwangtung until April 1, 1917.[22] This agreement was never consummated, however, and as a result, a new contract was entered into in January 1917 whereby the Chinese government promised to purchase the remaining 2100 chests of opium held by the Shanghai combine at 8200 taels per chest to be paid for by 6 percent Chinese government bonds guaranteed and secured by revenue from the stamp duty and tax.[23] Two months later the Chinese parliament passed a bill prohibiting the government from purchasing the opium, but the president refused to sign it. Nevertheless, the agreement fell through, and a new one was signed in 1918 providing for the transfer of 1700 chests of opium in bond at 6,000 taels per chest to the Chinese government. These chests were then to be resold to a Chinese opium syndicate consisting of certain leading officials of the Peking government and former Canton opium monopolists who were to sell their own stocks of opium as well as other foreign opium. It was claimed that the opium purchased would be used only for medical purposes.[24]

In the eyes of most observers, Chinese and foreign, the deal, involving as it did transactions in opium for profit by Chinese officials, was a scandalous affair. Protests from both domestic and foreign sources poured in on Peking. The United States had already defined its attitude as early as 1913 toward the plight of the opium merchants. It had ordered its consuls not to forward to the diplomatic corps at Peking the letters and petitions of these merchants and the foreign banks—including the International Banking Corporation, an American concern—which had financed their shipments from India, requesting the ministers at Peking to protest to the Chinese government the practice by provincial officials of prohibiting the sale and use of opium in their provinces, and thus closing the market for the Indian drug. The State Department took the position that the forwarding of such communi-

22. For the dealings of the Chinese government with the opium combine see "Summary of Correspondence re Opium and Morphine Situation in China," memorandum of the Division of Far Eastern Affairs, Dec. 19, 1918, SDR 893.114/190.
23. *Ibid.*   24. *Ibid.*

cations was contrary to the American policy expressed in the treaty of 1880.[25] It was therefore natural that the United States, after being prodded by Mrs. Hamilton Wright, would join in the condemnation of the deal. Upon ascertaining that the British government had no part in the transaction and that furthermore it highly disapproved of it, the United States secured the cooperation of that government in making almost simultaneous and very strong protests against the transaction on the grounds that it would jeopardize the progress already made in the national and international reform movement as well as that contemplated under the Hague Opium Convention which the United States and China had already put into effect.[26] Faced with vigorous opposition from various quarters and groups in China as well as the representations of the British and American legations, the Chinese government decided to burn the opium it had purchased from the Shanghai combine. The burning was carried out with great ceremony and fanfare from January 18 to January 25, 1919, at Shanghai, an affair to which various interested individuals were invited. Symbolic of United States interest was the fact that the American consul general at Shanghai was the only member of the consular body present at the ceremonies. About 14 million dollars' worth of opium was thus destroyed.[27]

While the foreign opium was burning at Shanghai, China was experiencing a recrudescence of poppy cultivation which both accompanied and was the result of the outbreak of civil strife throughout the provinces. Military governors in the various provinces permitted and even encouraged poppy cultivation in order to enable the farmers to pay taxes to finance their troops. The efforts of the central government to enforce prohibition were of little avail, as its authority was not respected. In 1924 the International Anti-Opium Association of Peking reported that opium was being produced in seventeen of the eighteen provinces of China proper and that in fourteen of these provinces the cultivation was extensive.[28] It was estimated that by 1925 China was

25. Minister William J. Calhoun (Peking) to the Secretary of State, July 8, 1912, NA, RG 43, E 40. Secretary of State Knox to the American Legation (Peking), Feb. 13, 1913, SDR 893.114/41.

26. "Summary of Correspondence re Opium and Morphine Situation in China," *op. cit.* Also *Foreign Relations,* 1918, pp. 209–13.

27. Consul General Thomas Sammons (Shanghai) to the Secretary of State, Jan. 29, 1919, SDR 893.114/211.

28. Foreign Policy Association, Committee on Traffic in Opium, "Opium Production in China," Opium Series, No. 1 (July, 1925), pp. 6–7, enclosed in Helen Howell Moorhead to Nelson T. Johnson, Oct. 30, 1925, SDR 511.4A2/409.

producing half as much opium as in 1905 and that she was probably the largest opium producer in the world.[29]

There was very little that the United States could do in this situation. China's retrogression was naturally regrettable and embarrassing. The United States found its efforts to persuade the European powers to suppress the traffic in prepared opium in their Far Eastern territories undermined, for these powers claimed that no effective measures could be taken in this regard until China had curbed her production and thereby ceased to be a major source of the Far Eastern illicit traffic in the drug. Given the political chaos in China, this was manifestly impossible, and when World War II broke out, the situation in regard to opium smoking in the Far East was virtually the same as prior to the First World War. The United States found its ability to influence the situation in China reduced to alternately protesting to and encouraging the central government on the problem. The American legation was instructed to impress continually on the Chinese government the American expectation that China would fully comply with her treaty obligations.[30] From time to time the legation as well as American consuls protested against the conduct of military officials in the provinces in forcing Christian Chinese farmers to plant the poppy on the grounds that this was contrary to treaty provisions granting Christian converts immunity in the practice of their religion.[31]

The American government also made known its opposition to a proposal backed by the British suggesting the establishment of an opium monopoly by the Chinese government.[32] It will be recalled that such a system for China had been seriously considered in the State Department prior to the Hague Opium Conferences. The United States had reversed its attitude on the wisdom of this step and now subscribed to a policy of strict prohibition. This was also the official policy of the Chinese government. The American view was that as the central government was actually too weak to bring the cultivation of the poppy and the trade in opium under its exclusive control, the effect of the monopoly would be merely to add another agency to the mili-

29. *Ibid.*, p. 7.

30. Secretary of State to the American Legation (Peking), Oct. 15, 1924, SDR 893.114/487.

31. Jacob Gould Schurman (Peking) to the Secretary of State, April 5, 1924, *ibid*.

32. Acting Secretary of State Norman Davis to the American Embassy, London, Dec. 1, 1920, SDR 893.114/266a; Consul General G. E. Gauss (Tientsin) to the Secretary of State, July 6, 1922, SDR 893.114/407, and Feb. 24, 1924, SDR 893.114/522.

tary governors promoting such activities. Over a decade was to elapse before China decided to establish the monopoly.

One result of the revival of opium production in China was the quieting of a growing agitation on the part of missionaries and other reformers who had been urging the United States to take action to prevent American liquor interests from establishing firms in China to supply the Chinese with a substitute for the opium habit. It was charged that as a result of national prohibition in the United States, American brewers were seeking to relocate themselves in China, and that they were conducting a massive propaganda campaign in the treaty ports and some interior ports as to the profitability of the liquor business. As an inducement to the Chinese they were even advertising beer as a "sure cure for opium."[33] Church groups, prohibition societies, and reformers in general protested vigorously against these developments, declaring that the United States should not allow its brewers, whom it would not tolerate on its own soil, to set up the business in China. In the absence of any antiliquor action on the part of the Chinese government, it was by no means clear what the American government was to do except to instruct its consuls, as suggested by a former consul general to Shanghai and Hong Kong, not to promote or encourage the trade.[34] The United States took no action, however, because the renewal of the opium traffic in China claimed its attention.

Another issue touched by the Chinese opium question was the remission of the Boxer indemnity. In 1924 Stephen G. Porter, chairman of the Foreign Affairs Committee of the House of Representatives, suggested to the State Department, at the instigation of T. Z. Koo, a representative of the National Anti-Opium Association of China, that a portion of the remitted Chinese indemnity funds be given to the Association to help finance the antiopium educational campaign in China.[35] In 1925 and 1926 Porter repeated the request,[36] and great pressure was

---

33. Silas Bent, "American Beer in China," *Asia*, XIX (June, 1919), 597–598. Shailer Mathews, "Shall We Make the Chinese Drunkards?" *The Independent*, CIV (Nov. 5, 1920), 186; Charles Stelzle, "Uprooted in the United States the Brewery Interests Turn to China," *World Outlook*, V (Nov., 1919), 16–17.

34. Amos P. Wilder, "The Danger of Strong Drink in China," *Missionary Review of the World*, XLII (July, 1919), 530–31.

35. Porter to the Secretary of State, Dec. 11, 1924, SDR 511.4A2/1346 and 493.11/1160.

36. Porter to the Secretary of State, May 26, 1925, SDR 511.4A2/347 and 493.11/1159; also memorandum by Nelson T. Johnson of a conversation with Porter, April 9, 1926, SDR 493.11/1233.

put on the China Foundation for the Promotion of Education and Culture, the organization established by the Chinese government to handle the funds accruing from the indemnity. The State Department took the position that the United States should not interfere with the way the Chinese disposed of the fund, thereby avoiding the possibility of the charge that the United States government was imposing conditions on the remission of the fund.[37] Another consideration advanced in opposition to the proposal was the fear that it might create the impression that the Anti-Opium Association was an agent of the American government designed to discredit Great Britain, Japan, and other countries in China allegedly connected with the opium and narcotic traffic, for opium was smuggled from India while morphine and cocaine came from Japan and Japanese-held territory.[38] Since the matter of the appropriation for the indemnity fund was taken up in Congress as an item in a deficiency appropriation bill, no new legislation was required, and the matter therefore went before the appropriation committee instead of before Porter's committee. The State Department was thus able to sidestep the issue and avoid taking action on it.[39]

Although by 1918 China had, for the time being, virtually ended native poppy cultivation and the legal importation of foreign opium, at no time were Chinese consumers lacking in a supply of narcotics. Another dimension to China's drug problem was the illicit traffic in manufactured drugs, especially morphine and cocaine, whose main sources were western Europe, the United States, and Japan. Thus with the resumption of poppy cultivation in 1918, only one aspect of the old drug problem since 1900 remained expunged from the Chinese drug picture: the legal Indian-Chinese trade. Since early in the century attention had been drawn to the traffic into China of the manufactured drugs. After the putting into effect, in 1909, of the antimorphine clauses of the treaties of 1902 and 1903 with Britain and the United States, the traffic in morphine was illegal in China. Nevertheless the traffic continued. Japan and territory under Japanese control were the immediate sources of the drug. As early as 1913 it was intimated to the State Department that there appeared to be a concerted movement by the Japanese to spread morphine throughout China.[40] From 1917 on,

37. Secretary of State Kellogg to Porter, June 5, 1925, SDR 511.4A2/340.
38. Memorandum, Johnson to the Secretary of State, April 10, 1926, SDR 493.11/1233.
39. Memorandum, Johnson to Wilbur Carr, April 30, 1926, SDR 493.11/1233.
40. Yamei Kin to Hamilton Wright, Sept. 29, 1913, SDR, RG 43, E 36.

increasing reports of the illicit traffic in morphine in China, under the auspices of the Japanese, came from both official and unofficial sources.[41] Private observers and American consuls in China reported that China was being flooded with opium and opium products through the medium of Japanese post offices, drugstores, shopkeepers, and Chinese, Korean, and Japanese peddlers in China, and that in the Japanese concessions opium dens were flourishing under Japanese protection. In Korea it was reported that the Japanese were encouraging opium cultivation for the specific purpose of smuggling it into China, and that Manchuria was fast becoming a center of the dope traffic. In China the port of Tsingtao was held to be the chief center of the Japanese trade from which morphine and opium were distributed throughout the provinces of Shantung, Anhui, and Kiangsu. This was made possible through control of the customs and military domination of the area.

Paul S. Reinsch, American minister in China, saw the Japanese activity as part of a general scheme "to aggravate all weakness and corruption so that instead of being helped to pass the dangerous transition from old to new the Chinese people are to be rendered utterly helpless by having the disorganization incident upon that transition deepened into actual demoralization of every part of social and political life."[42] He strongly denounced the Japanese action as "criminal," "vicious," "in defiance of humanity and treaty obligations," and as "a nefarious scheme to corrupt a nation." Other actions of Japan along the same line included the "debasing of currency," "ruining of credit," "complicity with bandits," and the encouragement of the most corrupt elements in the Chinese government. He suggested that the State Department ask the Japanese government to explain the situation.[43]

But Japan was not alone responsible for the situation in China. John Dewey, the American educational philosopher, who was visiting China in 1919, reported that the United States and Great Britain were both directly and indirectly involved. The United States was indirectly participating in the traffic through permitting the shipment of drugs,

---

41. See, for example, "Summary of Correspondence re Opium and Morphia in China: Illicit Trade in Opium and Morphia in China under Protection of Japanese," Memorandum in the State Department, Dec. 19, 1918, SDR 893.114/190; also "A Chinese Charge Against Japan," *Literary Digest*, LXI (April 12, 1919), 20; "Poisoning the Chinese," *ibid.*, LXVIII (Feb. 26, 1921), 30.

42. Reinsch to the Secretary of State, Dec. 21, 1918, SDR 893.114/195.

43. *Ibid.*

especially morphine, from Britain to the United States which were placed in bond and then subsequently transshipped to Japan and smuggled by the Japanese into China. America's direct involvement was through the shipment by American manufacturers of large quantities of morphine to Japan which subsequently found its way into China. He reported that Japanese customhouse returns for the first five months of 1919 showed 25,000 ounces of morphine reaching Kobe from American ports and that a Japanese newspaper in Kobe stated that 90,000 additional ounces entered the port which were not registered in the customs returns. Great Britain was by far the larger participant in the traffic. Prior to 1912 the annual export of morphine from Great Britain to Japan was 30,000 ounces. By 1917 this had increased twenty times over. It was obvious that this morphine was destined for China, as Japan was manufacturing more than enough morphine for her own medical needs.[44] To remedy the situation the British government, after representations from various missionary and antiopium groups in both China and England, publicly announced in late 1917 that the exportation of opium products to Japan and Manchuria would be conditioned upon the receipt of a certificate from Japanese officials stating that the drugs were for actual consumption and for medical use only in Japan and Manchuria (Darien).[45] This effected a significant reduction in the export to Japan, but as Japan actually needed no morphine from abroad for her own domestic needs, any quantity at all shipped from abroad was destined for China.

Not until several years later did the United States take steps to end its complicity in the traffic. By the Narcotic Drugs Import and Export Act of 1922 a strict system of control designed to restrict the exportation of manufactured narcotic drugs to medical use was established.[46] Other than this measure, the United States took no direct action aside from urging the parties to the Hague Convention to carry out their obligations under the Convention to stop the illicit Sino-Japanese traffic. No direct approach was made to Japan by the American government, and the repeated urgings of the International Reform Bureau

44. John Dewey, "Our Share in Drugging China," *New Republic*, XXI (Dec. 24, 1919), 114–117.

45. *Ibid*. See also J. H. Oldham, Secretary of the Conference of Missionary Societies (Edinburgh) to Bishop Brent (Edinburgh), Oct. 1, 1917, and Jan. 22, 1918, Brent Papers, Box 14.

46. See above, p. 132.

and other interested persons to the Chinese and American delegates to the Washington Naval Conference of 1921 that the opium question should be brought up at the conference were rejected. The American delegates said it was up to China or Japan to introduce the question. The Chinese refused to act on the grounds that the program of the conference was already crowded.[47]

In the meantime the world public outcry against the situation was having repercussions in Japan. The issue was extensively debated in the 1922–1923 session of the Japanese diet, and members of the opposition party demanded suppression of the illicit traffic. The Japanese public, having become aware of the situation, condemned official connivance at the traffic. By the end of the Geneva Opium Conferences of 1924 the Japanese government had become extremely sensitive to the criticism.[48] Although Japan made some efforts to correct the situation, the problem remained and in the 1930's added to the friction between the United States and Japan on other issues.

After the First World War the opium question became more and more involved in the political relations of the United States. The degree and manner in which the United States participated in the international campaign often depended to a large extent upon the country's current political relations with other nations and particularly the prevailing official attitude toward the League of Nations. The opium problem even figured to a small degree in the controversy in the United States over the ratification of the League Covenant.

That the peace treaties ending the war might furnish a convenient vehicle by which most of the nations of the world could be brought into the antiopium movement was realized long before the war ended. Sir William Collins, a member of the British delegation to the Hague Opium Conferences, had suggested in his final report on the Hague Conference that the peace conference might be the means by which the nations could be committed to the Hague Opium Convention.[49] In identical notes addressed to the American ambassadors in Tokyo, London, Paris, and The Hague in the spring and early summer of 1918,

---

47. Paul Lee, "Drug Addiction in America and China," *Zion's Herald* (Feb. 15, 1922), 203.

48. Jefferson Caffery, Chargé d'Affaires ad interim (Tokyo) to the Secretary of State, Sept. 20, 1924, SDR 511.4A2/103.

49. Matthew Bodson to Bishop Brent, Yorks, Feb. 15, 1917, Brent Papers, Box 13.

the State Department urged the powers to ratify and put into effect the Hague Opium Convention despite the exigencies of the war.[50] At that time only the United States, China, the Netherlands, Honduras, and Norway had put the Convention into effect. Belgium and Luxembourg put it into effect on May 14, 1919.

The American representation evoked from the British Foreign Office the suggestion that to secure wider adhesion to and enforcement of the Convention the question should be raised at the Peace Conference with the idea of the adoption of a resolution binding all the belligerents to enact legislation immediately to carry out the terms of the Convention.[51] The special advantage in this procedure would be the securing of the effective cooperation of the important producing and manufacturing countries, including especially such defeated states as Germany, Austria, Hungary, and Turkey, whose recalcitrance was largely responsible for the refusal of other governments to ratify and put the Convention into effect. It was felt that if all the belligerents were brought within the purview of the Convention, the neutral states would eventually be forced to follow suit. In a surprisingly short-sighted reply, the State Department disagreed with the British suggestion on the ground that the conference should deal only with questions growing out of the war,[52] but fortunately it decided not to object to the proposal. Jealous, however, for the American position of leadership in the antiopium movement, the State Department cabled the American peace mission in Paris to the effect that while it still adhered to its belief regarding the British suggestion, "it would . . . seem unfortunate for any other country to receive the sole credit for bringing this matter to the attention of the Peace Conference."[53] In Paris, Secretary of State Lansing took the position that while believing that the narcotics question did not belong in the Peace Conference, the United States should not commit itself in advance on the point, but should await the actual bringing up of the matter in the conference.[54]

50. Acting Secretary of State Adee to Roland S. Morris (Tokyo), June 14, 1918, SDR 511.4A1/1529a; Acting Secretary of State Frank L. Polk to Walter Hines Page (London), William G. Sharp (Paris), and John W. Garrett (The Hague), July 16, 1918, SDR 511.4A1/1530a, 1530c, and 1530b, respectively.

51. Irvin Laughlin, American Embassy (London) to the Secretary of State, Dec. 14, 1918, SDR 511.4A1/1535.

52. Polk to the American Embassy (London), Jan. 25, 1919, *ibid.*

53. Polk to the American Peace Mission, Feb. 4, 1919, SDR 511.4A1/1538a.

54. American Peace Mission to the Secretary of State, Feb. 6, 1919, SDR 511.4A1/1539. See also *Foreign Relations, Paris Peace Conference, 1919,* XI, 18.

Nevertheless, the British and American delegations to the Peace Conference subsequently agreed that the time and occasion were quite opportune for taking steps to put the Hague Convention into operation.[55] By that time China had already raised the question by demanding that Germany and Austria ratify the Convention as a condition of making peace with her.[56] Thus when on April 15, 1919, the British presented to the Council of Ministers a draft of an article concerning the opium traffic for insertion in the peace treaty, the American mission was ready with a substitute.[57] The significant differences between the two drafts were that in the British draft article the powers would promise to ratify the Convention immediately and put it into effect, while the American draft provided for the signing and ratification of the Convention by the very act of signing the peace treaty. Another difference lay in the fact that the British draft called for bringing the Convention into force immediately after its ratification by the signing of the Special Protocol of the Third Hague Opium Conference and the passage of the necessary legislation, while the American draft called for the passage of legislation giving effect to the provisions of the Convention not later than three months *after the deposit of ratifications of the peace treaty.* Thus the American draft was subject to being construed so as to make the effectuation of the Convention await the exchange of ratifications of the peace treaty with the last depositing power. To iron out the differences, the two drafts, on Lansing's suggestion, were referred to the Drafting Committee, whose draft was read and accepted without controversy by the Council of Foreign Ministers on April 19 for insertion into the peace treaty. The draft became Article 295 of the Treaty of Versailles:

Those of the High Contracting Parties who have not yet signed, or who have signed but not yet ratified, the Opium Convention signed at The Hague . . . agree to bring the said Convention into force, and for this purpose to enact the necessary legislation without delay and in any case within a period of twelve months from the coming into force of the present Treaty.

Furthermore, they agree that ratification of the present Treaty should in the case of the Powers which have not yet ratified the Opium Conven-

55. American Peace Mission to the Secretary of State, March 31, 1919, SDR 511.4A1/1545.
56. American Peace Mission to the Secretary of State, March 18, 1919, SDR 511.4A1/1544.
57. *Foreign Relations, Paris Peace Conference,* 1919, IV, 552–53.

tion be deemed in all respects equivalent to the ratification of that Convention and the signature of the Special Protocol which was opened at The Hague in accordance with the resolutions adopted by the Third Opium Conference in 1914 for bringing the said Conventions into force.

For this purpose the Government of the French Republic will communicate to the Government of the Netherlands a certified copy of the protocol of the deposit of ratifications of the present Treaty, and will invite the Government of the Netherlands to accept and deposit the said certified copy as if it were a deposit of ratifications of the Opium Convention and a signature of the Additional Protocol of 1914.[58]

An identical article was inserted in the peace treaties with the other defeated powers. Thus the war which had interrupted the international antiopium movement served to give renewed impetus to that movement. It is doubtful whether Germany could have been persuaded otherwise to ratify and put the Convention into effect. Without action by Germany, other powers would undoubtedly have refused to put the Convention into effect.

In still another way the war resulted in a new momentum for the antiopium campaign. Article 23c of the Covenant of the League of Nations gave the League general supervision over the execution of agreements dealing with opium and other narcotic drugs. Thus the problem was placed within the purview of virtually the whole community of nations.

The drug problem figured in two other aspects in relation to the Treaty of Versailles and the attitude of the United States. Those who opposed the Covenant of the League and United States entrance into the League naturally seized upon any aspect of the peace treaty which might discredit it. One of the more controversial provisions of the treaty was that relating to the granting of German rights in Shantung to Japan. Most Americans thought this unfair to China and therefore opposed it. Even those favoring the peace treaty generally, but interested in the drug question, pointed to the Japanese flooding of China with morphine, using the town of Tsingtao as a base for the traffic, as sufficient reason for not allowing the province to come under Japanese domination.[59] In the debate in the Senate on the Treaty, Senator Henry Cabot Lodge castigated the Shantung provision as one of the many ways in which Japan was trying to get control of all of China.

58. *Ibid.*, p. 595.
59. Elizabeth Washburn Wright, "The Injustice to China," *The Outlook*, CXXII (Aug. 20, 1919), 601–602.

Another method, he declared, was Japan's deliberate fostering of the opium traffic in China in order to weaken China physically and morally. He inserted in the *Record* under the title "Shantung and Opium" the testimony of W. E. Macklin, a long-time resident of China and head of the College of Nanking, before the Foreign Relations Committee concerning Japanese complicity in the drug traffic in China. He pointed to this situation along with other factors in the Shantung question as sufficient reason why the United States should not consent to the peace treaty.[60]

The other way in which the traffic in opium and other dangerous drugs was involved in the debate on the peace treaty was the inclusion of this subject in the fourth of the Lodge reservations by which that traffic and a host of other issues were declared to be domestic matters solely within the jurisdiction of the United States and not to be brought within the province of the League or any other power.[61] Since the United States, including Senator Lodge, had repeatedly emphasized the necessity of international action to control the narcotics traffic and had stressed the fact that no country through its own laws could effectively meet its own internal drug problem, the inclusion of the narcotics traffic in the reservation was something of a contradiction. To withdraw what was considered this nonpolitical matter from the League's competence was a graphic expression on the part of the League's opponents of their lack of confidence in that body. It is therefore not surprising that the United States cooperated only hesitantly with the League on the drug question throughout the nineteen-twenties.

---

60. *Congressional Record*, 66th Cong., 1st Sess., 1919, LVIII, Part 7, 6877–6878.
61. *Ibid.*, Part 9, 8773, 8777.

Chapter six

Tentative cooperation with the League of Nations, 1921–1924

Throughout the 1920's and 1930's the participation of the United States in the antidrug campaign was complicated by the question of the degree to which this country would participate in League of Nations activities. In the early months of the Harding administration, the probability of cooperation with the League appeared to be slight, for communications from the League were not even acknowledged.[1] Gradually, however, indirect communication was established by a tortuous route beginning with the League Secretariat and leading via the Swiss Minister for Foreign Affairs to the American minister at Berne and finally to the State Department.[2] Later, an alternate route was established, from the League Secretariat to the American consul at Geneva to the State Department. Matters relating to narcotics were routed at first through the government of the Netherlands, which still served as the channel of communications regarding the traffic among parties to the Hague Convention who were not members of the League. Under that Convention the Dutch government was charged with taking the initiative in obtaining the deposits of ratifications and in instituting negotiations to solve disputes growing out of the Convention, and with acting as an intermediary for the exchange of information among the parties in regard to regulations and statistical data on opium and other narcotic drugs.

About a month before the Wilson administration went out of power, the State Department responded to a query from the Dutch legation as to whether the Department approved of the decision to accept the

1. The most comprehensive study of the relations of the United States with the League is Denna F. Fleming, *The United States and World Organization, 1920–1933* (New York: Columbia University Press, 1938). A briefer summary is that of Clarence A. Berdahl, *The Policy of the United States with Respect to the League of Nations* (Publications of the Graduate Institute of International Studies, No. 4; Geneva: Libraire Kundig, 1932).

2. Berdahl, *ibid.*, pp. 97–103.

deposit of ratifications of the Versailles Treaty as ratification of the Hague Convention as provided for by Article 295 of the Treaty of Versailles, expressed gratification at the procedure, and asserted its inability to see why any other party to the Hague Convention should object to it.[3] In the light of the subsequent attitude of the Harding administration it may be interesting to conjecture what its reply might have been, for about a month and a half after the Harding administration took office, the Netherlands government requested American concurrence in the transfer of its obligations under the Hague Convention to the League and asked if the United States would cooperate with the League in this regard.[4] Thus the United States was faced inescapably with the question of what its relations with the League would be. The Division of Far Eastern Affairs of the State Department, which had charge of international matters concerning narcotics, did not feel competent to give an answer to this basic question.[5] The Solicitor's office suggested that the United States might avoid embarrassment by interpreting Article 23c of the League Covenant, entrusting the League with supervision of the Hague Opium Convention, as implying the necessity of future agreement among the members of the League to entrust it with such functions. The possibility would then exist that the League members would not vote to do this and the Convention would be administered, as in the past, among both members of the League and nonmembers. Thus the United States would escape the dilemma of having to decide whether or not to cooperate with the League.[6]

The suggestion from the Solicitor's office appeared to be based largely on wishful thinking. Feeling that the United States was not yet ready to recognize the League, even in the matter of narcotics control, the Far Eastern Division drafted a reply signed by Secretary Hughes declaring that the United States would not acquiesce in the proposed transfer and would continue to look to the government of the Netherlands for the execution of the Convention. Reasons given for the position taken were that the United States had signed but had

3. Secretary of State Bainbridge Colby to Jonkheer W. H. de Beaufort, Chargé d'Affaires ad interim of the Netherlands, Feb. 5, 1921, SDR 511.4A1/1565.

4. W. H. de Beaufort to the Secretary of State, April 19, 1921, SDR 511.4A1/1568.

5. Memorandum by Nelson T. Johnson (Division of Far Eastern Affairs) to the Secretary of State, May 18, 1921, SDR 511.4A1/1572.

6. Memorandum from the Office of the Solicitor to the Division of Far Eastern Affairs, June 11, 1921, SDR 511.4A1/1568.

not ratified the Treaty of Versailles, but that it did sign, ratify, and put into force the Hague Opium Convention and was thus bound by it. Thus "any departure from its terms . . . would be in the nature of an Amendment to the Convention the acceptance of which would require the sanction of the Senate."[7] The Netherlands government therefore replied that it would continue to fulfill its duties in regard to states not members of the League, but would cooperate with the League as much as possible.[8] No other major state, however, took the position that the United States did.

Meanwhile the League of Nations was proceeding to assume the duties entrusted to it by the Covenant. In accordance with a resolution adopted by the First Assembly on December 15, 1920, the Council appointed an Advisory Committee on the Traffic in Opium and Other Dangerous Drugs consisting of representatives of China, France, India, Portugal, Japan, Siam, Great Britain, and the Netherlands—nations held to be most interested in the opium problem. Three assessors were also appointed, not as representatives of governments but in their individual capacities as experts on the drug problem. They were Henri Brenier of France, Sir John Jordan of Great Britain, and Mrs. Hamilton Wright of the United States. The Committee was charged with "general supervision over the execution of agreements with regard to the traffic in opium and other dangerous drugs and the consideration of all such international questions relative to the traffic in opium which may be submitted for consideration."[9] At its first meeting, in May 1921, the Committee issued an appeal to all countries to become parties to the Hague Convention and drew up and sent to all countries a questionnaire on the cultivation, production, and manufacture of opium and other narcotic drugs. At its second meeting in April of 1922, the Committee drew up a draft importation certificate which it requested all states to accept and put immediately into force; prepared a form of an annual report which it recommended to all countries for adoption, giving information for each country as to the general control of the drug traffic, import and export regulations, control of specified drugs and all prepared opium, and statistics on the production, manufacture, and trade in the various manufactured

7. Secretary of State Charles E. Hughes to W. H. de Beaufort, June 18, 1921, SDR 511.4A1/1568.
8. Netherlands Legation to the Secretary of State, Dec. 9, 1921, SDR 511.4A1/1580.
9. For a brief summary of the establishment of the Opium Advisory Committee and its work up to October 1922, see *Foreign Relations, 1923*, I, 90–93.

drugs; and requested information from all governments as to their requirements for domestic consumption of the various drugs in order to determine the quantity needed for the world's legitimate consumption.

For nearly a year the United States refused to respond to the Advisory Committee's request for information. The Netherlands government had sent the first forms of the Advisory Committee requesting information on July 14, 1921. The State Department took the position that the United States should have nothing to do with the League machinery in regard to the opium question but should continue to rely solely on the Netherlands government.[10] Finally it decided to furnish the information requested to the government of the Netherlands for transmission to the signatories of the Hague Opium Convention, thus establishing the fiction that it was communicating with the Hague Convention signatories, but not with the League.[11] This was the procedure followed for a considerable period in the communications between the League and the United States in regard to narcotics. The State Department tried to act as if the League did not exist.

The League could not long be ignored, however. On September 19, 1922, on the basis of a recommendation of the Advisory Committee, which felt that lack of information from the United States was hampering its work, the Third Assembly of the League adopted the following resolution:

The Assembly, convinced of the urgent necessity of securing the fullest possible cooperation in the work of the Advisory Committee on Traffic in Opium and Other Dangerous Drugs, and considering the fact that the United States of America is one of the most important manufacturing and importing countries, recommends to the Council of the League that it should address a pressing invitation to the Government of the United States to nominate a member to serve on the Committee.[12]

On September 26, 1922, the Council instructed the Secretary General of the League to issue the invitation. It was sent on October 14, 1922.[13]

Before receipt of the invitation, the State Department, having been

10. Memorandum of the Office of Assistant Secretary of State Fred M. Dearing, Jan. 27, 1922, SDR 511.4A1/1584.
11. Secretary of State Hughes to the Secretary of the Treasury, April 8, 1922, SDR 511.4A1/1575. Hughes to J. C. A. Everwijn, Minister of the Netherlands, April 28, 1922, SDR 511.4A1/1584.
12. *Foreign Relations*, 1923, I, 89.
13. Eric Drummond, Secretary General of the League of Nations to the Secretary of State, Oct. 14, 1922, SDR 511.4A1/1687.

apprised on September 20 of the Assembly's resolution,[14] was already considering its response. Edwin L. Neville, who was charged with the international aspects of the narcotics problem in the Division of Far Eastern Affairs of the State Department, urged acceptance of the invitation, pointing out that the presence of an American representative on the Advisory Committee would strengthen the hand of the committee in getting its recommendations for control of the traffic accepted by the League Assembly and Council. Furthermore, this would redound to the benefit of the United States, since its efforts at control were thwarted by widespread smuggling.[15] After the receipt of the invitation, Neville reiterated his stand, adding that as the Advisory Committee contemplated recommending the calling of a conference, the United States should be represented on the committee so as to influence the nature and scope of such a conference and also to smooth the way for American participation in such a conference without offending the members of the League and without "arousing political susceptibilities" in the United States. He recommended, however, that in order to avoid the necessity of obtaining the consent of Congress to such representation, there should be appointed an informal and unofficial representative to the committee to serve in an advisory capacity, preferably someone in the Public Health Service who would be familiar with both medical and administrative aspects of narcotics control.[16]

Meanwhile, the State Department was receiving communications from other sources urging it to resume active leadership in the anti-narcotics campaign. Prior to the receipt of the League invitation, various individuals and groups in the United States had urged the government to call an international conference to be held in the United States. After receipt of the invitation, many voices were raised urging its acceptance.[17] One who had consistently pressured the Department to cooperate with the League from the very beginning was Mrs.

14. Minister Joseph C. Grew (Berne) to the Secretary of State, April 12, 1922, SDR 511.4A1/1599.

15. Memorandum by Edwin L. Neville to William Phillips, Sept. 21, 1926, SDR 511.4A1/1687.

16. Memorandum by Neville to Phillips, Oct. 27, 1926, *ibid.*

17. Missionary and other religious organizations, antiopium societies, governors and congressmen from Pacific coast states, civic and social organizations, and private individuals all urged active participation by the United States either in cooperation with or without the League. See decimal files SDR 511.4A1/1570, 1571, 1583, 1591, 1604, 1663, 1688, 1689, 1707, 1710, etc.

Hamilton Wright, who brought to the movement a dedication and zeal which seemed to surpass even that of her late husband.[18] Within the State Department itself, largely as a result of Mrs. Wright's representations, influential voices were raised in support of the resumption of actual leadership on the part of the United States in the antiopium movement.[19] Thus it appeared that the government would have ample public support for a decision to send a representative to sit on the Advisory Committee. From abroad too came pressure for United States cooperation. Sir John Jordan, former British minister to China, a veteran of previous opium conferences, and now an assessor to the Advisory Committee, sent an urgent appeal to the State Department not to turn the invitation down. He pointed out that since the Committee as then constituted represented countries which were "immediately and vitally interested in the production of opium," and which were at that very moment favorably considering the establishment of an opium monopoly in China as the best means of controlling the traffic there, the influence of the United States—the only large and influential country not interested in opium production—was desperately needed on the committee, or the future results in regard to the opium traffic would be disastrous.[20]

The arguments of Sir John Jordan, especially his appeals to the American desire to thwart any movement for the establishment of an opium monopoly in China; public opinion in favor of American representation on the committee (or at least the lack of opposition to the idea); Germany's representation on the committee; and the desire of the United States to reestablish American preeminence in the international movement—all combined to make it easy for the Division of Eastern Affairs to gain the consent of Secretary of State Hughes and President Harding to sending someone in an informal and unofficial capacity to represent the United States at the next session of the Advisory Committee.[21] Undoubtedly the government's decision was also

18. Mrs. Elizabeth Wright to Phillips, July 24, 1922, SDR 511.4A1/1660; also memorandum by William R. Castle, Acting Chief, Division of Western European Affairs, Feb. 25, 1922, SDR 511.4A1/1596.

19. Memorandum by Castle to the Secretary of State, March 20, 1922, SDR 511.4A1/595.

20. Memorandum by Nelson T. Johnson to John V. A. MacMurray, Chief, Division of Far Eastern Affairs, Nov. 21, 1922, SDR 511.5A1/1700.

21. Memorandum by MacMurray to the Secretary of State, Nov. 21, 1922, SDR 511.4A1/1700; Secretary of State Hughes to the President (Harding), Nov. 25, 1922, SDR 511.4A1/1687.

influenced by its earlier selection in October 1922 of Miss Grace Abbott, Chief of the Children's Bureau in the Department of Labor, and Dr. Morison Dorset of the Bureau of Animal Industry in the Department of Agriculture to serve, respectively, on the League's Advisory Committee on the Traffic in Women and Children and on the Anthrax Committee of the International Labor Office.[22] At the suggestion of the Treasury Department, Dr. Rupert Blue, Assistant Surgeon General of the Public Health Service, was chosen to "serve in an unofficial and consultative capacity" as the American representative.

Dr. Blue attended the fourth session of the Advisory Committee at Geneva held from January 8 to 14, 1923. In its instructions to him, the State Department set forth the reasons for its current interest in the drug problem and therefore the reasons why the United States deemed it advisable to participate, though unofficially, in the meetings of the Advisory Committee. Of primary importance was the desire of the United States to protect its own nationals. In this regard the first concern was with domestic measures to prevent narcotic drugs from reaching its nationals for illicit purposes. Of subsidiary interest were the regulations of other manufacturing and producing countries to control the export of the crude and manufactured products, and measures for the prevention of the accumulation within any territory of a surplus which would supply the illicit traffic. Second in importance was the desire to prevent American nationals from engaging in the illicit international traffic. To achieve these ends the United States placed emphasis on the control of the manufacture of narcotics with a view to inducing other powers to bring their domestic and export regulations up to the standards proposed and adopted by the United States. Stressed third in order of priority was the desire of the United States to continue its historic efforts to help China eliminate her opium problem. It was therefore declared that "the American policy remains committed to the complete suppression and prohibition of the production and traffic in narcotics except for scientific and medical purposes and is therefore opposed to any legitimization of the traffic for other than scientific and medicinal purposes by the establishment of a government monopoly in China." Finally, it was felt that American participation would constitute a recognition of and response to the historic interest of Americans in efforts to control the

22. Berdahl, *The Policy of the United States*, p. 105.

traffic in narcotics through the participation of the United States in international conferences, conventions, and bilateral agreements.[23]

Blue was instructed to avoid "apparent acquiescence" in the actions of the Advisory Committee that were contrary to the traditional policy of this country and to let the committee know that the United States interpreted the term *production of opium*, as referred to in the Hague Opium Convention, as the growing of the poppy for the production of raw opium as well as the manufacture and refining of the raw product. Thus, stated in simple terms, the American position in regard to the traffic in opium and other dangerous drugs embraced the principles that production and manufacture should be limited to the legitimate needs of the world; that the only legitimate use of these products was for scientific and medical purposes, any other use constituting an abuse; that the best system for the suppression of the misuse of these drugs was prohibition; and that the solution to the problem lay in strict control by each country concerned of the production (including cultivation of the raw plant), manufacture, and distribution of the drugs.

The United States had now notably reversed its order of priorities since the pre-World War I conferences. Before the war the main emphasis was on helping China solve her problems; the problem in the United States and its possessions was considered secondary. Now China stood third in the list of priorities, behind the concern with America's own domestic problem and the desire to prevent Americans from engaging in the illicit traffic. This change in attitude reflected the growing realization that at this time the problem in the Orient and that in Western countries were not necessarily one and the same, but actually constituted two separate though related and sometimes overlapping phases of the worldwide problem.[24] The United States and other Western countries suffered primarily from manufactured products compounded in western Europe from raw opium produced in Turkey, Persia, and the Balkan states and from the coca leaf produced in South America—Bolivia and Peru. The use of prepared opium produced in the Far East constituted a very minor factor in the problem. The Orient, however, suffered from both aspects of the drug evil—the use of raw and prepared opium, whose source was both indigenous and foreign, and also the traffic in the manufactured products whose source

23. Hughes to the Secretary of the Treasury, Dec. 14, 1922, SDR 511.4A1/1707a.
24. Memorandum in Division of Far Eastern Affairs, Oct. 16, 1922, SDR 511.4A1/1720.

was western Europe and Japan. It was thus believed that through the control of the manufacture and the distribution of alkaloids the problem of Western countries, and especially the United States, might be considerably mitigated even though the Far Eastern problem remained chronic. Furthermore, because of the stability of the governments in the Western countries involved with manufacture and distribution, the Western phase of the problem appeared to be more susceptible of solution. Then too, there was a growing shift in the concern of the American public from China to America's own internal situation. This can be adduced from the fact that to the voices of the missionary and religious groups were added increasingly, after the war, the voices of individuals and groups of a civic and secular nature, most of whom were specifically organized to protect and combat the dope menace in America—hence the top priority claimed by America's domestic problem.

At its session in January the Advisory Committee had before it two major subjects for discussion. One was a resolution of the Assembly of the League that governments party to the Hague Opium Convention should boycott imports from nonsubscribers to the Convention who had not adopted the system of import-export certificates approved by both the Council and the Assembly in 1921 for the control of the international traffic in narcotics. The object of the resolution was to force certain countries, particularly Turkey and Persia, which were major producers of raw opium, and Switzerland, which was a major manufacturing country, to ratify and put the Convention into force. In the ensuing lively discussions several objections were made to this proposal, the principal of which were the contentions that it would give India a monopoly of the production of raw opium, increase the illicit traffic, increase prices, and deprive countries of necessary medicines. Blue did not take much part in this discussion. No decision was reached and the matter was carried over to the next meeting of the Committee.[25]

The second important item on the agenda was the report of the Mixed-Subcommittee, consisting of members of the Health Section of the League and the Advisory Committee, whose function was to examine questions of a medical nature. In their report the subcommittee undertook to answer two questions: (1) What was the object of the

25. Rupert Blue to Joseph C. Grew, Jan. 25, 1923 and Blue to the Secretary of State, Feb. 28, 1923, SDR 511.4A1/1743.

League's work in regard to dangerous drugs? and (2) What constitutes abuse of these drugs? In answer to the first question, the subcommittee held that the object of the League's work was to limit and prevent the abuse of opium, morphine, and cocaine and their products. Here Blue intervened to set forth the American position that investigation of production was one method by which this object might be attained and that the United States understood production of raw opium to include the growing of the poppy. The first part of Blue's contention was acceptable to the committee, since it had already discussed this point in previous meetings. The League had refused to accept the contention, however, that control of production of raw opium as mentioned in Article I of the Hague Convention embraced the idea of control of poppy cultivation.[26]

Blue took vigorous exception to the Mixed-Subcommittee's endorsement of the use of opium and cocaine as stimulants in the unfavorable climate and social conditions of the Far East. As a physician he could speak with some authority. He declared that these products were dangerous habit-forming drugs which should be administered only under the orders of a physician. As a result of his observations the subcommittee's position was thrown out of the report and a directly opposite viewpoint was incorporated which declared that only the medical use of opium should be considered legitimate, and that any other use of opium could not be considered legitimate even in tropical countries. Discussion of this part of the subcommittee's report was postponed to the next session of the Advisory Committee. Thus in two respects the meeting of the Advisory Committee revealed a possible rift between the United States and some of the other members as to what constituted control of production and legitimate use of opium and other drugs. A definitive statement by the committee on these subjects had to await its next session.

Indicative of the probable results was the great difficulty experienced by Mrs. Wright and Sir John Jordan, two of the assessors, in getting the American point of view on the legitimate use of opium incorporated in the Advisory Committee's report to the Council.[27] Sir Malcolm Delevingne, the chairman of the committee, and John Campbell, the Indian delegate, led the opposition to their efforts, the latter insisting that Blue's opinion should be confined to the minutes. Blue

26. *Ibid.*
27. Mrs. Wright to William Phillips, Feb. 7, 1923, SDR 511.4A1/1751.

himself declined to press the issue. The matter was important, however, for the members of the Council read and considered the report, but few read the minutes of the committee's meetings. Therefore, in order for the American position to be given proper consideration by the League, it would have to be brought before the Council and perhaps eventually before the Assembly through the medium of the Advisory Committee's report, unless, of course, some member of the Council or the Assembly wished to raise the issue. All efforts at this having failed in the committee, Mrs. Wright, on the occasion of the meeting of the Council in Paris after the committee session had adjourned, protested to Lord Balfour, the British Foreign Secretary, and Sir Eric Drummond, the League Secretary General, at the treatment accorded to Blue's statement and pointed out the possible repercussions in America. Agreeing that the suppression of the American position was a serious mistake, Sir Eric and the secretary of the Advisory Committee persuaded the rapporteur of the committee, M. Hymans of Belgium, to point out in a foreword to the report to the Council the importance of American participation in the committee's work and to draw attention to the annexed report of the Mixed-Subcommittee and to the fact that the question of the definition of the legitimate use of opium had been placed on the agenda of the next session of the Advisory Committee at the request of the American representative.[28]

Thus the first contact between the United States and the Advisory Committee was not altogether a satisfying one. With a more forceful representative from the United States it might well have soured the two bodies on each other. As a matter of fact, a more definite and forceful position on the part of the United States had been expected.[29] The reason that such a position was not taken lay in the absence in Blue's instructions of a clear and definitive statement of that position, as well as the lack of orders to present vigorously the American viewpoint. It must be remembered, however, that the United States was taking only a tentative and somewhat tremulous step toward cooperating with the League. Blue had been confidentially instructed to "report very carefully his considerations as to whether the League affords the proper machinery to effect the desired international cooperation for the suppression of the opium evil."[30] In a confidential report on this matter,

28. *Ibid.*   29. *Ibid.*

30. Phillips to Grew, Dec. 16, 1922, SDR 511.4A1/1736a. This paragraph was deleted from the original draft of Blue's instructions because his instructions and report would become public documents.

Blue declared that in the Advisory Committee the League had quite the proper machinery, but that as then constituted and directed, it would not likely deal with the root of the opium problem—the growth of the poppy for raw opium production. He pointed out that on this matter the committee operated under a ban imposed indirectly by the Assembly when it reversed a decision of the Council in 1921 to investigate the production of opium in the Far East with a view to its eventual restriction. He pointed out further that of the nine voting members of the Advisory Committee only the representatives of China and Siam favored restricting production, while the representatives of Great Britain, France, India, Holland, Japan, Portugal, and Germany were opposed to it. Furthermore, under the League's interpretation of the term *control of production* the establishment of a government monopoly for the control of the acreage devoted to poppy cultivation would meet the terms of the Hague Convention regardless of the amount of opium produced.[31]

As a result of the above situation and the unsatisfactory response of the Advisory Committee to the American viewpoint on poppy cultivation and the nonmedical use of narcotic drugs, Blue recommended that the American observer make it clear at the next meeting of the committee that further United States cooperation with the League on narcotics would be contingent upon the League's recognition and acceptance of the American principles.[32] Mrs. Wright made the same observations and recommendations.[33]

Although the Advisory Committee accomplished little at the session in which the United States made its debut, its net effect upon the issue of American cooperation with the League was salutary. It impressed upon the State Department the necessity of American representation on the committee if the American viewpoint was to be understood and given proper consideration by the nations most concerned with the narcotics question.[34] There was no outcry in American isolationist circles against such participation. As a matter of fact the State Department had received an unexpected ally in Representative Stephen G. Porter, chairman of the House Foreign Affairs Committee, who was

31. Blue to Grew, Feb. 7, 1923, enclosed in Grew to Phillips, Feb. 19, 1923, SDR 511.4A1/1743.
32. *Ibid.*; also Blue to Grew, Jan. 25, 1923, *ibid.*
33. Mrs. Wright to Phillips, Feb. 7, 1923, SDR 511.4A1/1751. It is obvious that Mrs. Wright influenced Blue in making his assessment of the Advisory Committee as well as in making the above recommendations.
34. Memorandum by MacMurray to Phillips, Feb. 8, 1923, SDR 511.4A1/1743.

anti-League in sentiment. Prior to Blue's embarkation for Geneva for the January 1923 meeting of the Advisory Committee, Porter had called on Undersecretary of State William Phillips and implicitly endorsed the step by revealing his plan to introduce in Congress a resolution on opium calling on the President to make direct representation to foreign governments to cooperate in the suppression of poppy cultivation and of the production and traffic in opium and other dangerous drugs. In support of the resolution the Congressman planned to hold hearings and to prepare a "formidable document" embodying the most up-to-date information on drug production and traffic throughout the world. Such action, he thought, would strengthen Blue's hand at Geneva. Although promising to keep the State Department fully informed on his actions, Porter expressed the desire to remain independent of the Department in this regard, so that it might not be held responsible for any steps he took which might prove embarrassing.[35]

With Porter's backing as well as the support of various pro-League organizations and antidrug groups the government did not hesitate to prepare to send a delegation to the fifth session of the Advisory Committee, which was to meet in May 1923. To give the American position due weight, an impressive delegation was appointed consisting of Porter as chairman, Bishop Brent, Dr. Blue, and Edwin L. Neville as technical assistant. The necessity for such a delegation had been clearly revealed in the fourth session of the Advisory Committee when Blue, whose experience in American legislative work in regard to narcotics was certainly not meager, had still found himself at a great disadvantage in contending with the representatives of other nations, most of whom were long-time experts in the field.[36] Since the American position before the League was primarily based on American legislation and administrative measures, the need for someone thoroughly grounded in the details of those measures and their effects was apparent. Edwin L. Neville filled this requirement admirably, and as a result, proved to be perhaps the most valuable member of the delegation. Porter, Brent, and Blue lent political, moral, and scientific prestige to the delegation.

35. Memorandum by Phillips of conversation with Stephen G. Porter, Nov. 29, 1922, SDR 511.4A1/1730.

36. This was attested to by numerous observers at the meeting, including Blue himself, all of whom urged that thereafter the United States be represented on the committee by an expert who would have a position of permanence. See Mrs. Wright to Phillips, Feb. 7, 1923, SDR 511.4A1/1751; MacMurray to Phillips, April 7, 1923, SDR 511.4A2/90; Phillips to the Secretary of State, April 5, 1923, SDR 511.4A1/1757.

This time the American representatives were fortified with a specific set of instructions which set forth the American view on the items on the agenda of the Advisory Committee as well as on the narcotics question as a whole with clarity and vigor. The principles there laid down constituted a summation of the American position as it had developed over the previous years and as it was to be maintained throughout the remainder of the period covered by this study.

The American position rested upon two pillars—the Hague Opium Convention and the legislation which the United States enacted to carry out its provisions and to deal with the domestic drug problem. The United States maintained that it would cooperate in the international movement and with the Advisory Committee only on the basis of the Hague Convention, the only convention common to all the powers, and that therefore it could not acquiesce in any interpretation of that convention which weakened it. Where it was defective the American government favored measures to strengthen it. The American legislation carrying out the provisions of the Convention, it was asserted, represented "the conviction of the American public that the best method of controlling the traffic in narcotic drugs is to do so by means of control at the source; that is, . . . that control should begin with the new product and should be carried on through all the processes of manufacture so as to prevent the illicit or non-medical use of narcotic products at any stage of their manufacture."[37]

In a statement drawn up to be delivered by Porter at the meeting, the provisions of the Hague Convention, the American interpretation of them, and the American legislation putting them into effect were summarized at some length. On the basis of this statement, five resolutions embodying the American viewpoint were presented with the request that they be adopted and embodied in the committee's report and recommendations "as the basis upon which the effective international cooperation can be expected." The resolutions set forth the following propositions:

1. If the purpose of the Hague Opium Convention is to be achieved according to its spirit and true intent, it must be recognized that the use of opium products for other than medicinal and scientific purposes is an abuse and not legitimate.

2. In order to prevent the abuse of these products it is necessary to exercise the control of production of raw opium in such a manner that

37. Secretary of State Hughes to Porter, Brent, and Blue (the American Delegation), May 10, 1923, SDR 511.4A1/1777a, see also *Foreign Relations*, 1923, I, 103.

there will be no surplus available for non-medical and non-scientific purposes.

3. The nations which are parties to the Hague Opium Convention are urged to bend every effort to induce the nations which are not parties to the Convention, or which have not yet enacted legislation to put it into effect, to do so at once.

4. Those nations which have well developed chemical and pharmaceutical industries are urged to prohibit the importation of all narcotic drugs except such quantities of crude opium and coca leaves as may be necessary to provide for medicinal and scientific needs.

5. All nations are urged to prohibit the exportation of narcotic drugs, including opium in whatever form and coca leaves and derivatives of these drugs, to those countries which are not parties to the Hague Opium Convention and which do not have domestic systems of control—including import and export certificates.[38]

The first two resolutions were the crucial ones, as they were the ones upon whose acceptance by the Advisory Committee future American cooperation with the League depended. The first draft of the instructions drawn up by Neville contained a statement which the American delegation was to make in case the resolutions were not adopted, expressing disappointment and regret, and grave doubt as to the utility of further attendance by the United States at the meetings of the committee and therefore the necessity for independent action by the United States to obtain the desired international cooperation.[39] This was deleted from the final instructions, however, at the suggestion of William Phillips, who thought that it would be better to await action by the committee and then instruct the delegation by telegraph as to what to do in case the committee rejected the American proposals.[40] Nevertheless, this was the card which the United States was prepared to play, and it showed that it was the intention of this government not to cooperate with the League in regard to the problem except on American terms.

The third resolution had already been recommended by the Advisory Committee and endorsed by the other League organs. The fourth and fifth resolutions represented legislative and administrative measures of the United States already in force.

38. *Ibid.*

39. Memorandum by MacMurray to the Secretary of State, April 24, 1922, SDR 511.4A1/1777.

40. Memorandum by Phillips to the Secretary of State, April 27, 1923, SDR 511.4A1/1777.

The other principal item on the League's agenda was the question of boycotting the imports of nonadherents to the Hague Convention. On this the State Department adopted Mrs. Wright's view that the better policy would be to continue the efforts to get these countries to adhere rather than attempt a boycott, especially in view of the fact that in the Balkans and Asia Minor, the principal American sources of raw opium, political conditions in regard to the restoration of peace and the fixing of territorial boundaries were in such a fluid state that a boycott would not affect the illicit traffic which was the source of American difficulties.[41] Emphasis was thus placed on withholding manufactured drugs from nonadherents to the Hague Convention rather than boycotting the raw products of such countries as Turkey and Persia.

In addition to a prestigious membership and a set of clearly stated principles, the American delegation was buttressed by resolutions from both the American and Pan American Congresses. Porter had succeeded in getting his resolution passed, the preamble of which contained a lengthy dissertation on the world narcotics problem and its effect on the United States. The resolution called on the President to urge the producing nations to limit the growth of the poppy and the coca leaf and the production of the raw drugs to medicinal and scientific purposes as the only effective way to control the traffic in and use of these drugs.[42] During the meeting of the Fifth Pan American Conference in April 1923, the State Department instructed the American delegation to that conference to secure the supporting views of the conferees in order to strengthen the American position before the Advisory Committee.[43] This assignment, in effect, had already been carried out two days earlier when the conference had unanimously adopted a resolution submitted by the delegation of the United States declaring its approval of the Hague Convention and urging the American states which had not done so to ratify the Convention and enact legislation to put it into force.[44]

Although the American delegation on the Advisory Committee was limited by its instructions to a "consultative" role, the activities of the

41. Secretary of State Hughes to the American Delegation, May 10, 1923, SDR 511.4A1/1777a.
42. Lewis, *Opium and Narcotic Laws*, pp. 20–22.
43. Secretary of State Hughes to the American Delegation to the Fifth Pan American Conference, April 28, 1923, SDR 511.4A1/1769.
44. Henry Fletcher to the Secretary of State, April 29, 1923, SDR 511.4A1/1814.

delegation came under extensive scrutiny. The entrance of the United States into League opium activity had attracted the attention of various interested groups and individuals in America. Prominent among those observing and attempting to influence the delegation at Geneva were Mrs. Helen Howell Moorhead of the Foreign Policy Association; Miss Ellen La Motte, author of several books and articles on the subject of opium; and a representative of the Hearst newspaper chain, which was violently anti-League in its sentiments. These individuals were to play an influential role in the issue of cooperation between America and the League on the drug problem.

League officials welcomed the American delegation to Geneva with some trepidation. They expected that the Americans would insist on the acceptance of the first two proposals in their program, and if successful, would then present detailed measures to carry them out. The League officials felt that as these proposals would constitute a revision of the Hague Convention, a matter beyond the Advisory Committee's power, the committee would find it impossible to accept them unreservedly, and thus a stalemate would ensue and future cooperation between the League and the United States on the drug problem would be jeopardized.[45] Although subsequent events were to relieve the officials of their fears, the initial action of the American delegation seemed to justify their apprehension. Porter, who headed the delegation, became the dupe of his own anti-League inclinations and propaganda when on his arrival in Geneva he committed the naïve blunder of approaching the League as a sovereign entity in itself, a superstate, to be dealt with on an equal basis by the United States as one sovereign power with another. He therefore laid the American proposals before Sir Eric Drummond, the Secretary General, with the idea that their acceptance by Drummond on behalf of the League would be binding on the member states. Drummond was both astonished and perturbed at Porter's naïveté and with some difficulty managed to explain to him that the League was not a superstate, that he was merely the Secretary General of an organization in which over sixty sovereign states were represented, and that Porter would therefore have to deal with the nine member states of the Advisory Committee in their capacities as individual sovereign states.[46]

45. American Legation (Berne) to the Secretary of State, July 12, 1923, SDR 511.4A1/1814.
46. This incident was later reported confidentially and with some consternation to the State Department by the American legation at Berne and by Mrs. Moorhead. See

Drummond's explanations were not sufficient to cause Porter to surrender entirely his concept of the nature of the League. After their initial speeches and the presentation of the American proposals in the Advisory Committee, the American representatives, taking care to avoid acting in a way that could be interpreted as an acknowledgment that they were a constituent part of the committee, refused to participate in the committee's discussions. They regarded the committee and themselves as separate entities, the committee negotiating on behalf of the League, and the American delegation on behalf of the United States. Thus they presented the American proposals as "the settled position" of the United States, leaving it up to the committee on behalf of the League to present counterproposals, if any, to the American delegation for consultation.[47] Later Porter went so far as to suggest to Sir Eric Drummond the idea of forming a new committee or commission consisting of five members from the United States and five from the League. Sir Eric cryptically informed Porter that the members of the League would not agree to being equaled by one sovereign state, even if that country was the United States.[48]

The Americans did not attend the first meetings of the Advisory Committee on May 24, which were devoted to organization, because they had not received a reply to their communication to the Secretary General informing him of their desire to present the American proposals at the committee's convenience. The following day, however, in speeches by Brent and Porter, the American views were laid before the committee. In a masterly statement, Bishop Brent stressed the moral and humanitarian considerations which underlay the need for the limitation of the production of the narcotic drugs and the raw material from which they were derived to the medical and scientific needs of the world. The main barrier to such limitation, he asserted, was revenue considerations, which if eliminated would likewise end the interest of governments in the production of such products. As science had clearly established that the nonmedical use of opium was an abuse, and as nine-tenths of the world's production was for revenue and in

ibid., "Confidential Report on Trip to Opium Commission of the League of Nations, Geneva, May 1923," Moorhead to Castle, received July 23, 1923, SDR 511.4A1/1816; Confidential Memorandum from the Division of Western European Affairs to the Secretary of State, June 22, 1923, SDR 511.4A1/1938.

47. Porter to the Secretary of State, May 27, 1923, SDR 511.4A1/1788; Brent to the Secretary of State, June 16, 1923, SDR 511.4A1/1799.

48. Moorhead to Castle, received July 23, 1923, SDR 511.4A1/1816.

excess of medical and scientific needs, the nations concerned, for the sake of their colonies as well as for themselves, and to help rather than take advantage of weaker nations, should subordinate all economic considerations and administrative difficulties in coping with the evil to the moral, humanitarian, religious and scientific determinations. He called for limitation at the source—restriction of poppy cultivation—and made a special plea in behalf of China, which, he declared, was the "victim of former exploitation and her own present weakness." He therefore urged the committee to dissuade China from the idea of establishing a government monopoly of the traffic in opium.[49]

In his speech, Porter, after assuring the committee that the purpose of their presence was not to criticize but to establish common strategy, read the statement in his instructions setting forth the provisions of the Hague Convention, the American interpretation of that Convention, the American legislation putting it into effect, and the views of the United States as to the legitimate use of opium and the control of production. He urged the committee to adopt and to recommend to the Council and the Assembly the adoption of the American resolutions which declared that the only legitimate use of opium products was for medicinal and scientific purposes and which called for the restriction of the production of raw opium to those purposes. In support of the two resolutions he presented a statement which the delegation itself had drawn up at Geneva citing and interpreting Chapters II and III of the Hague Convention and referring to them as "the heart" of that Convention.[50]

The Advisory Committee, having expected a more vigorous presentation, was both impressed and relieved by the two speeches; Brent's on moral grounds and Porter's setting forth the legal position.[51] As already mentioned, after taking part in the discussion of items connected with the Hague Convention, the American delegation withdrew when the American proposals came up for discussion, holding that as the United States was not part of the Advisory Committee, they would not act until the committee accepted or declined the proposals. The initial reaction to the proposals saw Germany, Portugal, Siam, and China ap-

---

49. A copy of this speech is in Brent Papers, Box 18.

50. Porter to the Secretary of State, May 25, 1923, SDR 511.4A1/1787; May 22, 1923, SDR 511.4A1/1785; Aug. 2, 1923, SDR 511.4A1/1824.

51. American Legation (Berne) to the Secretary of State, July 12, 1923, SDR 511.4A1/1814.

proving them without reservation; Japan, India, the Netherlands, and France opposing them; and Great Britain taking a noncommittal attitude. The Indian delegate, John Campbell, declared that the American propositions were contrary to the Convention; France insisted on a dictionary definition of the term legitimate; and the Dutch held that effective action could be taken only after the contraband traffic was ended.

Since India led the opposition to the American proposals, Porter wished to challenge Campbell's right to vote on the ground that India, as a part of the British Empire, had no independent relationship to the Hague Convention. Great Britain had signed, ratified, and put the Convention into effect on behalf of her colonies and possessions, and India was thus not an independent signatory. The State Department, however, while agreeing with the validity of Porter's objection, pointed out to him the embarrassing position in which the American delegation would be placed if, representing the United States only in a consultative capacity and being unable to vote, it nevertheless challenged India's right to vote in a committee of the League.[52] Thus Porter did not pursue the matter.

The question for crucial consideration was what constituted the legitimate traffic in and use of opium. The powers with Far Eastern possessions insisted that under the Hague Convention the traffic in and use of prepared opium were legitimate. The Indian delegate contended that the customary manner in which opium was used in India—primarily eating—was also legitimate under the Convention. The British and German representatives initially upheld the Indian position, but later abandoned it. Campbell, however, remained adamant. The other major opposition to the American principles came from the French representative, who adopted an obstructionist attitude not only toward the American proposals but also to the British resolution calling for stricter police measures to bring about the suppression of the traffic in prepared opium as called for in Chapter II of the Hague Convention. The British, in general, were inclined to support the American viewpoint.[53]

After several days of heated discussion, the Advisory Committee drew up a series of resolutions which embodied only in part the American principles. This was unacceptable to the American representatives,

52. Porter to the Secretary of State, May 27, 1923; Secretary Hughes to Porter, May 29, 1923, SDR 511.4A1/1788.
53. Moorhead to Castle, received July 23, 1923, SDR 511.4A1/1816.

and they presented a counterproposal based on an earlier British resolution. But this too was rejected by the committee. Thereupon Porter presented an ultimatum to the committee threatening cessation of American cooperation with that body.[54] As a result, Sir Malcolm Delevingne, the chairman of the Advisory Committee, appointed a drafting committee on which Porter and Neville were included, but from which the obstructionist Indian representative, Campbell, was excluded, to bring forth a formula that would be acceptable to all.

The resolutions drawn up by the drafting committee were adopted by the Advisory Committee with the approval of the American delegation. They were divided into four parts. In Paragraph 1 the American proposals were recommended to the League "as embodying the general principles by which the Governments should be guided in dealing with the question of the abuse of dangerous drugs, and on which, in fact the International Convention of 1912 is based. . . ."[55] This statement was modified by the reservation of the representatives of Great Britain, France, Germany, Japan, the Netherlands, Portugal, and Siam to the effect that "the use of prepared opium and the production, export and import of raw opium for that purpose are legitimate so long as that use is subject to and in accordance with the provisions of Chapter II of the Convention."[56]

Paragraph 2 consisted of an expression of appreciation for the cooperation of the United States with the League and of the desire of the governments concerned to cooperate with the United States in "giving the fullest possible effect to the Convention."

Paragraph 3 recited the ways the Advisory Committee had already worked toward the goals expressed in the American proposals, such as trying to secure the adhesion of all countries to the Hague Convention; seeking information in regard to the world medical and scientific needs for manufactured drugs with a view to restricting production to those needs; attempting to suppress the illicit traffic by recommending the system of import certificates, arranging for exchange of information among countries concerned, and suggesting other measures for inter-

54. *Ibid.*; also Brent to the Secretary of State, June 16, 1923, SDR 511.4A1/1799.
55. "Resolutions of the Advisory Committee on Traffic in Opium of the League of Nations (June 5, 1923), Accepting the Proposals of the United States with a Reservation Reaffirming Chapter II of the Hague Opium Convention relating to Prepared Opium," enclosed in Porter to the Secretary of State, June 6, 1923, SDR 511.4A1/1793. All the resolutions adopted are contained in this document.
56. *Ibid.*

national cooperation; attempting to get China and the powers with Far Eastern possessions to consider measures to solve the problem of the use of prepared opium; and the collection and publication of information from the various countries as to the conditions in their respective territories and the measures taken by them to carry out the provisions of the Convention. This particular paragraph had been drawn up through the instrumentality of Sir Eric Drummond at the instigation of Mrs. Moorhead of the Foreign Policy Association, who wanted this recitation for the benefit of the American delegation in order to show them and the American government and people that the League and the United States were seeking and working toward the same objective, and that therefore they should cooperate with each other.[57]

Paragraph 4 recommended to the Council that to give effect to the American principles as well as to the policy of the League, a conference consisting of the manufacturers of opium and coca leaf products and the producers of raw opium and the coca leaf for export, and a conference of the powers in whose territories prepared opium was used should be held with a view to reaching an agreement providing for (1) the limitation of the production of manufactured drugs and their raw materials to medicinal or scientific needs, (2) the reduction of the quantity of raw opium to be imported for smoking purposes where it was presently used, and (3) the suppression of the illegal production and use of opium in China. To this recommendation India appended a reservation specifying that "the use of raw opium, according to the established practice in India, and its production for such use are not illegitimate under the Convention."

The resolution was indeed a forward step in the relations between the United States and the League. But it was not wholly on American terms. For the sake of agreement the American delegation was forced to concede the reservations modifying the American definition of legitimate use by accepting the view of all the member states of the Advisory Committee except China that the use of prepared opium was legitimate under the terms of the Hague Convention. Although they opposed the Indian contention that opium eating was legitimate, they finally accepted a negative statement of that same argument to the effect that such use of opium was "not illegitimate." The delegates justified their concessions on the ground that they merely constituted

57. Moorhead to Castle, received July 23, 1923, SDR 511.4A1/1816.

a reaffirmation of Articles 6 and 7 of the Convention.[58] In this the delegates were undoubtedly correct, but their instructions had interpreted these articles differently.

If the original positions of the Advisory Committee and the United States are interpreted as being contradictory, the American representatives did score a moderate victory. In addition to getting qualified acceptance of the American principles in regard to the legitimate traffic in and use of opium, they succeeded in getting incorporated in the resolution of the Advisory Committee the American suggestion for the inclusion of producing nations in a conference for the purpose of devising means to reduce the supply of raw opium and coca leaves—reduction at the source.

Yet, as Paragraph 3 of the resolution and the discussions in the committee revealed, the United States and the committee were together on many issues. Most of the governments seemed to favor strict international control of the traffic in manufactured drugs. The British were particularly keen on this. The complicating factor, however, was the fear of nonmanufacturers that restrictions on the existing basis of manufacture would give a monopoly to the few countries which were then manufacturing. The British likewise were responsible for the inclusion of a call for a conference of states in whose territories prepared opium was used. These states, however, including British India, seemed to the American delegation to be more interested in protecting their opium revenue from the competition of the illicit traffic in and consumption of opium for smoking. Their representatives contended that efforts to suppress opium smoking would be nullified by the cultivation and smuggling of opium in China and by the importation of Persian opium into the Far East. Only Siam frankly admitted that it opposed the suppression of opium smoking because opium was a source of necessary revenue.[59] Thus the American delegation was able to make virtually no headway where the interests of particular members of the committee appeared to be entrenched.

The session of the Advisory Committee was fruitful in several respects. Aside from the modified acceptance of the American position, the groundwork was laid for another conference covering all aspects of the narcotics problem—cultivation, manufacture, and trade. Also the discussions opened Porter's eyes to the complexity of the problem—to

58. Porter to the Secretary of State, Aug. 2, 1923, SDR 511.4A1/1824.
59. *Ibid.*

considerations other than mere desire for revenue that hindered its solution. Furthermore, Porter gained a new understanding of the nature of the League to the extent that he was moved to praise the work of its permanent staff.[60] Although there was some grumbling in regard to Porter's dictatorial methods and the refusal of the American delegation to enter fully into the discussion of the Advisory Committee, those who honestly desired progress in regard to the solution of the drug problem realized more than ever the desirability and necessity of American cooperation. Further steps in this direction awaited the action of the Council and the Assembly of the League.

On the recommendation of the Council, the Secretary General invited the United States to send a representative to sit in on the meetings in September of the Fifth Committee of the Assembly (the committee of the Assembly concerned with social and humanitarian questions) at which time the report of the Advisory Committee containing the American proposals would be considered. The presence of an American representative was desired so that the United States might explain its views and to enable the members of the Fifth Committee to consult with the American representatives.[61] The United States accepted the invitation and sent the same delegation that attended the Fifth Session of the Advisory Committee to the meeting of the Assembly to act in a consultative capacity. They were given no detailed instructions, but were merely advised to make clear that the American position was the same and to try to secure the acceptance of that position as embodied in the recommendation of the Advisory Committee.[62]

At the beginning of the discussion in the Fifth Committee on September 18 some confusion arose as to the meaning of the Advisory Committee's resolution calling for the conferences. The American, French, and Dutch representatives thought the resolution contemplated two conferences: one concerned with the production and export of the raw materials, the international restriction of their derivatives, and the production and export of raw opium for smoking; the other to be confined to the consideration of the opium smoking problem in the Far East. On the other hand, the British also thought that the

60. *Ibid.*
61. American Legation (Berne) to the Secretary of State, Aug. 9, 1923, SDR 511.4A1/1821.
62. Secretary Hughes to Porter, Brent, and Blue, Aug. 24, 1923, SDR 511.4A1/1832a.

resolutions called for two conferences, but that one would be a conference on manufacturing and the other a conference on the production of raw materials, while the production of and traffic in raw opium for smoking purposes would constitute only a tentative agenda on one phase of the narcotics problem.

The American delegation was prepared to support a proposal for one conference to deal with different aspects of the question, but when Porter's suggestion to this effect was put as a motion by the South African delegate, it was amended by the British to call for two conferences. The issue was then referred to a subcommittee, which after two days of deliberations reported back a recommendation for two conferences. The Fifth Committee of the Assembly endorsed this in the form of two resolutions requesting the Council to call first a conference on prepared opium and the illegal production and use of opium in China, to be followed immediately by a conference of all the member states of the League and the parties to the Hague Convention. The subjects to be considered by the latter conference would be the limitation of the manufacture of derivatives and limitation of imports of raw materials for that purpose, and the restriction of the production of raw materials for export to medical and scientific purposes, thereby giving effect to the principles of the United States and the policy of the League.[63] The Fourth Assembly adopted the resolutions of the Fifth Committee, and in December 1923 the Council instructed the Secretary General to take steps to put them into effect.

By its participation in the discussions of the Advisory Committee and the Fifth Committee of the Assembly the United States bridged the gap that had occurred in the international antinarcotics campaign during the years of World War I and the early hesitant steps of the League. During this period American interest had been largely dominated by its own internal problem and the situation in China. Antipathy toward the League served to delay a vigorous reentry into the international movement. By 1924, however, the United States seemed prepared to reassert its leadership in that movement, whose center was now Geneva, just as it had pushed through the work at the Hague from 1911 to 1915.

---

63. These were Resolutions 5 and 6 adopted by the Fifth Committee. For the report on the proceedings of the committee in regard to narcotics, see Porter to the Secretary of State, Oct. 20, 1923, SDR 511.4A1/1860.

Chapter seven

The Geneva opium conferences

The Council of the League had called for the convening of two conferences in November 1924. At the suggestion of the Assembly, and over the objection of the British, the Council specified that the parties to the Hague Convention and all members of the League should be invited to participate in the second conference. The British had opposed this on the grounds that the inclusion of nonmanufacturing and nonproducing countries, which were not directly concerned with the drug problem, might hamper, through the presentation of impractical proposals, the reaching of satisfactory and speedy conclusions. The decision to invite these states was made to meet the question raised by Porter as to what would happen if after the manufacturing and producing countries had reached agreements, countries not parties to the agreement began production of the raw materials and the manufacture of their derivatives. The British maintained that the simpler solution would be merely to invite these states to adhere to the agreements reached.[1] As the issue was of little interest to the United States, it did not insist on the inclusion of these states in the Conference.[2] Nevertheless the decision of the Council to invite them stood.

The Geneva Opium Conferences which met in 1924–1925 established a high water mark in the relations between the United States and the League of Nations. For the first time the United States was formally and officially represented in a League activity. The government cast itself wholeheartedly into the preparations for the conferences. It was not invited, however, to the first conference, as this was confined to the subject of opium smoking and to nations in whose Far Eastern territories such use of opium was permitted. Nevertheless, the United States interpreted the original resolutions of the Advisory Committee as supporting the assumption that the second and larger conference dealing

1. Memorandum by Edwin L. Neville to Undersecretary of State William Phillips, Nov. 12, 1924, SDR 511.4A2/1.
2. H. G. Chilton, Chargé d'Affaires ad interim, British Embassy (Washington) to Secretary of State Hughes, Nov. 8, 1923, SDR 511.4A2/1.

with production and manufacture would have the results and conclusions of the first conference before it for study.[3]

To prepare the American program for the forthcoming deliberations
the State Department appointed Porter, Neville, and Mrs. Wright.
Neville attended the sessions of the Preparatory Committee called for
by the Council, which was to draft a program for the second conference. Because of the highly technical nature of much of the work before the committee and the great stress in Geneva placed upon the
desirability of an American delegate of "expert knowledge and well
trained in negotiations," he had at his disposal the assistance of M. R.
Livingstone, the assistant secretary of the Narcotic Control Board;
H. F. Worley, customs narcotic representative in Zurich; and Surgeon
W. W. King of the Public Health Service, who was then in Paris.
Other members of the committee were Sir Malcolm Delevingne of
Great Britain, Gaston Bourgois of France, W. G. Van Wettum of
the Netherlands, and the two European assessors of the Opium Ad-
visory Committee, Sir John Jordan and Henri Brenier.

Neville's instructions, which he drew up himself, laid down in
general terms the items which the United States insisted should be
included in the program for the conference. In regard to the production of raw materials the American proposals called for the restriction
of the cultivation of the opium poppy and the coca leaf to medicinal
and scientific needs and no encouragement of such cultivation by the
state; no reliance by governments on the revenue derived from the control of opium and coca leaf production and trade, except to regulate
the narcotics traffic; the consideration of treaty provisions preventing
certain states from substituting increased customs taxes for the taxes
on opium and coca leaves and their products; and the application to
coca leaves of the provisions of the first five articles of the Hague Convention. As for the transportation of drug products, it was proposed to
confine the international trade in them to medicinal and scientific purposes, except for the temporary traffic in prepared opium, which should
cease after a fixed period of about ten years through the strict application of the import-export license system among the parties to the
Hague Convention. In addition, strict measures to control the transshipment of drugs and their transportation on the high seas, including
the reciprocal right of search, were recommended. With respect to

3. Phillips to Chilton, Nov. 30, 1924, SDR 511.4A2/1.

manufacture, the instructions called for the application of Articles 9
through 13 of the Hague Convention to all derivatives and preparations
of opium and coca leaves, the prohibition of the importation by manufacturing countries of manufactured drugs, and the restriction of the
exportation of manufactured drugs and preparations to only those
parties to the Hague Convention having "adequate" systems of domestic control. Several administrative measures were also suggested. The
most important of these called for the establishment of "a permanent
central organization" with sufficient powers to carry out the administrative features of the agreement arrived at; the submission of annual
reports by all the powers showing the amounts of raw materials and
their derivatives "produced, imported, exported or used for local consumption"; making illegal possession of the various forms of the drugs
a penal offense; and bringing within the scope of the convention drugs
subsequently discovered to be dangerous as narcotics.[4]

From March 6 to July 16, 1924, the Preparatory Committee held
several meetings without being able to agree on a draft program for
the conference. A significant drawback was the lack of sufficient data
to ascertain the quantity of the world's needs of raw materials for the
production of the world's requirements of drugs for medicinal and
scientific purposes and for the production of prepared opium. Another obstacle was the view of many of the delegates that conditions
in China, Turkey, and Persia precluded effective measures to bring
about a reduction in the production and exportation of raw opium.
Sir Malcolm Delevingne favored confining their efforts to a restriction
of manufactured drugs and coca leaves, the less difficult problem.[5] The
French delegate, Bourgois, however, was less than keen on the idea
of the restriction of manufacture, and it was only after representations
at Paris by both the British Foreign Office and the American State Department[6] that he came forward with any proposals at all.

Five different plans were finally presented, of which the most important were those of Neville, the British, and the Dutch. The main
features of Neville's plan, based on and supplementing the principles

4. The Secretary of State to Neville, Feb. 21, 1924, SDR 511.4A2/31b.
5. American Embassy (Paris) to the Secretary of State (from Neville), April 3,
1924, SDR 511.4A2/46.
6. Aide-mémoire from the British Embassy (Washington) to the State Department,
May 7, 1924, SDR 511.4A2/55; Secretary Hughes to the American Embassy (Paris),
May 12, 1924, SDR 511.4A2/55; Ambassador Myron T. Herrick (Paris) to the Secretary of State, May 21, 1924, SDR 511.4A2/58.

laid down in his instructions, were the establishment of a fixed quantity
for all countries or for each country individually of opium and coca
leaves to be produced for export and the restriction of such production
to states then producing; the confining of the importation of a fixed
quantity of raw materials for manufacture to the countries then manufacturing, and the restriction of manufacture for export to the states
then manufacturing for export; and the establishment of a permanent
central board, consisting of two members each from producing and
manufacturing countries in Europe, the Americas, and Asia plus an
expert jurist, a board which would collect, collate, and publish statistics
in regard to production, manufacture, importation and exportation,
consumption, stocks on hand, and the domestic requirements of each
state for raw and manufactured drugs and which would regulate and
adjust necessary modifications in the schedules of quantities allotted on
the basis of estimates of needs submitted to manufacturing and producing states.[7]

Numerous and varied objections were raised in the committee to
Neville's scheme. The more prominent criticisms were that it was
impossible to determine the per capita need for the various forms of
the drugs; that a rationing of quotas of production, manufacture, and
export would be difficult, would inhibit fair competition, and would
deprive purchasing countries of the right to choose their markets; that
the scheme would cause a too sudden decrease in production with a
consequent rise in prices which in turn would cause an increase in
smuggling and in the manufacture of drugs for consumption by countries not then manufacturing; and that varying conditions between
countries producing opium and countries producing coca leaves would
preclude the same measures for control of excessive production of
both these products. Other objections to the scheme were that it would
result in too much official interference with trade, necessitate the appointment of too many new government officials, and would incur too
much expense.[8]

The British plan was similar in many respects to that of Neville,
except that it contemplated only the control of the production of coca
leaves and of the manufacture of opium and coca leaf alkaloids and
derivatives. The principal steps called for were the manufacture on the

7. League of Nations, *Report of the Opium Preparatory Committee*, C.348.M.119.
1924. XI (Geneva, 1924), pp. 24–25.
8. *Ibid.*, pp. 25–27.

basis of the estimated needs of each state of a fixed quantity of drug products and the proportionate distribution of the amount to be manufactured among the manufacturing states; the restriction of the importation of raw materials to the amount needed to meet the manufacturing quota, and of the importation of manufactured drugs by consuming countries to the quantity stated in their estimates; the setting of a fixed export quota of coca leaves for each producing state; the institution of a system of import certificates and export licenses; the providing of means for future new manufacturing and producing countries to enter the quota system through agreements with the old manufacturing and producing states revising the quotas; and the establishment of a permanent board consisting of representatives of the manufacturing and producing countries to administer and supervise the scheme. The British felt that of the two parts of their plan, the part relating to control of manufacture was the more important and could operate without the part relating to control of production.[9]

The British scheme attracted virtually the same criticisms as those directed against the American plan. Additional objections, however, were the contentions that it would be impossible for new producers and manufacturers to get an agreement with the old producers and manufacturers for a share of the quotas, and that the supervisory body's composition would not lend itself to impartial decisions.[10] Thus a central objection to both the American and British plans was the fear of the establishment of a monopoly of the production of raw materials and manufactured drugs by the then producing and manufacturing countries.

The difficulty of the opium problem led the Dutch to bypass its consideration. Their plan of control was therefore confined to the production of the coca leaf and the manufacture of cocaine. Like the British scheme, it called for the establishment of a monopoly of the international trade in coca leaves and the production of cocaine among the existing producing and manufacturing countries. Unlike the British plan, however, it placed the major emphasis on the restriction of the raw material rather than on the rationing of factories, which the Dutch considered impractical. Specifically, their scheme called for the prescribing of fixed amounts to be exported by each producing state, the restriction of the exportation and reexportation of the raw material to

9. *Ibid.*, pp. 14–20.   10. *Ibid.*, pp. 20–24.

countries then manufacturing for export purposes, the reduction by not more than 10 percent of the amount then produced for export, and the establishment of a permanent committee to supervise exports.[11]

The Dutch proposals were criticized on the grounds that a mere 10 percent reduction in production would not limit output to medicinal and scientific needs, that control of manufacture would be easier than control of production, that a monopoly of producers and manufacturers would be unacceptable, and that there would be no assurance that manufacturers would receive a fair share of the raw product for export, especially since Holland occupied a dual role as a producer—through its possession of Java—and as a manufacturer and could thus establish a monopoly of the trade.[12]

Bourgois, the French representative, and Brenier, one of the assessors, also presented proposals,[13] but like those of the American, British, and Dutch, they were found unacceptable. Thus the grand result of the work of the Preparatory Committee was five different schemes. At its meeting in August 1924, the Advisory Committee, on the motion of Mrs. Wright, appointed a subcommittee consisting of those who had served on the Preparatory Committee and representatives of Germany and India to try to reconcile the different projects. After extensive discussions and a great deal of hard work, the subcommittee brought forth a draft scheme which was accepted by the Advisory Committee. In brief, the scheme called for the establishment of a central board composed of experts to be chosen by the Council of the League on the advice of the Advisory Committee. The board would receive the reports of governments on estimates of their annual import requirements of raw opium, coca leaves, and certain of their derivatives and preparations for medicinal and scientific purposes and annual statistics on imports, exports, consumption and stocks on hand. It would be empowered to set the requirements for countries which failed to submit estimates or submitted estimates which appeared to be greatly in excess of their requirements. Each government would pledge that it would not import drugs in excess of its estimates and that it would limit exports to a country to the quantity set by the board. The scheme also provided for amendments to the Hague Convention which would

---

11. *Ibid.*, pp. 8–13. As there were only three territories in which the coca leaf was extensively produced—Bolivia, Peru, and Java—it was assumed that regulation of the trade in this product would be relatively simple.

12. *Ibid.*, pp. 12–13.   13. *Ibid.*, pp. 28–34.

place coca leaves in Article 2 and include synthetic cocaine in the definition of cocaine in Chapter III; establish a system of import certificates and export licenses for the international trade in both raw materials and their manufactured products; and institute measures to prevent drugs stored in bonded warehouses or free ports or shipped in transit across a country from being diverted to the illicit traffic. Finally, the plan suggested that governments adopt specific measures to prevent their subjects from promoting the illicit traffic in other countries and to prevent the use of their merchant marine for carrying unlicensed shipments of drugs.[14]

The Advisory Committee's plan represented the very maximum on which agreement could be obtained in the committee. The American proposals for direct limitation of the production of raw materials and the British scheme for direct limitation of manufacture were both rejected because of the objections raised to giving a monopoly of production and manufacture to the countries currently engaged in these activities and because of opposition to any degree of coercion. In return for dropping his insistence on direct limitation of production, Neville was able to get accepted the idea of a central board to which estimates of needs and reports on consumption would be submitted as an indirect approach to the same goal.[15]

The Dutch and French representatives opposed the suggestion that the board be composed of representatives of the producing and manufacturing countries on the ground that it would lead to the suspicion that they would favor large sales of narcotics to benefit their respective countries. These objections were responsible for the decision that the board should be chosen by the Council on the advice of the Advisory Committee.[16] Five months were thus consumed in arriving at a scheme that would serve as an acceptable basis for discussion in the Second Conference. The difficulty involved in this achievement augured ill for the success of the conference.

The forthcoming deliberations were in the meantime arousing interest in the United States. While general sentiment appeared to be in favor of American participation, there were some objections to holding the meetings in Geneva because Switzerland, an important manufacturing country, despite repeated urgings from the United States

14. Neville to the Secretary of State, Aug. 14, 1924, SDR 511.4A2/83; and Aug. 28, 1924, SDR 511.4A2/85.
15. *Ibid.*   16. *Ibid.*

and others, had failed to ratify the Hague Convention.[17] As the conferences were being held under the auspices of the League of Nations, however, Geneva was the logical site, and there was little that the American government could or wished to do about it. Of more significance was the work of Congressman Porter, who undertook the mission of securing a congressional appropriation to finance American participation. He therefore introduced a joint resolution in Congress which, after reviewing the role of the United States in the international movement and setting forth the American principles for the control of the narcotic drug traffic—the use of drugs for only medicinal and scientific purposes and the limitation of production of the raw material to amounts needed for such purposes—called for an appropriation of $40,000 for American participation in the conference.

The resolution, considered in the House on April 7, 1924, brought up the issue of the relations of the United States with the League, but surprisingly aroused only slight controversy. Representative Thomas L. Blanton, Democrat of Texas, chided Porter for sponsoring a proposition for cooperation with the League, since Porter and the Republican Party "have not only ignored and disregarded it [the League] but turned it down."[18] Instead of the $40,000 appropriation Blanton recommended first $10,000 and then $20,000 as being adequate for the purpose. On the other hand, Representative J. Charles Linthicum, Democrat of Maryland, came out wholeheartedly for the resolution, regarding it as indicative of one among many steps toward further American cooperation with the League. He deplored the halfhearted pace at which such cooperation was proceeding and urged that the United States become a full member of the League and thus assume the responsibilities and leadership in world affairs to which it was entitled.[19] Porter, however, was by no means willing to have his actions interpreted as favoring closer American ties with the League—of going into the League, as some of his colleagues suggested, by the back door. He explained that the basis of the dealings of the United States with the League were treaties with the member states, treaties that had been in existence long before the League came into being. Thus, he con-

17. See for example the resolutions forwarded to the State Department in the following communications: Senator Samuel M. Shortridge to the Secretary of State, Feb. 19, 1924, SDR 511.4A2/28; Senator G. W. Pepper to the Secretary of State, Feb. 23, 1924, SDR 511.4A2/30; and Representative Scott Wolff to the Secretary of State, March 24, 1924. SDR 511.4A2/37.

18. *Congressional Record*, 68th Cong., 1st Sess., 1924, LXV, Part 6, 5767.

19. *Ibid.*, 5770.

tended, the United States was merely asserting "our rights and discharging our obligations under the terms of these treaties." "In every instance," he declared, "where the United States representatives have negotiated with the league it had been to assert a right or perform a duty under an existing treaty, and I confess frankly I cannot see any distinction between negotiating with those nations en bloc and negotiating with them individually."[20] Thus Porter revealed that he still had not disabused himself of the notion of the League as an entity with which the United States should deal on a basis of equality.

The resolution received the overwhelming approval of the House. The Senate, however, on the recommendation of the Foreign Relations Committee, attached what came to be a crucial qualification whereby the American representatives were forbidden to sign any agreement which did not embody the American position in regard to the legitimate use of opium and other dangerous drugs and the necessity for the limitation of the production of raw materials. As adopted unanimously by both houses in early May, the resolution, with the exception of the preamble, resolved:

That the appropriation of such sums as may be necessary, not to exceed $40,000 for the participation of the United States in one or both of these conferences . . . to be expended under the direction of the Secretary of State, is hereby authorized: Provided, That the representatives of the United States shall sign no agreement which does not fulfill the conditions necessary for the suppression of the habit-forming narcotic drug traffic as set forth in the preamble.[21]

Since the United States placed most emphasis on the curtailment of the production of raw materials, the State Department approached the various producing states prior to the conferences and expressed the hope that they would attend and agree to reduce their production to medicinal and scientific purposes.[22] Typical of the position of the producing countries and illustrative of the complexity of the problem as well as of the task that would face the American delegation at the conference was the reply of Bolivia. The Bolivian foreign office

20. *Ibid.*

21. U.S. Congress, House, Committee on Foreign Affairs, *Hearings . . . on H.J. Resolution 195, The Traffic in Habit Forming Drugs*, 68th Cong., 1st Sess., 1924 (Washington: Government Printing Office, 1924); see also Lewis, *Opium and Narcotic Laws*, pp. 23–24.

22. Secretary of State Hughes to the American Embassy (Lima) and to the American Legation (La Paz, Bolivia), Sept. 11, 1924, SDR 511.4A2/90a; to the American High Commissioner (Constantinople), Sept. 11, 1924, SDR 511.4A2/93; and to the American Legation (Teheran), Sept. 15, 1924, SDR 511.4A2/93a.

promised to be represented at the conference but stated emphatically that they could not agree to restrict the production of the coca leaf.[23] Their position was explained to the State Department by the American legation, which pointed out that the coca leaf was such an integral part of the Bolivian economy that it would be very difficult to even get an agreement not to *increase* production and quite impossible to extract a promise to reduce production. Aside from the fact that the Bolivian government depended upon coca leaf cultivation for a large part of its revenue, prominent political leaders of both political parties were great producers of the commodity, and employers universally believed that the Indians needed it to work.[24] This attitude of the producing states signified another ill omen for the American position at the conference. In regard to the coca leaf the situation in Peru was like that in Bolivia, while the major opium-producing countries could see no way of effecting restrictions on their product without incurring disastrous political and economic consequences.[25]

Although the United States did not participate in the work of the First Geneva Opium Conference, it watched its proceedings with great interest. As the moral champion, historically, of the East on the opium question, it regarded the suppression of the traffic in prepared opium as only slightly less vital than the solution of its own domestic problem. Besides, the United States was under the impression that the results of the First Conference would be open to review by the Second Geneva Opium Conference, a view largely responsible for the controversy which characterized the deliberations of the latter assembly.

The major work of the First Conference was done in its first twenty meetings from November 3 to December 5, 1924. The final four meetings, from December 13, 1924, to February 11, 1925, were closely bound up with the deliberations of the Second Conference and consisted of efforts to alleviate some of the dissatisfaction in that body with the results of the previous performance of the First Conference.[26] The

23. W. Russell Baker, Third Secretary of the American Legation (La Paz) to the Secretary of State, Sept. 19, 1924, SDR 511.4A2/106.

24. *Ibid.*

25. W. Smith Murray, Chargé d'Affaires ad interim, American Legation (Teheran) to the Secretary of State, Oct. 9, 1924, SDR 511.4A2/129, encloses "Memorandum on Opium" by D. W. MacCormick, Director of Internal Revenue, Persia.

26. League of Nations, *First Opium Conference, Geneva, November 3rd, 1924–February 11th, 1925: Minutes and Annexes*, C. 684. M. 244. 1924. XI (Geneva, 1924). Cited hereafter as *Minutes of First Geneva Opium Conference*. A convenient summary of the work of the First Conference is contained in the Foreign Policy Association,

mandate of the First Conference, as expressed in Resolution 5 of the Fifth Committee of the Assembly, was the consideration of measures to carry out the obligations assumed under Chapter II of the Hague Opium Convention calling for the gradual suppression of the use of prepared opium. Its agenda, therefore, based on the proposals of the Advisory Committee at its fifth session in May 1923, included the examination of conditions in the Far East relative to the use of smoking opium and its suppression, the consideration of measures to suppress more effectively such use of opium, and the discussion of the situation in China in regard to the illegal production and use of opium and measures to be recommended to China for the solution of the problem. The conference, which consisted of representatives of Far Eastern nations or of nations with Far Eastern possessions,[27] had before it specific measures, suggested by the Advisory Committee, for discussion. These called for the replacement of the farm system by a government monopoly, the establishment of a maximum quantity of opium to be imported, the inauguration of a system of registration and rationing of addicts, the institution of a system of uniform retail prices for the drug and of uniform penalties for violation of the laws, and the holding of periodic reviews of the opium situation.[28]

For a considerable period the work of the First Conference was overshadowed and even hindered by the controversy between the British and Japanese delegates over the import certificate system as applied to imports into Formosa from Hong Kong. The British had recently begun to follow the practice of refusing to honor suspicious import certificates issued by Japanese authorities for the export or transshipment of opium from Hong Kong to Formosa because much of this opium had found its way into the illicit traffic. The Japanese contended that they were being discriminated against on national grounds in the application of the system. They maintained that the powers should allow the export or transshipment of opium on the presentation of import tickets without question and that they could not sign an agreement unless their demand was met. As the matter threatened to break up the conference, the British urged that it be made the subject of direct negotiations between the two governments. They

---

International Control of the Traffic in Opium: Summary of the Opium Conferences Held at Geneva, pp. 7–9.
27. China, France, Great Britain, India, Japan, the Netherlands, Portugal, and Siam.
28. Foreign Policy Association, *op. cit.*, p. 7.

appealed to the United States for representations at both Geneva and Tokyo in this regard.[29] As the United States was not a producer of raw opium and did not allow its re-exportation from the country, it was not directly concerned. Nevertheless, the State Department responded to the British request.[30] Meanwhile the First Conference adjourned from November 16 to November 21 to enable the two disputants to reach an accord. The result was embodied in Article 6 of the Agreement of the Conference as follows:

1. The export of opium, whether raw or prepared, from any Possessions or Territory into which opium is imported for the purpose of smoking shall be prohibited.

2. The transit through, or transshipment in, any such Possessions or Territory of prepared opium shall be prohibited.

3. The transit through, or transshipment in, any such Possessions or Territory of raw opium consigned to a destination outside the Possession or Territory shall also be prohibited unless an import certificate, issued by the Government of the importing country, which can be accepted as affording sufficient guarantees against the possibility of illegitimate use is produced to the Government of the Possessions or Territory.[31]

It can be seen that the British were able to retain essentially what they had insisted on, while the Japanese apparently obtained satisfaction through the extension of the demand for trustworthy import certificates to other powers, thus removing the onus of being discriminated against.

In regard to the major problem under consideration—steps to suppress gradually the use of prepared opium—the delegations showed little inclination to take significant action. Aside from the Chinese, the Japanese delegation was the most vigorous in pressing for strong measures. They urged that the Formosa system of control, characterized by the registration and rationing of habitual users, should be adopted. The representatives of the other powers demurred, on the ground that the mobility of their populations would render such a system ineffective. The British suggestion calling for a system of government monopoly of all transactions in opium, even including retail sales, met with more general approval. But other progressive measures to suppress the use of smoking opium were generally opposed. China served as the con-

29. Acting Secretary of State Grew to the American Consul (Geneva), Nov. 20, 1924, SDR 511.4A2/164d.

30. Grew to the American Consul (Geneva) and the American Embassy (Tokyo), Nov. 22, 1924, SDR 511.4A2/164.

31. *Minutes of the First Geneva Opium Conference*, p. 107.

venient scapegoat, for all the other delegations, except the Japanese, maintained that as long as China continued to be a major producer of opium and the principal source of the illicit traffic, efforts to suppress the use of prepared opium in adjacent territories would be futile.[32] The Chinese naturally opposed this view, but they could only promise that the problem would be ended as soon as conditions permitted. Most of the powers simply preferred to maintain the status quo so far as systems of control in their own territories were concerned. In the light of this attitude it is not surprising that the agreement reached consisted of innocuous provisions that would have little effect, if any, on the opium problem in the Far East.

The First Conference completed its Agreement by early December. In essence, it called for a government monopoly of the importation, sale, and distribution of opium; prohibition of the sale of opium to minors and exclusion of minors from opium dens; prohibition of the export of prepared opium from, transit in, and transshipment through territories which imported such opium, and a similar prohibition of the same kind of traffic in raw opium with respect to such territories except on the furnishing of a valid import certificate; exchange of information and views among the various territories in the efforts to suppress smuggling; and the holding of joint periodic reviews of the situation in regard to prepared opium—the first such review to be held not later than 1929.[33] December 13 was set as the date for the signing of the Agreement. In the meantime, the work of the First Conference had come under the surveillance, though not within the competence, of the Second Conference, and thereafter the deliberations of the two assemblages were inextricably bound up with each other.

The American delegation to the Second Geneva Opium Conference consisted of Porter as chairman; Bishop Brent, who reluctantly consented to serve just once more; Mrs. Hamilton Wright; Edwin Neville; and Rupert Blue. William B. Morris, the Assistant Solicitor of the State Department, accompanied the delegation as an expert in international law. Whereas only eight powers, including India, participated in the First Conference, forty-one powers, including the participants in the First Conference, were represented in the Second Conference. The American delegation was privately opposed to the separate representation of India, both because India was not a sovereign entity and her

32. *Ibid.*, pp. 117–118.   33. *Ibid.*, pp. 115–116.

representation gave Great Britain an additional vote in the conference, and also because the most vigorous and bitter opposition to the American proposals came from the Indian delegate, John Campbell. The Second Conference held thirty-eight plenary sessions, beginning November 17, 1924, and ending February 19, 1925. An extended Christmas recess was taken in the proceedings from December 16 to January 19 in order to permit the settling by the governments involved of the controversies which had arisen in the conference. In fact controversy characterized by bitter recriminations, especially between the American and the British delegations, was the most notable feature of the Second Conference. The roots of the conflict lay in the American proposals which led to the raising from the very beginning of the conference of the question of the competence of the conference to consider certain matters.

The proceedings of the Second Conference revolved around the draft conventions submitted by the United States and the Opium Advisory Committee. The American scheme incorporated, in the form of amendments to the Hague Opium Convention, the principles and proposals previously enunciated by the United States and covered all matters in that convention except Chapter IV relating to China. Its main points were (1) the restriction of the production and distribution of raw opium and coca leaves to medicinal and scientific needs; (2) the gradual suppression of the traffic in prepared opium within a period of ten years by means of a 10 percent reduction per year in the importation of raw opium for the purpose of making prepared opium; (3) the establishment of a permanent central board to which governments would submit annual estimates of their narcotic drug needs and quarterly statistics of their production, importation, exportation, and consumption of narcotic drug products, and with authority to question the estimates of countries deemed to be in excess of reasonable requirements and to recommend the cessation of the export of drugs to such countries; and (4) the adoption of an import-export system for controlling the international traffic.[34]

The scheme of the Advisory Committee, which served as the basis of the work of the Second Conference, was very similar to the Ameri-

---

34. A convenient comparison of the Hague Opium Convention and the draft conventions of the United States and the Advisory Committee is contained in a printed document in the State Department entitled *International Control of the Traffic in Habit-Forming Narcotic Drugs, Fourth International Conference*, SDR 511.4A2/315.

can proposals with respect to the import-export certificate system, the permanent central board, and minor amendments to the Hague Convention.[35] It did not contain, however, proposals for the limitation of the overall production of raw opium and the suppression of the traffic in prepared opium. This was due to the fact that the committee put emphasis on the first part of Resolution 6 of the Fourth Assembly authorizing the Second Conference. This part of the resolution specified as subjects to be considered

limitation of the amounts of morphine, heroin or cocaine and their respective salts to be manufactured; the limitation of the amounts of raw opium and the coca leaf to be imported for that purpose and for other medicinal and scientific purposes; and . . . the limitation of the production of raw opium and the coca leaf for *export* [italics added] to the amount required for such medicinal and scientific purposes. . . .[36]

The American program, on the other hand, involved emphasis on the latter part of the resolution which requested the Council

as a means of giving effect to the principles submitted by the representatives of the United States of America, and to the policy which the League, on the recommendation of the Advisory Committee has adopted, to invite the Governments concerned to send representatives with plenipotentiary powers to a conference for this purpose. . . .[37]

Thus, there were two different approaches to the agenda of the Second Conference: that of the Advisory Committee, which was based on the view of most of its members that the matters to be discussed should be confined to the subjects listed in the first part of the resolution, and the American viewpoint which held that any proposals designed to give effect to the principles of the United States as endorsed by the League were within the competence of the conference and that the subjects mentioned in the first part of the Assembly's resolution were not intended to be exhaustive but suggestive as to the measures to be taken to carry out those principles. Out of these different interpretations came the first major difference of opinion in the conference.

The American delegation presented its complete program to the conference at the fourth meeting on November 19.[38] In a statement

35. *Ibid.*
36. Porter to the Secretary of State, Oct. 20, 1923, SDR 511.4A2/1860.
37. *Ibid.*
38. League of Nations, *Records of the Second Opium Conference*, Vol. I: *Plenary Meetings: Text of the Debates*, C. 760. M. 260. 1924. XI (Geneva, 1925), pp. 34-36. Cited below as *Records of Second Geneva Opium Conference*, I.

preliminary to the presentation of the proposals, Bishop Brent emphasized the need to help China and asserted that the crux of the drug
problem was money. He urged the conferees to place morality above
practical and material considerations and to adopt the same measures
for the welfare of other nationalities and races as for their own.[39] The
American proposals regarding limitation of production of raw materials and the suppression of prepared opium immediately raised the
question of the competence of the Second Conference as prescribed in
Resolution 6 of the Fourth Assembly to consider these matters. Several
days were spent in discussing this question in relation to Article 1 of
the American suggestions calling for the limitation of the production
of raw materials to medicinal and scientific needs. The Indian delegation, supported by the British and the Dutch, maintained that as the
American proposal envisaged limitation of production for internal
consumption, it was beyond the competence of the conference, for the
agenda adopted permitted only the discussion of limitation of the production of raw materials for export. The American response to this
contention was that Resolution 6 of the Assembly "constituted in
effect the agenda of the conference" and that as the resolution stated
that the conference was called to give effect to the principles of the
United States and the policy of the League, these principles and policy
called for the limitation of production so that there would be no surplus
available for nonmedicinal and nonscientific purposes. Thus, the American proposal was clearly within the purview of the conference. After
a lively discussion, the conference upheld the American position by a
vote of 26 to 1 with 9 abstentions, and Article 1 was referred to the
appropriate subcommittee for consideration.[40]

Productive of much more difficulty was Article 8 of Chapter II of
the American scheme, which called for the suppression of opium smoking within ten years. At the first plenary session of the Second Conference the American delegation served notice that they would move
to amend the agenda of the Second Conference so as to provide for
the consideration of the problem if no significant progress was made

39. *Ibid.* The work of the Second Conference is thoroughly and objectively summarized in the "Report of the Delegation of the United States in Attendance at the
Geneva Conference held at Geneva, Switzerland, November 27, 1924," typed copy
submitted to the State Department, April 3, 1925, SDR 511.4A2/315. Cited below as
Report of the American Delegation to Geneva Opium Conference.

40. For the competence of the conference to consider Article 1 of the American
proposals, see *Records of Second Geneva Opium Conference,* I, 68–97.

in the First Conference. At that time the First Conference had reached no agreement, but the probability was strong that no meaningful measures would be forthcoming. Nevertheless, when the Agreement was finally brought forth the American delegation was shocked at its weakness. In a written communication to the participants of the conference, Bishop Brent unleashed a scathing attack upon the provisions of the document. He examined each provision clause by clause and pointed out their various deficiencies. In his view the principal weaknesses of the Agreement were the failure to establish a time limit in which the use of prepared opium would be suppressed, lack of a call for measures to prevent the spread of the habit to adults, the establishment of a government monopoly of transactions in opium, thereby giving governments an interest in revenue from this source, and the failure to recommend measures for the cooperation of neighboring territories in the solution of the opium problem in China. In language full of sarcasm Brent flayed the results of the First Conference as follows:

When we contemplate the tremendous machinery called into being for the creation of the document that lies before me—Advisory Committee, Council, Assembly of the League of Nations, International Conference with plenipotentiary representatives—it is like requisitioning a steam hammer for splitting a rock and then cracking a walnut with it . . . . I fear the best I can say about the document is in the terms of a Latin proverb—Montes parturiunt, nascitur ridiculus mus [the mountains are in the pangs of birth; there is born a ridiculous mouse].[41]

Bishop Brent urged that the Second Conference disregard the question of competence and proceed to do what the First Conference failed to do; that it not confine itself to dealing with only the 10 percent of the subject which affected Europe and America, but that it also seek a solution of the 90 percent of the problem affecting Asia; and that in the interest of good relations between the East and West, the Western powers adopt the same standards for their Eastern territories and peoples as for their own nationals. He implored the participants in the First Conference not to sign the Agreement.[42]

Bishop Brent conducted a virtual one-man campaign against the Agreement. After addressing his "Appeal to My Colleagues" he left Geneva on December 7 for France and England in an effort to persuade

41. Copy of Brent's "Appeal to My Colleagues" in SDR 511.4A2/—. Also in Brent Papers, Box 16.
42. *Ibid.*

the officials of those countries not to sign the document. In Paris he saw Premier Herriot. In London he saw various officials of the British Government—Waterlow of the Foreign Office, Sir Arthur Stelle Maitland, Secretary of Labor, Lord Cecil, and the Archbishops of York and Canterbury, and he corresponded with the Foreign Secretary, Sir Austen Chamberlain.[43] While there he took advantage of the occasion to answer the charges against the American delegation, printed in the London *Times*, of John Campbell, the Indian delegate, who had preceded him to London. Campbell had severely criticized the American delegation and its program. He charged them with having presented in their draft convention matters that went beyond the scope of the agenda of the Second Conference and which they had previously agreed specifically to exclude from the agenda. He contended further that the American principles on which their draft convention was based represented an incorrect interpretation of the Hague Opium Convention, and he criticized the American delegation for refusing to accept his suggestion to refer the question of the meaning of the Convention to the Permanent Court of International Justice or to an *ad hoc* conference of the signatory powers. Finally, he complained that Article 1 of the American draft convention interfered with the domestic concerns of India. He could not agree, he asserted, that "the only thing which can solve the opium problem is the reduction of the original crops," for the production of opium in India did not affect in any way the amount of opium available for consumption. He concluded that the action of the American delegation on these matters jeopardized the success of the conference.[44]

In a letter to *The Times* dated January 13, Brent denied Campbell's charges. He pointed to the fact that the Second Conference had already decided that it had competence in regard to two articles of the American suggestions, including the controversial Article 1. Besides, not only the United States but other nations also had presented proposals in addition to those of the Preparatory Committee, since it was never understood that the proposals made in that committee were exhaustive. Furthermore, he argued, the American interpretation of the Hague Convention had been "explicitly accepted by the Advisory Commit-

43. Brent to Sir Austen Chamberlain, London, Dec. 11, 1924, SDR 511.4A2/251, also in Brent Papers, Box 16. Brent to Porter, en route to United States aboard S.S. *Leviathan*, Dec. 14, 1924, Brent Papers, Box 16. Brent to Secretary of State Hughes, S.S. *Leviathan*, Dec. 16, 1924, SDR 511.4A2/207. Also in Brent Papers, Box 16.

44. Clipping from *The Times* (London), Dec. 12, 1924 in Brent Papers, Box 16.

tee, the Council, and the Assembly of the League, . . . India's reservation being duly recorded." Finally, the American representatives had never agreed in any form that certain subjects included in the American scheme would be excluded from discussion, and if they had, such an agreement would have been repudiated by the American government. Brent concluded that Campbell's whole position was weak and his statement without foundation.[45] Thus, the differences between the participants in the conference were placed in the arena of public opinion where, because of the nature of the problem, the United States, as the champion of morality, had the advantage.

Brent's efforts to persuade the powers to reject the Agreement of the First Conference were temporarily rewarded with success. The day (December 13) when the First Conference participants were to sign passed with only the signature of the delegate of India, who had signed on December 6, attached to the Agreement. At the last moment the British and French delegations had received instructions from their governments not to sign.[46] The other governments followed suit. Thus hope remained within the American delegation that the Second Conference might salvage something of substance from the discussions on the problem.

The most obvious explanation for the decision of the British and French to postpone the signing of the Agreement of the First Conference was their hope that they could persuade the United States to withdraw its controversial proposals, both in regard to limiting the production of raw opium and suppressing the traffic in prepared opium. As early as December 3 the British Foreign Office appealed to the State Department not to insist on bringing these proposals before the Second Conference, as they were clearly beyond its scope. They suggested instead that as a compromise, the United States endorse a proposal which the British would bring forth and which would call for the appointment of an impartial commission, headed by an American and not containing nationals of the powers with Far Eastern possessions, to conduct an investigation in all the Far Eastern Territories concerned, including China, as to the nature of the opium problem and the feasibility of measures for its suppression. A full knowledge of the nature of

45. Copy of Brent to the Editor of *The Times* (London), Dec. 13, 1924, Brent Papers, Box 16.

46. Brent to Porter, S.S. *Leviathan*, Dec. 14, 1924, Brent Papers, Box 16. For a summary of Brent's activities and their results, see memorandum by F. P. Lockhart to the Secretary of State, Jan. 5, 1924, SDR 511.4A2/339.

the problem, and of British administrative difficulties in dealing with it, would, in the opinion of the Foreign Office, induce sympathetic understanding on the part of Americans of the British position.[47]

The State Department rejected the British plea. It cited House Joint Resolution 195 instructing the American representatives not to sign any agreement which failed to fulfill the American principles as the reason for its inability to acquiesce in the British suggestions.[48] However, the Department suggested to Porter that in order to facilitate a compromise with Great Britain and thereby avoid jeopardizing the success of the conference, he might become more flexible about the fixed term of ten years for the suppression of the traffic in prepared opium.[49] Porter agreed not to insist on the ten-year limit, but held that if the menace of prepared opium was to be eliminated, the United States would have to insist on some time limit in which this would be brought about.[50]

On December 12 the American delegation presented its suggestions on prepared opium and moved their referral to the appropriate subcommittee. As predicted, this aroused a storm of protest from many nations represented in the First Conference, particularly the British, the French, and the Dutch. They contended that the proposal was outside the competence of the Second Conference. Furthermore, they did not wish to repudiate an agreement they had just completed and had authority to sign. Although, as already mentioned, the signing of the Agreement was postponed, the battle over the competence of the Second Conference to consider the American proposal continued to rage. On December 16 the conference voted to adjourn all plenary sessions until January 12, when the discussion of the issue would be resumed.[51] It was hoped that in the meantime the major disputants would be able to work out some compromise. If a vote had been taken on the question at this time, the Americans could probably have carried the conference by a large majority.[52] This might have availed them nothing, however,

47. Esme Howard, British Embassy (Washington) to the Secretary of State, Dec. 3, 1924, SDR 511.4A2/178.

48. Secretary of State Hughes to the American Consul (Geneva) (for Porter), Dec. 5, 1924, SDR 511.4A2/178.

49. *Ibid.*

50. Consul Tuck (Geneva) (from Porter) to the Secretary of State, Dec. 8, 1920, SDR 511.4A2/185.

51. For the discussion of the issue to December 16, see *Records of Second Geneva Opium Conference*, I, 110–114.

52. Tuck (from Porter) to the Secretary of State, Dec. 17, 1924, SDR 511.4A2/197.

because the British and several other delegations might then have withdrawn from the conference.

Had the State Department been willing to exert firm control over the American delegation at Geneva, a compromise might have been worked out. While in London, attempting to persuade the British to postpone the signing of the Agreement of the First Conference, Brent was fully exposed to the considerations underlying the British position. Sir Austen Chamberlain, the Foreign Secretary, set forth convincingly that position in a letter to Brent. The situation in India was the root of the difficulty. Chamberlain pointed out that the reports of both the American and British delegates on the Hague Opium Conference in 1912 agreed with India's present interpretation of Article 1 of the Hague Convention to the effect that the purely domestic production and use of opium in India was not open to international consideration. He also pointed out the difficulties standing in the way of confining "by a single stroke of the pen" the production and export of opium to medicinal and scientific purposes. Prominent among these were the opium situation in China, lack of controls in other producing states, the illicit traffic and the absence of measures by certain countries to suppress it, the presence of large numbers of Chinese in Britain's Far Eastern possessions, and the customs of the people in these territories and the need for a proper regard for them. Chamberlain cited Britain's withholding of its signature to the Agreement of the First Conference and the proposal for sending an impartial commission of inquiry to India and other British possessions as evidence of the serious concern of the government with the problem and the desire to do what was right about it.[53]

Brent was almost completely won over by Chamberlain's arguments. He suggested to the State Department that the United States should refrain from interfering in India's internal affairs, but should confine its importunings to the restriction of production for export, a position which he had urged on the American delegation before he left Geneva for France and England. He likewise recommended that the United States support the British proposal for a League of Nations investigatory commission to the Far East. Finally, he endorsed Chamberlain's view that the complexity of the opium smoking problem precluded solution by a "simple stroke" and that because of chaotic conditions in

53. Chamberlain to Brent, Dec. 19, 1924, enclosed in Brent to the Secretary of State, Jan. 7, 1925, SDR 511.4A2/251.

China the fixing of a specific time when adjacent territories should begin to reduce imports would not be feasible.[54]

In the State Department the views of Chamberlain and Brent were given respectful consideration. In a memorandum from the Division of Far Eastern Affairs it was recommended that Porter be sent excerpts of their remarks and also selections from the Department's instructions to Blue on December 14, 1922, disavowing the desire or intention of the United States to interfere in the internal and purely domestic measures of governments in regard to the drug traffic in their own territories. It was hoped that these statements would induce Porter to refrain from risking the loss of British cooperation by insisting on a fixed number of years in which the use of prepared opium in India and other British possessions should be suppressed. It was suggested that the adoption of the British proposal for a commission of inquiry to the Far East might be the maximum which the American delegation could obtain if it was not to risk wrecking the conference.[55]

The State Department endorsed the views set forth in the memorandum, but merely contented itself with sending the recommended excerpts to Porter for his careful consideration in the light of the attitude of the government and the provisions of House Joint Resolution 195 authorizing American participation in the conference.[56] No specific instructions were sent, nor was Porter apprised of the recommendation in the memorandum on the possibility of the American delegation abandoning its insistence on a fixed time limit for the ending of the traffic in prepared opium. The Department preferred to leave matters to Porter's discretion.

During the period of adjournment, the British, French, and Dutch governments appointed new men to head their delegations. The British first chose Lord Salisbury to succeed Sir Malcolm Delevingne as head of the British delegation, but after failing to recover from a riding accident in sufficient time for the resumption of the Second Conference, Salisbury was succeeded in turn by Viscount Cecil. Because of the accident, the reconvening of the conference was postponed from January 12 to January 19. The French appointed Edouard Daladier, Minister of Colonies, to head their delegation. The Dutch appointed

54. Brent to the Secretary of State, *ibid.*
55. Memorandum by F. P. Lockhart to the Secretary of State, Jan. 14, 1925, SDR 511.4A2/251.
56. Secretary of State Hughes to the American Consul (Geneva) (for Porter), Jan. 15, 1925, SDR 511.4A2/251.

as their chief delegate Jonkheer Loudon, who was formerly Dutch minister to the United States and who later became the head of the Dutch foreign office. The appointment of these men was obviously designed to give greater prestige to their respective delegations. At the same time, it gave a heavier political cast to the deliberations and constituted as well the recognition of the political importance of the conference and the possibly harmful repercussions, especially to the League of Nations, if the conference should fail.

When the Second Conference reconvened on January 29, the discussion of its competence to consider the question of prepared opium continued. It soon became clear that there was no change in the basic positions of the principal contending nations. The plenary sessions from January 19 to January 22 were dominated by the chiefs of the American and British delegations, who defended the positions of their respective countries with angry words and mutual recriminations. Viscount Cecil's statement that the per capita consumption of opium in the United States was greater than that in India was characterized by Porter as "a vile slander upon the American people."[57] Although Cecil later withdrew the allegation, Porter's subsequent remarks strongly implied that Great Britain, motivated primarily by financial consideration, had disregarded her obligations under the Hague Convention and was seeking further to evade them. Cecil replied angrily to the charge as wounding to the national feeling, honor, and reputation of his country and ample justification for the withdrawal of his delegation from the conference.[58]

Out of the heat of these three days of discussion there emerged the virtual certainty that the positions of the American and British delegations were irreconcilable. The British were adamantly opposed to being placed under the obligation of reducing the production and consumption of prepared opium and the traffic in that commodity so long as China remained a huge producer and a major source of the illicit traffic. They were not prepared to repeat the sacrifice they had made in the prewar period for the benefit of China. They therefore insisted that the question of prepared opium was not within the competence of the conference. They based their argument on the fact that the Fourth Assembly of the League had in two separate resolutions called for two

57. *Records of Second Geneva Opium Conference*, I, 148, for Cecil's statement; p. 162 for Porter's charge.
58. *Ibid.*, 178–181.

separate conferences. Resolution 5 had called for a conference of those powers with Far Eastern territories in which prepared opium was used, while Resolution 6 had called for a second conference to follow to deal with the manufacture, production for export, and the international traffic in the various narcotic products. They therefore concluded that since the issue of prepared opium was being considered by the First Conference as authorized by Assembly Resolution 5, it had no place in the deliberation of the Second Conference, whose agenda had been defined by Resolution 6.[59] The French, Dutch, Portuguese, and Indian delegations fully supported the British view.

Porter was just as unyielding as the British. Obviously the not too subtle hints sent him by the State Department in the form of excerpts from the letters of Brent and Sir Austen Chamberlain and from the Department's instructions to Blue in 1922 failed to impress him. By rather tortuous reasoning the American delegation contended that the conference did have competence to consider the question of prepared opium. They maintained that in accordance with Resolution 6, in order to provide for the reduction of the production of raw opium to world medicinal and scientific requirements through the establishment of machinery for the determination of these needs, the amount of raw opium needed for the manufacture of prepared opium and the time when the use of such opium would be ended had to be ascertained. In support of this contention they referred back to the fact that in the Fifth Committee of the Assembly the American representatives had favored one conference to cover all phases of the drug problem. They tacitly admitted, however, that on technical grounds the British had the better case. They therefore urged that technicalities be put aside in view of the fact that the subject of prepared opium was covered by the Hague Convention and could not be separated from the general problem.[60]

While not yielding their basic positions, the two sides did make an attempt at compromise. The maximum British concessions were their proposals for a commission of inquiry to the Far East and an agreement to suppress the traffic in prepared opium and the use of the product within a fifteen-year period beginning *after* China had suppressed the illicit production of and traffic in opium within her borders.[61] On the other hand, the Americans expressed their willingness to extend

59. *Ibid.*, 146–154.
60. *Ibid.*, 163–168.   61. *Ibid.*, 153.

the period during which the traffic in prepared opium should be suppressed to fifteen years beginning immediately.[62] Thus the crucial issue was when the fifteen-year period should begin.

After several days of deadlocked discussion the conference adopted a resolution offered by the Finnish delegation which provided that the American proposal and all other suggestions and declarations in regard to it be referred to a mixed commission of sixteen to be composed of representatives of the eight nations constituting the First Conference and of eight nations participating in the Second Conference. This committee was then to submit a report to both conferences. The British, French, Dutch, Indian, and Portuguese delegations accepted the resolution, with the observation that they still maintained their position on the question of competence and reserved the right to bring it up later.[63]

The Committee of Sixteen held four meetings. At the third meeting a subcommittee of five consisting of representatives of Great Britain, France, Finland, Japan, and the United States was appointed in an effort to reconcile the two conflicting plans embodied in the British and American compromise proposals. In a tentative protocol to the prospective agreement of the Second Conference the British had proposed a five-year period in which producing nations would suppress smuggling, a fact to be determined by a League commission. Thereafter, presumably, the Far Eastern powers would take steps to abolish the use of smoking opium within a period of fifteen years. Porter's maximum concessions were to grant to any contracting party the right to appeal to the Council if internal and external difficulties prevented it from carrying out its obligations, to extend to three years the period of grace which would precede the fifteen-year period, and to allow provision to be made for addicts who, as certified by competent medical authorities of the states concerned, could not be deprived of the drug without a serious danger to health and life.[64] The crux of the argument of the British, French, Dutch, and Portuguese was that Articles 1 and 3 of the Hague Convention calling for the control and

62. *Ibid.*, 167. For a summary of the respective positions of the Americans and British, see Report of the American Delegation to the Geneva Opium Conference, pp. 11–13, 19–20.

63. Report of the American Delegation to the Geneva Opium Conference, p. 12.

64. League of Nations, *Records of the Second Opium Conference ... Vol. II: Meetings of the Committees and Sub-Committees*, C. 760. M. 260. 1924. XI (Geneva, 1924), pp. 53–54, 59.

regulation of raw opium production and distribution had to be carried out before Article 6, calling for the gradual suppression of prepared opium, could be carried out. The United States contended that these obligations were independent of each other. No agreement could be reached in the subcommittee, and this fact was reported to the Committee of Sixteen at its fourth meeting on February 6.[65] The United States was not present at this meeting; it had already withdrawn from the conference.

The question of the suppression of prepared opium was the most controversial of the conference, but the proceedings were by no means confined to it. Most of the heated discussion took place in the plenary sessions, but the bulk of the work was done in the various subcommittees. Subcommittee A considered the problem of the limitation of manufacture, the importation of manufactured drugs, and the importation of raw materials for manufacture. All of the manufacturing countries were represented on this subcommittee. Its discussions were confined to various suggestions for a central board to which estimates of requirements and statistics of production, consumption, importation, and exportation were to be submitted. On this matter the suggestions of the United States and the Advisory Committee were nearly identical. Both called for the submission of advance estimates by states of their annual requirements of raw material and manufactured drugs to be imported annually, such estimates to be binding on the respective governments. The central board would have the power to revise any estimates of a government which it considered to be greatly in excess of requirements and to recommend the cessation of exports to a country in excess of that country's needs.

Objections to these ideas were forthcoming from the French, Swiss, and Dutch delegations, who wanted the powers of the board confined to that of an information bureau. The French held that it would be impossible to submit estimates in advance that would be binding in view of the fluctuations in the annual opium crop and the speculative character of the drug trade, which made it impossible for a country manufacturing for export to determine in advance its requirements for export purposes. They also contended that limitation of imports to a country would necessitate rationing so that particular dealers could not corner the market. The proposal of these governments was

65. For the work of the Committee of Sixteen see *ibid.*, pp. 47–79.

that the central board should examine the statistics of the trade at the end of each year for the preceding year and call attention to cases of what seemed to be excessive imports indicating that a country might be a center for an illicit traffic. The resulting compromise provided for a central board whose main function was reduced to watching the international traffic, that is, noting the source and destination of drug products, and to requesting explanations for the accumulation of excessive quantities of drugs and recommending the suspension of exports to the accumulating country if no satisfactory explanation was received. To aid in carrying out this main function each country would submit to the board quarterly statistics of imports and exports, annual estimates at the end of each year of requirements for the ensuing year which would not be binding, and annual statistics on production, manufacture, consumption, and stocks.[66]

The American delegation naturally opposed the watering down of its suggestions and those of the Advisory Committee. One of its principal objections was to the failure to give the central board the right to comment on the quantity of prepared opium manufactured and sold in a country and the quantities purchased by governments. A more substantial objection was raised in regard to the way the central board was to be constituted. The American delegation had wanted the board to be as independent of the League as possible, with the power to make its own regulations. The subcommittee provided, however, for the appointment of the seven members of the board by the Council of the League in cooperation with Germany and the United States. The secretary and the staff of the board were to be appointed by the Secretary General subject to the approval of the Council. Furthermore, the board had to make its reports to the Council and its requests for explanations in regard to excessive accumulation of drugs had to be made through the instrumentality of the League. This connection of the board with the League organization was deemed sufficiently close, in the eyes of the American delegation, to destroy its independence.[67]

Subcommittee B dealt with the subject of the limitation of the production of raw opium. It was composed of representatives of the producing and consuming countries. The principal proposal before it was Article 1 of the American suggestion calling for the limitation of production of raw opium to medicinal and scientific needs so that

---

66. For the work of Subcommittee A see *ibid.*, p. 97–137.
67. Report of the American Delegation to the Geneva Opium Conference, pp. 13–15.

there would be no surplus for illegitimate use. This constituted the second most difficult proposal before the conference. After two months of discussion, only two producing nations—China and Egypt—were prepared to accept the American suggestion unconditionally. This was small comfort, for China could not carry out the obligations and Egypt produced no opium for export. The principal producing nations frankly stated that they could not accept the American suggestion. The Persian delegate cited economic reasons for his country's inability to limit production. He declared that in order for Persia to agree to such limitation she would first have to obtain a 10,000,000 tomans loan for twenty years with no interest charges for the first five years and only 5 percent thereafter, a moratorium on foreign claims against Persia, and a revision of treaties with her so as to give her liberty of action in regard to tariffs. Turkey likewise cited the need for financial assistance for the substitution of other crops for the poppy in order to reduce opium production. Yugoslavia declared that further reduction on her part would cause "serious economic disorders"; while India declared that Article 1 constituted "an unwarranted interference with the internal affairs of the country." The Indian delegation offered a proposal embodying substantially the provisions of Articles 1 and 3 of the Hague Convention. This was dropped, however, when the Persian and Turkish delegates said they would have to make reservations to it. The American delegation opposed it on the grounds that "it marked no advance over the Hague Convention, and did not require the limitation of production to medicinal and scientific purposes."

The only concrete achievement of Subcommittee B was the unanimous adoption of a proposal submitted by Mrs. Wright calling for the appointment of a commission of inquiry to visit certain producing countries in order to study the nature of their problems in regard to opium production, use, and traffic with reference to the feasibility of promoting other economic activities as a substitute.[68] The subcommittee did accept the Australian proposal that countries not currently producing should be prohibited from producing in the future; but as this same proposal, when considered in Subcommittee D, consisting solely of consuming countries, brought forth the condition that the present producers reduce their production, a condition the producing

68. For the work of Subcommittee B see *Records of the Second Geneva Opium Conference*, II, 153–194.

countries could not accept, nothing came of it. The principal concern in Subcommittee D was the desire to bring about the limitation of the production of raw materials and the manufacture of their derivatives in such a way as to avoid placing the consuming countries in a position of complete dependence on the manufacturing countries.[69]

Subcommittee C had before it the question of limiting coca leaf production. As Peru was not represented at the conference, the only interested countries were Bolivia and the Netherlands. Taking a cue from Subcommittee B, they concluded that because of conditions in South America the restriction of the production of coca leaves to medicinal and scientific purposes would be impossible, a conclusion the substance of which the Bolivian government had informed the United States prior to the Conference.[70]

Subcommittee E was concerned with the national and international distribution of narcotic drug products. It therefore had before it the rather detailed suggestions of the United States which were based on America's own narcotic legislation, and the similarly detailed proposals of the Advisory Committee. There was little opposition to these suggestions, and the subcommittee adopted substantially what was recommended. The conference was therefore urged by the subcommittee to incorporate in the convention provisions putting into effect the import-export certificate system and calling for national legislation which would have the effect of preventing the illicit transportation of unlicensed drugs and providing punishment for illicit transactions carried on by individuals in one country while residing in another.[71] The work of this subcommittee was more satisfactory to the American delegation than that of all the other subcommittees.

Subcommittee F dealt with the scientific and medicinal aspects of the drug question. While recommending a number of measures which represented an advance over the Hague Convention, including the restriction of the use of Indian hemp to medicinal and scientific purposes, it failed to accept two proposals which the American delegation considered important. One was the suggestion that all opium and coca leaf derivatives be subject to the same control as morphine and cocaine and that the manufacture of heroin be prohibited. The other was that the morphine and cocaine content of preparations dispensed without

69. *Ibid.*, pp. 233–248.
70. *Ibid.*, pp. 225–232.   71. *Ibid.*, pp. 249–280.

medical prescription be reduced to one-fourth grain to the ounce. The American delegation filed a minority report on the latter suggestion taking exception to the failure of the subcommittee to endorse it.[72]

To the American delegation, Porter particularly, the results of the work in the subcommittees and in the plenary sessions of the conference were quite unsatisfactory in four major respects. First and foremost was the refusal of the producing nations to agree to limit the production of raw materials and their export to medicinal and scientific needs—the cardinal point of the American program. Equally disappointing was the unwillingness of the nations with Far Eastern possessions to begin to take measures to bring about the abolition of the traffic in prepared opium by limiting the importation of raw opium for the manufacture of smoking opium—another chief point in the American program, and one which the American delegation believed would help force a reduction in the production of raw opium by limiting the market. The failure of the First Conference to formulate effective measures in this regard was disheartening, and the refusal of the Second Conference to remedy the situation was even more regrettable. Less disappointing was the character of the organization and functions of the central board, whose close connection with the League made it, in the eyes of the American delegation, susceptible to political influences, especially to the influence of members of the League whom the Americans suspected of being opposed, because of financial considerations, to any effective steps to deal with the drug problem. It was also felt that the imagined subservience of the central board to the League Council would defeat ratification of the Convention by the Senate, or at least provoke a bitter fight in that body. Finally, there was dissatisfaction with the lack of provisions for the control of the alkaloids and derivatives of opium and the coca leaves other than morphine and cocaine. Aside from the fact that some of these commodities were considered dangerous by the United States, another factor for consideration was the difficulty the uncontrolled market in these products would cause in efforts made to arrive at an accurate determination of the overall world medical and scientific requirements of raw opium and coca leaves.

The only provisions with which the American delegation expressed

72. *Ibid.*, pp. 281–332. For the work of the various subcommittees and the attitude of the American delegation toward the results, see Report of the American Delegation to the Second Geneva Opium Conference, pp. 13–24.

unconditional satisfaction were those relating to the giving of statistical information to the central board and the import/export certificate system and other measures for the control of transportation. These were regarded as representing a distinct advance over the provisions in the Hague Convention, but not sufficient to overcome the other weaknesses in the proposed convention to the extent of warranting American approval.[73]

The above dissatisfaction with the work of the Second Conference, and the unlikelihood that the deficiencies would be corrected, convinced Porter, even before the Committee of Sixteen had completed its deliberations, that further participation of the United States in the conference was useless. Therefore, on February 1 Porter cabled the State Department for permission to withdraw the American delegation from the conference, citing the above factors and "the political aspect of the proposed agreement, the small gain to be hoped for over the control of the traffic and the terms of the resolution of Congress under which the delegation proceeded to Geneva," as reasons for the request. He contended that the United States might promote greater progress in the control of the narcotics traffic by remaining aloof from the League and retaining its liberty of action—asserting its rights and demanding performance of the obligations of the parties to the Hague Convention.[74] The State Department sent a reply the next day giving him authority to withdraw at his discretion, but with the admonition that in order to avoid damaging the relations of the United States with the other nations or causing irritation, the statement of withdrawal giving the reason for the action should be so drafted as not to cause offense.[75] Porter then waited to ascertain the results of the work of the subcommittee of five (of which he was a member) of the Committee of Sixteen on the problem of prepared opium. When, after three days of discussion, the subcommittee reported back to the parent committee on February 6 that it could reach no agreement, it was met with the announcement that the American delegation had withdrawn from the conference.[76]

On February 7 the announcement of the American withdrawal was made to the plenary session of the conference by the president of the

73. Consul Tuck (from Porter) to the Secretary of State, Feb. 1, 1925, SDR 511.4A2/263.
74. *Ibid.*
75. Secretary of State Hughes to Tuck (for Porter), Feb. 2, 1925, SDR 511.4A2/263.
76. *Records of the Second Geneva Opium Conference*, II, 69.

conference, Herluf Zahle of Denmark. He likewise announced the withdrawal of the Chinese delegation on the grounds of the failure of the conference to arrive at a satisfactory agreement on measures for the suppression of prepared opium.[77] In the letter of withdrawal, dated February 6, and the accompanying memorandum the American delegation gave as its principal reasons for the action the failure of the conference to provide for the restriction of the production of raw opium and coca leaves to medicinal and scientific needs of the world, due to the refusal of the producing countries to agree to such limitation, and the reluctance of nations in whose territories the use of smoking opium was temporarily permitted to take steps to suppress such use and thereby limit the market for raw opium. Thus, under the terms of House Joint Resolution 195 the American delegation had no alternative but to withdraw, since it could not sign the agreement proposed.[78]

Despite signs of the impending breakup of the conference as early as January 21, the withdrawal of the American delegation nevertheless came as a shock. President Zahle, speaking with emotion, declared it to be the greatest tragedy and disappointment of his life, while Lord Cecil, on hearing the news, buried his head in his hands.[79] Many feared that more was at stake than the antidrug movement. There was much apprehension among the members and proponents of the League that the failure of America's first official and formal participation in League activities might fatally jeopardize further cooperation in other and more important areas by furthering anti-League sentiment in the United States.[80]

Reaction within the conference was varied. The delegations which had opposed the American proposal were unanimous in their condemnation of the withdrawal. In a somewhat bitter speech, Jonkheer Loudon, former Dutch minister to the United States, traced the source of the misunderstandings to the failure of the American delegation to take into account the reservations of India in regard to raw opium production and those of other powers relative to prepared opium which were made two years previous at the Fifth Session of the Opium Advisory Committee and which, he contended, clearly showed that the American principles in regard to Chapters I and II of the Hague Convention were not accepted. He blamed the rigid instructions under

77. *Ibid.*, I, 201–204.
78. *Ibid.*, pp. 201–202.

79. *New York Times,* Feb. 7, 1925, p. 1.
80. *Ibid.*, p. 3.

which the American delegation operated as precluding the necessary give and take, goodwill, and cooperative atmosphere within which a successful conference must be conducted.[81] Lord Cecil likewise refuted the American charges on the purpose of the conference and the reason for the difficulties experienced. He asserted that the chief object of the conference was to find ways to arrest the traffic in dangerous drugs and that this goal had been largely attained. He reiterated the British position that the most effective way to control the drug traffic was by the control of manufacture, not control of the production of raw materials.[82] Monsieur Daladier of the French delegation criticized the refusal of the American delegation to give due consideration to the illicit traffic in opium from which consuming countries bordering on producing countries suffered and which, in his view, rendered "futile" and even "dangerous" any measures for the suppression of consumption. He chided the American delegation for trying to obtain its objectives all at once and contended that more progress could be made step by step.[83]

Despite the general condemnation of the American withdrawal, Zahle, in his closing speech to the Second Conference some two weeks later, credited the "boldness," "directness" and "devotion" of the American delegation with giving the "supreme impetus to the whole antidrug campaign," but he characterized their withdrawal as "the most serious and most unfortunate incident of the Conference." He believed that had they remained to the end, a better convention would have been formulated.[84]

The one nation other than China which consistently backed the proposals of the American delegation throughout the conference was Japan. In wooing their support, the Americans took special pains to be friendly to their delegation socially,[85] and Porter, in the interest of Japanese-American friendship, even went so far as to cable the ranking member of the House Foreign Affairs Committee urging that committee to condemn a bill calling for a conference of white nations bordering on the Pacific which the Japanese feared was directed against

81. *Records of the Second Geneva Opium Conference,* I, 204–205.
82. *Ibid.,* pp. 205–206.
83. *Ibid.,* pp. 206–207.   84. *Ibid.,* p. 362.
85. Helen Howell Moorhead, "The Opium Problem and the League of Nations; An Address . . . Before the Democratic Women's Luncheon Club, Philadelphia, April 27, 1925," *Democratic Women's Luncheon Club of Philadelphia Addresses 1–48,* No. 22 (1922–1930), p. 14.

them. The chief Japanese delegate, Sugimura, thanked Porter for this action and pledged Japanese support, with minor reservations, for the American position.[86] After the American delegation withdrew from the conference, the Japanese praised them for their stand and expressed the hope for continued friendly relations between their two countries.[87] Thus, by the slender reed of cooperation in the antiopium campaign the two delegations hoped to contribute to the reestablishment of the accord between the two nations that had been somewhat damaged by the barring of Japanese immigration to the United States in 1924.

The departure of the American delegation from the conference and the events leading up to it were, of course, the most publicized aspects of the Geneva conferences. Press opinion in Europe and Asia generally followed the policy lines of their respective governments. Most of the prominent English newspapers, even before the American exit, criticized the uncompromising attitude of the American representatives. They defended the practice of opium eating in India and dwelt upon the "alarming growth of the drug habit" in the United States. Many attributed that growth to liquor prohibition and pointed to the ineffectiveness of that experiment as indicative of the probable ineffectiveness of a prohibitory system in the Far East for opium, whose use, they maintained, was as much a part of the habits of the people as the consumption of alcohol in the United States. They defended their government's view that the solution of the problem in China must precede efforts to abolish the use of prepared opium. They argued that America's opposition to the growth of the poppy in India was predicated upon the false assumption that Indian opium was the source of the American drug problem.[88] This was, of course, a misrepresentation of the American position, as the emphasis of the United States upon the situation in the Far East was not based at this time on the concern for her domestic problem, but stemmed from an altruistic concern for the Far Eastern peoples and the belief that control of opium production in India was part of the necessary pattern of universal control. The British-owned papers in the Far East followed the same line as the home papers in criticizing the American position.[89]

86. *New York Times,* Jan. 19, 1925, p. 1.   87. *Ibid.,* Feb. 9, 1925, p. 5.

88. See excerpts from the London *Times,* Jan. 20, 1925; Manchester *Guardian,* Jan. 19 and 21, 1925; London *Daily Mail,* Jan. 22, 1925; and *Westminster Gazette,* Jan. 21, 1925, enclosed in American Embassy (London) to Assistant Secretary of State John V. A. MacMurray, Jan. 27, 1925, SDR 511.4A2/319.

89. See for example the Madras *Mail,* Jan. 31, 1925, in Alfred R. Thompson, American Consul (Madras) to the Secretary of State, Feb. 7, 1925, NA 511.4A2/297; the

Native and American-owned papers in the Far East generally supported the American stand, however.[90] Some press opinion, notably the Dutch and the Swiss, while castigating the actions of the American representatives as doctrinaire and unrealistic, nevertheless saw in their withdrawal facilitation of the arrival of the conference at a realistic agreement.[91]

In the United States and among Americans the reaction to the American withdrawal was most varied. The anti-League Hearst press naturally applauded the action.[92] The pro-League *New York Times*, which had hoped for the success of the conference so that a precedent might be set for closer American cooperation with the League on other problems, took a somewhat equivocal position. While acknowledging that the "dramatic performance" of Porter and the American delegation had made the American position clear and emphatic in regard to the opium traffic and had given impetus to the antinarcotics campaign, the *Times* regretfully pointed out that if the central board was set up, "it will be another international institution of American conception and suggestion but without immediate American cooperation, to add to the list that begins with the League of Nations and the World Court."[93] The paper later expressed great misgivings at the position taken by Porter at Geneva in regard to limitation of cultivation and at his undue concern with the Far Eastern problem, and urged close cooperation between the United States and the League on the opium question.[94]

Many prominent Americans were quite critical of the action of the American delegation. John Palmer Gavit, a newspaper correspondent,

Peking and Tientsin *Times*, Feb. 9, 1925, in Consul General C. E. Gauss (Tientsin) to the Secretary of State, Feb. 9, 1925, SDR 511.4Q2/297; the *North China Daily Herald*, Feb. 10, 1925, in Consul General Edwin S. Cunningham (Shanghai) to the Secretary of State, Feb. 21, 1925, and the *Far Eastern Times* in Minister Jacob G. Schurman (Peking) to the Secretary of State, Feb. 11, 1925, SDR 511.4A2/308; and *The Englishman*, Feb. 9, 1925, in Consul General Julius Lay (Calcutta) to the Secretary of State, Feb. 12, 1925, SDR 511.4A2/296.

90. Such papers as the *Far Eastern Times*, Feb. 10, 1925; the *China Press*, Feb. 10, 1925; and *The Hindu* castigated the British and praised the American stand. See excerpts from these papers enclosed in Schurman to the Secretary of State, Feb. 11, 1925; Cunningham to the Secretary of State, Feb. 21, 1925, SDR 511.4A2/308; and Thomas to the Secretary of State, Feb. 17, 1925, SDR 511.4A2/297, respectively.

91. See excerpts from the *Journal de Genève*, Feb. 8, 1925, in Alan Winslow, American Chargé d'Affaires ad interim (Berne), to the Secretary of State, Nov. 25, 1925, SDR 511.4A2/291; the *Handelsblad*, Feb. 7, 1925, in American Legation (The Hague) to the Secretary of State, Feb. 27, 1925, SDR 511.4A2/304.

92. New York *American*, Feb. 16, 1925, p. 24.

93. *New York Times*, Jan. 29, 1925, p. 18. For the quotation, Feb. 8, Sec. II, p. 6.

94. *Ibid.*, Sept. 25, 1925, p. 20.

summed up the views of most Americans critical of the American withdrawal. He pointed out that international negotiations require compromise and concessions and therefore delegations should not be shackled by congressional resolutions and acts of Congress. Even so, he contended, the American delegation should have remained to the end of the conference and lent their support to the strengthening of those provisions of the Convention relating to the control of manufacture and the international traffic. They still would have been free to refuse to sign the Convention at the end of the conference.[95] In the same vein, Professor Quincy Wright, an authority on international law, pointed out that in international negotiations where important interests are not involved, and common ends are sought, the spirit of the procedure is one of cooperation rather than competition, and national desires are subordinated, if that is necessary, to advance the general object. Citing the instructions of Secretary of State Root to the American delegation to the Second Hague Peace Conference in 1907 as an example, Wright pointed out that where a nation's direct interests in the proceedings of a conference are not involved, vis-à-vis the interests of other participants, the emphasis should be on coming to an agreement on what can be presently achieved with a view to further progress toward the common goal through later discussions. By withdrawing from the Second Geneva Conference when they could not get all that they wanted, he contended, the American delegation acted contrary to the procedure of cooperation. Professor Wright placed the major responsibility for this action on the joint resolution of Congress authorizing the participation of the United States in the conference. He expressed the opinion that such congressional resolutions attempting to direct international negotiations were of both doubtful constitutionality and doubtful expediency.[96]

There is some evidence that the American representatives were not unanimous in the decision to withdraw from the conference, but were forced to follow the lead of their chairman. Mrs. Hamilton Wright said later that she was opposed to the American withdrawal, but whether she indicated this emphatically to Porter before the event is unknown. Bishop Brent was likewise opposed to the American withdrawal, but he was not in Geneva at the time, not having returned after the Christmas adjournment. He was not aware of the action until it was pub-

95. *Ibid.*, Feb. 19, 1925, p. 18; see also John Palmer Gavit, *Opium* (London: G. Routledge and Sons, Ltd., 1925), pp. 225–228.
96. Quincy Wright, "The Opium Conferences," *AJIL*, XIX (July, 1925), 348–355.

licized in the press.[97] It is doubtful whether his presence in Geneva would have altered the situation, since he had earlier failed to persuade Porter to modify some of his demands.

There is no definite evidence as to opinion in Congress of the developments at Geneva. There appears to have been only one occasion when the proceedings of the conference aroused comment in Congress. This was educed by the bitter arguments that raged in Geneva between the American and British delegates from January 19 to January 22. Representative Blanton of Texas again raised the issue of the propriety of the presence of the American delegation at a League-sponsored conference. He charged that the American representatives were merely on a junketing trip without value to the nation, against the wishes of the European powers, and without the authorization of Congress; that the position of the United States was embarrassing in that while it refused to join the League to stop war, it sent an unauthorized representative without power to Europe to "sit with a bunch of bullyraggers in a conference over narcotics"; that Porter was being insulted, the American delegation and their plan were being sneered at, and Porter was simply causing friction and ill feeling with foreign governments. Blanton contended that the United States should confine its efforts to its domestic opium problem, especially since ill feeling resulting from interference in European affairs might eventually cause war, which Porter and the Republicans refused to join the League to prevent.[98] Blanton appeared to be alone in his views, however, as no other Congressman spoke in endorsement of them. Several Congressmen, however, took exception to them. Representatives William D. Upshaw of Georgia, Theodore Burton of Ohio, Fiorella La Guardia of New York, and Otis Wingo of Arkansas all backed the Porter mission, pointing out that it was properly authorized by House Joint Resolution 195 and that Porter's efforts were endorsed and supported not only by Congress but by the American people.[99] Except for this irresponsible and partisan outburst from Representative Blanton, there was no expression of disapproval of the American activities in Geneva from either House of Congress, neither before nor after the delegation left Geneva.

Aside from the Hearst press there were some other defenders of the

97. *New York Times*, Feb. 7, 1925, p. 3.
98. *Congressional Record*, 68th Cong., 2nd Sess., 1924, LXVI, Part 3, 2295–2299, 2316–2318.
99. *Ibid.* Upshaw and Wingo were Democrats; Burton and La Guardia, Republicans.

departure of the American delegation from Geneva. Among them was
Miss Ellen N. La Motte, the author of several books and articles on
the opium question. She ridiculed the argument that effective cooperation on the part of the representatives of the United States was precluded by the rigid character of their instructions by contending that
other nations were bound by equally inflexible instructions. She
charged that the British, Dutch, Portuguese, and Swiss representatives
had secret instructions to protect the opium trade at all hazards.[100]
Another defender of the American action was W. W. Willoughby, a
prominent international lawyer, who served with the Chinese delegation at the conference.[101] His viewpoint may well have been colored
by that service. Yet the general consensus among Americans who were
not professionally hostile to the League was that the American delegates should have remained to the end, even if they could not have
signed the resultant convention.

The withdrawal of the American delegation was greeted by some
participants in the conference with dismay, by others with relief. The
conferees continued their work, but with considerably lessened interest. The First Conference brought its work to a close on February
11, having added to the earlier agreement a protocol drafted by the
British and French delegations in the Committee of Sixteen. The
main points of the Protocol called for the suppression of the consumption of prepared opium within a fifteen-year period to begin after the
producing countries had established effective control over exports
and had suppressed smuggling, a fact to be determined by a commission appointed by the League. This was closely tied up with the
Protocol adopted by the Second Conference calling for the suppression of the illicit traffic in raw materials within five years. As China
had withdrawn, the only nation to protest this arrangement was Japan,
who repeated the American objection to making the obligation to take
measures to abolish the use of prepared opium dependent on measures
taken by producing countries to control export.[102] Nevertheless Japan,
along with the other participants in the First Conference, signed the
Agreement, Protocol, and Final Act of the Conference.

100. Ellen La Motte, "The Americans Wouldn't Compromise!" *The Nation*, CXX
(May 6, 1925), 511–512.
101. Westel W. Willoughby, *Opium as an International Problem: The Geneva
Conferences* (Baltimore: The Johns Hopkins Press, 1925), pp. 452–464.
102. *Minutes of the First Geneva Opium Conference*, pp. 117–119.

The Second Conference met for approximately two weeks after the American departure. Its deliberations thus covered a period of seventy days, the longest a League conference had convened up to that time. While some nations would have been happy to adopt an agreement of ineffective platitudes now that the American delegation was no longer present to prod them, others, notably Great Britain, sought concrete achievements. The result was a convention which in most aspects was a considerable improvement over the Hague Convention, whose Chapters I, II, and V it supplanted. Through its thirty-nine articles, coca leaves, crude cocaine, Indian hemp, and ecogonine, substances not covered by the Hague Convention, were brought under control, and provisions were made for the inclusion of new drugs in the controls on the advice of the Health Committee of the League and the International Health Office; an intricate system of import and export certificates to control the international traffic and designed to curb the illicit trade in both raw materials and manufactured drugs was established; a Permanent Central Board was set up to receive and disseminate information on drug production, consumption, requirements, trade, and legislation, and also to watch the international traffic; the control of drugs in and transit through free ports, free zones, and bonded warehouses was provided for; and measures to remove national boundaries as a barrier to the prosecution of narcotic law violations were called for. The Convention was to come into force after it had been ratified by ten signatories, seven of which had to be states which were designated to nominate members of the Central Board and two of which had to be permanent members of the Council. The principles which underlay the Convention and which were stated in the preamble—"the limitation of the amounts of morphine, heroin, or cocaine and their respective salts to be manufactured; . . . of the amounts of raw opium and coca leaf to be imported for that purpose and for other medicinal and scientific purposes; and . . . of the production of opium and the coca leaf for export to the amount required for such medicinal and scientific purposes . . ."—though only partly effected in the provisions of the Convention, nevertheless made more definite and extensive the principles of the Hague Convention.[103]

103. For the text of the Convention see *Records of the Second Geneva Opium Conference*, II, 502–519.

Chapter eight

Sequel to Geneva: American isolation
from the antidrug campaign

The United States did not sign the Convention and Protocol of the Second Geneva Conference but was invited to adhere to them. Its refusal to do so was based more on political and face-saving considerations than on dissatisfaction with the Convention, for the United States was eventually forced to admit that the treaty was a forward step in the drug control movement. However, American withdrawal from the Geneva Conference precluded early acceptance of the Convention. Such acceptance would have constituted a dramatic reversal of the American position and a repudiation of the American delegation, especially Porter. As long as Porter was opposed to American adherence to the Convention, the State Department did not dare to take action. The initial rejection of the League invitation to become a party to the Geneva Opium Convention was not so emphatic, however, as to debar future consideration of the step.[1] Bishop Brent confidently expected that the United States would accept the Convention and had so informed responsible people in Europe and England.[2] Mrs. Wright, however, was definitely opposed to this step and even urged the government to take steps to prevent its ratification by other powers.[3] Porter, on the other hand, while unalterably opposed to American acceptance of the Convention as it stood, nevertheless did not object to its ratification by other governments, holding that this would facilitate the divorcement of the United States from it.[4]

For a brief period the State Department toyed with Mrs. Wright's suggestion of actively opposing the ratification of the Convention by

1. Secretary of State Frank Kellogg to Porter, Jan. 25, 1926, SDR 511.4A2/445a.
2. Memorandum by Nelson T. Johnson of conversation with Mrs. Wright, July 7, 1926, SDR 500.C1197/18.
3. *Ibid.*; see also memorandum by Johnson to the Secretary of State, Dec. 16, 1927, SDR 511.4A2/557.
4. Mrs. Wright to Johnson, Jan. 25, 1928, SDR 511.4A2/563; memorandum by Johnson, Jan. 27, 1928, SDR 511.4A2/564.

other powers. On the occasion of the meeting of the Sixth International Conference of American States in January and February, 1928, the State Department, at the instigation of Mrs. Wright, instructed the American delegation to that conference to make known the American position on the Geneva Opium Convention if the question of opium was brought up, and to urge the Latin American states to cooperate with the United States in carrying out the Hague Opium Convention.[5] Calling on other states to cooperate with the United States in carrying out the obligations of the Hague Convention was the principal means by which this government sought to undermine the Geneva Convention and to block its going into force. This approach was not confined to Latin American countries but extended to European powers as well.

As it became clear that these efforts were not producing the desired results, the State Department began to reconsider its position. In a lengthy confidential memorandum drawn up in the Division of Far Eastern Affairs and dated March 3, 1928, the Hague Convention was compared with the Geneva Opium Convention and the superiority of the latter was clearly admitted in virtually all respects. "The only respects in which the Geneva document is definitely inferior to the Hague Convention," declared the memorandum, "are its connection with the League of Nations and the substitution of a *recommendation* for an *obligation* to apply the restrictions of the convention to dangerous new drugs."[6] In regard to the American program at Geneva for the limitation of raw material production to medicinal needs, the memorandum did point out that the Geneva Convention fell far short. However, the statement which followed showed clearly the metamorphosis in the Department's thinking, when it was declared that because of the situation in the producing countries it would probably be impossible in the foreseeable future to realize the American principle. Therefore, the United States should direct its attention to securing a more attainable object—the limitation of manufacture—toward which the Geneva Convention had made a promising advance and which would largely solve America's and the world's most serious problem, smuggling. That the Geneva Convention likewise failed to incorporate the American goals of bringing under the same control as morphine

5. Secretary of State Kellogg to Charles Evans Hughes, Chairman of American Delegation to the Sixth International Conference of American States, Feb. 4, 1928, SDR 511.4A2/563.

6. Confidential memorandum of Division of Far Eastern Affairs, "The Geneva Opium Convention," March 3, 1928, SDR 511.4A2/570.

and cocaine all the other derivatives and preparations of opium and the coca leaf and of taking measures for the suppression of opium smoking was also pointed out. It was admitted, however, that "the Hague Convention likewise fails to do each and every one of these things. It is repeated that no principle is weakened by the Geneva Convention and administrative and restrictive measures are made more effective."[7]

The memorandum simply constituted the official recognition of what had been quite evident ever since the Second Geneva Conference had finished its labors: that the Convention was a significant though not a giant step forward. Recognized here too was the fact that the United States, when comparing the Convention with what had existed before, could have no valid objection to it. The designation of its connection with the League as a defect was, of course, a most debatable assumption. Others could claim with considerably more reason that this very connection with a body composed of almost all the nations of the world was a source of strength. It must always be kept in mind, however, that on the narcotics problem the American antipathy to the League stemmed not only from political considerations but also reflected the suspicion that the leading members of the League were not sincerely interested in the restriction of the drug traffic.

The memorandum was designed to stimulate discussion within the State Department and among other interested officials as to the feasibility of American adherence to the Convention. For the Convention to be acceptable to the United States the following conditions were laid down: (1) the extension of the provisions of the document to new drugs on the recommendation of the International Office of Public Health, (2) the settlement of disputes involving the United States as to the interpretation or application of the Convention by diplomatic negotiations between the parties concerned or by referral to the Hague Convention for the Pacific Settlement of International Disputes, (3) the divorcement of the functions of the Central Board from the League, and (4) the recognition that adherence by the United States implied no legal relation to the League or assumption of obligations under the Treaty of Versailles nor involvement in the Agreement of the First Geneva Opium Conference. If the other signatory powers accepted these reservations by an exchange of notes, it was recom-

7. *Ibid.*

mended that the United States adhere to the Convention in order to better promote the fight against the illicit traffic than it could by "heading a faction outside the group." If association with the League precluded American adherence to the Convention, it was suggested that in order to regain its leadership in the antidrug movement, the United States should call a new conference whose agenda could be confined to the limitation of manufacture, as it was not likely that producing countries would be able to accept the American proposals for the limitation of production. If it proved unfeasible to take either of these suggested steps, it was recommended that the United States nevertheless cooperate with the other nations by fulfilling all the obligations of the Geneva Convention.[8]

This straightforward and unbiased look at the Geneva Convention was not sufficient to cause the State Department to abandon its timid policy. The chief factors in the decision to take no action for the present were the unlikelihood that the signatories of the Geneva Convention would accept the American reservations in regard to the removal of the Central Board from League control; the likelihood that the American reservations, constituting as they did a fundamental revision of the Geneva Convention, might be more easily obtained through the negotiation of a new convention; the fact that American adhesion would indicate a recession from its position in 1924;[9] and most important, the division of opinion in the United States among those interested in the narcotics problem. The last point reflected the fact that there was much sentiment in the United States for American adhesion to the Convention,[10] but that the State Department dared not act without the approval of Porter. When the matter was referred to him, Porter turned thumbs down on the idea.[11] The Department realized that it could hardly prevail against his wishes, as his influence in Congress could easily block the contemplated step. Thus the idea was abandoned. After the Convention went into effect in September 1928, the United States did cooperate to the extent of submitting the desired information to the Central Board. The suggestion that the United States call a new conference was likewise tabled when it was realized that the United

8. *Ibid.*
9. Memorandum by John K. Caldwell to Johnson, March 9, 1928, SDR 511.4A2/570.
10. The Treasury Department, for instance, favored American adhesion. See memorandum by Caldwell to Johnson, March 10, 1928, SDR 511.4A2/569.
11. Memorandum by Caldwell of conversation with Porter, March 8, 1928, SDR 511.4A1/2064.

States did not have a program to offer beyond that of 1925, which most likely would suffer the same fate in a new conference as it did in 1925.[12]

In judging the American action at Geneva and in assessing the net effect upon the antinarcotics movement of that action, one is forced to conclude, in retrospect, that the United States failed to make the most of the opportunity to advance that movement. This failure stemmed from the very nature of the American approach to the problem. This approach was characterized by the desire to deal with the whole problem in all its aspects, and all at once. It was also characterized by the holier-than-thou attitude which the delegation took toward other member nations of the Second Conference. This attitude did have much to justify it. Undoubtedly many of the other nations were not responsive to the moral considerations that enveloped the American proposals. On the other hand, the Americans failed to take into full account the fact that their high morality was not complicated by other factors that other nations had to take into consideration; that in demanding the full acceptance of their program they were asking other countries to make considerable sacrifices in regard to revenue, domestic peace, independence in domestic jurisdiction, and even sovereignty, while the United States had nothing to lose and everything to gain from such action. To charge other nations with bad faith and disreputable motives, even though the charges may have been partly warranted, could not under these circumstances advance the cause for which the conference was striving. Furthermore, while castigating the powers with Far Eastern possessions for the refusal to commit themselves to definitive measures to suppress the traffic in prepared opium, the American delegation played down the role of China in the situation. The refusal to look objectively at conditions in China and at their effect upon surrounding territories was one of the weaker aspects of the American argument. Although little could be done about these conditions by China or by anyone else at the time, it was most unrealistic to refuse to face up to the problem that they presented to other Far Eastern territories. To adopt a policy based on moral considerations which would have no real effect on the existing situation in these territories would provide no solution to the problem, but might merely serve to camouflage the situation. An equal failing on the part of the

12. Memorandum by Johnson to Caldwell, March 10, 1928, SDR 511.4A2/569.

American delegation was its refusal to face the fact that the international movement which had been initiated to force other nations, principally Great Britain, to help China solve her opium problem, had in its results so far failed. It might have been better appreciated that Great Britain would be skeptical of making further sacrifices in the interest of China, sacrifices that might again prove of no value to China and might, on the other hand, intensify the traffic in Great Britain's possessions.

The American delegation was quite justified in pushing for the full acceptance of its program. But in view of the foregoing it should have been more amenable to compromise, more willing to accept what was then possible, reserving for future discussions the effectuation of the rest of its program. Few international conferences achieve what they set out to do. The Geneva Opium Conferences were no exception, nor were the Hague Opium Conferences which preceded them. The Second Conference did make significant progress, though not to the point that the United States desired. This, however, was not sufficient reason for the American delegation to withdraw from the conference. The congressional resolution did not require this step; it merely prohibited the delegation from signing any unsatisfactory agreement arrived at. The withdrawal was motivated as much by political antipathy toward the League of Nations and irritation with the refusal of the members of that organization to be dictated to in matters affecting their important interests as to dissatisfaction with the work of the conference. It is fairly safe to assume that had the chairman of the American delegation been one who was free of anti-League bias, the suggestion that the delegation withdraw would not have arisen. The American withdrawal was, in effect, an expression of no confidence in the League.

While the behavior of the American delegation at Geneva was characterized by boldness and vigor, the behavior of the United States in regard to the ratification of the resulting Convention was exactly the opposite. While forced to admit the great superiority of the Geneva Convention over the Hague Convention, the State Department was nevertheless afraid to advocate its implementation. This, of course, was the natural result of the action of the American delegation at Geneva. Instead, the government called for continued international cooperation on the basis of what it admitted was an inferior document, the Hague Convention. Thus the United States found itself occupying an illogical and somewhat embarrassing position.

The result was the lack for the first time of a clear-cut policy in dealing with the drug problem. From 1925 to 1930 the United States virtually marked time so far as significant cooperation in the international movement was concerned. It could not resume the leadership in the movement, despite urgings from various quarters, foreign and domestic, because it simply did not know what to do, what to propose, what steps to take which would differ from its Geneva Conference program, which the crucial nations had already repudiated. At the time, for fear of congressional disapprobation symbolized in the person of Stephen J. Porter, it dared not cooperate fully with the League on the basis of the Geneva Convention. The dilemma was somewhat mitigated by the fact that because of its own legislation, which though somewhat advanced over the measures called for in the Geneva Convention, was similar in intent, the United States could march in time with the other nations and demand the enactment of measures similar to its own which would at the same time carry out the provisions of the Convention. Furthermore, in purely administrative matters, the United States deigned to cooperate with the League—for instance, in submitting information to the Central Board. It is significant, however, that the United States did not regain a position of leadership in the international movement until the League itself began to take new steps in which the United States, subordinating its traditional animosity toward that body, agreed to participate.

Aside from the impetus given to the fight against the narcotics traffic through publicity for the evil and the measures adopted to cope with it, the Geneva conferences were significant in several other respects.

First was the political significance of the American participation in the Second Conference. This action constituted a complete reversal, though brief, of the initial attitude and approach of the United States toward the League of Nations. In 1919 the majority of the Senate had declared that the narcotic drug question was not to be submitted to any agency of the League for consideration. Five years later the submission of this question to a League-called conference had the specific endorsement of virtually the same Senators who had opposed such a step in 1919. The United States never did retrogress to the position taken by the Senate in 1919 nor to that of the early Harding administration in refusing to cooperate at all with the League on the drug problem.

Secondly, the conference revived the old animosity and suspicion in regard to the opium problem between Great Britain and the United States. Once again the United States came forward as the champion of Oriental peoples against what it regarded as a degrading aspect of Western influence. This was the major theme of Bishop Brent's remonstrances to the British and the other Far Eastern Powers—the demand for the same consideration for the welfare of Eastern as well as for Western people. Once again India was the main source of controversy between the two nations, this time as a major producer and consumer of opium beyond medicinal and scientific requirements. The Americans charged the British with being callous towards the welfare of Oriental peoples where revenue considerations were concerned, while the British responded with the old charge of impractical idealism against the Americans.

Thirdly, the real complexity of the narcotics problem was finally brought home to the United States, which grudgingly came to realize that its solution could not be obtained by a stroke of the pen, but that the problem would have to be attacked piecemeal. The realization of the dilemma of the producing countries made some Americans also understand eventually that the problem was not simply one of morals, but that these countries had to consider matters which vied with the moral aspect of the opium question in order of importance, which in fact stood above and apart from moral considerations in many cases. For example, for such countries as Turkey and Persia, interference with opium production might very well undermine the foundation of the government.

The Geneva conferences sought to deal with all aspects of the narcotics traffic—in the words of Professor Quincy Wright, with "smuggling, smoking and surplus production" of both raw materials and manufactured drugs. In regard to smoking and the surplus production of raw materials the results were minimal. Some progress was made in the control of manufacture, that is, in giving publicity to excess manufacture. The most progress was made toward the control of smuggling. In none of these areas, however, were the measures adopted altogether adequate. In fact, the desired goal of confining the use of narcotic drugs to medicinal and scientific purposes could not be achieved by concentration on a single aspect of the problem. Smoking, smuggling, and surplus production and manufacture had all to be brought under control before this objective could be realized. The Geneva conventions made a start; the most important work remained to be done. And in fact, thereafter no attempt was made to deal with all the aspects of the problem at once, but each was dealt with in separate discussions as part of a unified effort toward progressive solution of the overall problem.

The passivity which characterized America's international narcotics policy in the five years after the Geneva conferences was largely the result of two conflicting goals. On the one hand the United States wished to avoid entanglement with the League of Nations; on the other hand it wanted to reestablish American leadership in the international antidrug campaign. In pursuit of the first goal the United States maintained only a tenuous relationship with the Opium Advisory Committee. From August 1925 to April 1928, the United States was represented "unofficially" on the committee by Pinkney Tuck, the American consul at Geneva, except at the eighth session in 1926, when the vice-consul, Stanley Woodard, substituted for him. By the admission of the State Department, Tuck was to serve only as an "unofficial spectator," reporting on the activities and discussions of the committee and responding to questions put to him, but not taking an active part in the work.[13] By his own admission, Tuck, because of his lack of technical knowledge of the subject of narcotics, was quite unqualified to serve on the committee. He repeatedly urged the State Department to appoint someone more qualified who could effectively represent the United States on the committee, as other countries still looked to the United States for leadership.[14] The Department demurred, however, taking the position that the restoration of good relations between the Advisory Committee and the United States depended on the willingness of the committee to back the American efforts to restrict to medicinal and scientific needs the production and manufacture of raw and refined drug products.[15]

This attitude of the American government, expressed in the dispatch of an unqualified unofficial observer, finally aroused the ire of the League Secretariat. The announcement by the United States in February 1928 that Tuck would again represent this country as unofficial

13. Nelson T. Johnson, Chief, Division of Far Eastern Affairs, to Tuck, March 3, 1926, SDR 511.4A2/477.
14. Tuck to the Secretary of State, Sept. 5, 1925, SDR 511.4A2/390; Tuck to Johnson, Nov. 25, 1925, SDR 511.4A2/477.
15. Johnson to Tuck, March 3, 1926, SDR 511.4A2/477.

observer drew forth pronounced expressions of dissatisfaction from League officials at America's uncooperative attitude and indifferent behavior. They pointed out that the virtual withdrawal of the United States from collaboration with the League was hamstringing that body in its efforts to deal with a common humanitarian problem, the solution of which should transcend party politics or any question of League membership. Until the United States put forth a sound and clear-cut policy in keeping with her traditional role and her obligations under the Hague Convention, they declared, the chance of convening another international conference was very small.[16] This criticism, as well as pressure from prominent Americans active in the narcotics movement, finally led the State Department to assign John K. Caldwell, who replaced Edwin L. Neville in the narcotics work of the Division of Far Eastern Affairs, to the American consulate at Geneva to become acquainted with the League machinery on drug matters and to attend with Tuck, as unofficial observer, the eleventh session of the Advisory Committee in April 1928. Caldwell was instructed to answer inquiries on the control of narcotics in the United States and to become acquainted with the members of the committee and other League personnel concerned with the drug problem and to ascertain their views on all aspects of the problem.[17] Caldwell remained thereafter the principal representative of the United States not only on the Advisory Committee until the early nineteen thirties but also in the League-sponsored conferences on narcotics.

The touchiness of the United States on League matters was further illustrated by its refusal to become connected formally in any way with the League Commission of Enquiry sent to Persia in 1926 to investigate the growth of the poppy there and the possibilities of substituting other crops. This commission was primarily the brainchild of Mrs. Hamilton Wright which the League had adopted as she had recommended in the Final Act of the Second Geneva Opium Conference. Great pains were taken by the League to find an American to head the commission. The State Department refused to help in this effort and even declined to give formal assurance of its approval of the

16. Clipping from the *New York Times*, Feb. 12, 1928, enclosed in C. K. Crane to John K. Caldwell, Acting Chief, Division of Far Eastern Affairs, Feb. 21, 1928, SDR 511.4A1/2047.

17. Wilbur J. Carr (for the Secretary of State) to Caldwell, March 26, 1928, SDR 500.C1197/165; Secretary of State to the American Consul, for Caldwell (Geneva), April 27, 1928, SDR 500.C1197/171.

commission and the American finally chosen to head it. It did offer to give any informal assistance, however, that could not be construed as official involvement in a League matter.[18]

A similar motivation prompted the United States to refuse to cooperate with the Council of the League in selecting the members of the Permanent Central Board as provided for by the Geneva Convention. That instrument had received the requisite number of ratifications by the end of June 1928 and went into effect on September 25. According to the Convention, the eight members of the Central Board were to be chosen by the Council in concert with the United States and Germany. Thus, when on September 7 the Secretary General invited the United States to name its representative to sit with the Council to participate in the appointment of the board,[19] the State Department was faced with a long anticipated dilemma. On the one hand the Department realized that as the Central Board would have considerable power with reference to the control of the narcotics traffic, the character of the members of the board would be of great importance to the United States and the antidrug campaign as a whole. On the other hand, for the United States to participate in the selection of the members of the board would mean the government's active participation in a meeting of the League Council, a matter susceptible to great controversy.[20]

The extensive discussions in the State Department on the issue brought forth two points of view. The Undersecretary of State, Reuben J. Clark, was in favor of American cooperation with the Council in the selection of the board so as to secure the appointment of an American who would keep the United States fully informed on the board's activities. He recommended that the acceptance of the Secretary General's invitation be coupled with a statement expressing the intention of the United States to call a conference at an opportune time. This statement, he felt, would furnish the means by which the United States might regain the leadership it had lost after the Geneva conferences.[21] But Clark stood virtually alone in his views. The opinion of Congressman Porter was conclusive in the matter. He endorsed the

---

18. See below, p. 311–312.

19. Minister Hugh Wilson (Berne) to the Secretary of State, Sept. 7, 1928, SDR 511.4A2A/2; transmits telegram from Sir Eric Drummond.

20. Memorandum by Nelson T. Johnson, June 20, 1928, SDR 511.4A2A/—.

21. Memorandum of "Conversation Between Representative Stephen G. Porter and Doctor Rupert Blue with Mr. Clark, Mr. Johnson and Mr. Caldwell," Sept. 24, 1928, SDR 511.4A2A/9½.

position taken by Nelson T. Johnson and Caldwell that the United States should decline the invitation, and Clark deferred to Porter's wishes.[22] The reasoning underlying the refusal to cooperate with the Council was based on the considerations that acceptance of the invitation would imply a renunciation of the American objections in regard to the subservience of the Central Board to the League and in regard to other aspects of the Geneva Convention as stated in 1925; that it would weaken the American position relative to the narcotics problem as a whole; that it would be inappropriate in view of the American refusal to sign the Geneva Convention; that it would appear to be contrary to the official attitude of the United States toward the League; and most important, that it would be opposed by Congress as Porter's attitude indicated.[23] Furthermore, it was expected that other member countries of the Council would try to have an American elected to the board. Thus American participation in the selection would not be necessary and would not materially affect the board's composition.[24]

In reply to the League and in declining the invitation to sit with the Council, the State Department sought to use language that would not arouse ill feeling. Therefore the Department acknowledged that in regard to manufactured drugs and the control of transportation the Geneva Convention was an improvement over the Hague Convention. It nevertheless maintained that Porter's objections to the Geneva Convention, because of its failure to provide for the limitation of the production of raw materials to the world's medicinal and scientific needs and for the control of all opium and coca leaf derivatives, were still valid and of sufficient importance to offset the improvements made by the Convention. The Department concluded with the statement that the United States could not participate in the selection of the members of the Central Board because "the Geneva Convention tends to destroy the unity of purpose and joint responsibility of the Powers accomplished by the Hague Convention . . ." and that therefore the United States believed that the desired ends might better be achieved through the strict observance of the Hague Convention.[25] Though refusing to sit with the Council, the State Department was careful not to close the

22. *Ibid.*
23. Memorandum by Maxwell M. Hamilton and John K. Caldwell, Aug. 17, 1928, SDR 511.4A2A/2½.
24. *Ibid.*
25. Secretary of State Kellogg to the American Legation (Berne), Sept. 29, 1929, SDR 511.4A2A/7.

door on American cooperation with the Central Board and also possibly with the League itself. The Secretary General was assured that the United States would continue to cooperate in the international efforts to suppress the abuse of narcotic drugs and that it would submit to the board any information it might request.[26] Significantly, the State Department did not repeat the objections to the Central Board previously made. In fact, these objections never constituted major obstacles to American acceptance of the Geneva Convention. The promise to furnish the board with any information requested did not constitute, therefore, a change in the American attitude toward the Convention, but was made to avoid the probable charge, if such information were withheld, that the United States was attempting to prevent any progress through that instrument.[27]

Despite the effort of the Americans to phrase the reply to the League's invitation in an amicable manner, the Council was much exercised over the American statement. In a memorandum adopted December 14, 1928, it refuted the American views on the Geneva Convention. The Council asserted that the treaty should be regarded as strengthening and supplementing the Hague Convention rather than weakening it. The Council took sharpest issue with the American charge that the Geneva instrument tended to "destroy the unity of purpose and joint responsibility of the Powers accomplished by the Hague Convention." It maintained that, on the contrary, the best way to preserve and strengthen the unity of purpose and joint responsibility of the powers was to press for the widespread adoption of the Geneva Convention in addition to urging the strict enforcement of the Hague Convention.[28]

As the State Department had earlier anticipated, the anxiety of the League for an American on the Permanent Central Board made American participation in the selection of the Board's members unnecessary. Though taking no official position on the matter, the Department approvingly acquiesced in the putting forth of the names of Herbert L.

26. *Ibid.*

27. Memorandum by Caldwell, Sept. 29, 1928, SDR 511.4A2A/7½.

28. Minister Wilson (Berne) to the Secretary of State, Dec. 15, 1928, SDR 511.4A2A/24. What the State Department really meant by this statement was that the unity of purpose and joint responsibility of the powers were destroyed by the separation into special groups—countries in whose territories opium smoking was allowed and powers concerned with the narcotics problem—and the separation of one phase (use of prepared opium) of the general problem from the problem as a whole. See memorandum by Maxwell M. Hamilton, Jan. 8, 1929, SDR 511.4A2A/38.

May and Frederic A. Delano as nominees for the Central Board by Mrs. Moorhead of the Foreign Policy Association, a private organization.[29] Mrs. Moorhead approached Sir Malcolm Delevingne of the British Home Office and thereby obtained the assistance of the British Foreign Office in arranging for New Zealand to nominate May as a candidate for membership on the board.[30] May was elected by the Council in its December session, along with seven other persons from a list of sixteen candidates.[31] These individuals were to serve in their individual capacities and not as representatives of governments. Nevertheless, May maintained informal contact with the agencies of the American government concerned with narcotics and played an invaluable role in explaining the American statistics submitted to the board.[32]

As far as possible the United States sought to ignore the connection of the Central Board with the League. In transmitting information to the board efforts were made to avoid going through League channels. Therefore information coming under Article 21 of the Hague Convention was sent to the board through the Dutch government. Other information was transmitted through the American legation at Berne and addressed in the following manner: "The Secretary of State . . . encloses herewith for transmission in the usual informal manner, a note to the President of the Permanent Central Opium Board . . ."[33]

In still another way the United States sought to maintain the fiction that it was in no way collaborating with the League. On adopting in 1926 the import and export certificate forms specified by the League, the United States carefully pointed out that this was being done to facilitate cooperation with other nations and not the League, and that this did not imply any approval of the Geneva Convention. The United States adopted these forms on the basis of a suggestion of Arthur Woods, the American assessor on the Advisory Committee who had

29. Memorandum by Johnson of conversation with Mrs. Moorhead, Oct. 30, 1928; memorandum by Caldwell of conversation with Mrs. Moorhead, Oct. 31, 1928, SDR 511.4A2A/11; memorandum by Johnson of telephone conversation with Arthur Woods, May 16, 1928, SDR 511.4A2A/17.
30. Memorandum by Stuart J. Fuller to Pierrepont Moffat, Sept. 5, 1933, SDR 511.4A2A/300.
31. Other persons selected were Dr. O. Anselmino (Germany), Dr. C. J. Bonin (France), Professor Giuseppe Gallavresi (Italy), L. B. Lyall (Great Britain), Sir B. K. Mullick (India), Henrik Ramsey (Finland). See American Consulate (Geneva) to the Secretary of State, Jan. 14, 1929, SDR 511.4A2A/39.
32. Memorandum by Fuller to Moffat, Sept. 5, 1933, SDR 511.4A2A/300.
33. Memorandum by Caldwell to Johnson, July 17, 1929, SDR 511.4A2A/53.

succeeded Mrs. Wright, and the desire of the Treasury Department for closer cooperation with the League on administrative matters,[34] as uniform procedures facilitated its task of carrying out the narcotics laws and regulations of the United States and of suppressing the illicit traffic.

While trying to maintain a proper degree of aloofness toward the League, the United States found itself at a loss as to how to regain its leadership in the international movement. For a while it appeared that its role was being progressively assumed by Italy, a member of the League. At the meeting of the Fifth Committee in September 1926 the Italian representative, Cavvazoni, had shocked the representatives of the other powers by bitterly assailing the Geneva Convention. He also criticized the composition of the Opium Advisory Committee, which up to this time consisted of representatives of drug-producing and drug-manufacturing countries, and demanded a seat on the committee for Italy as a consuming country. His demand was met, and he became Italy's representative on the committee. At the ninth session of the committee in January 1927, Cavvazoni laid down the Italian policy as embracing the following points: the strict and full enforcement of the provisions of the Hague Convention, entrusting solely to the League of Nations the control of the narcotics traffic and manufactured drugs, the rationing of the manufacture of drugs among the manufacturing countries, an intensive study of the smuggling problem as to its causes and the penalties imposed on offenders, and the extension of the Hague Convention to cover all narcotic substances.[35] Cavvazoni later implemented these principles with a detailed scheme for the strict supervision of the traffic in and manufacture of narcotic drugs. This scheme, he declared, was designed to strengthen the Hague Convention, for he was very skeptical of the efficacy of the Geneva treaty.[36]

The American government manifested considerable interest in Cavvazoni's plan. The element of attraction in the scheme was the appeal for the control of the narcotics traffic on the basis of a strengthened

34. Undersecretary of State Grew to the Secretary of the Treasury, May 22, 1926, and enclosures, SDR 511.4A2/499.

35. Stanley Woodward to the Secretary of State, Feb. 23, 1927, SDR 500.C1197/71. See also Tuck to the Secretary of State, Sept. 10, 1926, SDR 511.4A2/515. For text of Cavvazoni's statement before the Advisory Committee, see League of Nations, Advisory Committee on Traffic in Opium and Other Dangerous Drugs, *Minutes of the Ninth Session Held at Geneva from February 17th to March 3rd, 1927*, C.86.M.35, 1927. XI (Geneva, 1927), pp. 11–15.

36. Caldwell to the Secretary of State, May 25, 1928, "Report on the Eleventh Session of the Advisory Committee," SDR 500.C1197/199.

Hague Convention rather than on the defective Geneva instrument. This one point was sufficient to arouse American sympathy for the Italian position, despite the failure of the scheme to embrace the American principles of limitation of production of raw materials and the suppression of the traffic in prepared opium. The Italian plan also called for strict League supervision of the trade, something to which the American government was averse. Nevertheless, on the basis of the Italian dissatisfaction with the Geneva Convention, the United States looked ahead to the reestablishment of its leadership in cooperation with Italy in an effort to bring about stricter control of the drug traffic through the implementation of the Hague Convention.[37] This idea collapsed, however, when Italy ratified the Geneva Convention in December 1929. Thus the United States was left virtually isolated among the major powers on the narcotics question.

In the meantime, the American government was casting about for some means by which it might regain the initiative it had lost by withdrawal from the Geneva Conference. This desire for action was intensified by pressure from various sources, both within and outside the United States. As already mentioned, even officials of the League castigated American lethargy. But as the United States maintained that only the Hague Convention furnished a proper basis for international action to solve the narcotics problem, the choice of means available to reestablish its prominence in the movement was limited. The idea that the United States should call a conference on its own initiative was several times broached, but there was little likelihood that this would meet with any significant response from other nations. The hope that the Geneva Convention would not be ratified by the requisite number of nations for it to go into effect was fatuous. It was not likely that the adherents to that convention would agree to a new conference without having given the instrument a trial. Furthermore, the matters in which the United States was most interested—limitation of the production of raw materials and suppression of the traffic in prepared opium—were not amenable to early accomplishment, as there was no fundamental change in the positions of the nations directly involved in these activities from the stand they had taken in 1925. The United States appeared to be trapped by its own principles and position as enunciated at the Geneva Conference. It could do little more than seek bilateral agreements with other powers on administrative matters.

37. For interest of American officials in the Cavvazoni proposal, see *ibid.* and memorandum of Caldwell to Johnson, May 8, 1929, 511.4/31½.

Gradually, however, the United States began to concentrate increasing attention on the aspect of the narcotics problem which appeared to be most susceptible of melioration—the manufacture of excess quantities of drugs. Arthur Woods, the American assessor on the Opium Advisory Committee, had urged the committee during its eighth session in May and June 1926 to recommend to the Council of the League that the manufacture and distribution of derivatives of opium and the coca leaf be permitted only in factories owned or effectively controlled by governments. As there were less than fifty factories in the world, and most of these were in five countries—the United States, Great Britain, Switzerland, Germany, and Japan—Woods maintained that such control could easily be achieved and would result in the effective suppression of illicit traffic in manufactured drugs.[38] Although the committee did not adopt Woods's resolution, it was strongly endorsed by the Dutch foreign minister, Jonkheer Loudon, and Lord Cecil. The latter suggested that the American ambassador in London take up the matter with the British foreign secretary, Sir Austen Chamberlain.[39] A favorable reception from the British was assured, for this proposal represented a position which the British had long held in regard to the solution of the drug problem. In line with Woods's proposal the State Department decided to urge the parties to the Hague Convention to establish stricter control over the factories manufacturing and selling narcotic drugs.[40] In the communication sent to the other powers the United States cited its own legislation controlling drug transactions and pointed out that only a small part of the drugs manufactured in the United States got into illicit channels. Therefore, in order for the American system of control to be effective in preventing the smuggling of narcotics into the United States and their illicit consumption, there was a great need for the other countries to adopt similar control measures. The United States was prepared to cooperate with any other government to achieve the ends aimed at by the Hague Convention.[41]

38. League of Nations, Advisory Committee on Traffic in Opium and Other Dangerous Drugs, *Provisional Minutes of the Eighth Session Held at Geneva from May 20th to June 8th, 1926*, C.393.M. 136.1926.XI (Geneva, 1926), pp. 52–53.

39. Arthur Woods to Undersecretary of State Grew, July 15, 1926, SDR 500.C1197/20.

40. Secretary of State Kellogg to the American Embassy (London), Aug. 26, 1926, SDR 500.C1197/26a.

41. The Secretary of State to the Diplomatic Officers of the United States Accredited to the Governments Party to the Hague Convention of January 23, 1912,

It is significant to note that no mention was made of prepared opium or the desirability of limiting the production of raw materials.

A year later the attention of the American government was again drawn to the feasibility of limiting its immediate objectives to the manufacturing phase of the drug question. Assuming that the American note of October 1926 to the parties to the Hague Convention indicated that the United States was prepared to subordinate temporarily its demands relative to prepared opium and coca leaf and poppy cultivation in favor of measures to control manufactured products, Charles K. Crane, a private American citizen who had given extensive thought to the narcotics situation,[42] proposed a plan to the American government for the achievement of the latter. The plan, which came to be known as the Scheme of Stipulated Supply, was the work of A. E. Blanco, a member of the Opium Section of the League Secretariat and a Spanish national.[43] Crane's scheme was quite simple in its general outline and contained only two main features. Each country, through the machinery of the League, was "to notify in advance, for a determined period, their requirements of each narcotic substance" and "to state from which country they will purchase these requirements."[44] Limitation of manufacture to these requirements would be effected in that having stated their needs beforehand, the purchasing countries would obtain the stipulated supply only from the countries designated, and the manufacturing countries would produce only the quantities necessary to meet their own domestic needs and to fill the previously publicized orders of the purchasing countries. The purchasing country would have a guaranteed supply while the selling country would have a guaranteed definite market.

Washington, Oct. 14, 1926, SDR 511.4A1/1972a. Also in *Foreign Relations*, 1926, I, 250–253.

42. Crane was a retired American businessman who had resided in England for a number of years up to 1924. After the Geneva Conference he had made an intensive study of the drug problem. See Crane to the President of the United States, Oct. 14, 1927, SDR 511.4A1/2037.

43. Crane did not reveal the authorship of the plan for almost a year after presenting it to the State Department, although he did specify that the scheme was not original with him. By this time Blanco, because of personality and policy differences with other members of the Opium Section, had resigned from his position. He remained in Geneva, however, and established the Anti-Opium Bureau, a one-man operation, for the propagandizing of his views on measures for the solution of the narcotics problem. Because of the glare of publicity which it directed toward the Opium Advisory Committee and other agencies of the League concerned with the drug question, the Bureau was not uninfluential.

44. Crane to the President, Dec. 14, 1927, SDR 4A1/2038.

Crane's scheme appeared to be ingenious, and the State Department evinced much interest in it.[45] The only other plans for the limitation of manufacture which had thus far been put forward embodied the principle of the allocation or rationing of quotas of the drugs to be manufactured among the existing manufacturing countries. Because of the difficulty of finding a satisfactory basis on which an equitable allocation of quotas could be made and the fear that the current non-manufacturing countries which might later wish to manufacture for export might have great difficulty in obtaining such quotas, the rationing plans had not generated much enthusiasm. The advantages claimed for the Scheme of Stipulated Supply lay in the apportionment without rationing of the manufacturers' export market, the freedom of choice allowed to consuming countries to determine the extent of their drug requirements, and the dissociation of the plan from the difficult problem of the production of raw materials. The plan was later modified, however, to include raw materials to the extent that governments of manufacturing countries would prevent their manufacturers from overproducing by restricting the importation of raw materials to the amounts necessary for legitimate manufacture. The boycott was contemplated as the principal instrument for enforcing the scheme. A manufacturing country which refused to cooperate in the plan would be subject to a boycott not only of its drug products but of other commodities as well, on the assumption that all of its exports were suspect as containing narcotics, a system which prevailed informally and temporarily between the United States and Switzerland.[46] Consuming countries which refused to submit estimates and otherwise cooperate would be denied drugs by the manufacturing countries. Countries which were both producers of the raw materials and the manufacturers of derivatives could be similarly subjected to an economic boycott.

Together with its creditable features, Crane's proposal had several potential shortcomings. One of these was the impossibility of binding nations which were both producers of the raw materials and manufacturers of the refined products in the same way as other countries. Although a boycott might be instituted against such countries if they refused to cooperate, excess quantities of drugs could be built up in

45. Stanley K. Hornbeck, Chief of Division of Far Eastern Affairs to C. K. Crane, March 3, 1928, SDR 511.4A1/2044.

46. Gavit, *Opium*, p. 238.

these countries which would find an outlet in the illicit traffic. Then too, there was the likelihood that countries with small drug requirements would consider the scheme as involving too much effort, and by refusing to submit estimates, they would frustrate the accurate determination of the world's legitimate drug requirements, which could only be ascertained through the cooperation of all purchasing countries. Furthermore, as the plan required dealing in futures, there would be restriction on competitive buying; once a country had designated the nation from which it would buy, its purchases would be confined to the factories of that one nation. From the point of view of the United States the principal defects of the plan were the stipulation that it should be administered by the Opium Advisory Committee and the lack of concrete provisions for the control of raw material used in manufacture. Aside from these "defects," the State Department saw real merit in the scheme.[47] To meet the American objections Crane offered to modify his plan so that it might be administered by a board established by the manufacturing countries to collect, collate, and transmit the information received from the various governments rather than by the Advisory Committee. The scheme might also be made to cover the importation of raw materials by the manufacturing countries.[48]

From the fall of 1927 to the end of 1929 Crane kept up a continuous correspondence with the State Department in an effort to secure American sponsorship of his plan and possibly the convening of an international conference by the United States to obtain its adoption by the international community.[49] The State Department, being still uncertain about concentrating its efforts on this one aspect of the narcotics problem, and fearing that an international conference could not be obtained on American initiative, demurred. It contented itself with transmitting the scheme, "without comment and without responsibility," to the Dutch government for communication to the parties to the Hague Convention, and with allowing Crane to send copies of the plan, if he wished, to the American consulate at Geneva for informal transmission to the League Secretariat, making it absolutely clear that it was Crane and not the State Department who was sending

47. Memorandum by Caldwell of conversation with Porter, March 8, 1928, SDR 511.4A1/2064.
48. Crane to Caldwell, May 21, 1928, SDR 511.4A1/2087.
49. The principal correspondence is contained in the following files: SDR 511.4A1/2037, 2038, 2039, 2040, 2044, 2052, 2057, 2058, 2059, 2062, 2070, 2087, 2090, 2091, 2101, 2121, 2122, 2131, 2134, 2135.

them.[50] Despite the Department's efforts to dissociate itself from Crane's proposal, the plan eventually came to be known as the American scheme. Blanco was largely responsible for this, for he used every opportunity to convey the impression that the United States was backing the proposal.[51] Newspaper correspondents also contributed to this fiction by referring to the plan as the "American Scheme."[52]

Although Crane failed to gain American support for his plan, several other governments did endorse it. By the end of 1929 Germany, Spain, Hungary, Uruguay, Belgium, Costa Rica, and Italy had all approved the scheme. Except for Germany, however, most of these countries could be classified as nonmanufacturers. By the time the conference on manufacture convened in 1930, several other governments had given the plan their tentative endorsement. One of the reasons for lack of wider approval of the scheme was the cool reception accorded it by the Opium Advisory Committee. At its twelfth session in January and February 1929 the majority of the members, while admitting that the plan was ingenious, nevertheless considered it to be impractical. They therefore decided to take no action on it, but to wait to see the results of the Geneva Convention which had just recently come into force. A minority of the members of the Advisory Committee, however, wanted the scheme taken as a starting point for discussion in the next session of the committee when the question of measures for the limitation of manufacture would be taken up.[53]

The decision of the Advisory Committee to examine seriously the possibility of circumscribing the manufacture of narcotic drugs to the

50. Memorandum of conference between Johnson, Hornbeck, and Caldwell, March 9, 1928, SDR 511. 401/2065; memorandum by Caldwell to Hornbeck, Sept. 10, 1928, SDR 511.4A1/2096. Also enclosed is copy of Caldwell to American Consul (Geneva), Sept. 25, 1928.

51. Memorandum by Caldwell to Johnson, March 13, 1929, SDR 500.C1197/266½. Gibson C. Blake to Secretary of State, Dec. 14, 1929, SDR 511.4A1/2141.

52. See, for example, the New York *Herald Tribune*, Oct. 24, 1929, p. 3.

53. League of Nations, Advisory Committee on Traffic in Opium and Other Dangerous Drugs, *Report to the Council on the Work of the Twelfth Session Held at Geneva, from January 17th to February 2nd, 1929* C.33. 1929.XI, OC.943 (1) (Geneva, 1929), pp. 5–6. The Dutch government had forwarded the scheme to the League Secretariat which had printed and distributed it as a League document to the Advisory Committee just before its eleventh session. At this session the committee demonstrated a hostile attitude toward the plan largely because Blanco, with whom the committee was having considerable difficulties, was the author. The committee therefore postponed discussion of the scheme on the grounds that Crane disclaimed authorship and thorough familiarity with it. See memorandum by Caldwell to Hornbeck, Sept. 10, 1928, SDR 511.4A1/2096.

world's medical and scientific needs stemmed from the realization that the illicit traffic in these products was reaching extremely dangerous proportions. Not only was this the phase of the narcotics problem which most seriously affected Western countries, but during the 1920's it had also become the major problem in the Far East, constituting a more serious menace to Orientals than the use of prepared opium. The principal sources of these manufactured drugs in the illicit traffic were certain countries of western Europe and Japan. Two developments spurred the League to action. At the twelfth session of the Advisory Committee the Dutch government disclosed that it had suppressed a huge center of illicit traffic in narcotic drugs. The Naarden firm, a Dutch concern, had amassed during a fifteen-month period covering 1927 and the first half of 1928 about 850 kilograms of morphine, 3,000 kilograms of heroin, and 90 kilograms of cocaine, the bulk of which went into the illicit traffic to China. Most of the supplies came from three firms in Germany, Switzerland, and France. It was estimated that this center of the international traffic had probably dealt with half the total annual world production of heroin.[54] The Naarden case received extensive publicity in the British and American press and led to the publicizing of other disclosures in the Advisory Committee of illicit drug transactions.[55] As a result, public pressure developed in many countries for measures to control the manufacture of these products.

The other development which prompted League consideration of the surplus production of manufactured drugs was the sudden reversal in the French attitude toward this phase of the narcotics problem. It will be recalled that in the preparations for the Second Geneva Conference and in the conference itself, the French had opposed suggestions for strict measures to regulate the production of opium and coca leaf derivatives.[56] The members of the League were thus caught by surprise when the French representative announced in a meeting of the Fifth Committee of the Assembly in 1929 that his government had decided to impose limitations on the quantity of narcotics manu-

---

54. League of Nations, *Traffic in Opium and Other Dangerous Drugs, Report of the Fifth Committee to the Assembly*, A.86.1929.XI (Geneva, 1929), p. 4.

55. For clippings from British papers dated Jan. 26, 1929, on the Naarden case and subsequent press reports, see American Embassy (London) to the Secretary of State, Jan. 29, 1929, SDR 500.C1197/257; Feb. 5, 1929, SDR 500.C1197/260; and Feb. 18, 1929, SDR 500 C.1197/264.

56. See above, p. 173.

factured in France and to adopt other strict measures to suppress illicit traffic.[57] This change in the French attitude apparently stemmed from alarm over recent disclosures of the participation in illicit transactions of French manufacturers, wholesalers, and other dealers in narcotics. The absence of adequate regulations covering the drug trade was largely responsible for this situation. As the discussion of the situation in the League organs concerned with the problem would have proved highly embarrassing to France, the French announcement was made to rectify the weaknesses in the French system of control.[58]

To take immediate advantage of the new French approach, Duncan Hall of the Opium Section of the League Secretariat and Sir Malcolm Delevingne, the British representative on the Advisory Committee, approached the representatives of the principal manufacturing countries as to the possibility of reopening the question of direct limitation of manufacture. These countries responded favorably. The result was the adoption by the Fifth Committee of the British proposal calling for acceptance of the principle of the limitation of the manufacture of those drugs covered by the Geneva Convention of 1925, the preparation of a plan of limitation by the Advisory Committee, and the convening by the Council, on the basis of the Advisory Committee's report, of a conference of the manufacturing and principal consuming countries to consider steps supplementing the Geneva Convention to restrict the manufacture of dangerous drugs to the amount required for medical and scientific purposes.[59] The Assembly adopted the resolution on September 24, 1929.

57. *Report of the Fifth Committee to the Assembly*, A.86.1929.XI, pp. 4–5.

58. The motives behind the French change of attitude were confirmed in several communications to the State Department from disparate and reliable sources. See Consul Gilson G. Blake, Jr. (Geneva), to the Secretary of State, Nov. 1, 1929, SDR 500 C111/418; memorandum of Conversation between Mrs. Helen H. Moorhead, Herbert L. May, Hornbeck, and Caldwell, Nov. 4, 1929, SDR 511.4A6/6; memorandum by Caldwell to the Undersecretary, Dec. 9, 1929, SDR 511.4A6/16.

59. *Ibid*. See also *Report of the Fifth Committee to the Assembly*, A.86.1929.XI, p. 6.

Chapter nine

American cooperation with the League in limiting manufacture

When the call came from the League of Nations for a new conference, the issue of the resumption of American collaboration with that body on the narcotics problem could no longer be evaded. If the United States refused to participate in an obviously sincere endeavor to solve one major aspect of the problem, it would open itself to severe and justifiable criticism and possibly end for a long time any chances it had of exerting any significant influence on the movement as a whole. Therefore, the initial reaction among those in the State Department concerned with the subject was in favor of American participation in the pending conference on manufacture. They regarded the conference and the preliminary meetings of the Advisory Committee leading up to it as affording a propitious opportunity for the United States to resume its active and leading role in the international antidrug campaign. Other phases of the problem might be dealt with in later conferences.[1] But again Congressman Porter stood as the major obstacle to the resumption of active American cooperation with the League. Porter warned against the possible political repercussions from what might appear to be abandonment of the American position of 1924–1925. He therefore initially expressed opposition to American participation in a conference so long as China's interests were not taken care of and the Far East situation with respect to prepared opium was not dealt with.[2] Thus the main task of the State Department was to overcome Porter's objections.

The arguments in favor of American participation in the conference on manufacture were compelling. Manufactured drugs from Europe

---

1. Memorandum by Caldwell to Johnson, Oct. 8, 1929, SDR 511.4A6/1½.
2. "Memorandum of a Conference Held in the Office of the Honorable Stephen G. Porter on Wednesday, October 16, 1929," between Porter, Johnson, Caldwell, Tennyson of the Narcotics Unit of the Treasury Department, and John D. Farnharne, representative of Arthur Woods and the Bureau of Social Hygiene, Oct. 17, 1929, SDR 511.4A6/4.

constituted a far greater menace to the United States than raw or prepared opium from the Orient. As a result of strict enforcement of the American control system, the price of morphine in the illicit traffic had risen from $12 or $13 per ounce in 1927 to $90 per ounce in New York and $130 per ounce in San Francisco in 1929.[3] The quantity of American-made drugs, compounds, and preparations containing narcotics which found their way into the contraband traffic was negligible. For the fiscal year ending June 30, 1929, the value of such products exported from the United States amounted to only $20,931, constituting only one-half of 1 percent of the total value of narcotic drugs manufactured in the United States in 1928.[4] As for China and the Far East, the control of the manufacture of drugs in Europe and Japan would have as much or more value than the abolition of opium smoking, for China was a major victim of illicit traffic in opium and coca leaf derivatives, as the Naarden case indicated. Furthermore, the Chinese delegate in the Fifth Committee of the Assembly had stated that China would support efforts to limit manufacture.[5] In addition, restriction of manufacture was embodied in the American program at the Geneva Conference, and the achievement of this objective would be giving effect to Article 9 of the Hague Convention relating to the restriction to medicinal and scientific purposes of the manufacture, sale, and use of certain narcotic drugs. Finally, while participating in a conference on manufacture, the United States could still make it clear that its attention to this phase of the narcotics problem did not mean the abandonment of its often stated position relative to prepared opium and the limitation of the production of raw products. These arguments were sufficient to cause Porter to modify his opposition to the extent of approving the attendance of Caldwell at the session of the Advisory Committee which would consider a plan of limitation, provided he took no active part in the work of preparation.[6]

Caldwell attended the thirteenth session of the Advisory Committee in January and February 1930 and served on the subcommittee consisting of representatives of the manufacturing states which was ap-

3. Memorandum by Caldwell of telephone conversation with Harry Anslinger of the Narcotics Unit of the Treasury Department, Oct. 23, 1929, SDR 811.114 N16/1701.
4. Memorandum by Caldwell to Ward, Dec. 18, 1929, SDR 511.4A6/20.
5. Memorandum by Caldwell to the Undersecretary of State, Nov. 15, 1929, SDR 511.4A6/23½.
6. Memorandum by Caldwell of conversation with Porter, Dec. 14, 1929, SDR 811.114N16/1718½.

pointed to prepare a plan of limitation. He confined his activities to help on technical questions, however, and refrained from taking a prominent role in controversial matters.[7] The plan which the sub-committee drew up was adopted by the Advisory Committee after only cursory discussion. It provided for the determination of the world requirements of manufactured drugs on the basis of the esti-mated needs of each country, the division of the manufacture of these total requirements either by agreement among the manufacturers them-selves or by the governments concerned, and the establishment of a central organization to make necessary readjustments in the quotas allocated and to ensure that the consuming countries received the amounts they required.[8] In essence the plan proposed an international cartel of European narcotic drug manufacturers. As the attitude of the United States was opposed in general to cartels, and as the plan of the Advisory Committee would not provide a system of limitation more strict than that in force in the United States, the State Department con-cluded initially that American participation in the pending conference would be of no special benefit and should therefore be confined merely to sending an observer to watch the proceedings.[9]

At its session in May 1930 the League Council approved the plan of the Advisory Committee and authorized the sending of invitations to twenty-five major producing, manufacturing, and consuming coun-tries to participate in the limitation conference to be convened on December 1. The Council also accepted the British suggestion that a preliminary conference among the governments of the manufacturing countries be summoned by Great Britain for the purpose of agreeing upon the establishment of an international cartel and the allocation of quotas among the component nations or firms. It was expected that the preliminary conference would be held in July, to be followed by a special session of the Advisory Committee in August to draw up a

7. Consul Blake (Geneva) (from Caldwell) to the Secretary of State, Jan. 25, 1930, SDR 500.C1197/340.

8. League of Nations, Advisory Committee on the Traffic in Opium and Other Dangerous Drugs, *Report to the Council on the Work of the Thirteenth Session*, C.138.M.51.1930.XI (Geneva, 1930), pp. 20–24. See also Blake (from Caldwell) to the Secretary of State, Feb. 7, 1930, SDR 500.C1197/347, and Feb. 8, 1930, SDR 500.C1197/348.

9. Memorandum by Caldwell to Cotton and Shaw, March 21, 1930, SDR 511.4A6/46; memorandum by Caldwell to the Secretary of State, May 23, 1930, SDR 511.4A6/57½; Secretary of State Stimson to the American Legation (Berne), July 22, 1930, SDR 511.4A6/100.

draft convention. Because of the delay in the conclusion of private negotiations among European drug manufacturers on the rationing of quotas among them, the preliminary conference did not meet until October. In September the Council endorsed the decision of the Fifth Committee of the Assembly to invite all countries to the main conference and the date of its convening was changed to May 27, 1931, and that of the next session of the Advisory Committee to January 9, 1931. In the meantime, the United States had accepted the August 22 invitation of the British government to attend the preliminary discussions.[10]

The Preliminary Conference on the Limitation of the Manufacture of Narcotic Drugs met in London from October 27 to November 11, 1930. Representatives of eleven countries attended,[11] including Caldwell for the United States. Caldwell was instructed to make clear the narcotics situation in the United States and to emphasize the American desire to see other countries establish effective controls. He was admonished to avoid committing the United States to any particular scheme or to participation in any further conference.[12] For additional guidance Caldwell had before him the views of American manufacturers on the subject of limitation. They had not participated in the discussions held by the European manufacturers on the question, but they vigorously disapproved of the formation of a cartel on the grounds that participation by American firms in such a cartel would be illegal under the antimonopoly laws of the United States. Such a system would also place them at a disadvantage in competing for a share of the world market. Although their drug exports were small, and there was no anticipation of any immediate increase in these, the American manufacturers were opposed to any scheme which would preclude such an increase if it were made possible by economic conditions and factors relative to the control of distribution. They claimed that the paucity of American drug exports was due less to the strict control over distribution provided in the Import and Export Act than to the American import duty on raw opium of $3 per pound. The latter

10. For the steps leading up to the convening of the preliminary conference, see memorandum by Caldwell, Oct. 2, 1930, SDR 511.4A6/141. See also *Foreign Relations, 1931,* I, pp. 646–648.

11. France, Germany, Great Britain, India, Italy, Japan, Netherlands, Switzerland, Turkey, United States, USSR.

12. J. P. Cotton (for the Secretary of State) to Caldwell, Oct. 10, 1930, SDR 511.4A6P43/8.

was responsible for the price of American drugs being higher than that of their European competitors, who had the advantage of a lower import duty on the raw materials plus the ability to take advantage of certain other features of the drug traffic. They also doubted the practicality of the Scheme of Stipulated Supply. The only system of control satisfactory to them was that in effect in the United States. They therefore urged the American government to recommend the adoption of similar control measures by European countries as being most effective for worldwide control of the manufacture and distribution of drugs.[13] This was the position which American drug manufacturers had maintained ever since the passage of the Import and Export Act in 1922. By placing their European counterparts under restraints similar to those imposed on them, the Americans hoped to gain a better competitive position in the world market. They emphasized, however, that they still would not be able to compete until the tariff on raw opium was reduced.[14]

The London Preliminary Conference had two principal items on its agenda: the apportionment of quotas among the manufacturing countries and the formulation of a system which would ensure a proper distribution of the drugs manufactured among the consuming countries. As president, Sir Malcolm Delevingne initially dominated the conference, and it was on his insistence that the work of the conference was delayed for over two weeks until the European manufacturers could come to some agreement on quotas. Then, when the manufacturers submitted their agreement, all the governments present whose nationals were to be included in the proposed cartels of the manufacturers were willing to accept the manufacturers' allocations except the British. The principal objections voiced were that the quotas did not conform to the plan of the Advisory Committee; that they were quotas of company rather than national production, and some companies were established in more than one country; and that there was no relation between the quotas and the figures of legitimate export in recent years. The failure of the quotas to cover all narcotic drugs and to deal adequately with the conversion of morphine into codeine was another objection. As revealed in private conversations, it appeared

---

13. Memorandum by Caldwell of conference held at Anslinger's office on Oct. 7, 1930, Oct. 10, 1930, SDR 511.4A6/155. See also the transcript of the conference in SDR 511.4A6/168.
14. *Ibid.*

that the dissatisfaction of the British delegate stemmed principally from his belief that the morphine quota assigned to British firms was too small.[15]

Perhaps the most discordant note of the deliberations was struck by the Turkish representative when he demanded that his country be assigned a quota of one-third of the entire world production of manufactured drugs. This demand was based on Turkey's position as the principal producer of the raw material used by European and American manufacturers and Turkey's claim that it had exported for the first six months of 1930 over six tons of morphine and heroin. The latter disclosure raised a very serious question. It was clear that these exportations, though legitimate by Turkish law, had gone into the illicit market, for no imports of these drugs from Turkey had been reported to the Permanent Central Board, and the countries to whom the Turkish delegate said the exports had been made—France, Germany, and Italy—denied having received the shipments.[16] The delegate promised that if his demand were met, Turkey would become a party to the international opium conventions, all of which that country had so far refused to adhere to.

Dissentient voices to the manufacturers' quota plan were also raised by the delegates of Russia and Japan. Championing the position taken by the United States at the Geneva Conference, the Russian representative suggested that the scope of the conference should be expanded to include discussion of the issues of limiting the production of raw material. This proposal was of course rejected. On the subject of manufacture, he stated several times during the conference that the situation in Russia was similar to that in the United States—manufacture for domestic needs and very small export to neighboring territories—and that his government wanted this situation maintained. He was opposed to Russian participation in an international cartel.[17] On the same issue, the Japanese representative, whose countrymen had not been assigned quotas by the European manufacturers, took a similar position.[18]

As instructed, Caldwell's major efforts at the conference were directed toward making clear the position of both the American gov-

15. "Report on the Preliminary Conference . . . ," Caldwell to the Secretary of State, Dec. 12, 1930, SDR 511.4A6/184. pp. 3–5.
16. *Ibid.*, pp. 8–9.
17. *Ibid.*, pp. 11, 12.   18. *Ibid.*

ernment and American drug manufacturers and in getting a draft scheme formulated that would be acceptable to the United States as a basis for discussion at the forthcoming May conference. For a part of the Preliminary Conference a representative of the American drug interests was present in London and kept in touch with Caldwell. He did not participate in the discussions of the European manufacturers, and when it became clear that the plan they brought forth would not affect the position of American manufacturers unless they wished to become large producers for export, he returned to the United States.[19] Caldwell was thus left free to point out to the conference that the main interest of the United States was in seeing improvements in the conditions of the narcotic drug traffic rather than in the protection of its own export trade. Nevertheless, his principal objection to the plan under discussion related to the difficulty that new manufacturing or exporting countries would be likely to experience in negotiating for a share of the quotas which would have already been allocated to the existing manufacturing countries, especially since the latter would not constitute a unity, but would be five different countries which would not even be in agreement among themselves.[20]

Several different drafts of a limitation convention as well as amendments and suggestions were presented to the Preliminary Conference. The draft convention which received the greatest attention was that presented by Sir Malcolm Delevingne, the British delegate. The manufacturers' quota arrangements were designed to fit this scheme. The principal features of the British plan were as follows: each country was to submit to a central office estimates of its annual domestic and re-export requirements of manufactured drugs; a mixed commission consisting of representatives of the Permanent Central Board, the Opium Advisory Committee, and the Health Committee of the League would examine these estimates and determine the medical and scientific requirements of the countries which failed to furnish estimates; the percentage of the world's requirements which each exporting country would be allowed to manufacture would be specified; the mixed commission would inform the central office and each government of the

19. *Ibid.*, pp. 13–14.
20. Conference on the Limitation of the Manufacture of Dangerous Drugs, *Preliminary Meeting of Manufacturing Countries, London, October, 1930, Verbatim Report,* M. C. (Lond.), pp. 1–20, mimeographed, PV 4, p. S.7; PV 17, p. 1.

total amount of the world's requirements each year and the quantity each quota country would be allowed to manufacture; the quota countries would pledge to have available for export the quantities which they were allowed to manufacture for that purpose and to prevent any unwarranted increase in prices; and finally, nonmanufacturing countries or countries which manufactured but exported little would nevertheless furnish the central office with information relative to the quantity manufactured or exported, and if they desired to become large exporters, they would negotiate with the quota countries for a share of the quotas.[21] As already mentioned the main objection to this sort of scheme was the granting of a monopoly of the export trade to the existing manufacturing-exporting countries with which countries deciding in the future to manufacture for export would have to negotiate in order to participate.

No agreement could be reached in the Preliminary Conference on any particular scheme. The conferees therefore prepared a report to which the British plan was annexed and brought their work to a close on November 11. The accomplishment of the conference was largely confined to a sharper delineation of the issues in controversy, and as a result, some of the governments began preparations on schemes for presentation to the forthcoming main conference that might provide a satisfactory solution. A secondary achievement was the bringing of Russia and Turkey once again within the orbit of international cooperation on the drug question, from which they had been for some time excluded by international situations and internal conditions in their own territories. Caldwell did not formally accept any of the results of the Preliminary Conference. Although he made no formal reservations for incorporation in the report of the conference, he did make it clear that the United States was not committed to any of the plans discussed. In fact, no government was bound by anything said or done at the conference, for their representatives did not have plenipotentiary powers. Thus all governments were free to present amended or entirely different proposals in the forthcoming discussions in the Advisory Committee and in the conference in May.[22]

At its fourteenth session in January and February 1931 the Advisory Committee devoted most of its time to drafting a scheme of limitation.

21. Caldwell's Report on the Preliminary Conference, pp. 15–16, SDR 511.4A6/184.
22. Secretary of State Stimson to the American Consul (Geneva), Dec. 23, 1930, SDR 511.4A6/194. Also in *Foreign Relations*, 1931, I, 649–650.

The plan finally adopted was based on the principles set forth by the committee during the preceding session, and it contained essentially the features of the British plan annexed to the report of the London Preliminary Conference.[23] The Advisory Committee's scheme and the report to the Council were sent to the interested governments by the Secretary General on March 11. The United States had decided by this time, after considerable soul searching in the State Department, to participate fully in the May conference.[24] Most private groups and individuals consulted on the matter had urged American representation at the conference. The procrastination in the State Department had not been a result of the narcotics question per se, but was owing to the relation of that question to other issues.[25] It was because of these other issues that Porter and Kenneth Clark, a correspondent for the Hearst newspapers, had opposed American attendance.[26] Porter's death in June 1930 removed the major obstacle to the participation of the United States in the conference. Thereafter, the State Department carefully sought to prevent any one Congressman from becoming so closely connected with its negotiations in regard to the drug problem as to dominate American policy on the matter. Thus the efforts of Representative Hamilton Fish, the second-ranking member of the House Foreign Affairs Committee, to take Porter's place in representing the United States in international conferences on the subject were thwarted.

The Conference on the Limitation of the Manufacture of Narcotic Drugs met at Geneva from May 27 to June 13, 1931. The American delegation to the conference consisted of Caldwell as chairman; Harry Anslinger, the head of the recently created Bureau of Narcotics; Dr. Walter L. Treadway, Assistant Surgeon General of the United States; and Sanborn Young, a member of the legislature of California. Accompanying the delegation as disbursing officer and secretary, respectively, were Marc Smith, the American vice-consul at Geneva, and

23. For the discussion of the plan and its formulation, see League of Nations, Advisory Committee on Traffic in Opium and Other Dangerous Drugs, *Minutes of the Fourteenth Session* . . . , C.88.M.34.1931.XI. Vol. I (Geneva, 1931), pp. 10–85. For the Draft Convention itself see the Annex 4 to Vol. 2, pp. 242–250.

24. Secretary of State Stimson to President Hoover, Jan. 20, 1931, SDR 511.4A1/210. Also in *Foreign Relations*, 1931, I, 650–651; see also *Foreign Relations*, 1934, I, 653.

25. Undersecretary of State Cotton to Arthur Woods, Dec. 26, 1929, SDR 511.4A6/28.

26. Memorandum by Caldwell of conversation with Kenneth Clark, Dec. 20, 1929, SDR 511.4A6/25.

Winthrop Greene, the Third Secretary of the American legation at Berne.[27] So this time, except for Young, the United States was represented only by officials of the federal government concerned with the narcotics problem.

The American delegation had no plan of its own, nor was it pledged to support any particular scheme, despite the efforts of Crane and Blanco to obtain such a commitment. It was prepared to "support any plan or combination of plans" that would effect the desired limitation either directly or indirectly and which was "not clearly unacceptable" to the American government.[28] Since the United States assumed that it already had an effective system of control, the government was primarily concerned with eliminating the excess production abroad from which the illicit traffic to and within the United States was supplied. The delegation was therefore prepared to support a convention which though unacceptable to the United States in certain particulars was nevertheless acceptable to other countries if it appeared capable of effecting the desired restriction of manufacture in those countries. The American delegation would work for a convention based on either the quota system, the Scheme of Stipulated Supply, a combination of the two, or any other plan so long as it provided for a direct limitation of the quantities to be manufactured, adequate measures for the control of distribution, the limitation of the quantities of raw material available to factories (the American system), the establishment of a central office to receive governmental estimates of drugs required for domestic consumption and to check these estimates against exports from manufacturing countries, and the strict control and limitation of the re-exportation of drugs.[29]

For the first time the American government had to take into consideration the economic interests of a segment of its population directly involved in the problem under discussion—the manufacturers of narcotic drug products. In its participation in the previous international conferences, there had been virtually no economic concerns whose views had to be taken into account. This handicap had been confined

27. Department of State, United States Delegation to the Conference on the Limitation of the Manufacture of Narcotic Drugs, Geneva, May 27–July 13, 1931, *Report of the Delegation to the United States Secretary of State* (Washington: Government Printing Office, 1932), p. 1. Cited below as *Report of the American Delegation on the Narcotics Limitation Conference.*

28. Memorandum by Caldwell, May 5, 1931, SDR 511.4A6P43/103.

29. *Foreign Relations,* 1931, I, 657.

to other governments. Fortunately, however, the views of the American manufacturers were generally in accord with those of the government, despite their dislike of both the quota system and the Scheme of Stipulated Supply. As already pointed out, their opposition to the quota system was based on the fear that they would be foreclosed, by the allocation of the quotas on the basis of existing exports of countries, from significant future participation in the export trade if conditions ever permitted an increase in this phase of their activities. As for the Scheme of Stipulated Supply, they feared that they would come out second best in the competition for the market of the consuming countries, which, they felt, would not be willing to commit themselves in advance as to the countries from which their drug supplies would be purchased. The principal weakness in both plans in the view of the American drug interests was the lack of adequate provisions for the control of distribution, which they regarded as the vital point of the control problem, much more important than the curtailment of the quantities produced. They therefore urged that the American delegation push for the adoption of the American system of control, which they regarded as the only effective method. Its virtue, besides providing effective regulation of distribution, lay in allowing freedom of competition within the sphere of the legitimate trade as to markets, source of supplies, and prices.[30] As they had indicated before the London Preliminary Conference met, what the American manufacturers really wanted was to place their European competitors under the same system of regulation as themselves, for they claimed that the profits of the European factories were partly based on drugs which went into the contraband traffic.

All the governments of the world were invited to attend the full conference, and fifty-seven did participate. The plan of the Advisory Committee was accepted as the basis for discussion, but it was agreed that amendments or entirely different projects were in order. The Advisory Committee's plan was vigorously championed by the British delegate, Sir Malcolm Delevingne. He spent several weeks of fruitless efforts to work out quota percentages that would be acceptable to all the manufacturing countries. There was little optimism among the

---

30. *"Statement Presented to the American Delegation to the Conference on the Limitation of the Manufacture of Narcotic Drugs on Behalf of the American Manufacturers of Narcotics by Oscar R. Ewing, Esq., Washington, D. C., April 9, 1931,"* SDR 511.4A6/271.

other delegations that such could be achieved, and there was thus an early disposition to consider other plans.

The attitude of Turkey was a major stumbling block to any agreement on quota allocations. In recent years Turkey had furnished up to 61 percent of the raw opium imports of the manufacturing countries. The Turkish delegate therefore insisted privately on a large percentage of the world's export trade in manufactured drugs and demanded publicly a guaranteed market at a predetermined price for Turkey's raw opium supplies.[31] The Turkish government claimed that to allow its citizens the right to manufacture opium derivatives from the raw materials in their own country was "but logical and fair" and certainly as justifiable as the manufacture of these products in other European countries which had to import the raw materials.[32] Efforts throughout the conference to get Turkey to modify its demands failed, but some progress was made toward inducing Turkey to ratify the Hague Convention. Anslinger gave the Turkish delegation a copy of a bill concerning narcotics which had been introduced in the American House of Representatives and explained that an amendment would likely be introduced to the bill which would call for the prohibition of the importation of raw opium from countries which had not applied the principles of the Hague Convention. This information was communicated to the Turkish government, which in turn instructed its delegate to inform the American delegation that as Turkey did not wish its legitimate export market for raw opium cut off, it would very probably ratify the Hague instrument.[33] Largely as a result of this threat and the repeated urgings of American diplomatic officials in Turkey, the Turkish government announced on April 27, 1932, its intention to adhere to both the Hague Convention of 1912 and the Geneva Convention of 1925.[34]

Major opposition to the quota plan of the Advisory Committee came also from the delegates of Russia, Yugoslavia, Japan, and France. The Russian delegate reiterated the position his government had taken in the London Preliminary Conference. He insisted that the conferees

31. *Report of the American Delegation on the Narcotics Limitation Conference*, p. 5. For percentages of raw materials furnished by Turkey and other countries to manufacturing countries, see *Records of the Narcotics Limitation Conference*, II, 37.

32. Ambassador Joseph C. Grew (Istanbul) to the Secretary of State, May 23, 1931, SDR 511.4A6/347.

33. Caldwell to the Secretary of State, SDR 511.4A2/654.

34. Consul Gilbert (Geneva) to the Secretary of State, April 27, 1932, SDR 511.4A2/2210.

consider the question of the restriction of the production of raw materials, and he proposed an amendment to this effect. Any other measures short of this, he maintained, would be futile. The American delegates expressed sympathy with this Russian promotion of the old American principles, but refused to support the contention that this phase of the question was within the competence of the conference. Caldwell promised that he would later propose an amendment for the limitation of the supplies of raw materials allocated to factories, thereby dealing with the issue of raw material production in an oblique way. By a vote of 43 to 3 with 3 abstentions the conference voted not to discuss the Soviet proposal.[35] The Yugoslav delegate did not object to the quota plan per se, but his insistence on a large share in the system for his country contributed to the failure to reach agreement on the percentages to be apportioned among the manufacturing countries. The same was true of Japan, whose delegation demanded an equal allocation of quotas among the manufacturing states. As Japan had not previously manufactured for export, and as one country had furnished up to 40 percent of the world's requirements, this demand was patently unacceptable. The Japanese therefore proposed that manufacture by each country be limited to the annual estimate of its domestic requirements for medical, scientific, and conversion purposes plus an amount to fill actual export orders accompanied by an import certificate. The French introduced a brief amendment to the Japanese proposal calling for the filling of drug orders of a nonsignatory country by signatories only with the permission of a central authority. The amendment, by agreement between the two delegations, was added to the Japanese plan.[36]

At the fifth meeting of the conference, Caldwell, at the specific request of the president of the conference, made a brief statement of the American position which was "well received" and pointed out that no plan thus far suggested was entirely acceptable to the United States.[37] The delegation had early reservations concerning the Ad-

35. For the Russian proposal and the discussion on it, see League of Nations, *Records of the Conference for the Limitation of the Manufacture of Narcotic Drugs, Geneva, May 27th to July 13th, 1931*, Vol. I: *Plenary Meetings, Text of the Debates*, C.509.M214.1931.XI. (Geneva, 1931), pp. 51–52, 77, 80. Cited below as *Records of Narcotics Limitation Conference*, I.

36. For the presentation of the Japanese and French proposals, see *ibid.*, pp. 42, 102, 104.

37. *Ibid.*, p. 44. The statement of the American position was made in response to the request of the president of the conference, who hoped that it would accelerate the proceedings, for it seemed that many delegations were waiting for the United

visory Committee's quota scheme, but refrained from acting upon a too hurried inclination to reject it. Thus for two weeks after the opening of the conference the delegation confined its major formal activities to introducing amendments embodying the American principles to the quota plan in order to obtain a discussion of basic alterations in the plan or the consideration of other alternatives. On June 13, however, the delegation came out squarely for the Japanese-French plan, which in its essentials embodied most of the American principles, as a preferable basis for a limitation convention.[38]

The American delegation also submitted a plan of its own which it had worked out after the conference had begun. The scheme, known as the Stock Replacement or Rotating Stock Plan, was based on two fundamental principles: the limitation of the quantity of raw material available to factories to amounts necessary for the production of the strictly medical and scientific requirements of narcotic drugs as estimated by countries, and the extension of such limitation to all harmful derivatives of opium and the coca leaf. The main features of the plan called for:

> Submission to the Permanent Central Board by each country of advance estimates of its annual needs for domestic consumption;
>
> Submission to the board by each manufacturing country of annual estimates of its needs for raw opium, coca leaves, and drugs obtained from these commodities for manufacturing or conversion purposes;
>
> Restriction by each country of its imports of raw materials and their derivatives to the quantities appearing in their estimates and the limitation of the export of these materials to the estimates of the countries receiving them;
>
> Freedom of each country to manufacture for domestic consumption and for a "reasonable working stock," with manufacturers being allowed to maintain a stock of drugs for export equal to 50 percent of their exports of the previous year, provided, however, that manufacturers were not to be permitted additional supplies of raw materials for manufacture and drugs for conversion until export orders had been shipped from the country;

States to state its position before stating theirs. Caldwell to the Secretary of State, May 30, 1931, SDR 511.4A6/341. See also *Foreign Relations*, 1931, I, 657–658.

38. *Foreign Relations*, 1931, I, 659–660. See also *Records of the Narcotics Limitation Conference*, II, 31–32.

The right of countries not currently manufacturing or manufacturing only for domestic consumption to fill legitimate export orders out of their stocks for domestic consumption and to replace these depleted stocks by subsequent manufacture;

Coverage of the trade in all dangerous narcotic substances by the import and export certificate system.[39]

In short, the American scheme provided for a free competitive market in opium and coca leaf derivatives. Their manufacture was to be limited to quantities needed for medical and scientific purposes by restricting the raw products available to factories to the quantities necessary for the production of the required refined products.

Although the Crane scheme was given no independent consideration by the conference, the American and the Japanese-French plan did embody some of its concepts. Annual estimates of drug needs, manufacture up to these needs for domestic consumption and to fill export orders, a free competitive market and the right to choose the source of supply, and even the control of the importation of raw materials were all encompassed in the Scheme of Stipulated Supply.

On June 20, the conference voted 27 to 3 to scrap the quota plan and to adopt the Japanese-French plan as a basis for discussion. At informal conferences among the Japanese, French, Spanish, German, and American delegations, the first draft of a convention based on the Japanese-French plan was drawn up. From this draft the final convention was soon developed.[40]

The American delegation devoted most of its energies during the course of the deliberations on the new scheme to getting the bulk of its plan incorporated in the convention. It especially desired the coverage by the convention of all dangerous and potentially dangerous drugs currently being produced or which might be produced in the future, including such products as codeine and synthetic drugs. It also sought the coverage of solutions and preparations containing narcotics and the inclusion in the estimates submitted by countries of the preparations exempted in the previous conventions. Limitation of the factory stocks of raw materials was a cardinal point in the American plan, and the delegation also wanted the convention to provide for an assay of these

39. For the plan see, *Records of the Narcotics Limitation Conference*, I, 308–315.
40. *Report of the American Delegation on the Narcotics Limitation Conference*, pp. 8–9.

raw materials to determine the quantities of derivatives they would yield. And finally, a stricter control of the distribution of drugs was sought.[41]

The American delegation did not get all it wanted. It was not until near the end of the conference that an agreement to apply the import and export certificate system to codeine was extracted from the German delegation, which heretofore had absolutely refused to agree to such a step.[42] Other manufacturing countries had strongly opposed this step also. But the Americans did not win their point without a concession. As the result of including codeine in the list of drugs to be brought under control, the final convention divided these drugs into two groups. Group I consisted of the more dangerous drugs, to which the strictest degree of limitation and control was applied. In Group II the less dangerous drugs, including codeine, were subjected to a less severe system of control.[43] Another difficult issue was what disposition to make of heroin. The insistence by the Austrian and Polish delegates that its manufacture be totally prohibited was strongly supported by the Americans, but was vigorously opposed by the British and Swiss delegates.[44] A compromise proposal was finally incorporated in the convention which prohibited the export of the drug except on the request for it for medical and scientific purposes by the government of a country where the product was not manufactured. The importing government was required to consign it to a government department for distribution.

The American proposal to limit the amount of raw materials allowed to factories also met with much opposition, especially from the German delegation. As a result, direct limitation of these commodities was not provided for in the convention. Nevertheless, the Americans achieved essentially what they wanted, for the convention did call for the strict supervision of the quantity of raw materials in the possession of each manufacturer and the prevention of the accumulation of excess stocks of these products.[45] In regard to drugs seized in the illicit traffic, the American delegation supported proposals for their destruction. When these proposals were opposed, the Americans were

41. *Ibid.*, pp. 7–8.
42. Caldwell to the Secretary of State, July 12, 1931, SDR 511.4A6/388.
43. *Report of the American Delegation on the Narcotics Limitation Conference*, pp. 12–13.
44. *Ibid.*, pp. 14–15.   45. *Ibid.*, p. 17.

satisfied with the arrangements for alternative methods of disposing of these drugs, such as converting them, under government control, into nonnarcotic substances or using them for medical and scientific purposes under government supervision and accounting for them, if not destroyed, within a country's estimates.[46] The Americans failed to bring all preparations containing narcotics under the import and export certificate system. In addition, they were disappointed that preliminary authorization by a central office was not required for drug shipments to countries which applied the system and for shipments of less than five kilograms to any country.[47]

Although they worked energetically for their objectives, the American delegation did not insist on an absolutely perfect convention. Rather, they sought a practical and effective treaty that could be accepted generally. They deliberately avoided a repetition of the discord which had characterized the Geneva conferences. Even Porter had eventually admitted that "while the methods of the American delegation in 1924–1925 were proper at the time," these methods should not be followed a second time.[48] As a matter of fact, a view had long prevailed in the State Department that the withdrawal of the American delegation from the Geneva Conference had been unwise and that continued participation by the delegation might have resulted in a better convention. Furthermore, the action had created an atmosphere of hostility which had made subsequent cooperation between the United States and other nations on the narcotics problem more difficult. By precluding American adherence to the Geneva Convention, it was felt that the withdrawal had very much weakened the international position of the United States in the antidrug campaign.[49]

The American delegation at the Conference on the Limitation of Manufacture therefore abstained from extended speeches and sought to avoid exchanges of recriminations. An occasion for the latter had been presented by Sir Malcolm Delevingne's hostile criticism of the Americans for opposing the quota plan and suggesting amendments to it. Caldwell, realizing that Delevingne's cooperation was needed and could be eventually obtained, wisely refrained from replying in a similar vein. This attitude paid off, for Sir Malcolm was subsequently very

46. *Ibid.*   47. *Ibid.*, p. 7.
48. Memorandum by Caldwell to the Secretary of State, Sept. 27, 1931, SDR 511.4A6/444.
   49. *Ibid.*

helpful in putting the American points across.[50] The maintenance of such decorum, however, was not without certain risks. The Hearst press accused Caldwell of buckling under to Delevingne and was very critical of the American proposals. During the course of the conference and after, it headlined its criticism of the delegation by such phrases as "Caldwell Colorless," his "Attitude Apologetic," "Britain Leading America by the Nose," "U.S. Yields at Geneva on Limitation of Dope," "Caldwell Backed Down," and similar expressions.[51] Similar criticisms were later echoed by A. E. Blanco and Miss Ellen La Motte.[52] These attacks on the conduct of the American delegation were patently unjustified. The delegation achieved by quiet diplomacy nearly all the objectives laid down in their instructions. This was indeed a commendable achievement in a conference of fifty-seven participating states. The State Department and the rest of the American press in general realized this and praised the resultant convention.[53]

The Narcotics Limitation Convention consisted of seven chapters and thirty-four articles.[54] Chapter I (Article 1) defined the terms used in the Convention and divided the drugs covered by the instrument into the two groups mentioned above.

Chapter II (Articles 2–5) dealt with the estimate system. It provided for the submission by each country of annual estimates of the quantities of drugs needed for medical and scientific purposes, for conversion, and for the maintenance of reserve and government stocks to the Permanent Central Board. These estimates were to be examined by a Supervisory Body consisting of four members, one each appointed by the Opium Advisory Committee, the Permanent Central Board,

50. Memorandum by Caldwell to Hornbeck and Stuart J. Fuller, Sept. 14, 1931, SDR 511.4A6/447. For Delevingne's criticism and Anslinger's calm and reasoned reply, see *Records of the Narcotics Limitation Conference*, II, 37–38, 41–46.

51. For an analysis of the newspaper clippings from the Hearst press, see Helen H. Moorhead to Dr. Stanley Hornbeck, Dec. 14, 1931, SDR 511.4A6/481.

52. For Blanco's criticism see Anti-Opium Information Bureau, Geneva, *Communiqué No. 16* (Aug. 20, 1931) in 511.4A6/447. For Miss La Motte's statement see "Limiting Drug Manufacture," *The Nation*, CXXXIV (April 13, 1932), pp. 418–419; for Caldwell's replies to these criticisms see Caldwell's memoranda of Sept. 14, 1931, SDR 511.4A6/447, and of April 20, 1932, SDR 511.4A6/560.

53. Memorandum by Hornbeck to the Secretary of State, Sept. 23, 1931.

54. A convenient summary of the major provisions of the Convention, Protocol of Signature, and Final Act as well as the text of these are contained in the *Report of the American Delegation on the Narcotics Limitation Conference*, pp. 29–76. *Foreign Relations*, 1931, I, pp. 675–699 also carries the text of the Convention and the Protocol of Signature. All three documents are contained in *Records of the Narcotics Limitation Conference*, I, 367–421.

the Health Committee of the League, and the Office International d'Hygiène Publique, and by a secretariat provided by the Secretary General of the League. The Supervisory Body was empowered to make estimates for countries which failed to furnish them and to forward to the signatory powers a statement of the annual estimates of each country accompanied, if it so desired, by any comments it cared to make on them.

Chapter III (Articles 6–9) dealt with the limitation of manufacture. It specified that manufacture by each country was to be limited to the quantities stated in its estimates and quantities needed to fill export orders, minus imports and confiscated drugs used for domestic consumption or converted into other products.

Chapter IV (Articles 10–12) covered the subject of prohibitions and restrictions. It called for the prohibition of the export of heroin except at the request and on the responsibility of an importing country which did not manufacture the drug and which ensured that it would be used only for medical and scientific purposes. The production or manufacture of narcotic drugs of no scientific value was prohibited, and the control of newly discovered narcotic drugs was provided for.

Chapter V (Articles 13 and 14) dealt with the subject of control and provided for the application of provisions of the Geneva Convention, or measures in conformity with it, to the drugs listed in the Limitation Convention. The Permanent Central Board was authorized to check the import and export returns of governments, and in the likelihood that exports to a country would create a supply in excess of that country's estimates, further exports to that country were to cease for that particular year. In addition, the exportation of quantities of drugs of more than five kilograms to any country not applying the import certificate system was prohibited until authorization had been obtained from the Permanent Central Board.

Chapter VI (Articles 15–19) consisted of administrative provisions. The chapter called for the creation by each country of a special narcotics administration to apply the provisions of the Convention, to regulate, supervise, and control the trade in narcotic drugs, and to organize a campaign against drug addiction. In addition, strict supervision of the quantity of raw materials and manufactured drugs in the possession of each manufacturer was required, and the accumulation of quantities of raw products by a manufacturer in excess of the amount necessary for manufacture during the ensuing six months, unless under exceptional conditions as determined by the government, was prohibited. The chapter also required the strict supervision of the quantities of drugs and preparations produced, the destruction or conversion into nonnarcotic substances or the appropriation for medical or scientific use of confiscated drugs, the destruction or conversion of seized heroin, and the labeling of packages containing drugs as to the kind and percentage of the drug contained.

Chapter VII (Articles 20–34) contained general provisions relating to such matters as the exchange of information among the signatory powers, the sending of annual reports to the Permanent Central Board in regard to drugs used to make preparations for which export authorizations were not required, the settlement of disputes over the interpretation of the Convention, and the signing, ratification, and coming into force of the Convention. The Convention was to be open for signature until December 31, 1931, after which date it might be acceded to and ratifications might be deposited with the Secretary General of the League. The Convention was to come into force ninety days after the deposit of ratifications or the accession of twenty-five governments, including any four of the following: France, Germany, the United Kingdom, Japan, the Netherlands, Switzerland, Turkey, and the United States. The Protocol of Signature provided that if the Convention had not come into force by July 13, 1933, the Secretary General should so inform the Council of the League, which would either summon a new conference, which the signatory powers would be obligated to attend, or take other measures it considered necessary.

The Final Act consisted of the following ten recommendations to the League Council:

Creation of a single narcotics agency by each country;

Preparation by the Opium Advisory Committee of a model code for the application of the Convention;

Coverage of certain drugs not currently covered by the Geneva and Hague Conventions;

Establishment of government monopolies of narcotic drug transactions;

Conclusion of a convention for the prosecution and punishment of narcotic law violators;

Prohibition of the use of heroin;

Application of the system of control of the Geneva Convention to all preparations containing any of the drugs listed in Group I of the Limitation Convention;

Exclusion of substances covered by the Geneva and Narcotics Limitation Conventions from the benefits of the most-favored-nation clause in future commercial treaties;

Publication of certain statistics prepared by the League Secretariat concerning the world medical and scientific requirements of morphine, heroin, and cocaine;

Awarding of prizes for research into possible substitutes for addiction-producing drugs.

The American government thoroughly approved of the Convention. In addition to having secured most of the points it advocated, the government realized that because the United States was the worst sufferer among Western countries from illicit traffic in drugs fed by the excess manufactured in Europe, the strict control over the manufacture and distribution of these drugs in European and other countries as provided for by the Convention would make the United States the greatest beneficiary of its provisions. Many of the features of the Convention were similar to American legislation, and all were in accord with the American system of control. American drug manufacturers found the Convention "highly satisfactory" and private Americans interested in the narcotics problem hailed it as a great advance over the previous agreements.[55] For these reasons the State Department was anxious to have the Convention signed and ratified by the United States as quickly as possible.[56]

Two questions not necessarily related to the narcotics problem still appeared capable of complicating matters. One was the perennial issue of the nature of proper American relations with the League of Nations. The other was whether American adherence to a convention to which the Soviet Union would also probably become a party would constitute de facto recognition of the Soviet regime. Closely related to these two

55. Wilson (Berne) to the Secretary of State, July 14, 1931, SDR 511.4A6/395. As already indicated, the greatest dissatisfaction with the Convention was expressed by the Hearst press and Miss La Motte. In her article condemning the Convention, Miss La Motte invalidated most of her criticisms by expressing the fear that the Convention would not be ratified because "it was so good that the scoundrels in the manufacturing countries would never stand for it." See above, p. 250.

56. State Department press release, July 17, 1931, SDR 511.4A6/412.

questions was the problem of the attitude the Senate would choose when the treaty was submitted to it for ratification.

Since various provisions of the Convention were to be carried out by the Council and Secretary General of the League, and by the Permanent Central Board and the Supervisory Body through the instrumentality of the League Secretariat, the question of whether American endorsement of these arrangements would involve the United States in such intimate relations with the League as to jeopardize Senate approval of the Convention was a disturbing issue to the State Department. Yet examination of the issue led to the conclusion that the United States had already acquiesced in activities of the League similar to those provided in the Convention. The American government had signed the Protocol of Accession to the Permanent Court of International Justice under which the United States might participate in the proceedings of the Council or the Assembly for the election of judges to the Court. The United States had also ratified the Convention for the Abolition of Import and Export restrictions, which provided for the communication of the parties with each other through the medium of the Secretary General, the settlement of disputes concerning the convention by referral to the Permanent Court of International Justice, and the receipt of ratifications, accessions, denunciations, and requests by the Secretary General. Finally, the United States had already cooperated with the organs of the League concerned with narcotics matters. Thus on the issue of association with the League, the State Department concluded that ample precedents existed for validly assuming that the Convention could be safely signed. Furthermore, Senate reaction to the Convention would furnish the Department with guidelines on how to proceed on other League-connected matters, especially in regard to the negotiations on disarmament and participation in the Permanent Disarmament Commission.[57]

Extensive consideration of the relationship of signature of the Convention to recognition of the Soviet regime did not take place until after the United States had signed the instrument. When the American delegation signed the Convention and the Final Protocol on July 18, 1931,

57. For the discussions leading up to this conclusion see Minister Wilson to the Secretary of State, July 14, 1931, SDR 511.4A6/395; memorandum by Stuart J. Fuller to the Division of Western European Affairs, July 16, 1931, SDR 511.4A6/407; memorandum by Pierrepont Moffat of the Division of Western European Affairs, July 15, 1931, SDR 511.4A6/406; and memorandum by the Division of Western European Affairs, July 16, 1931, SDR 511.4A6/408.

thirty-five other countries had already signed, including such major manufacturing states as Germany, Great Britain, France, Japan, the Netherlands, and Switzerland. The United States did not sign the Final Act, since this consisted of recommendations to the Council of the League which the government thought it would be improper for the United States, not being a member of the League, to make. Instead, the United States assured the president of the conference that its failure to sign the Final Act "should not be construed as indicating any lack of sympathy with the general objectives of the recommendations themselves."[58]

Despite the warm approval given the Convention, six reservations were attached to the American signature of the instrument. In the first two the United States reserved the right to impose measures stricter than those in the Convention for the control of the domestic and international traffic in narcotic substances and of the transit of these products through its territories. In resolutions three and four the United States objected to the period allowed in which statistics of imports and exports were to be submitted to the Permanent Central Board as too short, and complained that the necessity of designating separately the quantities of drugs purchased or imported for government purposes was impractical. The last two reservations were aimed at the Soviet Union and were designed to forestall the misconception that American signature of the Convention and participation in its provisions constituted de facto recognition of the Communist regime. The reservations therefore stipulated that

The plenipotentiaries of the United States of America formally declare that the signing of the convention for limiting the manufacture and regulating the distribution of narcotic drugs, by them on the part of the United States of America, on this date, is not to be construed to mean that the Government of the United States of America recognizes a regime or entity which signs or accedes to the convention as the government of a country when that regime or entity is not recognized by the Government of the United States of America as the government of that country.

. . . The plenipotentiaries of the United States of America further declare that the participation of the United States of America in the convention . . . does not involve any contractual obligation on the part of the United States of America to a country represented by a regime or entity which the Government of the United States of America does not recognize

58. *Report of the American Delegation on the Narcotics Limitation Conference,* p. 10. *Foreign Relations,* 1931, I, 673.

as the government of that country, until such country has a government recognized by the United States of America.[59]

The necessity and practicality of making these reservations in regard to the Soviet Union were the subject of much discussion and some controversy in the State Department. The American minister to Switzerland, Hugh Wilson, urged that these reservations be withdrawn. He maintained that Russia was not contemplating signing the Convention, and that even if it did, logic would demand that the United States attach similar reservations to all multilateral treaties which it had signed or might sign in the future and to which Russia might be expected to accede. Furthermore, he felt that the procedure followed would cause a problem with the Senate in regard to more vital treaties and might also discourage Russian adherence to future treaties to which her accession would be essential or desirable.[60] Dr. Wallace McClure, Assistant Chief of the Treaty Division, concurred in Wilson's views. He maintained that the reservations were unnecessary and that "unnecessary provisions which complicate treaties should be avoided." He also pointed out that the actual practice of the United States in regard to this issue was inconsistent in that the United States had signed in 1928 the Kellogg-Briand Pact of Paris for the Renunciation of War without such reservations even though it knew that Russia would be invited immediately to adhere.[61] McClure's views were also those of the Chief of the Division of Far Eastern Affairs, Stanley K. Hornbeck. Hornbeck had doubted the wisdom of the reservations from the beginning, but had approved the instructions to the American delegation containing them on the grounds that they represented a matter involving general policy which he presumed had already been decided on. However, Hornbeck believed that it would be unwise to withdraw the reservations since they had already been made, but that in the future, if America's overall policy in regard to Russia was clear, such reservations should not be made.[62]

It had been the policy of the American government not to recognize the Soviet government ever since that regime had been established. There was no conclusive authoritative opinion on whether participation in a multilateral convention implied recognition of the other par-

---

59. *Report of the American Delegation on the Narcotics Limitation Conference,* pp. 9–10. See also *Foreign Relations,* 1931, I, 672–673.
60. Wilson to the Secretary of State, July 1, 1931, SDR 511.4A6/413.
61. Memorandum by McClure to Frank X. Ward, July 15, 1931, SDR 511.4A6/421.
62. Memorandum by Hornbeck, July 25, 1931, SDR 511.4A6/423.

ticipants, but the view that such was not the case was supported by most writers on the subject as well as by international practice. The State Department had also generally adopted this view. However, it had found the policy of attaching reservations to conventions to which the Soviet Union was or might become a party to the effect that American signature, ratification, and implementation of such conventions did not imply recognition of the Communist regime, a desirable means of preventing a misconstruction of the United States' position. This procedure had been first adopted in May of 1925 in relation to American participation in the Arms Traffic Conference and was subsequently endorsed by the Department in the same year when the issue was raised as a matter of policy. After this date, the treaties signed by both the United States and Russia to which such reservations were made were the International Sanitary Convention signed on June 21, 1926; the Kellogg-Briand Pact; the Convention for the Safety of Life at Sea, signed on May 31, 1929; and the International Load Line Convention, signed on July 5, 1930. The only convention signed by both powers during this period to which such reservations were not made was the Convention for the Suppression of Counterfeiting Currency signed at Geneva on April 20, 1929. On this occasion the question of reservations was not even considered.[63] Thus since 1925, American policy and practice on this matter had been relatively unvarying.

To maintain the relative consistency of this policy, the State Department, on the advice of the chiefs of the Division of Eastern European Affairs, the Treaty Division, and the Solicitor's Office, decided that the reservations to the Narcotics Limitation Convention should not be withdrawn. Nevertheless, they proposed that such reservations should be considered desirable only in the case of the signature or probable signature of a treaty by both the United States and an unrecognized regime and not in cases of the later adherence of an unrecognized regime to a treaty already signed by the United States.[64] Other factors influencing the Department's decision were the views that withdrawal of the reservations might be interpreted as the adoption of a policy by the United States contrary to that expressed

63. For this summary of American policy to 1931, see the memorandum by Frank X. Ward, July 24, 1931, SDR 511.4A6/419. See also *Foreign Relations*, 1931, I, 674.

64. *Ibid*. See also memorandum by Robert F. Kelly, Chief of the Division of Eastern European Affairs, to Ward, July 25, 1931, SDR 511.4A6/422.

in the reservations, an interpretation which "might give rise to undesirable public discussion," and that since the reservations merely repeated the well-known position of the United States, Russia was not likely to refuse to sign or ratify the Convention merely because of them. Furthermore, the Senate had already approved two treaties containing such reservations, and another treaty with similar reservations was currently before that body.[65]

The Russians did not entirely ignore the American reservations. On July 22, 1931, the Moscow *Izvestiia*, in an article entitled "A Clumsy Policy of 'Stipulations,'" blamed the American action on the government's attempt to indicate a policy that would refute the contention made by John Bassett Moore in 1930 that the signing of the Kellogg-Briand Pact by both the United States and Russia constituted recognition of the Soviet government. It castigated the American reservations as part of the ridiculous and ineffectual effort of the United States to aid its European debtors and American bankers by the manifestation of an unfriendly attitude toward the Soviet Union.[66] Several months later the Soviet government explained its refusal to sign the Limitation Convention not only because of what it considered to be the Convention's inadequacy, but also because of the refusal of the United States to enter into contractual relations with the Soviet Union on the "purely humanitarian" problem with which the Convention sought to deal.[67] American recognition of the Soviet government (in November 1933), however, was not followed until two years later by Russian adherence to the Convention.[68]

Indicative of the general endorsement of the Convention by the United States was the ease with which ratification was achieved. Var-

---

65. *Foreign Relations*, 1931, I, 674–675. Another argument presented in the Department against the withdrawal of the reservations was that if both the United States and Russia became parties to the Convention without these reservations, the United States would be bound to allow the transit of narcotic substances through American territory to and from Russia; and that as transit shipments were the favorite method of smuggling manufactured narcotics, Russia, which was "notorious for its disregard of contractual obligations" and very badly in need of cash, might take advantage of the situation in order to promote smuggling into the United States to secure cash. See memorandum by Stuart J. Fuller, July 24, 1931, SDR 511.4A6/420.

66. Translation enclosed in Felix Cole, Chargé d'Affaires (Riga, Latvia) to the Secretary of State, July 28, 1931, SDR 511.4A6/433.

67. Winthrop S. Greene, Secretary of the American Legation (Berne), to the Secretary of State, April 14, 1932, SDR 511.4A6/559.

68. Stanley Hawks, Secretary of the American Legation (Berne), to the Secretary of State, Nov. 25, 1935, SDR 511.4A6/1421.

ious segments of American society interested in the drug question—the drug interests, religious and humanitarian organizations, labor groups, antinarcotics organizations, and political groups—all urged prompt American ratification of the instrument.[69] The Convention, contrary to expectations, sailed smoothly through the Senate. The Senate Foreign Relations Committee, under the chairmanship of the isolationist and anti-League Senator Borah, manifested much interest in the document. Many questions were asked as to the nature and extent of the narcotics problem in the United States, the probable effect of the Convention upon it, the sources of the illicit traffic, and the purpose and effect of the American, Japanese, and Swedish reservations to the Convention. It was pointed out to the committee that the only objection to the Convention by anyone in the United States was to the failure to provide for the absolute destruction of all drugs seized in the illicit traffic. It was contended, however, that this objection was not valid in that confiscated drugs were useful for the accumulation of emergency war stores, for during World War I the United States had been dependent largely on England for drug supplies. No hostility was displayed toward the Convention by any member of the committee, and it was approved unanimously.[70] In presenting the treaty to the full Senate for ratification, Senator Borah called it "an exceedingly important treaty," and Senator Robinson of Arkansas commended it as representing "a distinct forward movement in the control of the manufacture of narcotic drugs and the distribution of such drugs through the channels of commerce."[71] There was no opposition to ratification expressed in the Senate, and that body approved it unanimously on March 31, 1932. It was signed by the President about a week later.

The United States deposited its ratification of the Convention with the Secretariat of the League on April 28, 1932, and was thus the second nation to do so.[72] It then set about the task of helping to secure the ratifications and accessions of other nations. From March 18, 1932,

69. For statements of representative groups see SDR 511.4A6/473, 477, 478, 495, 497, 503, 505, 509, 516, 521, 523, 528.

70. For the account of the reception accorded the Convention in the Foreign Relations Committee, see memorandum by Caldwell to Rogers and Hornbeck, March 30, 1932, SDR 511.4A6/553.

71. *Congressional Record*, 72d Cong., 1st Sess., 1932, LXXV, Part 7; see p. 7101 and 7207 for Borah's comments, and p. 7208 for Robinson's statement and Senate approval of the Convention.

72. Nicaragua was the first on March 16, 1932.

to April 1, 1933, the State Department sent a series of communications to other governments urging them to ratify or accede to the Convention and to appeal to other countries to do likewise.[73] The Department also pressured the Secretary General to work toward the same end, but ever mindful of the possible hazards of a too intimate association with the League, it refused to permit the circulation by the League Secretariat of an American appeal for early ratification.[74] The purpose of these activities was to secure enough accessions to the Convention by April 13, 1933, to enable the instrument to go into effect ninety days later without the necessity of convening another conference. These efforts met with success, for as early as April 10 twenty-nine states had ratified or acceded to the Convention, including the required number of manufacturing countries—France, Germany, Great Britain, Turkey, and the United States.[75] The Convention was thus to go into force on July 9, 1933, ninety days after the necessary twenty-five ratifications and accessions had been made. It was generally acknowledged that the activities of the United States were primarily responsible for this achievement.[76]

The Narcotics Limitation Convention, when put into effect among a sufficient number of powers and properly applied, effectively achieved its purpose—the limitation of the legitimate manufacture of narcotic drugs to the world's medical and scientific needs and the restriction of the quantity of these drugs available to each country. It therefore constituted a significant advance in the antidrug campaign.[77] At the same time it also represented an important development in international law and administration. As the Twelfth Assembly of the League of Nations pointed out: "This is the first time that an

73. For these representations see SDR 511.4A6/862–866, 909–915; memorandum by Fuller to Undersecretary Phillips, March 9, 1933, SDR 511.4A6/835; and *Foreign Relations*, 1932, I, *General*, 897–898.

74. *Foreign Relations*, 1932, I, *General*, 897–900.

75. State Department press release, April 10, 1933, SDR 511.4A6/981.

76. Blanco to Cordell Hull, April 10, 1933, SDR 511.4A6/963; American Legation (Berne) to the Secretary of State, April 12, 1933, SDR 511.4A6/1006; and Secretary of State Hull to Fuller, April 12, 1933, SDR 511.4A6/984. The going into force of the Convention was heralded in the United States with speeches and a radio broadcast in a celebration sponsored from New York City by the World Narcotics Defense Association, a private antidrug organization headed by Captain Richmond P. Hobson, a former naval officer and Congressman and Spanish-American War hero. See the *New York Times*, July 10, 1933, p. 15.

77. Bertil A. Renborg, *International Drug Control: A Study of International Administration By and Through the League of Nations* (Washington, D.C.: Carnegie Endowment for International Peace, 1947), p. 24.

industry has been brought under international regulation, and that manufacture in its economic aspect has been wholly subordinated to higher humanitarian and moral aims."[78] The parties to the Convention gave up a not inconsiderable degree of their authority when they agreed to extensive restrictions on their right to manufacture and distribute narcotic drugs. Moreover, by providing for an embargo on exports of drugs to states which imported in excess of their requirements, the Convention provided for the coercion of noncooperative states.[79]

For the United States, the Convention was significant in a special way. It gave the country a legal basis for cooperation with the League on the narcotics problem, and through such cooperation, for reassuming its leadership in the international movement. It was thus only through the relinquishment of the goal of avoiding entanglement with the League that the United States was able to enter once again the vanguard of the campaign to control the traffic in dangerous drugs.

Having committed itself to a degree of collaboration with the League, the United States nevertheless sought to confine this collaboration to what it considered to be proper limits. In implementing the Convention, the United States tried to cooperate fully with the international administrative agencies specified in that instrument. On the other hand, the government sought to make these agencies as independent of the League as possible. The two agencies primarily involved were the Permanent Central Board and the Supervisory Body. The Supervisory Body had been established under the Limitation Convention, and as the United States was a party to this treaty, there was little hesitation as to whether the United States should fully cooperate with that body, even to influencing the selection of its members. The appointment of an American to the agency was regarded as crucial to the creation of "an international balance of control" and to the prevention of severe criticism of the government by Americans interested in the drug question.[80] Of the four bodies which were to appoint the members of the Supervisory Body—the Opium Advisory Committee, the Permanent Central Board, the Health Committee of the League, and the Office International d'Hygiène Publique at Paris—the United States had membership only on the last. But it was through the Permanent Central Board that the United States, by tactful influence,

78. Quoted in *ibid.*, p. 26.   79. *Ibid.*, p. 25.
80. Anslinger to Ernest L. Ives, May 4, 1933, SDR 511.4A6/4.

obtained the selection of Herbert L. May, already a member of the board, to membership on the Supervisory Body.[81]

The Permanent Central Board had been established under the Geneva Convention of 1925 and had been given additional functions by the Narcotics Limitation Convention. Participation in the nomination and selection of its members raised a more difficult problem. The United States began to consider this matter as early as September 1933, as the terms of the current members were to expire on January 1, 1934. Although the United States had cooperated fully with the board in the matter of furnishing information, it had balked at submitting nominations and sitting with the Council of the League in electing its members. This refusal was based on dissatisfaction with the Geneva Convention, the assumption that the board was in reality an organ of the League and would therefore lack the independence necessary for the vigorous and objective performance of its duties, and fear of the domestic political repercussions that might ensue from American participation in the work of the League Council.[82] Under the new situation created by the Limitation Convention, the first objection was considered to be no longer valid. The Convention had assigned additional duties to the board, and the United States was a party to the Convention. This constituted American approval of the current international narcotics policy and the role assigned to the Central Board in carrying it out. As to the second objection, the United States had become convinced by 1931 that the Central Board, as evidenced by its conduct, was capable of resisting undue interference in its work by the League, despite the fact that the League Council chose its members and the League Secretariat provided its clerical staff. Contributing to this confidence in the board's ability to be independent was the fact that the members of the board did not sit as representatives of governments but in their private capacities, and they received no compensation beyond a small allowance for expenses.[83]

The third point, however, was considered to be still a matter for concern. The appointment of an American representative to sit and

---

81. Consul Gilbert (Geneva) to the Secretary of State, May 10, 1933; Fuller to Ives and Hornbeck, May 10, 1933, SDR 511.4A6A/13.

82. See above, pp. 220–221.

83. For the new attitude of the State Department toward the feasibility of American representation in the Council for the election of members to the Central Board, see memorandum by Stuart J. Fuller to Pierrepont Moffat, Chief of the Division of Western European Affairs, Sept. 5, 1933, SDR 511.4A2A/300.

vote with the Council would constitute a new step in the relations between the United States and the League. The American consul at Geneva had sat with the Council in 1931 to discuss the Manchurian affair, but he did not vote. The question of the propriety of such action did not then arise.[84] The expediency of taking the step now contemplated was not confined to the question of American relations with the League on narcotics. It also had to be considered in connection with the general subject of overall American relations with the League, and more particularly, with the probable effect of such action upon the chances for ratification, without crippling amendments, of the World Court Protocols of Accession which the United States had signed and which provided for American participation in the proceedings of either the League Council or the Assembly for the election of the judges of the Court. In the opinion of the State Department, American participation in the selection of the members of the Permanent Central Board offered "an excellent opportunity" for determining the probable reaction of the American public to the carrying out of the World Court protocols. Considerable adverse reaction to American cooperation in the selection of the board would indicate to the government the inadvisability of currently pushing the World Court issue. If not much interest was aroused, "a useful precedent in favor of the provisions of the Protocol of Accession to the World Court" would be established.[85]

On the basis of these considerations and the conviction that America's position as the largest legitimate consumer of narcotic drugs and the worst sufferer from the illicit traffic gave it a vital interest in having an American on the board, the United States decided to submit nominations for membership on the board and to appoint the American minister to Switzerland to sit with the Council "solely in an electoral capacity."[86] At the meeting of the Council in October 1933, Wilson supported, as instructed, the reelection of all eight members of the board, and particularly that of Herbert L. May, with whose work the State Department and other interested officials of the American government were highly pleased.[87] With the exception of the

84. Memorandum by Fuller, Sept. 12, 1933, SDR 511.4A2A/303.
85. *Ibid*. See also memorandum by Moffat to Fuller, Sept. 6, 1933, SDR 511.4A2A/301.
86. Secretary of State Hull to the American Legation (Berne), Sept. 18, 1933, SDR 511.4A2A/298.
87. Memorandum by Fuller to Moffat, Sept. 5, 1933, SDR 511.4A2A/300. Memorandum by Fuller to Assistant Secretary of State Harry F. Payer, Sept. 8, 1933, SDR 511.4A2A/302.

selection of a replacement for a member who declined to serve again, the old board was reelected. Thereafter, the American minister at Berne sat with the League Council in all cases in which members were elected to the board. The principal qualification which the United States always stressed for such members was their "complete independence" of their respective governments.[88] This, however, was not entirely possible, for when Germany and Italy withdrew from the League in 1934 and 1938, respectively, and Japan severed all connections with League-connected organizations in 1939, they also recalled their nationals on the Central Board. In each case the United States urged these nations to continue to cooperate with the board, maintaining that the board was independent of the League, and pointing out how the United States, not a League member, nevertheless fully collaborated in the selection and work of the board.[89]

By 1939, then, the United States had become one of the major champions of the activities of both the Central Board and the Supervisory Body. When the War in Europe threatened to interrupt their work, the government expressed interest in the urgent necessity for arrangements for their continued functioning. The United States asserted that "it is upon the operations of these two boards, supplementing and coordinating the efforts of individual nations, that the entire fabric of international drug control ultimately and principally rests."[90] During the war the two agencies carried on their operations from the United States.

The United States did not regard its cooperation with the Permanent Central Board and the Supervisory Body as constituting a fundamental alteration in its policy toward the League. In fact, the government insistently proclaimed that these bodies were independent of the League. It sought to insure and bolster that autonomy in every way possible. Making financial contributions to support the activities of these agencies was one of the principal ways in which the United States

88. Secretary of State Hull to the American Delegate (Wilson), Sept. 27, 1933, SDR 511.4A2A/307. For American participation in subsequent elections to 1939, see Wilson (Geneva) to the Secretary of State, Sept. 26, 1935, SDR 511.4A2A/486; State Department press release, Sept. 2, 1938, SDR 511.4A2A/792; the Secretary of State to the Secretary of the Treasury, Jan. 31, 1939, SDR 511.4A2A/844.

89. William Phillips (for the Secretary of State) to the American Embassy (Berlin), April 9, 1934, SDR 511.4A2A/346; Consul Howard Bucknell, Jr. (Geneva) to the Secretary of State, Jan. 17, 1938, SDR 511.4A2A/722; and the Secretary of State to Ambassador Joseph C. Grew (Tokyo), May 8, 1939, SDR 511.4A2A/875.

90. State Department press release, Oct. 24, 1939, SDR 511.4A2A/916.

tried to do this. There were ample precedents for such contributions. Since 1922 the United States had paid to the League Secretariat a share of the extraordinary (secretarial) expenses of the League equal to that of Great Britain, the largest contributing League member, for conferences, commissions, and committees in which the United States had participated.[91] By the end of 1937 nearly $70,000 had been expended, either from specific appropriations or from the State Department's emergency fund, for this purpose.[92] There had been no public outcry against these expenditures. No money had been contributed, however, for the regular work of the League except for the secretarial expenses of the Opium Advisory Committee.

In 1934 the State Department decided that the United States should help defray the financial expenses of the Permanent Central Board, the Supervisory Body, and the Opium Section of the League Secretariat. This decision was based on two considerations: that as a party to the Narcotics Limitation Convention, the United States was morally and contractually obligated to help pay the cost of its implementation and that such payment was necessary to establish and carry out the principle that the operation of the Convention, especially in regard to the Central Board and the Supervisory Body, was not subject to the budgetary control of the League. The latter consideration was regarded as the most important. The United States had been much disturbed by the action of the Supervisory Commission of the League in striking from the League budget in the fall of 1932 sums for the functioning of these two bodies on the grounds that the Convention would not likely come into force in 1933, or even if it did, provisions for their expenses could be held over until 1934. The American government feared that the League, through its control over finances, was trying to undermine the independence of these organs. In response to this action of the League, the American representative on the Advisory Committee, Stuart J. Fuller, contended that the expense of the imple-

---

91. Among these were the Arms Traffic Conference of 1925, the Economic Conference of 1927, the Conference on Communications and Transit, 1927, the Conference on Import and Export Prohibitions and Restrictions of 1927, the Preparatory Commission on the Limitation of Armaments of 1926–1927, the General Disarmament Conference of 1932–1935, the International Monetary and Economic Conference of 1933–1934, the Opium Advisory Committee, and the Geneva Opium Conference of 1924–25. See memorandum of the Bureau of Accounts, State Department to Carr, March 12, 1929, SDR 500.C3/29; and memorandum by Achilles, Division of European Affairs, Dec. 28, 1937, SDR 500.C3/129.

92. Memorandum by Achilles, Dec. 28, 1937, SDR 500.C3/129.

mentation of the Narcotics Limitation Convention should be borne by the parties to it, and not by the League. He argued further that the work of the Permanent Central Board and the Supervisory Body, as independent agencies, could not be blocked by the refusal of any League commission to advance funds. As a result of this protest, the Supervisory Commission restored the funds to the budget.[93]

The United States remained suspicious of the motives of the League. These suspicions were strengthened when by the spring of 1935 the League still had not provided an independent staff for the Supervisory Body and from the American viewpoint had also failed to provide sufficient funds for an adequate staff for the Permanent Central Board.[94] The United States desired to contribute to the financial support of these organs and the Opium Section of the League Secretariat in such a way as to make it clear that the payments were being made as part of its obligation of implementing the Limitation Convention and not as a contribution to the general funds of the League.[95] It was decided that the United States should pay its proportionate share of the expenses of the body—the same as the British share of about 10 to 11 percent of the total—from the time the Convention came into force in 1933. This amounted to $12,086 for the calendar years 1933 and 1934 and was included in the urgent Deficiency Bill of 1935.

The government would have preferred and did try to make the payments directly to the Central Board and the Supervisory Body, but did not object to transmitting them to the Secretary General so long as they were not regarded as contributions to the League's general funds. The Secretary General, however, refused to permit the acceptance of the payments except as a voluntary contribution to these funds to be made directly to him. He maintained that the two bodies had no financial autonomy and were thus not empowered to authorize any person to receive payments in their behalf. His maximum concession to the American position was to describe the payments as a voluntary contribution towards the reimbursement of the cost of implementing the Narcotics Limitation Convention.[96] The United States

93. Memorandum by Fuller to Carr, July 5, 1934, SDR 4A6/1267.
94. Memorandum by Fuller, March 6, 1935, SDR 511.4A6/1371.
95. William Phillips to Minister Wilson (Berne), Oct. 14, 1935, SDR 511.4A2A/494; Carr to Wilson, Dec. 2, 1935, SDR 511.4A2A/512; and the Secretary of State to Wilson, Dec. 26, 1935, SDR 511.4A2A/536.
96. Stanley Hawks, Chargé d'Affaires of the American Legation (Berne), to the Secretary of State, Feb. 12, 1936, SDR 511.4A6/1446; July 1, 1935, SDR 511.4A6/1388.

refused to accept this formula, taking exception to the use of the terms *voluntary contribution*. Therefore no agreement could be arrived at. When the United States still insisted on the acceptance of its principle by sending the payments to the chairmen of the Central Board and the Supervisory Body in September 1925, the money was refused.[97] Further negotiations between the State Department and the Secretary General proved unsuccessful. The matter was finally turned over to the Supervisory Commission,[98] but the issue was still unsettled at the close of 1939. Meanwhile, the United States decided to pay the League a lump sum annually for its share in those activities, except narcotics, in which the United States participated officially, semiofficially, and unofficially which were of interest and benefit to the United States.[99] Narcotics activities were not included in these payments, for the United States refused to surrender its position on the matter and therefore preferred to treat the issue as a separate question.[100] There the matter rested until the eve of World War II, when it lost all significance along with the whole question of American relations with the League.

The important point to be remembered is that through the Narcotics Limitation Conference and the implementation of the resultant convention, the United States had regained its place of prominence in the international drug control movement. However, this achievement came only at what turned out to be the rather insignificant price of giving up its opposition to closer cooperation with the League of Nations. Increasing participation in League affairs was by no means confined to the drug problem, but was representative throughout the 1930's of American practice in other matters as well.[101]

97. C. M. P. Crass, District Accounting and Disbursing Office (Paris), to the Secretary of State, Sept. 5, 1935, SDR 511.4A6/1410; March 25, 1936, SDR 511.4A6/1449.

98. Memorandum by Achilles, Sept. 16, 1937, SDR 511.4A6A/141½.

99. Memorandum by Achilles, Aug. 11, 1938, SDR 500.C3/136; the Secretary of State to Howard Bucknell, Jr. (Geneva), April 19, 1939, SDR 500.C3/141A; Bucknell to the Secretary of State, May 4, 1939, SDR 500.C3/142.

100. Assistant Secretary of State G. S. Messersmith to Bucknell, May 6, 1938, SDR 500.C3/136.

101. Ursula P. Hubbard, "The Cooperation of the United States with the League of Nations, 1931–1936," *International Conciliation*, No. 329 (April, 1937).

Chapter ten

American cooperation with the League on the Far Eastern problem and illicit traffic

The trend toward greater collaboration between the United States and the League of Nations in the 1930's that was inaugurated by the Conference on Manufacture and the resultant Narcotics Limitation Convention embraced all phases of the drug problem. The United States played a prominent role in the deliberations of the League on such subjects as the traffic in and the use of prepared opium, the illicit traffic, and the excess production of raw materials—the suppression of which constituted the American program as laid down in the Geneva Conference of 1924–1925. Aside from the international conferences on these matters, the increased participation of the United States in League narcotic affairs was most evident in the work of the Opium Advisory Committee. As pointed out earlier, relations between the committee and the United States cooled considerably after the Geneva Conferences. By 1930, however, there was evidence of a tendency on the part of the American government to adopt a more cordial attitude toward this body. As early as 1929 the United States had decided to make a financial contribution to help defray the cost of printing the minutes of the committee's sessions. This was not a mere gesture but was designed to facilitate the prompt publication and distribution of these minutes so that public interest in the activities of the Advisory Committee would be maintained constantly.[1] Publicity was considered to be the most important weapon in the fight against the drug evil.

Much more indicative of the modification of the attitude of the American government toward the committee was the change in the

1. For the reasons underlying the American decision to make this contribution, see memorandum by John K. Caldwell to Nelson T. Johnson, Aug. 9, 1929, SDR 500.C1197/303; Aug. 17, 1929, SDR 500.C1197/304; Secretary of State Stimson to the American Legation (Berne), Aug. 21, 1929, SDR 500.C1197/304a.

designation and character of the American representative to that organ. Down to 1930 the American representatives had been variously designated as serving in an unofficial and/or consultative capacity, or as unofficial observers. For a lesser period, Americans serving with other League committees had been similarly described, but the realization of the absurdity of characterizing a representative of the government as unofficial caused an abandonment of this practice.[2] The incongruity was particularly apparent with reference to service on the Advisory Committee where, in most cases, the American representative was a regular official of the State Department. Therefore, in December 1929 the Department adopted the procedure that had been applied a few years earlier to Americans serving on other League committees, of instructing the American emissaries to serve in an "expert and advisory capacity."[3]

This new designation did not essentially change the legal relationship of the United States to the Advisory Committee, but it was accompanied by the renewal of more active participation in the committee's work. While under the existing arrangement the American representative could not vote, place questions on the agenda, nor act as chairman or vice-chairman of the committee, he could fully engage in the committee's deliberations, serve as chairman of the subcommittees, and act as rapporteur. The United States preferred this arrangement to having full membership on the committee. It viewed its limited representation as giving it the independence and liberty of action which it desired, especially since the majority of the most influential members of the committee often did not see eye to eye with the American representative. Being unable to vote, the American representative could dissociate himself and his government from any of the decisions or actions that the committee might take. The State Department also felt that the position of the United States on the committee was actually strengthened by the inability of the members of the committee to take the regular attendance of an American representative for granted. As to the matter of getting questions placed on the agenda, the United States experienced no difficulty in securing the good offices of other governments for this purpose. Thus several approaches which members of the committee and League officials made to the American representative

2. Memorandum by Caldwell to the Division of Western European Affairs, Dec. 5, 1929, SDR 500.C1197/631.
3. Johnson to Caldwell, Dec. 26, 1929, SDR 500.C1197/330a.

after 1931 as to the possibility of the United States accepting full membership were not seriously considered.[4] The State Department took the position that such a step should not be contemplated until the policy of the committee was more in accord with American views, especially in regard to the limitation of the production of raw materials.[5]

The degree of influence which the United States exerted on the Advisory Committee depended very largely on the personality of the American representative and the extent to which he was thoroughly grounded in narcotics matters. During the interregnum in American leadership after the Geneva conferences the American representatives were either unqualified or were prohibited by instructions from playing a commanding role. This situation was changed during the thirties. John K. Caldwell, who had performed most commendably in the Conference on Manufacture and who was largely responsible for nudging the State Department toward the resumption of a more active role in cooperation with the League in the narcotics movement, was succeeded in 1932 as American representative on the Advisory Committee and as the principal officer in the State Department concerned with the problem by Stuart J. Fuller. Prior to 1930 the narcotics work in the State Department had been handled as a part-time matter by one officer in the Division of Far Eastern Affairs. From July 1930 to June 1932 Caldwell and Fuller spent most of their time on this work. From July 1932 to July 1934 Fuller worked alone, with the occasional assistance of a field officer, while attending the sessions of the Opium Advisory Committee. After 1934 the narcotics work became a full-time job for two and later three officers of the Department. As Assistant Chief of the Division of Far Eastern Affairs, Fuller continued to head up the work. From 1932 on, Fuller, accompanied occasionally by Harry S. Anslinger, the Commissioner of Narcotics, represented the United States on the Advisory Committee. In 1935 he was made the regular representative of the United States on the committee.[6] Fuller, as his State Department and narcotics associates were quick to

4. Memorandum by Stuart J. Fuller to J. Pierrepont Moffat and Stanley K. Hornbeck, Jan. 27, 1934, SDR 500.C1197/663.
5. *Ibid.*
6. For a summary of the handling of the narcotics work in the State Department and of American representation on the Advisory Committee to 1939 see *ibid.*; memorandum by Hornbeck, Aug. 24, 1935, SDR 500.C 1197/894; and memorandum by George A. Morlock to R. Walton Moore, March 7, 1939, SDR 500.C 1197/1302.

acknowledge, brought boundless energy and devotion to the drug problem. He worked "incessantly at it, seven days a week, and with definite and very great efficiency."[7] He made the role of the American representative on the Advisory Committee a meaningful one, and through his activity on that body he demonstrated that the United States was once again the leader in the international campaign to suppress the abusive use of dangerous drugs.

One of the subjects to which Fuller gave a great deal of attention in the discussions of the Advisory Committee was the narcotics traffic in the Far East. In the thirties the Far Eastern drug situation had worsened to the extent of embracing not only the older problems of prepared opium and the contraband traffic in drugs manufactured in the West and Japan, but also the newer circumstance by which the Far East developed into the major source of illicit trafficking in manufactured drugs and raw materials to the West. After 1932 these problems, old and new, became matters of increasing concern to the international community, and Fuller took the lead in the Advisory Committee of pushing the policy of constant exposure of the situation and of calling for immediate and specific remedies.

The problem of suppressing the traffic in and use of prepared opium had been left somewhat in abeyance by the Geneva Agreement of 1925. In essence, except for minor measures to restrict the use of the drug and to control its transport, the Agreement left the existing situation undisturbed. Provisions were made, however, for a subsequent review of the situation not later than 1929. In August 1928 the British government, having experienced great difficulty in carrying out its obligations under the Hague Convention because of the illicit traffic stemming from China and the importation of Persian opium into the Straits Settlement, proposed to the League of Nations that a commission of inquiry be sent to the Far East to make "a fresh on the spot examination" of the drug traffic there.[8] The League Council and Assembly promptly endorsed the proposal, and the commission was appointed by the Council in March 1929.

In October 1928 the League Assembly queried the United States

7. Memorandum by Hornbeck, Aug. 24, 1935, SDR 500.C 1197/894.
8. Sir Eric Drummond to Hugh Wilson, Oct. 16, 1928, enclosed in Wilson to the Secretary of State, Oct. 18, 1928, SDR 500.C 1197/233. See also memorandum by Johnson to the Secretary of State, April 17, 1929, SDR 500.C 1197/273½.

whether the proposed commission would be permitted to visit the Philippine Islands.[9] This inquiry aroused considerable suspicion as to the real purpose of the commission. There was a view held in the State Department and by Americans associated with the international work on the drug problem that the object of the proposed investigation was to discredit the system of prohibition in the Philippines by comparing it unfavorably with the monopoly system prevailing in most of the other Far Eastern territories of the Western powers and Japan. It was suspected that the commission would merely whitewash the conditions existing in these territories and endorse the current systems of control.[10] Indeed, there was some fear that the investigation might turn up evidence that the prohibition system had not been effective in eliminating the opium problem, for there had been no comprehensive survey of the results of the system since it had been put into effect twenty years previously. Furthermore, some doubt had already been expressed in international circles of the effectiveness of the Philippine policy. The failure of the Philippine government to furnish adequate statistics on the extent of the opium traffic in the Islands, despite repeated requests from the League, the United States War Department, and interested individuals, lent substance to these doubts. In addition, Herbert L. May, after a year of investigating the opium smoking situation in the Far East, had stated in 1927 that the policy of prohibition in the Philippines was a failure. He had recommended a strong government monopoly system on the model of that which prevailed in parts of the Dutch East Indies as likely to be productive of the best results.[11]

Since refusal to allow the League commission to visit the Philippines would give rise to the view that there was something in the Islands to be concealed, the United States had little choice but to permit the visit. Therefore, after receiving assurances from the Governor General of the Islands that the commission would be welcomed and would be given all possible assistance, the State Department invited the League

---

9. Wilson to the Secretary of State, Oct. 18, 1928, SDR 500.C 1197/218.

10. Ellen La Motte to Johnson, Sept. 19, 1928, SDR 500.C 1197/225; memorandum by Caldwell to Johnson, Nov. 9, 1928, SDR 500.C 1197/226½; memorandum by Caldwell of conversation with Porter, Dec. 3, 1928, SDR 500.C 1197/240½; memorandum of conversation between Herbert L. May, Johnson, and Caldwell, Dec. 20, 1928, SDR 511.4A2/26.

11. Herbert L. May, *Survey of Smoking Opium Conditions in the Far East* (New York: Foreign Policy Association, 1927), pp. 11–12, 15, 21–26.

to send the commission to the Islands.[12] It had been initially decided that an American investigatory commission would either precede or accompany the League Commission to the Philippines, but it was subsequently agreed to postpone the American investigation until after the visit of the League commission.[13]

The Commission of Enquiry into the Control of Opium Smoking in the Far East was composed of persons who were presumably neutral as to the question of the most effective method of suppressing the traffic in prepared opium. Its chairman, Eric E. Ekstrand, was the Swedish minister to Argentina. The other members were Max L. Gerard, a Belgian, and Jean Havalasa, former Czechoslovakian minister to Brazil. Bertil A. Renborg, the Swedish member of the Opium Traffic and Social Questions Section of the League Secretariat, served as secretary.

The commission spent nearly eight months in its investigation (September 4, 1929, to May 11, 1930) and visited or covered by inquiry all the territories in the Far East where the smoking of opium was prevalent except China. The Chinese government refused to allow the investigators to enter its territory because of the refusal of the Ninth Assembly of the League to accept China's proviso that the inquiry be extended to all countries which produced or manufactured opium products and that China be represented on the commission.[14]

Nearly two weeks were spent by the commission in the Philippines, but only three places were visited—Manila, Cebu, and the town of Dirmaguete in Negros Oriental. The commissioners conducted a number of interviews, but left a general impression with Philippine officials that they were on a pleasure trip and that their investigation was a farce.[15] Obviously coloring the viewpoint of the officials in the Philippines was their firm expectation that the commissioners would be critical in their report of the prevailing policy of prohibition. Yet,

12. Secretary of State Kellogg to the American Legation (Berne), Dec. 8, 1928, SDR 500.C 1197/239.

13. Memorandum by Caldwell, Sept. 5, 1928, SDR 500.C 1107/218; memorandum by Caldwell to Johnson, Nov. 9, 1928, SDR 500.C 1197/226½.

14. League of Nations, *Commission of Enquiry into the Control of Opium Smoking in the Far East, Report to the Council*, Vol. I: *Report with Comparative Tables, Maps and Illustrations*, C.635.M.254, 1930.XI (Geneva, 1930), 9–10. Referred to below as *Report of Commission of Enquiry to the Far East*.

15. "Memorandum by Colonel C. H. Bowers of the Philippine Constabulary in Answer to Mrs. Wright's Questionnaire," Jan. 19, 1931, BIA 10233–95.

contrary to American presumption, the commission was eminently fair in its appraisal of the situation in the Islands. They pointed out in their report that the Philippines had been moderately successful in keeping the opium smoking vice under control, but that it was still a significant problem because of the inability of the prohibitive system to deal effectively with smuggling. The commission itself favored gradual suppression of the opium smoking habit by "legalizing smoking by confirmed addicts and by supplying such smokers with government opium," thus reducing individual consumption and preventing the spread of the habit to others. It pointed out, however, that regardless of the method of control, government monopoly or prohibition, success could only be achieved through the suppression of the illicit traffic, a problem common to all the systems of regulation.[16]

The commission's observations on the Philippines were later confirmed by an investigation conducted by Mrs. Hamilton Wright from the beginning of December 1930 to the last of March 1931. Mrs. Wright was sent to the Islands by the Bureau of Narcotics in lieu of the proposed American commission. She reported that the consumption of prepared opium had not been suppressed, that a great deal of this type of opium was smuggled into the islands, and that most of the contraband opium was a mixture of Persian and Yunnan opium which came from Hong Kong, North Borneo, and Amoy. She blamed the lack of an adequate and efficiently equipped preventive establishment in the islands as being responsible for this traffic.[17] Thus it was clear from her report and the observations of the League Commission that the Philippine government needed to take more vigorous steps to suppress smuggling if the system of prohibition was to be defended as being more effective than the government monopoly systems in the neighboring territories.

The Commission of Enquiry made a host of recommendations for dealing with the opium smoking problem. These included

Taking measures progressively and concurrently in each territory for the gradual suppression of the vice;
Scientific research into the opium smoking problem in each territory with government support and on an international basis;

16. *Report of the Commission of Enquiry to the Far East*, I, 53, 111.
17. Mrs. Wright to Harry J. Anslinger, May 8, 1931, "Report on Opium Situation in the Philippines," BIA 1023–401, Part 5.

Calling a conference by the League of Nations to secure the gradual
   restriction and control of poppy cultivation;

A public educational campaign against opium smoking;

Effective steps to suppress smuggling;

Reduction in the price of government opium so as to make smuggling unprofitable;

Extension of government monopolies to retail distribution;

Registration, licensing, and rationing of addicts, and the restriction
   of the consumption of the drug to smoking establishments owned
   and managed by the government;

Prohibition of smoking by minors;

Strict control over the residue (dross) left over from smoked opium;

Provisions for the cure of addicts and follow-up attention to cured
   addicts;

No budgetary dependence by governments on revenue derived
   from opium, and the application of such revenue to an antiopium
   campaign and other social and sanitary purposes;

Establishment in the Far East by the League of Nations as "part of
   the Opium Section of the Secretariat, a central bureau for the
   opium smoking problem which should serve as a distribution centre
   for information and facilitate cooperation between the Governments concerned."[18]

From the above recommendations, it can be seen that the commission,
like previous international groups which had studied the opium smoking problem, steered clear of proposing abrupt and drastic measures
for solution of the problem.

The study of the Commission of Enquiry was designed to be
preparatory to a conference on the prepared opium situation. As the
commission did not complete its work until the spring of 1930, the
Conference on the Suppression of Opium Smoking which, according
to Article 12 of the Geneva Opium Agreement, was to meet not later
than 1929, could not be convened until 1931. It met at Bangkok from
November 9 to 27, and was thus the second international conference
on the drug question to meet during that year. Great Britain, France,
Japan, the Netherlands, Portugal, Siam, and British India—the signatories of the Geneva Agreement—were represented at the conference.
China refused to attend. Although the United States was not a signa-

18. *Report of the Commission of Enquiry to the Far East*, I, 137–146.

tory of the Geneva Agreement, it accepted the League invitation to attend the conference, but only in the capacity of an observer. The United States decided to be represented at the conference, though in a restricted manner, because of its interest, historically, in the opium problem in the Far East, the bearing of the Far Eastern situation on the Philippines, and the desire to forestall the criticism that the United States would not cooperate in international action except on its own terms.[19] Caldwell and Colonel Lucien R. Sweet, Assistant Chief of the Philippine Constabulary, represented the United States at the conference. Caldwell's selection as the American delegate initially aroused protest, inspired by the Hearst press, from various individuals and groups in the United States because of the belief that he had failed to represent the United States in a competent and vigorous manner at the recently ended Conference on Manufacture.[20] In a release to the press, the State Department, however, fully backed Caldwell and credited his "quiet and effective persuasion" with achieving the incorporation of practically all the American principles of limitation and control of manufacturing in the resultant convention.[21]

The American government was not very sanguine about the probability of the conference taking any drastic steps to deal with the opium smoking problem. It was therefore certain that as the conferees would not be inclined to accept the American policy of strict prohibition, the United States would be unable to sign any agreement brought forth. The government hoped, however, that the American representatives, through both formal and informal discussions, would be able to promote closer cooperation among the territories concerned on measures for the suppression of both opium smoking and the smuggling of manufactured drugs.[22] Thus the formal activities of the American delegates were confined mainly to firm statements of the American policy on the question under discussion and explanations of the American system in the Philippines. The informal activities were largely devoted to trying to convince the other delegates of the soundness of the American position.[23]

---

19. Memorandum by Caldwell and Fuller to Hornbeck, Aug. 18, 1931, SDR 511.4R1/11. See also Department of State press release, Nov. 7, 1931, SDR 511.4R1/66.
20. Mrs. Moorhead to Hornbeck, Dec. 14, 1931, SDR 511.4A6/481.
21. Department of State press release, Nov. 7, 1931, SDR 511.4R1/66.
22. Secretary of State Stimson to Caldwell, Sept. 14, 1931, SDR 511.4R1/14.
23. "Report of John K. Caldwell, Observer on the Conference on the Suppression of Opium Smoking, Held in Bangkok, Siam, November 9, to 27, 1931," typed copy, p. 8, SDR 511.4R1/81. Cited below as Caldwell's Report on the Bangkok Opium Conference.

In order to prevent the Hearst press from accusing Caldwell of "buckling down to the British," the statement of the American position was written in the State Department after Caldwell had arrived in Bangkok, and was sent to him by telegram.[24] Caldwell delivered the statement at two of the early sessions of the conference. While expressing American support for any concerted action among the Far Eastern territories to suppress opium smoking, he qualified this pledge by stating categorically that the United States would not cooperate with any of the other governments in the perpetuation of the monopoly system and would not adopt such a system itself. He asserted that there was no moral justification for nations to prohibit absolutely the non-medical use of opium in their home territories and yet permit the use of smoking opium in their Far Eastern possessions. He maintained that the American system of absolute prohibition had worked satisfactorily in the Philippines despite the problem of smuggling, a problem common to any system of control, which could only be eliminated by the limitation and control of poppy cultivation. Nevertheless, even the problem of smuggling, he contended, would be considerably reduced if all the Far Eastern territories "conscientiously enforced" a policy of proscription of all phases of the opium traffic. In conclusion he declared that:

The Government of the United States most strongly urges frank recognition of the fact that there is but one real method by which to suppress the evil of opium-smoking in the Far East or anywhere else, and that this method is complete statutory prohibition of the importation, manufacture, sale, possession or use of prepared opium, coupled with active enforcement of such prohibition. Cooperation among the interested Governments in the suppression of smuggling is a necessary corollary. In measures of this kind, the United States is prepared wholeheartedly and cordially to cooperate.[25]

Caldwell's statements provoked no discussion, and the Philippines were seldom mentioned during the Conference. Caldwell reported, however, that in private conversations Ekstrand stated that the American position was the only sound one, and that even Sir Malcolm Delevingne appeared to admit as much.[26] But the prevailing attitude

24. Secretary of State Stimson to the American Legation (Bangkok) (for Caldwell), Nov. 5, 1931, SDR 511.4R1/59.

25. League of Nations, Conference on the Suppression of Opium Smoking, *Minutes of the Meetings and Documents Submitted to the Conference*, C.577.M. 284.1932.XI (Geneva, 1932), pp. 24–25, 43. Hereafter cited as *Minutes of the Bangkok Opium Conference*.

26. Caldwell's Report on the Bangkok Opium Conference, p. 8.

among the delegates throughout the conference was that nothing basic could be done or should be attempted until the problem of smuggling was eliminated. They were thus unprepared even to consider measures that might radically affect the use of prepared opium. There was little disposition to put into effect the recommendations of the Ekstrand Commission of Enquiry, most of which the delegates regarded, variously, as being either inconsistent one with another, or of little or no value, or as retrograde measures. Even some minor proposals put forward by the British were rejected. Van Wettum, the chief delegate of the Netherlands, led the opposition to proposals of novel measures. He maintained that the system of government monopoly in effect in the Dutch East Indies was the result of careful study and experience, was the best that could be devised, and was working well.[27] The interest of the conferees was mainly centered on the illicit traffic, and their discussions dwelt principally on the uncontrolled production of opium in China and the smuggling of the Chinese product into other Far Eastern territories. On this matter the delegates drew up an emphatic statement putting on record their view that "no strong measures for the suppression of the practice of opium smoking" would be practicable while the overproduction of opium and the illicit traffic from producing countries remained unchecked, a situation on which they hoped the governments concerned would immediately take action.[28] This was the only problem on which the conference did take a firm position.

The attitude displayed by the delegates made it a foregone conclusion that the resulting Agreement, signed by all the full participants on November 27, would contain no significantly new measures. It consisted of only four articles covering substantive matters; the last three articles dealt with territories covered by the Agreement and such procedural questions as ratification and denunciation. The Agreement merely provided for an end to retail sales on a commission basis, the sale of prepared opium for cash only, the prohibition of opium smoking or the entering of opium smoking establishments by minors, and the right of a government monopoly in one territory to be supplied with prepared opium from the factory of a government monopoly in another territory of the same power so that the number of opium factories

27. For the prevailing attitude in the conference see *ibid.*, pp. 5–6.
28. *Ibid.*, p. 7.

in the territory of one power might be reduced.[29] The Final Act, consisting of eleven recommendations to governments, likewise contained no radical suggestions for dealing with the opium smoking problem, except for the call for an international agreement to limit the production of opium. The other recommendations dealt with the rationing and licensing of addicts; the keeping of records, the making of reports, and the exchange of information on all aspects of the prepared opium traffic; the punishment of participants in the contraband traffic; and the treatment and aftercare of addicts and research into the effects of opium smoking and means of cure.[30]

The Bangkok Opium-Smoking Conference concluded the international action devoted primarily to this particular problem until after the end of World War II. The conferees simply endorsed the status quo with respect to carrying out the obligations of their governments under the Hague Convention to adopt effective measures for the gradual suppression of the traffic in and use of prepared opium. Absolutely no advance was made by the conference toward solution of the problem. No basically new proposals were brought forth to deal with it. From the American viewpoint, only two developments kept the conference from being a complete waste of time and effort. These were the general and implicit recognition and endorsement of the view that the final solution to the problem could only be achieved through the limitation of the production of the raw materials from which smoking and other forms of opium were derived, and the impetus which this recognition gave to the consideration by the Advisory Committee of measures to effect this fundamental result. The Agreement did not come into force until April 1937, and this in itself, in view of the fact that none of the signatories had expressed any serious objections to the document, indicates that few of the powers took the instrument seriously.

Paradoxically, full adoption of the American position on the problem of opium smoking came less as a result of international cooperation than as an outgrowth of international conflict. In 1942, several discussions were held at the Bureau of Narcotics in Washington with the nationals of several governments and international experts on the

29. *Ibid.*, pp. 17–19. See also *Minutes of the Bangkok Opium Conference*, pp. 105–106, for a brief summary of the Agreement.

30. Caldwell's Report on the Bangkok Opium Conference, pp. 19–21. See also *Minutes of the Bangkok Opium Conference*, p. 106.

question of abolishing government opium smoking monopolies in the territories held by Japan when these areas were liberated. In September 1943 the United States made representations in this regard to the governments concerned. Less than two months later, both the Dutch and British governments announced that a policy of absolute prohibition of opium smoking and the abolition of all smoking monopolies would be put into effect in their territories which were or had been conquered by the Japanese as soon as these territories were freed. The French government made a similar announcement in 1945. With the defeat of the Japanese, Japan's opium monopoly was also liquidated on orders of General Douglas MacArthur.[31] Thus war served as the instrument for the achievement of a goal for which the groundwork had been laid by nearly four decades of international discussion and peaceful cooperation. The policy which the United States had inaugurated in 1905 in the Philippines and subsequently urged upon other powers was thus ratified.

While the use of prepared opium was a serious problem in the Far East, it was overshadowed by far in international deliberations in the 1930's by concern with the rapid transformation of the Orient into the world's principal base for the clandestine manufacture of opiates and cocaine and the illicit traffic in these drugs. By 1934 the operation of the Geneva and Narcotic Limitation Conventions had virtually ended excess manufacture in the principal European manufacturing countries, but it had driven such activities to previously nonmanufacturing countries in southern Europe where the raw products were produced. Both licensed and clandestine factories were established in these countries for the purpose of feeding the illicit traffic. Pressure from individual governments and the League of Nations forced the respective governments to bring this situation under control.[32] As a result, the Far East, because of unstable political conditions, became the main center of the illicit activities.

The political instability which prevailed in China after World War I was accompanied by the increasing cultivation of the poppy and the production of raw and prepared opium. This situation continued throughout the 1930's. In the meantime the Chinese government was devoted to a system of prohibition which it could not enforce. Sug-

31. Helen H. Moorhead, "International Narcotics Control: 1939–1946," *Foreign Policy Association Report*, XXII, No. 8 (July 1, 1946), 94–95.
32. Bertil L. Renborg, *International Drug Control*, pp. 146–147.

gestions from various sources, foreign and domestic, that a government monopoly be established were opposed by such varied groups
as missionaries, the National Anti-Opium Association, illicit traffickers,
and the military leaders. The American government too, as the only
Western power with Far Eastern possessions in which the policy of
prohibition was in effect, also opposed the establishment of a government monopoly in China. Since there was no improvement in the situation, the Chiang Kai-shek government finally decided in 1934 to ignore
objections and to abandon the completely ineffectual prohibition system in favor of the monopoly. Under the new system a program for the
gradual but complete suppression of poppy cultivation and opium
smoking within a six-year period was instituted.[33] The United States
disapproved of this action,[34] but the progress which the Chinese government made during the next three years served to refute the American contention—at least as regards China—that the prohibition policy
was the only effective one.

As in the pre-World War I period the antiopium campaign was
infused with the spirit of Chinese nationalism, which was spearheaded
by the New Life Movement led by Madame Chiang Kai-shek. An
educational and propaganda campaign against opium which included
the contention that the use of the drug would aid China's enemy,
Japan, and the enactment of strict laws and their enforcement by determined leaders of the government had produced by 1937 significant
inroads on the traffic in and production and use of the drug. Unfortu-
nately, the outbreak of the Sino-Japanese War in 1937 reversed the
progress that had been made.[35]

Japan had long been accused of deliberately drugging China to
obtain money and to weaken the character and fiber of the Chinese people in order to gain political ends.[36] Prior to 1930, Japanese nationals
had been engaged in promoting the drug traffic in China from the
Japanese leasehold in Kwantung, and there was also an immense traffic
in drugs under the control of Japanese and Korean nationals in Manchuria. A new element was added to the situation when in 1932 the
Japanese transformed Manchuria and Jehol into the puppet state of
Manchukuo. In the same year the Manchukuo regime established a

33. For a discussion of the opium situation in China during the 1930's see Frederick
T. Merrill, *Japan and the Opium Menace* (New York: International Secretariat, Institute of Public Relations and the Foreign Policy Association, 1942), pp. 20–63.

34. Fuller to the Secretary of State, Feb. 1, 1935, SDR 500.C 1197/819.

35. Merrill, *op. cit.*, pp. 28–33, 42, 48–63.   36. See above, pp. 138–139.

government monopoly of smoking opium transactions, and eventually opium became one of the three main sources of the regime's revenue. Virtually no controls were placed on the traffic in other opium products, and the manufacture and distribution of morphine and heroin were freely permitted. Huge quantities of raw opium were imported from Persia.[37]

The Japanese adventure in Manchuria was followed by other incursions into China. As other areas of China came under Japanese political, administrative, or military control, the traffic in opiates followed a pattern similar to that in Manchukuo. The renewal of the Sino-Japanese conflict in 1937 accelerated both the Japanese occupation of Chinese territory and the spread of the drug traffic. Wherever the Japanese military went in China the virtually unrestricted traffic in opium and other narcotics followed. Restrictions which had been put in effect by the Chinese were removed by the puppet regimes established in China by the Japanese army. Thus, largely as a result of deliberate Japanese actions, the extensive production and use of prepared opium, the excess production and importation of raw opium, and the clandestine manufacture and consumption of opiates and cocaine characterized the Far Eastern drug situation in the decade preceding the Second World War. It was estimated that in China roughly 90 percent of the world's total raw opium supply was produced, and to this quantity were added the huge importations from Persia through Japanese-controlled territory and Macao. In addition to areas in China under Japanese control the British colony of Hong Kong, Portuguese Macao, and the French-leased territory of Kwangchowan became centers of the illicit traffic.[38] While the shipment of European manufactured drugs to the Far East practically ceased, the Far East became the major source of the illicit traffic to the West in raw and prepared opium and the refined products.[39]

The revival of the prominence of the Far East in the international drug traffic occasioned great alarm in Western circles. The American interest in the situation was direct and concrete. In early 1933 the State

37. Merrill, *op. cit.*, pp. 93–99.

38. For a discussion of the Far East as the producing, manufacturing and distributing center for drugs in the illicit traffic, see Merrill, *op. cit.*, pp. 64–101; and *Foreign Relations*, 1938, IV, *The Far East*, 561–567.

39. A convenient summary from the American point of view is contained in memorandum by Fuller to Morse, July 29, 1937, SDR 500.C 1197/1110; and Fuller to the Secretary of State, Sept. 3, 1947, SDR 500.C 1197/1115.

Department expressed grave concern at the appearance of increasing quantities of morphine of Japanese manufacture in the clandestine traffic on the Pacific Coast, and the American ambassador in Japan communicated this concern to the Japanese government.[40] As time passed, the illicit drug traffic from the Far East became somewhat reminiscent of the pre-World War I situation in that increasing though relatively small quantities of smoking opium consisting of a mixture of Chinese and Persian opium were smuggled into the United States from China. As there was little or no market for this type of smoking opium in China, the American government assumed that it was prepared for the illicit market in the United States. Heroin smuggled into the United States also came from China; after 1935 it came mainly from the Japanese concession in Tientsin. In addition, a contraband traffic to the United States in raw opium originated also in China, where Persian opium was imported for the clandestine manufacture of morphine and heroin and for smuggling into the United States, Canada, and some countries of western Europe.[41]

Although the United States protested unilaterally against this state of affairs to the Chinese and Japanese governments, its principal efforts at amelioration were made in conjunction with the League of Nations, mainly through the Opium Advisory Committee. By focusing "pitiless publicity" on the situation, the United States hoped that Japanese authorities could be induced by international public opinion to remedy conditions. Thus, after 1932, the American representative on the Advisory Committee, along with his Chinese and Egyptian colleagues—whose countries were major victims of the Japanese-sponsored traffic—called attention at virtually every session of the committee to the Far Eastern situation and demanded that Japan live up to its obligations under the various drug treaties to which it was a party. The earliest consideration was given to the conditions in Manchuria and was entwined with the question of the recognition of the state of Manchukuo. Both the League and the United States refused to recognize Manchukuo. The United States maintained that since it was the Japanese government which exercised de facto power in the territory, Japan was re-

40. Ambassador Joseph C. Grew (Tokyo) to the Secretary of State, Feb. 1, 1933, SDR 894.114 Narcotics/68, and Secretary of State Hull to the American Embassy (Tokyo), March 27, 1933, SDR 894.114 Narcotics/69.
41. For the effect of the Far Eastern Drug situation on the United States, see *Foreign Relations*, 1938, IV, *The Far East*, 563–564.

sponsible for any of the narcotics activities carried on there. Thus, early in 1933, the State Department instructed the American embassy in Japan to apprise the Japanese government informally of the American view that the establishment by the Manchukuo regime of a government monopoly for the sale of smoking opium was contrary to both the Hague Convention and the Geneva accords in that the monopoly system did not embody or envisage measures for the gradual suppression of the traffic in and use of such opium.[42]

The principal issue in regard to narcotics activities in Manchukuo was whether or not to legalize the trade in raw opium between that territory and Persia through the recognition of import certificates issued by the Manchukuo regime. The issue was raised by the British in May 1933 before the League Advisory Committee on the Sino-Japanese conflict. The British contended that the refusal to recognize these certificates might drive this phase of the opium traffic underground and thus impair the whole system of international drug control.[43] The feasibility of taking the step contemplated by the British required the answer to two questions: (1) whether the proposed acceptance of the Manchukuo import certificates would constitute de facto recognition of the Manchukuo regime and thus contravene the nonrecognition policy adopted by the League; and (2) whether, in fact, legalization of the Manchukuo-Persian raw opium trade would facilitate or prevent the use of Manchukuo as a base for the uncontrolled manufacture and distribution of narcotic drugs.

To get around the issue of recognition the Secretary General of the League suggested an ingenious procedure. A firm wishing to export opium to Manchukuo would secure a Manchukuo import certificate whose possession by the firm would be duly noted by the government of the exporting country and on the basis of which the exporting country would issue an export license to the firm but would not send a copy of the export license to Manchukuo.[44] The Advisory Committee on the Sino-Japanese Conflict unanimously approved of the procedure recommended.[45]

At the subsequent discussion of the issue at the seventeenth session of the Opium Advisory Committee in the fall of 1933, the American

42. *Foreign Relations*, 1933, IV, *The Far East*, 129–133.
43. *Ibid.*, p. 303.
44. *Ibid.*, pp. 351–352.   45. *Ibid.*, pp. 356–357.

representative came out vigorously against the proposal. The United States had opposed from the very beginning the British suggestion that the raw opium trade between Manchukuo and Persia be legalized. It took the position that the recognition of import certificates of Manchukuo would indeed constitute de facto recognition of the regime and that adherence to the principle of nonrecognition was more important than an attempt "to regularize in theory and in form shipments of narcotic drugs to and from Manchukuo."[46] The American government also maintained that instead of preventing a gap in the international system of narcotics control, the proposed legalization would produce just the opposite effect in that it would validate an already illicit traffic in narcotics. The government contended that the proposed legalization would facilitate the importation and accumulation of Persian and Turkish opium in the territory which, under the existing opium policy of the military regime there, would be transformed into manufactured and smoking opium and smuggled into the United States.[47] It regarded the procedure proposed by the Secretary General as contrary to Articles 3 and 15 of the Hague Convention and Article 6 of the Geneva Agreement of 1925, since Chinese sovereignty over Manchuria was still recognized by the powers and Chinese law prohibited the importation of raw opium.[48]

Aside from the political principles involved and the possible effects of the British proposal on the international narcotics traffic as a whole, the American opposition to the British suggestion was based on the strong suspicion that the motive behind the proposal and the support given it by several of the European governments was the desire to permit European shipping, importing, and financial interests to profit from the Persian-Manchukuo opium trade as carriers, financiers, handlers, and insurers of shipments of the drug.[49] Fuller, especially, believed this to be the case. His strong objections prevented the outright endorsement by the Opium Advisory Committee of the Secretary General's suggested procedure. Although many members indicated their ap-

---

46. *Ibid.*, p. 306.

47. *Ibid.*, p. 309. See also Fuller's Report on the Seventeenth Session of the Opium Advisory Committee, pp. 30–39, in Fuller to the Secretary of State, Jan. 9, 1934, SDR 500.C 1197/655.

48. Fuller's Report on the Seventeenth Session of the Opium Advisory Committee, pp. 33–35.

49. *Ibid.*, pp. 36–37.

proval of the scheme in a private session of the committee,[50] the committee as a whole recoiled from publicly supporting the project. Instead, in its report to the Council it asserted that "in accordance with Articles 3, 8, and 15 of the Hague Convention of 1912, exports of opium (raw and prepared) to the territory in question cannot be authorized."[51]

The continuous disclosures and denunciations in the Advisory Committee of the conditions prevailing in Manchuria and other areas in China under Japanese control aroused Japanese sensibilities. The Japanese denied responsibility for the situation on the grounds that the regimes set up in China by the Japanese army were independent governments which Japan recognized as such. In cases where it did admit responsibility, the Japanese government made only vague promises to reform its legislation to remedy the situation.[52] While Fuller's statements in the Advisory Committee were irritating, their accuracy was not successfully challenged, and on occasion it was even tacitly admitted by the Japanese representative on the committee.[53] Thus the Japanese government did not remain totally unresponsive to the appeals of the League and individual governments. In 1937 the Japanese authorities were reported to have begun a vigorous campaign against the Japanese and Korean drug traffic in China, especially in the Peiping and Tientsin areas, on instructions from the Foreign Office.[54] In the same year the Manchukuo regime, as a result of the criticism at Geneva and the realization that widespread addiction to opium was hampering the economic development of the area, put forth a plan to end the use of the drug within ten years.[55] Despite these pretentious steps, no measures were consistently followed up. The Japanese government in Tokyo, and especially the Foreign Office, seemed to be sincerely desirous of rectifying the drug situation, but its power over Japanese nationals and the army in China appeared to be limited. The civilian authorities in Tokyo were quite sensitive to the adverse publicity Japan received, but the military forces in China remained unaffected by it

50. *Ibid.*, pp. 30–31.
51. League of Nations, *Official Journal* (Feb., 1934), p. 159.
52. *Foreign Relations*, 1938, IV, *The Far East*, 566. See also memorandum by Fuller, Aug. 18, 1938, SDR 500.C 1197/1239.
53. See, for example, memorandum by Fuller of conversation with the First Secretary of the Japanese Embassy (Washington), Sept. 10, 1938, SDR 500.C 1197/1258.
54. Gilbert (Geneva) to the Secretary of State, June 16, 1937, SDR 500.C 1197/1091.
55. Merrill, *op. cit.*, pp. 102–106.

just as they were insensitive to the criticism of other aspects of their activities in China.[56]

Being either unwilling or unable to effect reforms, the Japanese government resorted to the expedient of responding to the criticism of Fuller and others on the Advisory Committee with the charge that their statements constituted a political attack on Japan. When the criticism continued unabated, the Japanese in 1939 withdrew their representative from the Advisory Committee on which they had been represented even after their withdrawal from the League in 1933. The cessation of cooperation with the committee was not an isolated event, however. As early as the fall of 1938 the Japanese government had come to a decision to sever all of its relations with the League and League-connected organizations.[57] Thus the decision to end participation in the Advisory Committee was part of the whole complex of political considerations in which the Far Eastern drug problem was entangled.

The onset of World War II interrupted efforts to deal with the narcotics traffic in the Orient. By that time the Far Eastern situation had amply demonstrated two major points of weakness in the existing system of international control. First, it was clear, as conditions in China had long made apparent, that in the absence of political stability in areas where the production and consumption of drugs were part of the economic and social fabric, effective suppression of the drug traffic there was impossible, regardless of the commitment to strict measures of control. Furthermore, any exposed point in the world scheme of control weakened the whole system. Second, it also became clear that "pitiless publicity," the basic weapon in the fight against the drug traffic, was inadequate for the task. Even in countries where political conditions were stable, world public opinion would not be sufficient if the social conscience of the people in the offending territory was not in accord with that opinion. Because of these facts it was impossible to make any substantial progress during the 1930's toward the amelioration of the drug traffic situation in the Far East.[58]

56. *Ibid.*, p. 133. See also *Foreign Relations*, 1938, IV, *The Far East*, 569–571, with reference to the great difficulty experienced by the Japanese Foreign Office on this matter.

57. Consul Bucknell (Geneva) to the Secretary of State, Nov. 2, 1938, SDR 500.C 1197/1390.

58. For a discussion of these points of weakness as demonstrated by the Far Eastern situation, see Merrill, *op. cit.*, pp. 132–133.

Despite the insoluble difficulties presented by the narcotics traffic in the Far East, the League of Nations continued its piecemeal approach to a mitigation of the drug problem. One aspect of the problem, the illicit traffic, had engaged a major share of the attention of the Advisory Committee ever since its inception. In 1931 the committee gave recognition to the prominence of this phase of the narcotics question by creating a Permanent Subcommittee on Seizures and Illicit Traffic. Prior to 1930 the emphasis was on the traffic as fed by the manufacture of excess quantities in legitimate factories in Europe. After 1930, as a result of the coming into force of the Geneva Convention in 1928 and the Narcotics Limitation Convention in 1933, attention shifted to the supplying of smugglers by clandestine factories established in various parts of the world, but particularly in southern Europe and the Far East. After the mid-thirties the matter became predominantly a Far Eastern problem.[59]

Aside from legalizing the use of drugs by addicts—an idea anathema to the United States—suppression of the illicit traffic in narcotic drugs required three main steps: the exchange of information among governments as to the nature, organization, and sources of supply of the traffic and the names and methods of operation of those participating in it; the cutting off of the sources of supply; and the severe punishments of offenders. All the existing international conventions had provided in some measure for the first step, and through the work of the Advisory Committee and the Permanent Central Board as well as bilateral cooperation among governments, the scrutiny of the international traffic was consistently, though inadequately, provided for. The Narcotics Limitation Convention had made a great contribution to the achievement of the second step so far as manufactured drugs were concerned. The supply of raw materials, however, remained uncontrolled. The international instruments of agreement covered the third point only by general admonitions to the signatories to take adequate steps to prevent transactions in dangerous drugs by unauthorized persons and to suppress illicit traffic. Thus, it was on this third point that international deliberations in the 1930's were concentrated.

The Advisory Committee began serious work on the problem of the illicit traffic at the beginning of 1930. At its thirteenth session in

59. A brief summary of the nature and extent of the illicit traffic and the international measures taken to deal with it is given by Renborg, *International Drug Control*, pp. 140–152.

January and February the committee addressed an appeal to governments to set up in their countries a centralized and unified police control of narcotic drugs so that international cooperation might be facilitated through the quick exchange of information on cases of illicit traffic. A year later the committee invited the delegates of the international Criminal Police Commission to the meetings of its fourteenth session in order to discuss means of obtaining effective international cooperation. At this session the Police Commission presented the committee with a draft convention providing for the establishment of a central police office for drug control in each country. These offices would maintain close contact with each other and with the League Secretariat. This draft convention and questions in regard to it were referred to a subcommittee for study.

Further impetus to action on the problem was the recommendation in the Final Act of the Narcotics Limitation Convention that a convention be concluded on the basis of the work already done by the Advisory Committee for the prosecution and punishment of violators of narcotic laws, and that the Council of the League call the attention of governments to the importance of such a step. Consideration of this recommendation by the Council and the committee led to the adoption of a draft convention by the committee at its sixteenth session in May 1933. The draft convention provided severe penalties for narcotic law violations and for punishment of persons who arranged or facilitated smuggling in territories outside the country in which they were residing. This draft and revised versions of it were presented in 1933 and again in 1934 to the respective governments for their views. On ascertaining that a large majority of governments favored the conclusion of a convention, the League Council decided definitely in May 1935 to call a conference for this purpose. In January 1936 the Council designated June 8 as the date for the convening of the conference. A special committee of experts was assigned the task of revising the text of the draft convention in order to bring it into conformity with certain of the views and suggestions of the interested governments.[60]

60. A convenient résumé of the steps taken by the Advisory Committee and other organs of the League which led up to the conference is contained in "Confidential Report to the Secretary of State of the Delegation of the United States to the Diplomatic Conference Held in Geneva in June, 1936, for the Purpose of Drafting a Treaty for the Suppression of the Illicit Traffic in Narcotic Drugs," pp. 7–19, typed copy in SDR 511.4T1/105. Cited below as Report of the American Delegation on the Illicit Traffic Conference.

The American government regarded these activities of the League without enthusiasm. As early as February 1932 it expressed a disinclination to participate in any new convention on the grounds that the provisions of existing treaties, if effectively carried out, furnished an adequate basis for measures to suppress the traffic. The United States maintained this view up to its reception in February 1936 of the invitation from the League to participate in the conference. The American position was based on the steps that the United States had taken to deal with the illicit traffic. As in other phases of the narcotics problem, the United States was well ahead of most other governments in control measures. In addition to its domestic legislation, the United States had concluded a number of treaties and bilateral agreements with foreign governments. In 1924, 1925, and 1926 model smuggling and extradition treaties covering the subject of narcotic drugs were concluded with Canada, Mexico, and Cuba, respectively.[61] By 1936 the United States was party to treaties providing for the extradition of narcotic drug offenders with twelve countries.[62] In addition, bilateral administrative agreements with twenty-three countries for the exchange of information and closer cooperation among their various preventive agencies had been concluded.[63] If other nations took similar steps, the United States maintained, no new convention would be necessary.

Despite this long-held position, the State Department decided that the League invitation to participate in the pending conference should be given friendly consideration. Most of the other governments had expressed a desire for a new convention and the American government did not want to appear uncooperative. Besides, a new convention might well strengthen existing measures and provide effective deterrent penalties for illicit transactions in all the drugs covered by the various conventions, including both raw and refined products.[64] The United

61. Edward J. Trenwith (compiler), *Treaties, Conventions, International Acts, and Agreements Between the United States of America and Other Powers, 1923–1937,* IV (Washington, D.C.: U.S. Government Printing Office, 1938), pp. 3984–3987 for Canada; 4039–4040, 4045–4048 for Cuba; and 4448–4449, 4452–4453 for Mexico. The smuggling treaty with Mexico was abrogated in 1927.

62. These countries were Albania, Canada, Cuba, France, Germany, Great Britain, Greece, Honduras, Lithuania, Luxembourg, Mexico, and Switzerland. See the Secretary of State to the American Minister (Berne), April 16, 1936, SDR 511.4T1/21.

63. U.S. Treasury Department, Bureau of Narcotics, *Traffic in Opium and Other Dangerous Drugs for the Year Ended December 31, 1936* (Washington, D.C.: U.S. Government Printing Office, 1937), p. 14.

64. Report of the American Delegation on the Illicit Traffic Conference, p. 3.

States was not satisfied, however, with the draft convention which was to serve as the basis for discussion at the conference, regarding it as much too limited in the subjects covered. Therefore, before deciding whether to participate in the conference, the State Department sought definite assurances from the Secretary General that additional matters might be included on the agenda. The Department was particularly desirous that the conference be competent to consider any subject connected with the prevention and punishment of illicit activities, especially questions involving cannabis (Indian hemp or marihuana), illicit traffic in raw materials, and the clandestine manufacture of derivatives.[65] When the Secretary General informed the United States that the scope of the conference was not limited to the draft convention but that any delegation could propose any matter for inclusion in the convention, the United States accepted the invitation to the conference.[66]

The Conference for the Suppression of the Illicit Traffic in Dangerous Drugs convened at Geneva from June 8 to June 26, 1936. Forty-two governments participated. Fuller and Harry S. Anslinger, with Frank S. Ward as legal adviser, composed the American delegation. Early in the conference the Americans proposed an amendment to the draft convention which sought to bring within the scope of the proposed convention all drugs covered by the existing treaties, including raw materials and smoking opium.[67] This amendment was designed to put into effect the American contention that the drug treaties already in effect required the parties to them to suppress the abuse of all narcotic drugs—raw opium and its derivatives, prepared opium, the coca leaf and its derivatives, and cannabis. The proposal in effect included in its scope all activities—cultivation, production, manufacture, and distribution—in relation to these drugs for nonmedical and nonscientific purposes within the meaning of the term illicit traffic and the imposition of severe penalties on anyone promoting or engaging in them.

The Portuguese delegation led the opposition to the proposed amendment, contending that those parts of it relating to raw and pre-

---

65. *Ibid.*, pp. 22–23.

66. *Ibid.*, pp. 23–24. See also memorandum by Fuller, Feb. 29, 1936, SDR 511.4T1/9; Secretary of State Hull to the American Legation (Berne), March 2, 1936, SDR 511.4T1/8; and Stanley Hawks (Berne) to the Secretary of State, March 24, 1936, SDR 511.4T1/13.

67. Report of the American Delegation on the Illicit Traffic Conference, p. 27.

pared opium were beyond the scope of the conference. But as this contention was contrary to the expressed assurances of the Secretary General to the United States as to the competence of the conference, it could not be sustained. Nevertheless, it was clear that the nations in whose territories the use of smoking opium was sanctioned and those which had a financial interest in the production of raw material regarded the idea of including smoking and raw opium transactions for nonmedical and nonscientific purposes within the convention with considerable disfavor.[68] They pointed out that the question of restricting all drug activities to medical and scientific purposes was not properly within the scope of the conference, for none of the previous conventions which the draft convention was designed to supplement went so far in providing for the control of the drug traffic except with reference to the manufacture of refined drugs. None had provided for the restriction of the production of raw materials or other transactions in such products to strictly medical and scientific purposes, and the use of prepared opium had been sanctioned as legitimate.[69]

The American delegation had anticipated the substantial opposition to their proposed amendment, and on the day the conference opened, it had requested authorization from the State Department to abstain from active participation in the conference if their proposal was refused. They would remain at the deliberations, however, in order to resume their participation if the achievement of an acceptable convention seemed probable.[70] But the State Department was averse to any action by the American delegation reminiscent of the situation at Geneva in 1925, which might undermine the principle of international cooperation on the drug problem and detract from the future usefulness of the United States in the movement and on other matters. Therefore, the American representatives were instructed to acquiesce in the disposition of the matter by its reference to a technical committee.[71] This was the very manner in which the amendment was disposed

68. *Ibid.*, pp. 26–27.

69. For the American proposal and the reaction to it, see Report of the American Delegation on the Illicit Traffic Conference, pp. 3–4, 26–28; and League of Nations, *Records of the Conference for the Suppression of the Illicit Traffic in Dangerous Drugs ... Text of the Debates*, C341.M.216.1936.XI (Geneva, 1936), pp. 26–31, 37–39.

70. Gilbert (Geneva) to the Secretary of State, June 8, 1936, SDR 511.4T1/41.

71. Acting Secretary of State Phillips to American Consul (Geneva) (for Fuller and Anslinger), June 9, 1936, SDR 511.4T1/42.

of. As a conciliatory gesture, however, the conferees agreed to embrace the principle of the proposal as a recommendation in the Final Act.

Their liberty of action thus limited by the State Department's attitude, the American delegation resigned itself to trying to obtain the best possible agreement within the framework of the draft convention before the conference. As the draft convention contained measures directly affecting constitutional and legal principles and procedures in the various participating countries, close attention to specifics was extremely important. The two issues most productive of controversy were whether willful commission or intent must be proved in order to punish offenders and whether conspiracy should be included among the punishable offenses. Contending that the requirement regarding intent would render the successful prosecution of many narcotics cases impossible, the American and Canadian delegates led the fight for the deletion of this stipulation from the draft. This was a difficult point to carry, for in most criminal codes proof of intent in criminal cases was required. As to the matter of conspiracy the American delegation supported the insistence of the delegate of Canada that it be included in the list of punishable offenses. They pointed out that since the important members of large narcotics rings did not personally handle the drugs, but confined their activities to promoting and financing illicit transactions, it would be impossible to prosecute them successfully without bringing the charge of conspiracy. Only at the last moment, and after the conference had agreed on the principles of the main articles of the final convention, did the Canadians and Americans win their points. When the Canadian delegate made it clear that his government would not sign the convention unless its demands were met, the British delegation, fearing for the future of an already weakened League, came to their aid. For this help, the British tried to secure from the Americans a promise that they would sign the convention, but failed. The Canadian delegate, however, gave assurance that he would sign.[72]

Throughout the conference, Fuller and Anslinger opposed the listing in the convention of the specific acts to be penalized. They maintained that such an enumeration was impractical and that it would be very difficult to describe such offenses in a manner that would accord with

72. For the discussion and final disposition of these controversial items, see Report of the American Delegation on the Illicit Traffic Conference, pp. 30–33.

the different systems of law in the various countries. They also pointed out the inadvisability of dictating in such detail to the legislative bodies the terms of legislation.[73] Their protests were ineffective, however. They were also unsuccessful in obtaining tight provisions for the extradition of narcotics law violators, the punishment of offenders in countries where extraterritoriality prevailed, and the confiscation of the profits derived by offenders from their illegal activities.[74]

The Convention for the Suppression of the Illicit Traffic in Dangerous Drugs as finally formulated covered three main subjects. First were the provisions specifying severe punishment, especially by imprisonment, for the commission in contravention of existing conventions of the following acts: "The manufacture, conversion, extraction, preparation, possession, offering, offering for sale, distribution, purchase, sale, delivery . . ., brokerage, despatch, despatch in transit, transport, importation and exportation of narcotic drugs." Intentional participation in, attempts and conspiracy to commit the offenses listed, and subject to the stipulations of national laws, preparatory acts were to be similarly punished. In addition, in countries having national laws regulating the cultivation, gathering, and production of raw materials, violations of such laws were also to be severely punished. Countries which had extraterritorial jurisdiction in the territory of another country were obligated to punish any of their nationals guilty of committing any of the enumerated offenses to the same degree as if the offense had been committed in the home territory. Furthermore, each of the acts, if committed in different countries, was to be considered as a distinct offense to be punished in each country where the act was committed, and foreign convictions for the offenses listed were to be recognized, for the purpose of establishing habitual criminality, in the countries where the principle of the international recognition of previous convictions was recognized. Finally, seizure and confiscation of narcotic substances and instruments intended for the commission of any of the offenses were stipulated.[75]

Secondly, the Convention contained measures aimed at preventing drug traffickers who moved from one country to another or who aided or promoted illicit activities in a country other than the one in which they resided from escaping punishment. Offenders taking refuge in

---

73. *Ibid.*, p. 4.   74. *Ibid.*, pp. 4–7, 30.
75. For the text of the Convention, see *Records of the Conference for the Suppression of the Illicit Traffic*, pp. 216–220.

another country to avoid punishment would either be prosecuted by the country of refuge or be surrendered up by it. Therefore all of the offenses listed, except those relating to the growth of raw materials, were made extraditable crimes for inclusion in extradition treaties already in effect or later concluded, or were to be recognized as extraditable crimes among the countries which did not make extradition conditional on the existence of a treaty or on reciprocity. The requirement of extradition was circumscribed by certain restrictions, however. The granting of extradition was to be in accordance with the law of the country to which application for extradition was made, and if the offense did not appear to be a serious one in the eyes of the competent authorities of that country, extradition did not have to be granted. In addition, a country which did not extradite its nationals was not obligated to prosecute its nationals for committing an offense in another country if, under similar circumstances, it could not grant the extradition of a foreigner. Furthermore, the prosecution and punishment of foreigners by a country to which they had fled for refuge after having committed an offense in another foreign country could be carried out only if extradition had been requested and could not be granted, and if the law of the country of refuge embraced the principle of prosecution of offenses committed abroad by foreigners.[76]

Finally, the Convention provided for cooperation and collaboration among national administrative services in efforts to suppress the illicit traffic. In this regard each party was required to establish a central office to supervise and coordinate all operations necessary to prevent and punish the commission of any of the enumerated offenses. These central agencies were to cooperate with each other to the greatest extent possible through the exchange of information regarding illicit drug transactions, the identity and description of drug traffickers, and the existence of secret factories and through other activities that would facilitate the suppression of the traffic.[77]

The Final Act consisted of four recommendations. The first was the principle underlying the amendment which had been proposed by the American delegation. Thus the governments were urged to abolish, without undue delay, the use of opium in their territories for other than medical and scientific purposes. The second recommendation called on countries which recognized the principle of extradition of

76. *Ibid.*   77. *Ibid.*

their nationals to grant the extradition of those nationals who committed offenses abroad even if the applicable extradition treaty contained a reservation on the subject. In the third recommendation the conference urged the parties to the Convention to create a specialized police service to help carry out its provisions. The final recommendation was simply a suggestion that the Opium Advisory Committee consider and give to the Council of the League its opinion on the question of the desirability of meetings among the representatives of the central offices of the various powers to facilitate the international cooperation provided for in the Convention.[78]

On the day the conference ended, twenty-six governments signed the Convention. The United States was the only nation which indicated that it would not sign.[79] Although the American delegates regarded the Convention as containing some worthwhile provisions which, if carried out by other governments, might effect some improvement in countries with weak systems of control and thus also improve the international situation, they were highly displeased with the loopholes in the Convention relative to extradition, the situation in countries where extraterritoriality existed, and the failure to provide for the confiscation of profits derived from the commission of the offenses enumerated in the document. They were also disappointed over the refusal of the conferees to agree to adequate coverage of the illicit traffic in raw materials, smoking opium, and cannabis. They maintained that the Convention weakened rather than strengthened the existing international arrangements for the suppression of the illicit traffic, and by failing to cover effectively all forms of narcotic drugs, limited the scope of the obligations imposed by the drug treaties already in force. They therefore recommended that the United States refrain from signing the instrument as it would require the United States to replace its existing system of control by a weaker system and might also imperil the effectiveness of America's extradition treaties. Because of the enumeration of the acts to be penalized as criminal offenses, Congress might also regard the Convention unfavorably as a "unwarranted invasion of the legislative field" by the executive branch. An additional reason offered for not signing the Convention was its failure to provide the one advance in America's own domestic legislation that the United

78. *Ibid.*, pp. 230–232.
79. Gilbert (Geneva) (from Fuller) to the Secretary of State, June 26, 1936, SDR 511.4T1/52.

States had hoped to derive from the Conference—a constitutional basis, by treaty, for the regulation by the national government of the production of opium and cannabis and the cultivation of the raw plants from which they were derived.[80]

This conference was the last that was held on the drug question until after the end of World War II. It did not provide a very auspicious conclusion, in the eyes of the American government, to the international movement up to that date. Like several of the preceding conferences, it served to reinforce the opinion long held by many Americans, officials and private citizens, that many of the nations involved in the narcotics traffic as producers and manufacturers or as beneficiaries of revenue derived from such traffic did not seriously desire to take effective steps to eliminate the drug problem.[81] This pessimistic view was strengthened by what the United States regarded as an inexcusable misrepresentation of its position as contained in the French translation, incorporated in the printed records of the conference, of the American statement explaining its refusal to sign the Convention. This misrepresentation was perpetuated by the Portuguese representative who, acting as rapporteur, stated in his report to the Council on the proceedings of the conference that the American Government had refused to sign the treaty "because it did not provide for the criminal prosecution of the habit of opium smoking."[82] "This preposterous misstatement" of the American position was subsequently corrected through the circulation by the Secretary General, at the American government's request, of the text of the American statement in English, French, and Spanish as prepared by the State Department.[83] It might be noted from this little controversy that international consideration of the drug problems had come full circle since the convening of the Shanghai Commission in 1909 and was once again focused on the Far East and the problem of opium smoking.

Like the other drug conventions, the Convention for the Suppression of the Illicit Traffic in Dangerous Drugs marked another milestone along the road toward the limitation of national sovereignty in the interest of the common welfare. It represented an admission by national

80. Report of the American Delegation on the Illicit Traffic Conference, pp. 4–7, 33–34; *Records of the Conference for the Suppression of the Illicit Traffic*, pp. 174–176; and the Department of State press release, Dec. 8, 1936, SDR 511.4T1/66.
81. Report of the American Delegation on the Illicit Traffic Conference, pp. 26, 34.
82. *Ibid.*, p. 37.
83. *Ibid.*, p. 38. See also Department of State press release, Dec. 8, 1936.

states that the full exercise of their own authority was not sufficient to protect and maintain the well-being of their citizens. Thus they sought to achieve through international criminal law what their own penal laws were unable to effect. However, the reluctance with which they gave up their freedom of action in this sphere was clearly illustrated by the fact that even after the relatively long period of five years in which the preliminary convention was drafted, the conference still had to iron out considerable differences in the points of view of the participating states. Yet, a treaty providing in many respects substantial modifications in national laws as well as innovations in international law did emerge with the endorsement of most of the participants. Unlike the other drug conventions, which were primarily concerned with the regulation and supervision of legitimate drug activities, the Convention of 1936 was directed exclusively against illicit transactions, making such activities an international crime.[84] The Convention went into force on October 26, 1939. There was no chance to ascertain how it would affect the illicit drug traffic as the war which soon engulfed the world interrupted the international control movement.

84. For the significance of the Convention from the point of view of international law, see J. G. Starks, "The Convention of 1936 for the Suppression of the Illicit Traffic in Dangerous Drugs," *AJL*, XXXI (Jan. 1937), 31–33, 43; and Renborg, *op. cit.*, pp. 27, 152.

Chapter eleven

American cooperation with the League
in limitation at the source

Primary emphasis within the international movement to deal with the abuse of dangerous drugs has been given to limiting the supplies of drugs available. Down to 1939 international measures dealt mainly with the regulation of the national and international legitimate trade, the suppression of illicit traffic, and the prevention of the production of surplus supplies of manufactured drugs. One area not adequately covered was the production of raw materials. This accounted for a major gap in the international system of control. Limitation of the supplies available could not be achieved unless limitation began at the source, with restricting the cultivation of the raw plants. In the American view, this was the basic problem, and it was the last to be tackled seriously by the international community.

In all of the international conferences held during the period under study some attention had been given to the necessity of limiting the quantities of raw material available for consumption and for use in the production of refined drugs. The Hague Convention had imposed upon its adherents the obligation to enact effective laws and regulations to control the production and distribution of raw opium, but no specific measures by which this was to be achieved or internationally supervised were stipulated. One of the reasons the United States withdrew from the Geneva Conference of 1924–1925 was the refusal of the producing countries to commit themselves to definite measures to restrict the production of raw opium and coca leaves to the medical and scientific needs of the world, and the resultant convention contained merely a provision similar to that in the Hague Convention with the added requirement that annual statistics on the production of these raw products be submitted to the Permanent Central Board. The question was raised in the Conference on Manufacture by the Russian delegate, but it was declared to be outside the scope of the conference. It was also briefly considered in the Conference for the Suppression of the Illicit

Traffic in 1936 in connection with the American amendment to Article I of the draft convention before that conference, but was shunted aside. By this time, however, the Opium Advisory Committee and interested governments had behind them several years of serious discussion on this phase of the drug problem, and plans for an international conference on the matter were being formulated. The impetus behind this development had come from the international deliberations on the highly perplexing question of opium smoking. Both the Commission of Enquiry to the Far East in 1929–30 and the Bangkok Opium Conference had concluded that the opium smoking problem could not be solved until poppy cultivation was under control. In 1931, as the result of their recommendations, the League apparatus was directed toward preparing for a conference on the matter.

As in other efforts at drug control during the period under study, political and economic considerations were highly involved in the problem of raw material production and trade. This was the reason for the timorousness with which this particular phase of the problem was approached prior to 1930. Rather than deal with the question of supplies at the source, the international conferees attempted to control the supplies themselves with the hope that as a result the source would automatically contract. Specifically, it was hoped that strict limitation of the traffic in and manufacture of narcotic drugs to the quantities necessary to fulfill the world's medical and scientific needs would, by lessening the demand for the raw material from which these drugs were derived, force a reduction in the production of the raw products to the legitimate market demand. In the early 1930's this hope appeared capable of being realized, for the application of the international instruments of control did produce a substantial drop in the demand for raw opium, with a consequent decline in the prices of the product to one quarter of what they had been in the late 1920's.[1]

A new element appeared in the situation which offered further promise of inducing the countries which produced raw opium to come to some agreement, as a measure of self-protection, to curtail production. This was the development and practical application of a method of extracting opium alkaloids, particularly morphine, directly from the dried poppy plant (poppy straw) without passing through the intermediate stage of raw opium.[2] The opium poppy was already extensive-

---

1. Renborg, *International Drug Control*, p. 158.   2. *Ibid.*, pp. 158, 170–171.

ly cultivated in many central, southern, and eastern European countries for its seed, and it could be grown in most warm and temperate climes of the world. Extensive use of poppy straw for the derivation of narcotic drugs could destroy the market for raw opium on which the major producing countries relied for a considerable portion of government revenue and the economic occupation of their people.

These factors were not enough, however, to move the producing countries to undertake voluntarily among themselves to restrict cultivation. What many optimistic persons had failed to consider adequately was the fact that since the poppy was an agricultural product whose cultivation was deeply imbedded in the economic fabric of the producing countries and was an economic habit with many of the cultivators, restriction of its production to market conditions was much harder to achieve than that of industrial products over which firm control could be exercised by the enterprises concerned. It had been amply demonstrated in various countries of the world that contraction of the market for agricultural products was not automatically followed by a reduction of production, but rather, often resulted in a continuing surplus that depressed both prices and the cultivators. In the case of opium, however, there was an outlet, for if the surplus could not be absorbed by the legitimate market, it could be siphoned off into the illicit market, international and national regulations notwithstanding.

The major producers of raw opium during the 1920's and 1930's were China, India, Turkey, Persia, Yugoslavia, and Russia. International concern with production in these countries was concentrated on production for export and only secondarily on the accumulation of surplus quantities of raw products in a country from which the illicit traffic might be supplied. A subsidiary issue was the production of raw opium for eating and for manufacture of prepared opium, both activities being legitimate under the existing international conventions, but unacceptable to such countries as the United States, which insisted on the restriction of the use of all forms of narcotics to strictly medical and scientific purposes. It was estimated that about 90 percent of the world's production of raw opium occurred in China.[3] Most of the opium was manufactured into prepared opium, but as both production and consumption in China were illegal until 1934, all of this opium went into the illicit traffic. The other major producer of raw opium

---

3. See above, p. 282.

in the Far East was India. In 1926 the Indian government announced a policy of gradual cessation of exports of opium for other than medicinal and scientific purposes until such export should cease altogether. This action was largely the result of accusations, especially by "impatient idealists" in the United States, that India was perpetuating the abusive use of opium and was feeding the illicit traffic to other territories.[4] Russia did not produce raw opium for export. Thus the principal producing-exporting countries were Turkey, Persia, and Yugoslavia. They were the nations whose cooperation was absolutely necessary to an effective movement for limitation of production at the source.

The view that the effective solution of the drug problem could not be achieved until raw material production corresponded with medical and scientific needs had long been the basic American approach to the problem. This view had been expressed at Shanghai in 1909 and had been followed up at the Hague Conferences. After World War I, this principle became the cardinal point in the American program and was referred to in international circles as the American plan. The United States in its earliest association with the League virtually demanded the acceptance of this principle as part of the price for continued American cooperation with the League on the drug problem. Failing to get little more than verbal support of its position from the international community, the United States temporarily withdrew from meaningful participation in the international movement. It was left up to Americans, working principally in their private capacities, to continue the efforts to put the American plan into effect. In no phase of the drug problem were individual Americans more active internationally than in trying to effect measures to secure limitation at the source.

After the First World War the one American holding no permanent official position with the government who was most active in the international drug-control movement was Mrs. Elizabeth Washburn Wright. Having worked up to the war on the problem with her late

4. League of Nations, Advisory Committee on Traffic in Opium and Other Dangerous Drugs, *Provisional Minutes of the Eighth Session Held at Geneva from May 26th to June 8th, 1926*, C.393.M.136.1926.XI (Geneva, 1926), pp. 36–37. See also *Council of State Debates, Monday and Tuesday, 8th and 9th February, 1926*, VII, No. 1 (Delhi: Government of India Press, 1926), enclosed in Consul General Julius G. Lay (Calcutta) to the Secretary of State, April 22, 1926, SDR 511.4A2/500.

husband, Dr. Hamilton Wright, she was intimately acquainted with its various aspects. In 1918 she decided to continue her husband's work.[5] She came from a family which had been very active in political and international affairs. Her father, William Drew Washburn, had represented Minnesota in both houses of Congress. Four of his brothers also served in that body as members of the House of Representatives, and one of these, Elihu B. Washburn, was Secretary of State for five days in March 1869, after which he served as minister to France until 1877.[6]

Mrs. Wright was keenly interested in the opium work and made numerous personal sacrifices to carry it on. In her own words she felt herself to be "a tool," "a medium being used by some outside force—for some definite purpose" in regard to the narcotics problem.[7] It was she who took the lead in calling the attention of the American government to the recrudescence of poppy cultivation in China after 1917. Like others, she realized that the peace negotiations following the World War would offer an ideal opportunity to secure broad adherence to the Hague Convention.[8] She therefore went to Paris during the Peace Conference to lend her voice to those supporting the idea of providing for such adherence through the peace treaties. She also attended the two Lausanne Conferences concerning Turkey for the same purpose. In 1920 she went again to the Far East to observe conditions there.[9] While in Paris during the peace negotiations, she urged American officials to take the initiative in the postwar international action on the drug problem.[10] Thereafter, she constantly sought some official position with the American government[11] so that she might have an influential platform from which to carry on her work. She was unsuccessful in securing a permanent position, however, despite the recommendations from time to time of such influential persons as

5. Memorandum by William McNeer to E. T. Williams, June 5, 1918, SDR 511.4A1/1525.

6. The *New York Times*, Feb. 14, 1952, p. 27, contains Mrs. Wright's obituary. For the activities of her father and uncles see *DAB*, XIX, 495–496, 502–506.

7. Mrs. Wright to William Philips, July 24, 1922, SDR 511.4A1/1660.

8. Memorandum by McNeer to Williams, June 5, 1918, SDR 511.4A1/1525.

9. Constance Drexel, "Are We Our Brothers' Keepers? How Our Country is Fighting the Drug Evil," *Harper's Magazine*, CXLIX (Nov., 1924), 740.

10. James Brown Scott to Lester H. Wooley, Feb. 25, 1920, SDR 511.4A1/1555.

11. See, for example, Mrs. Wright to Scott, Jan. 29, 1920, enclosed in Mrs. Wright to William Phillips, July 24, 1922, SDR 511.4A1/1660.

Bishop Brent, Stephen G. Porter, and Secretary of Commerce Herbert Hoover.[12] She did serve on the American delegation to the Second Geneva Opium Conference in 1924–1925, being thus the first American woman to receive plenipotentiary powers as a diplomat. She was also employed by the Bureau of Narcotics in 1930 to survey the Philippine opium situation, and she remained with the Bureau to help secure the enactment by the states of a uniform narcotic law. Most of her work, however, was carried on without any official connection with the American government.

Mrs. Wright continually urged the United States to appoint a permanent representative to the Opium Advisory Committee,[13] a position which she would have liked to have held herself. As an assessor on the committee from 1921 to 1925, she kept the State Department fully informed on the activities of the committee and bombarded the Department with her views and suggestions. Before the government did appoint a representative to the committee, the State Department had in her a useful source from which to obtain the most intimate details of the committee's attitude and work. As indicated by the similarity of their reports, Mrs. Wright greatly influenced the views of the first American representative to the committee, Rupert Blue, as to the policy which the United States should adopt toward that organ.[14] In fact, by her energy, zeal, and uncompromising dedication, she undoubtedly contributed in great measure to the formation of American drug policy in the 1920's. She was regarded by American officials as perhaps the most knowledgeable of the Americans working in the movement.[15] Her idealism, however, irritated many foreigners, particularly the representatives of countries which had financial interest in the traffic in prepared opium, and her presence on the Advisory Committee, which initially consisted primarily of the representatives of the so-called "opium bloc" countries, was often a source of discomfort to the committee.[16]

12. Porter to the Secretary of State, Dec. 28, 1923, SDR 511.4A1/1875. Hoover to the Secretary of State, June 9, 1921, SDR 511.4A1/1681.

13. *Ibid.* See also, memorandum by Undersecretary of State Joseph C. Grew of conversation with Mrs. Wright, Jan. 15, 1926, SDR 511.4A2/470.

14. See above, p. 157.

15. Hoover to the Secretary of State, June 9, 1921, SDR 511.4A1/1681; Secretary of State Hughes to the American Legation (Berne), April 14, 1923, SDR 511.4A1/1753.

16. Minister Joseph C. Grew (Berne) to the Secretary of State, April 12, 1923, SDR 511.4A1/1753; Consul Tuck (Geneva) to the Secretary of State, July 1, 1925, SDR 511.4A2/367.

The great emphasis which the United States placed on the theme of limitation of production, after World War I, was to a considerable degree the result of the persuasion and activities of Mrs. Wright. She had early concluded that restriction at the source was the only way to deal with the opium question.[17] In pursuit of this goal and with the blessings of the State Department, she visited Turkey and Persia in 1923 on her own initiative to investigate poppy-growing conditions with a view to discovering a practicable basis on which the countries might be persuaded to curtail cultivation.[18] Largely through her survey the United States gained a fuller understanding of the problems which beset the opium-producing countries.

The variety of uses to which the products from the opium poppy plant could be put was clearly demonstrated in Turkey. The growth of the poppy for oil was the major concern. The oil was extracted from the poppy seed and used domestically in soap and varnish, for lamps, and as a food oil. Some of the surplus seed not used domestically was exported for preparation and use as salad oil, as oil cake for cattle, for adulterating olive oil, and for artists' paints. The growth of the poppy for opium was, however, an extensive and profitable enterprise, but required much greater care in cultivation than poppy growth for oil. Its cultivation was essentially an economic issue, for opium smoking was not a common habit among the inhabitants of Turkey. Since the opium trade was primarily in the hands of Jews and Armenians, there was no great national attachment to the opium industry.[19] The principal markets for the Turkish product were Europe and the United States. Most of the American imports of raw opium came from Turkey. Because of its high morphine content, it was most sought after for the manufacture of derivatives. Although in 1928 control over imports and domestic drug transactions was established, exports of raw opium remained unsupervised.[20] It was not until 1932, as a result of American

17. Memorandum by W. R. Castle, Acting Chief, Division of Western European Affairs, Feb. 25, 1922, SDR 511.4A1/1596.

18. The State Department instructed its diplomatic representatives at Belgrade, Teheran, and Constantinople to give Mrs. Wright all possible assistance even though her mission was unofficial. Phillips to Mrs. Wright, Oct. 18, 1922, SDR 511.4A1/79a.

19. American Consul General G. Bie Ravndal (Constantinople) to the Secretary of State, March 21, 1923, SDR 511.4A1/1759.

20. League of Nations, Conference on the Limitation of the Manufacture of Narcotic Drugs, *Control of Narcotic Drugs in Turkey, Memorandum Forwarded by the Minister for Foreign Affairs of the Turkish Republic*, C.382.M.157.1931. VII (Geneva, 1931).

pressure, that Turkey finally agreed to ratify the Hague and Geneva Conventions.[21]

The American consul general at Constantinople, G. Bie Ravndal, convinced Mrs. Wright in 1923 that if a proper substitute crop could be found Turkey could be persuaded to reduce poppy cultivation. Such possible substitutes might be grain, cotton, tobacco, and silk. Certain American cigarette manufacturers had already helped to rehabilitate tobacco culture in Turkey by sending experts to that country to supervise the tobacco industry and help finance and direct the activities of growers. The consul general urged the broadening and continuation of activities such as these. He particularly urged that Americans help to reestablish sericulture and the silk industry in Turkey by setting up a school of sericulture, an agricultural bank to extend rural credits to farmers to grow mulberry plants, and a reeling factory.[22] On her return to America Mrs. Wright sought to give effect to Ravndal's suggestions by urging silk manufacturers and American bankers to help develop silk cultivation in both Turkey and Persia.[23] Her efforts were apparently of no avail.

Aside from China, opium production in Persia presented the most difficult problem from the international standpoint. The Persian opium situation is also most illustrative of the part played by Americans not officially connected with the American government in working for a solution to this particular aspect of the drug question. Persia's record in the field of international cooperation on the drug problem, like Turkey's, was not good. Although represented at the Shanghai Commission and the first Hague Opium Conference, the Persian government had refused to ratify the Hague Convention. At both meetings the Persian delegate had rejected the principle that countries should prevent at their ports of departure the shipment of the various forms of opium to countries which prohibited their entry. Thus, in signing the Hague Convention, he made a reservation to Article 3(a) in which this obligation was embodied. The reason behind the refusal to accept this principle was the desire not to interfere with the lucrative trade in Persian opium to China, which became even more extensive with the

21. See above, p. 244.
22. Ravndal to the Secretary of State, March 21, 1923, SDR 511.4A1/1759.
23. Mrs. Wright to Ramsey Peugnet, Dec. 2, 1923, attached to memorandum by Mrs. Wright entitled "The Opium Problem from the Angle of Production (Persia)," Jan. 28, 1925, SDR 511.4A2/448.

cessation of Indian exports to China. In keeping with this policy, Persia also refused to accept the import and export certificate system. Down to 1928 the only control which the Persian government exercised over opium exports was that necessary for the collection of export duties and other fees.[24] Even after this date, when certain limited measures were put into effect, Persian opium continued to feed the illicit traffic in the Far East and accounted for the bulk of the raw opium found in the illicit traffic in the United States even after the outbreak of World War II.[25]

In addition to Mrs. Wright, other Americans became intimately involved in the situation in Persia. The American Financial Mission to Persia from 1922 to 1927, headed by Dr. Arthur C. Millspaugh, a former economic adviser to the State Department, bore the greatest responsibility. In carrying out its assignment of reorganizing the Persian finances, the American Mission was given the task of collecting the opium revenues, which in turn required the enforcement of the Persian government's regulations for the control of the domestic traffic. At the same time the mission looked forward to the restriction of opium production and the eventual elimination of the rather widespread drug habit.[26] Following the statement of the American position on raw opium production in the Advisory Committee in May 1923, the American Mission proceeded to acquaint the State Department with conditions in Persia in regard to opium and the possible policy which Persia might be able to follow.[27] As administrator-general of the Persian finances, Millspaugh helped to formulate Persia's opium policy, and although the American Mission had no official connection with the American government, Millspaugh's views were given respectful attention by the State Department.

24. For Persia's opium policy and the part Persian opium played in the international traffic down to 1936 see Mohammed Chahkar, *Le Problème de l'opium en Iran* (Paris: Librairie Orientale et Américaine, G. P. Maisonneuve, 1936); Elizabeth B. MacCallum, *Twenty Years of Persian Opium (1908–1928)* (New York: The Foreign Policy Association, 1928); and Anthony R. Neligan, *The Opium Question, with Special Reference to Persia* (London: John Bale, Sons & Danielsson, Ltd., 1927).

25. United Nations, Economic and Social Council, Commission on Narcotic Drugs, *Illicit Traffic in Narcotic Drugs, Review of World Traffic from 1 January 1940 to 30 June 1946*, E/CN.7/68, 1947 (New York, 1947), pp. 3, 6.

26. Arthur C. Millspaugh, *The American Task in Persia* (New York and London: The Century Company, 1925), p. 260.

27. Persian Minister Hussein Alai (Washington) to Allen W. Dulles, July 29, 1923, SDR 511.4A1/1819. Encloses excerpts from letters of Millspaugh to Alai concerning opium in Persia, asking Alai to transmit their substance to the State Department.

In Millspaugh's view, economic and political conditions in Persia in the 1920's made absolutely impossible any immediate drastic measures to restrict opium production and to curtail the traffic in the commodity. The opium poppy was cultivated in eighteen of the twenty-six provinces, and in many of these provinces it was the only cash crop of any significance. Exclusive of oil, opium constituted from 20 to 25 percent of Persia's total export trade. It accounted for about 9 percent of the government's revenue. The wealthiest class in Persia and many of the most influential clergy were opium producers and merchants. The use of the drug in the form of smoking opium was widespread. Any sudden drastic restriction on the trade in and production of the drug would wreak havoc on an already depressed economy. It would result in an increase in the existing large deficit in the government's treasury, enlarge the already serious adverse balance of trade, worsen the extensive unemployment and poverty, and leave a considerable amount of capital idle. Such a step would most likely create political disturbances in a country where political instability was already rife and the control of the central government over certain areas tenuous. In short, efforts at sudden and drastic curtailment of opium activities in Persia were not likely to be effective, and the evils flowing from such attempts would far outweigh any progress made.[28]

Millspaugh compared the difficulty of the opium problem in Persia with the complexity of the liquor problem in the United States. He pointed out that prohibition was put into effect in the United States only after decades of discussion and trial on the state and local level, and that still it was not effective. He oppugned American impatience with Persia's refusal to ratify and put into effect the Hague Convention with the observation that, "if the United States had signed a liquor agreement, similar to the International Opium Agreement, it is very doubtful whether an impartial observer would say that the United States is at the present time fulfilling the obligation stipulated by that Agreement."[29]

28. *Ibid.* See also "Memorandum on Opium" prepared by Colonel D. W. Mac-Cormack, a member of the American Financial Mission and the director of the Persian internal revenue, for the Persian delegation at the Second Geneva Opium Conference. A copy of the memorandum was given to the American Government before the conference met. Therefore the United States knew well in advance and in detail what the Persian position at the conference would be. SDR 511.4A1/129.

29. Hussein Alai to Dulles, July 29, 1923, SDR 511.4A1/1819.

Although the American Mission defended the hesitancy of the Persian government to take the precipitate action which the Opium Advisory Committee of the League and the United States were urging it to take, they were clearly committed to the view that Persia should begin immediately to plan measures for the gradual restriction of opium production, consumption, and trade. By pointing out to the Persian government the possible political consequences that might accrue if Persia continued to decline to ratify the Hague Convention, Millspaugh was able to get the government to promise conditional acceptance of the instrument. Continued recalcitrance in this matter, he warned, would lead to hostility and censure and the "moral isolation" of Persia from other governments and people, which in turn would have a disastrous effect upon Persia's quest for foreign capital.[30] Persia's League representative was thus carrying out Millspaugh's suggestions when he informed the Fifth Committee of the Assembly in September 1923 that his government would begin immediately to take steps looking to the gradual restriction of the production and consumption of opium to medical and scientific purposes, and that Persia was prepared to withdraw its reservation to Article 3 (a) of the Hague Convention upon the condition that the other signatory powers and the League of Nations would agree to allow Persia a reasonable period of time in which to institute a program of crop substitutions for opium cultivation and to put other measures into effect.[31]

Persia's position at the Geneva Opium Conference was also formulated by the American Mission, and the memorandum submitted to the conference by the Persian delegate was the work of Colonel D. W. MacCormack, the Director of Internal Revenue. In inducing the Persian government to indorse the memorandum, MacCormack warned that in addition to the probable moral isolation of Persia and its consequent effect upon securing foreign loans, failure of the Persian delegate to indicate to the conference some progress toward carrying out the Hague Convention and the American principles might cause the parties to that convention which had accepted the import and export certificate system to boycott Persian opium. In addition, other

---

30. Millspaugh to the Persian Ministry of Foreign Affairs, May 25, 1923; copy enclosed in *ibid*.

31. *Ibid*. See also MacCallum, *op. cit.*, p. 19.

countries might follow the British in refusing to allow their ships to transport the Persian commodity.[32]

To forestall unfavorable reaction to Persia at the conference, the Council of Ministers approved MacCormack's memorandum with only minor changes.[33] Thus the Persian delegate was instructed to assure the conferees that Persia was in "full accord and sympathy" with the League's efforts to suppress the illicit traffic, and that it accepted the American principles of interpretation of the Hague Convention and was prepared to withdraw conditionally its reservation to Article 3(a) of that instrument. He was instructed to give unconditional assurances that Persia would continue to extend the measures already taken to control domestic traffic and consumption and to prevent smuggling. Moreover the government would take steps to bring cultivation under control, to prohibit the importation of opium for reexport to countries prohibiting its entry from the country of origin, to keep records of opium consumption, cultivation, and export, and to encourage the planting of mulberry trees, cotton, and tobacco as substitute crops for the opium poppy. To give full effect to the American principles, however, Persia would need a long period of preparation in which a program of crop substitution and the development of the mineral resources of Persia, requiring a large capital investment and adequate technical advice and direction, could be instituted. To finance such a project Persia would need a load of 10,000,000 tomans to be paid back within a period of twenty years at not more than 5 percent interest per year and with no interest charges for the first five years, a moratorium on foreign claims against Persia, and the removal of foreign restrictions on Persia's tariff policy. If such a program could be put into effect, then Persia would reduce opium cultivation by one-tenth annually until production coincided with the quantities needed for medical and scientific purposes, and production in a number of provinces would be eliminated entirely within three years. When cultivation had been reduced to medical and scientific requirements, then Persia would fully accept the system of import certificates.[34]

As a result of the work of Mrs. Wright and the formulation of Persian policy by the American Financial Mission, the United States was inclined to adopt a sympathetic attitude toward Persia's problem. At the

32. "Memorandum on Opium" by MacCormack, SDR 511.4A2/129.
33. Grew to the American Legation (Berne), Nov. 12, 1927, SDR 511.4A2/137.
34. "Memorandum on Opium" by MacCormack, SDR 511.4A2/129.

Geneva Conference the American delegation gave general support to the Persian stipulations.[35] Mrs. Wright had already sought to influence the League in Persia's behalf when at the fifth and sixth sessions of the Advisory Committee in 1923 and 1924, respectively, she had reported on the situation in Persia and had suggested that the League look into the matter of crop substitutes for opium cultivation.[36] It will be recalled that it was she who had proposed the resolution on behalf of the American delegation at the Geneva Conference calling for the sending of a commission of inquiry to the producing countries to study their problems relating to the production of and traffic in opium with the view to the feasibility of substituting other crops.[37] This recommendation was incorporated in the Final Act of the conference.

In May and June 1925 Mrs. Wright obtained assurances from Turkey and Persia that they would welcome a commission of inquiry to study the opium situation in their territory, although Turkey professed a preference for a strictly American commission rather than one sponsored by the League. In September 1925 the Assembly of the League, in accordance with the recommendation in the Final Act of the Geneva Opium Conference, adopted a resolution of the Fifth Committee providing for the sending of a commission to Persia to study the situation there in regard to the cultivation of the opium poppy and the possible replacement of a portion of this cultivation by other crops. It recommended that 100,000 gold francs be provided to finance the commission. The commission was to consist of three persons appointed by the League Council: a person to act as president, an expert on agriculture, and someone with experience in the business and markets of the East and with a knowledge of transportation problems.[38] Since the proposal had originated with the American delegation at the Geneva Opium Conference, the League was quite willing to accept an American to head the commission. But the State Department, despite its hearty approval of the project, refused to exercise any initiative in the matter. Seeking to avoid contamination by the League after the Opium Conference debacle, the State Department refrained

35. Chargé d'Affaires W. Smith Murray (Teheran) to the Secretary of State, Feb. 15, 1925, SDR 511.4A2/310; May 13, 1925, SDR 511.4A2/352.
36. See above, p. 161.
37. Ravndal to Mrs. Wright, May 18, 1925, and Millspaugh to Mrs. Wright, June 18, 1925, SDR 511.4A2/460.
38. For a convenient chronological summary of the steps leading to the Assembly's action, see Mrs. Moorhead to Dulles, Nov. 18, 1925, SDR 511.4A2/429.

from associating in any manner with the commission. It refused to give formal assurances of its approval of the investigation and barred any official of the government from serving on the commission. It limited its support to offering to give whatever informal assistance it could to the American finally chosen to head the commission.[39] Thus the burden of influencing the composition of the commission and of giving it open support was placed upon private citizens.

Even before the League had decided to send the commission to Persia, Mrs. Wright, feeling that the proposal would be rejected by the League, had secured a pledge from the Bureau of Social Hygiene that it would underwrite the project financially.[40] When the Sixth Assembly reduced the suggested 200,000 franc appropriation called for by the resolution of the Fifth Committee to 100,000 francs, Mrs. Wright and Mrs. Helen H. Moorhead persuaded the foundation to supply the extra 100,000 francs to bring the sum up to that originally suggested.[41] It was also Mrs. Wright who, after approaching some seven or eight persons, including such prominent Americans as Owen D. Young and Norman Davis, finally secured the services of Frederic A. Delano, a former member of the Federal Reserve Board, to head the commission.[42] The other members of the Commission of Enquiry to Persia were an Italian, Dr. Fridiano Cavaro, professor of botany at the University of Naples, and a Frenchman, Victor Cayla, an agricultural engineer. As his own personal staff, Delano chose J. B. Knight, an agricultural expert with experience in India and America, and Archibald MacLeish as his private secretary. The League furnished a secretary and stenographer for the commission.[43]

From March 24 to June 6, 1926, the commission traveled throughout Persia and compiled a study of Persia's physical geography, her economic and commercial history, existing conditions as to climate,

39. Memorandum by Dulles of conversation with Porter, Dec. 16, 1925, SDR 511.4A2/424; memorandum by Dulles of a conversation with Frederic A. Delano, Dec. 22, 1925, SDR 511.4A2/444; memorandum of conversations between George Gregg Fuller, Frederic Delano, and by Dulles of conversation with Dr. Taylor of the Department of Agriculture, Feb. 6, 1925, SDR 511.4A2/451.

40. Memorandum of a conversation with Mrs. Wright in the Division of Near Eastern Affairs, June 10, 1925, SDR 511.4A2/349.

41. Memorandum of conversation between Mrs. Moorhead, Dulles, and Murray, Nov. 5, 1925, SDR 511.4A2/349.

42. Memorandum by Dulles of conversation with Mrs. Wright, Nov. 2, 1925, SDR 511.4A2/410; memorandum by Dulles to Grew, Dec. 7, 1925, SDR 511.4A2/433.

43. League of Nations, Commission of Enquiry into the Production of Opium in Persia, *Report to the Council*, C.580.M.219.1926.XI (Geneva, 1926), p. 5.

water resources, agriculture, transport, commerce, labor, industries, land tenure, and taxation, and the current situation in regard to poppy cultivation and the feasibility of establishing substitute crops and industries.[44] It concluded that the institution of a program of curtailing opium production and of introducing substitute crops and other enterprises was not only practicable but would be economically beneficial to Persia and would not place any undue strain on Persia's economy.[45] Opium production could be replaced by the revival of various industries which were dying out, such as silk, wood, and cotton fabrics, pottery, tiles, earthenware, and bricks, artistic metal work, wood carving, and inlaying, painting miniatures, decorating, and engrossing parchment, sheep, lamb, and goat skins, hides, and leather goods. In addition, new industries such as those dependent on mineral oil, the preparation of vegetable oils from such products as rape seed, peanut oil, castor oil, and soya beans, the making and distribution of dried fruits, preserves, and similar products, the preparation of maple sugar cane, and gypsum, lime, and cement manufacture might be developed. Crops to supply the raw material for many of these industries might replace opium cultivation.[46]

The commission recommended that before inaugurating this adventuresome program Persia should be allowed a three-year preparatory period during which the government would institute an effective system of control over opium production and undertake experimental steps in crop substitution. During the same period, Persia would attempt to improve its internal economic conditions, inaugurate extensive improvements in transportation facilities, water resources, and agricultural methods, build up its sources of revenue, and adjust its import tariff system so as to encourage and protect home industries. After this three-year period of preparation, the government should then begin a program of gradually reducing the acreage devoted to poppy cultivation by 10 percent annually.[47] It should be noted that the commission failed to recommend the loan to Persia, which Persia had earlier suggested, to finance the project of poppy curtailment. This omission was due to the Persian government's subsequent decision

44. *Ibid.*, pp. 5–6.   45. *Ibid.*, p. 54.
46. For a convenient summary of the commission's report, see League of Nations, Commission of Enquiry into the Production of Opium in Persia, *Letter from the Chairman of the Commission*, A.16.1927.XL (Geneva, 1927).
47. *Ibid.* For the detailed recommendations see the commission's *Report to the Council*, pp. 54–56.

not to seek a loan "of any kind, for any purpose."[48] Both Delano and Millspaugh agreed that the proposal for a loan had been unwise, and the Persian government officially withdrew the request.[49]

The Persian government approved the general tenor of the commission's report and recommendations, but took vigorous exception to some of the features of the report. It criticized the commission for failing to take into consideration the legitimate demands for Persian opium. This was an important point, for as Persia had not accepted Article 3(a) of the Hague Convention nor the import and export certificate system, it did not regard the shipments of opium to the Far East uncovered by this system as illicit traffic. Another major criticism of the commission's report was the failure to suggest a corresponding limitation of production in other producing countries.[50] While approving the commission's recommendation of a 10 percent annual reduction in the area under poppy cultivation after a three-year preparatory period, the Persian government insisted that such a reduction should be carried on experimentally for three years to gauge its effects, and if the results were favorable, the reduction would then continue.[51] The Persian government also agreed to accept in part the import and export certificate system to be accompanied within at least three years by an annual reduction of 10 percent of the quantity of opium allowed to leave the country uncovered by such certificates and to study the feasibility of increasing the export duties on such opium.[52]

These observations of the Persian government were drawn up by Colonel MacCormack, who appeared personally before the League Council in March 1927 and before the Fifth Committee of the Assembly in September as a representative of the Persian government. The Council took no action on the commission's report or the Persian observations, but referred the matter to the Assembly. On September 20, 1927, the League Assembly adopted a resolution proposed by its Fifth Committee expressing its thanks to the Commission of Enquiry and requesting, at MacCormack's suggestion, the governments concerned to cooperate with Persia in removing restrictive tariffs on the

48. Minister Hoffman Phillip (Teheran) to the Secretary of State, April 7, 1926, SDR 891.114 Narcotics/60.

49. *Ibid.* See also memorandum by Wallace S. Murray of conversation with Delano, Sept. 9, 1926, SDR 891.114 Narcotics/67.

50. League of Nations, Commission of Enquiry into the Production of Opium in Persia, *Observations of the Persian Government*, A.8.1927.XI (Geneva, 1927), pp. 1–2.

51. *Ibid.*, p. 3.   52. *Ibid.*

Persian products which were to be substituted for opium and in granting Persia autonomy in regard to its own tariffs. Persia was requested to keep the League informed on the progress made in carrying out her suggested program, and other producing and manufacturing countries were urged to take similar steps to effect the necessary reduction of raw materials and manufactured drugs. The Advisory Committee later expressed disappointment at Persia's refusal to accept the entire program suggested by the commission, but recognized that the steps which Persia proposed to take constituted a marked advance.[53]

The American Financial Mission left Persia in 1927. It was thus unable to influence the enactment of the opium control program which it had laid out for the Persian government. Nevertheless, the government did take certain preliminary steps when in July 1928 it enacted legislation establishing a government monopoly over circulation, storage, and the domestic and international sale of opium. It also prohibited the importation of the drug except upon special license and instituted a program for the gradual reduction of consumption until it would be completely suppressed within ten years. It was hoped that these measures would increase revenue, suppress smuggling, and satisfy world opinion that Persia was trying to meet its international obligations.[54] However, these measures did not materially affect the situation with reference to the escape of Persian opium into the illicit traffic, and the failure to carry out the rest of the recommended program left opium production at a high level. The Persian opium situation therefore remained a matter for serious concern well beyond the 1930's.

The disinclination of the League after 1927 to pursue further the subject of limitation of raw materials and the American policy of avoiding collaboration with the League precluded any further progress in the 1920's toward control of poppy cultivation and raw opium production. Mrs. Wright continued her efforts in this regard, however. She sought support for investigation of raw material production in other producing countries similar to that which had been conducted in Persia.[55] As Turkey was not receptive to the idea of a League commission, Mrs. Wright tried to get the American government to send

53. The American Legation (Berne) to the Secretary of State, Nov. 8, 1927, SDR 511.4A2/556; MacCallum, *op. cit.*, pp. 34–37.
54. Vice-Consul David Williamson (Teheran) to the Secretary of State, July 28, 1928, SDR 891.114 Narcotics/79 and Sept. 17, 1929, SDR 891.114 Narcotics/81.
55. Memorandum by Grew of conversation with Mrs. Wright, Jan. 15, 1926, SDR 511.4A2/470.

a strictly American commission to that country.[56] She and Congressman Porter attempted to persuade Henry Ford to finance such a project inasmuch as the Rockefeller Foundation had backed the Commission of Enquiry to Persia; but Ford failed to respond.[57] Therefore, in response to the specific suggestion of Admiral Mark Bristol, the American High Commissioner in Turkey, she went again to Turkey in 1927 to conduct a preliminary survey of the opium situation there. Turkish officials expressed a willingness to endorse formally the American position on the necessity of restricting raw material production and to conduct an investigation of their own into the opium situation in Turkey if the United States would officially request a statement of Turkey's attitude on the subject. But as no such request was forthcoming from the American government, the statement drafted by Mrs. Wright expressing the attitude of the Turkish government was not endorsed by that government.[58]

Despite lack of encouragement from the State Department, Mrs. Wright continued her work to achieve the goal of limitation at the source. She consistently pressed the American government to begin preliminary work toward the convening by the United States of a conference of the opium and coca leaf producing countries and thus resume leadership in the international movement.[59] But the State Department, detecting no change in the attitudes expressed by the producing countries at the Geneva Conference, saw no merit in her proposal. The Department was undecided whether to continue to place major emphasis on the curtailment of production of raw material or to shift its attention to a goal more likely to be achieved, the limitation of manufacture. Having no concrete and practical proposals to offer as a basis for holding a conference of producing states beyond the principles enunciated in 1924–1925, the State Department believed that such a conference would be futile.[60] Therefore, the American government temporarily

56. Memorandum by G. Howland Shaw of conversation with Mrs. Wright, June 22, 1926, SDR 867.114/17.

57. Porter to Henry Ford, Jan. 10, 1926, attached to memorandum by Nelson T. Johnson of conversation with Mrs. Wright, Jan. 18, 1928, SDR 511.4A5/1. Mrs. Wright to Grew, Jan. 29, 1927, SDR 80 0.114 N 16/91.

58. Shaw to Ambassador Grew (Constantinople), Dec. 13, 1927, SDR 800.114 N 16/91.

59. Mrs. Wright to Secretary of State Kellogg, Feb. 15, 1928, SDR 511.4A5/5; March 23, 1928, SDR 511.4A5/8; memorandum by Caldwell of conversation with Mrs. Wright, March 17, 1930, SDR 511.4Q1/4.

60. Secretary of State Kellogg to Mrs. Wright, Feb. 24, 1928, SDR 511.4A5/6; memorandum by Caldwell of conversation with Mrs. Wright, SDR 511.4Q1/4.

relegated the question of limitation at the source to the background and concentrated its attention and efforts on achieving limitation of manufacture. As discussed in Chapter IX, these efforts culminated in the Narcotics Limitation Convention of 1931.

When the United States again took up the issue of restriction of production, it had renewed its collaboration with the League. The revival of the subject was initiated by the League. On September 16, 1931, the Fifth Committee of the Assembly adopted the following resolution:

Taking note of the wish of certain Governments that a conference should meet in the near future to consider the possibility of limiting and controlling the cultivation of the opium-poppy and the cultivation and harvesting of the coca-leaf; and,

Taking note also of the decision reached by the Council at its sixty-second session, in January 1931, to ask the Advisory Committee on the Traffic in Opium and Other Dangerous Drugs to consider the possibility of summoning a conference of the Governments concerned and to report to the Council on the subject:

Asks the Advisory Committee . . . and the competent sections of the Secretariat of the League of Nations to undertake, as soon as possible, the collection of all material that may serve as a basis for the discussions of a Conference on the Limitation of the Production of Opium and the cultivation and harvesting of the coca-leaf, and for that purpose to send a questionnaire to the Governments Members and non-members of the League.[61]

This resolution, which was subsequently adopted by the full Assembly, was based on a recommendation of the Commission of Enquiry to the Far East. It was originally presented by the representative of Panama at the instigation of A. E. Blanco, and was supported by the Italian, Spanish, and British representatives. While giving general endorsement to the resolution, the producing countries took care to call attention to the economic aspects of the subject which would complicate the achievement of the goal desired.[62] The resolution was the logical outcome of the preceding deliberations on the narcotics problem which had just culminated in the convention limiting the manufacture of narcotic drugs.

Because of the nature of this phase of the narcotics problem, extensive preparations for a conference were necessary. From 1932 to 1937

61. League of Nations Assembly, Fifth Committee, *Traffic in Opium and Other Dangerous Drugs, Report by the Fifth Committee to the Assembly*, A.65.1931.V (Geneva, 1931), p. 3.
62. Gilbert (Geneva) to the Secretary of State, Sept. 17, 1931, SDR 511.4A5/13.

the Advisory Committee devoted its activities on the matter primarily to collecting information on all aspects of raw material production, traffic, and use and the bearing these operations had on the social, agricultural, commercial, economic, and financial conditions in the producing countries.[63] In 1936 it recommended the separation of the problem of opium cultivation from that of the cultivation and harvesting of the coca leaf. This was necessary because the two problems differed considerably from each other in their economic and social aspects. While progress was being made in regard to the opium problem, the coca leaf producing countries were not yet prepared to cooperate. After 1936, then, the Advisory Committee, while continuing to collect and study data on both problems, concentrated on preparing for a conference on raw opium production and postponed to a later date consideration of the curtailment of coca leaf cultivation.[64]

The United States fully approved of these preparations by the League, and it cooperated fully where possible. While desiring that a conference be held as soon as practicable, the American government continued to resist pressure for its own initiation of such a conference. Despite the absence of poppy cultivation in the United States, the government did not feel justified in taking the initiative on this matter, for it had passed no effective legislation to control such cultivation. Constitutional difficulties stood in the way of such action, for under the federal system this subject was deemed to be exclusively within the domain of the states. An attempt to get state action on the matter had been made by the Porter Act of 1930, which authorized the Secretary of the Treasury to cooperate with the states to secure such legislation. The Uniform Narcotic Drug Act had been endorsed in 1932, and the Treasury Department sent Mrs. Wright and Mrs. Isabel O'Neil to officials of the various states to urge the enactment of the Act. Prior to the passage of the Act by Nevada in March 1933, no state prohibited or controlled in any way the growth of the opium poppy or the production of raw opium. By the fall of 1934 only eight states had passed the Act.[65]

---

63. See, for example, League of Nations, Secretariat, Opium Section, *Coca Leaf Questionnaire*, C.641.M.303.1933.XI and *Raw Opium Questionnaire*, C.640.M.302.1933. XI.

64. League of Nations, Advisory Committee on Traffic in Opium and Other Dangerous Drugs, *Report to the Council on the Work of the Twenty-First Session*, C.278.M.168.1936.XI (Geneva, 1936), pp. 16–17.

65. Memorandum by Fuller to Hornbeck, Sept. 7, 1934, SDR 511.4Q1/8.

Another view presented in the State Department was that governments deriving considerable revenue from the traffic in raw opium should refrain from assuming a leadership role in convening a conference. The American government might fall in this category in that it derived nearly a million dollars annually from such impositions as import duties, excise taxes, license fees, and fees for drug order forms.[66] This argument obviously carried little weight, for most governments which strictly regulated the raw opium traffic received revenue which was incidental to the system of control.

A weightier consideration was the State Department's opinion that the summoning of an early conference would be a waste of time. In such major producing countries as Turkey, Yugoslavia, and India, from which effective limitation might be expected, production was not much in excess of legitimate needs. In the problem countries such as China and Persia, however, there was little disposition, because of either the inability or unwillingness of the governments, to restrict cultivation. Furthermore, time was needed to study adequately the situation raised by the recently effected method of extracting morphine from poppy straw. The United States therefore preferred to work within the framework of the League, where presumably the necessary groundwork for a conference was being laid with thorough study and preparation.[67] In the meantime, however, the State Department instituted negotiations with Canada and Mexico with a view to concluding a trilateral treaty prohibiting the cultivation of the opium poppy and the production of raw opium in the three countries. Discussions on the subject began in 1936, and by the end of 1939 negotiations were well under way.[68] The treaty was never consummated, however.

The United States did not acquiesce in all the suggestions emanating from the League. The State Department took vigorous exception to a resolution adopted by the Assembly which called for the holding of two preliminary conferences, one consisting of countries producing raw opium and exporting it to manufacturing countries together with the manufacturing countries; the other consisting of producing countries which exported raw opium to countries which had established smoking opium monopolies together with these monopoly countries. This resolution revived the old controversy as to what should be re-

66. *Ibid.*   67. *Ibid.*
68. I was not permitted to use the State Department material on these negotiations.

garded as production for legitimate purposes. The United States had consistently maintained that only production for strictly medical and scientific purposes was legitimate, while the opium monopoly countries contended that under the Hague Convention and subsequently the Geneva Agreement, production for opium eating as practiced in India and for the manufacture of prepared opium was legitimate.

On the resolution proper, the United States took the position that the idea contemplated in it of restricting a conference on the limitation of production to producing and manufacturing countries was unwise. Since the opium poppy could be grown in most parts of the world and from it opiates could be derived without going through the intermediate stage of raw opium, surplus supplies of such products anywhere in the world would find their way into the illicit traffic. Therefore, a conference on limitation should be open to all governments. Furthermore, separate preliminary conferences were neither necessary nor desirable. Regardless of the purpose for which raw opium was produced—for medical derivatives or for smoking opium—an excess would go into the illicit traffic. The American government still adhered to the principle that the production of raw opium was a single question; production should be limited to medical and scientific requirements, any other use being an abuse. If provisions for supplying opium smoking monopolies with raw opium were "absolutely necessary temporarily" the United States contended that such measures should provide for a reduction by a definite percentage annually of the amount of raw opium to be made available for such purposes. Thus the United States was prepared to refuse to participate in any preliminary conference or in a later general conference unless it was clearly established in advance that the limitation of poppy cultivation for morphine extraction and of raw opium production for all purposes, including the manufacture, internal trade in, and use of prepared opium were to be considered.[69]

The Canadian representative had expressed views at the twenty-first session of the Advisory Committee similar to those of the United States on the necessity of suppressing raw opium production for all purposes, but Canada had not opposed the suggestions for holding preliminary conferences when the subject was discussed in the Fifth Committee of the Assembly. The United States therefore sought to

69. Secretary of State Hull to Norman Armour, American Minister (Ottawa), March 19, 1937, SDR 511.4A5/43.

get Canada's support in opposing in the next session of the Advisory Committee the plans for holding the preliminary conferences, and through Canada, to convince the British government of the inadvisability of such preliminary discussions.[70] Through conversations with the Canadian government this support was obtained. The Canadian government informed the British government of the American and Canadian views, thus obviating any American approach to Great Britain.[71] At the twenty-third session of the Advisory Committee, the American and Canadian representatives, as previously agreed, voiced their objections to the holding of the preliminary conferences. As a result of their protests, this idea was abandoned in favor of the British suggestion that the Advisory Committee resolve itself into a special preparatory committee to make a preliminary examination of the material on the problem.[72] At this session the Advisory Committee, sitting as a preparatory committee, drew up a set of principles on which a future raw opium limitation convention should be based.[73] At its session in 1929 a draft convention based on these principles was drawn up. Both the list of principles and the draft convention were presented to the interested governments for their views.

The system of limitation provided for in the draft convention was based on that of the Narcotics Limitation Convention covering manufactured drugs. Significant differences had to be provided for, however, since the control of the production of an agricultural product involved many variables. These included fluctuating yield brought on by weather and soil, the inability to adjust production rapidly to changes in demand, and for opium, the difference in the morphine content and consistence (percentage of anhydrous opium contained

70. *Ibid.*

71. Armour (Ottawa) to the Secretary of State, March 26, 1937, SDR 511.4A5/45; Armour to Fuller, April 15, 1937, SDR 511.4A5/50; memorandum by George A. Morlock to Hornbeck, April 26, 1937, SDR 511.4A5/53; Armour to Hornbeck, April 29, 1937, SDR 511.4A5/58.

72. For the discussions in the Advisory Committee on this issue, see League of Nations, Advisory Committee on Traffic in Opium and Other Dangerous Drugs, *Minutes of the Twenty-second Session . . . May 24th to June 12th, 1937*, C.315.M.211.-1937.XI (Geneva, 1937), pp. 68–77, 80–86.

73. League of Nations, Advisory Committee on Traffic in Opium and Other Dangerous Drugs, *Report to the Council Concerning Preparatory Work for a Conference to Consider the Possibility of Limiting and Controlling the Cultivation of the Opium Poppy and the Production of Raw Opium and Controlling Other Raw Materials for the Manufacture of Opium Alkaloids. Drawn Up by the Advisory Committee at Its Twenty-third Session (May–June 1938)*, C.221.M.123.1938.XI (Geneva, 1938).

in a given quantity of raw opium) of raw opium produced under different climatic and soil conditions and in different areas of the world. The draft convention and the principles underlying it covered five general topics: the purpose of poppy cultivation and raw opium production, methods of achieving limitation and at the same time providing for a constant supply, the allocation of production among the producing countries, internal control of cultivation and production, and the application of international controls.[74]

Poppy cultivation and raw opium production were to be confined to recognized world requirements of opium and opiates for medical and scientific needs, for the manufacture temporarily of prepared opium, subject to any limitations which might be provided for in the convention, and for other forms of nonmedical consumption (opium eating) currently authorized in certain countries. Limitation of production to such purposes was to be achieved through the estimate system. All countries would submit to an international controlling authority estimates of needs, and if such estimates were validated, the contracting parties would be required to purchase or import the full quantity, but no more, of their estimates. This obligation was necessary to protect producing countries, which were required to produce and export the quantities necessary to fill the estimates, from fluctuations in demand. The purchase of drugs for re-export were also to be included in the estimates. The producing countries had also to submit, annually, binding estimates of production on the basis of the area to be cultivated. To insure that estimates of needs would be filled despite variations in output and to meet emergency demands, regulating stocks were to be maintained by producing countries. Consuming countries might maintain stocks for the use of the military and for emergency situations.[75]

A major problem was how to allocate production and exports among the producing countries. The draft envisaged a choice between a quota system and a free order system.[76] Under the quota system each producing country would be allotted on the basis of the estimates of

74. League of Nations, Advisory Committee on Traffic in Opium and Other Dangerous Drugs, *Report to the Council Concerning the Preparatory Work for a Conference to Consider the Possibility of Limiting and Controlling the Cultivation of the Opium Poppy and the Production of Raw Opium . . . Drawn Up by the Advisory Committee at Its Twenty-fourth Session (May–June 1939)* C.175.M.104.1939.XI (Geneva, 1939).

75. *Ibid.*   76. *Ibid.*

needs a certain percentage of the total world production for export. This would guarantee the producing countries a market and contribute to the stablization of both markets and prices. The disadvantage in the quota system lay in the creation of a monopoly for the existing producing countries and in depriving the purchasing countries of freedom of choice in selecting their source of supply. To remedy this latter defect, as well as to guarantee to some extent a stable market for the producing countries, the quota system, as provided for in the draft convention, required the consuming countries to state in their estimates, in order of preference, the country or countries from which they would obtain supplies. Under the free order system each producing country would produce for export the amount the consuming countries had stated in their estimates that they intended to purchase from that particular producing country. Thus freedom of choice in selecting their source of supply would be allowed to purchasing countries, and competition for markets would be maintained among the producing-exporting countries. The disadvantage in this system lay in the probable lack of stability in raw opium production, for if large purchasing countries changed their sources of supply from year to year, the producing countries affected would be placed in the almost impossible situation of trying to keep agricultural production abreast of the rise and fall in demand.

To control domestic cultivation and production the draft convention provided for a government monopoly in the producing countries of all activities and transactions in opium, from cultivation to distribution. Aside from the activities of the controlling authorities with reference to the estimates, international supervision of the trade in raw opium was to be maintained through the application of the import and export certificate system.[77]

The draft convention did not deal with the important matter of poppy straw, for by 1939 no consensus had been reached among the countries producing raw opium and those using or contemplating using the poppy straw method of extracting opiates. The raw opium producers wanted to prohibit entirely the extraction of opium alkaloids from poppy straw in order to protect their declining market for raw opium for the manufacture of derivatives. The countries using the extraction method naturally opposed restrictions on their authority to

77. *Ibid.*

use domestically produced products to meet their own needs, and they were reluctant to give up their right to export. A possible solution to the controversy was to confine the use of poppy straw for the extraction of opium alkaloids to the domestic needs of countries already engaged in such activities. The whole question, however, was left for future consideration by the Advisory Committee or by the proposed conference.[78]

Agreement had not been reached by 1939 on two other important matters necessary for effective limitation of raw material production. An international system of control providing for a stable market and a stable but limited source of supply would also have to provide for some degree of price stability in order to protect both producers and consumers. Producers needed to be assured that they would receive reasonable prices for their products, especially since curtailment of production might entail a considerable economic sacrifice for them. Consumers likewise needed assurance that the limited supplies available to them could be obtained at equitable prices. In addition, price regulation was desirable, since opium transactions under the estimate system entailed dealing in futures, as orders for raw opium would have to be placed considerably in advance of delivery. Of equal importance was the need for a uniform standard on which to formulate and submit statistics of production and trade, for the morphine content and consistence of raw opium varied considerably according to locality and conditions under which the opium poppy was cultivated. The settlement of these two issues was also left to future discussions.[79]

In general the views of the United States corresponded with the principles and provisions of the draft convention. As usual, the United States was particularly insistent that any limitation scheme devised clearly provide for the early limitation of the production of both raw opium and the cultivation of the poppy plant for the extraction of opium alkaloids to strictly medical and scientific requirements. Therefore the government suggested that provision be made to reduce by a fixed percentage annually the amount of raw opium produced for transformation into prepared opium. The draft convention did not deal with this matter, but left it for future consideration. As a result of its controversy with the League Secretary General over the issue of the budgetary independence of the Permanent Central Board and

78. Renborg, *op. cit.*, pp. 172–173.   79. *Ibid.*, pp. 173–174.

the Supervisory Body, the American government was equally insistent that any control machinery given functions by the raw material convention be absolutely and completely independent, and that provision be made for the parties to the convention to pay an equitable share of the cost of its implementation. This subject, too, was not covered by the draft convention, for the drafters had not progressed to the point of stipulating detailed measures of how it should be implemented.

The United States indicated no particular preference as to whether the quota or free order system should be adopted. What it desired was a system that would provide a constant and equitable division of the legitimate market without discriminating against the consuming countries. Thus the consuming countries should be allowed to become producing countries, especially for their internal needs, in the event they were discriminated against in the matter of supply or in case the existing source of supply was diminished or cut off by an emergency. Furthermore, producing and consuming countries party to the convention should not engage in any transactions with countries not party to the convention.

Finally, the United States appealed for the incorporation of measures in the convention providing for a "complete and absolute" system of government control over the cultivation of the opium poppy, the distribution of its products, and the maintenance of stocks of these products.[80] The United States did not draw up a draft convention of its own, but limited its activity to informing the Advisory Committee of the general principles on which an acceptable convention should be based. It was undoubtedly gratified to see that in the draft convention of the Advisory Committee a real advance toward the American goal of limitation at the source was being made.

As in other matters, the outbreak of World War II interrupted progress toward the conclusion of an agreement on what was regarded as the basic step toward solution of the narcotics problem. The Advisory Committee, consisting as it did of representatives of governments, was unable to continue functioning. The United States therefore sought to keep the issue alive. In June 1944 Congress passed a resolution introduced by Representative Walter Judd, a former missionary to China, requesting the President to urge the opium-producing countries to take steps to limit production to strictly medical and scientific

80. For these views, see Secretary of State to the American Chargé d'Affaires (Berne), Feb. 24, 1935, SDR 511.4A5/90.

needs. In accordance with the resolution, notes were subsequently sent late in the same year to Afghanistan, Great Britain (for India and Burma), China, Iran, Mexico, the Soviet Union, Turkey, and Yugoslavia. Satisfactory replies were received from Afghanistan, which stated that it had prohibited all cultivation of the opium poppy as of March 21, 1945, and Turkey, which declared that it was fully prepared to continue its program of limiting production and would participate in any conference called for that purpose. Great Britain, in replying for India, reiterated its long-held position that it would *control* production and export, but as opium was used for quasi-medical purposes, it could not wholly meet the American request. No reply was received from Iran.[81] The United Nations took over the issue in 1945. In June 1953 an international agreement for the limitation of the production of opium at the source was concluded in a United Nations conference in New York.[82] Thus after thirty years, through the instrumentality of the United Nations, the principle which the United States had enunciated in its first association with the League of Nations on the drug problem finally won the acceptance of the international community.

81. Helen H. Moorhead, "International Narcotics Control: 1939–1946," *Foreign Policy Association Reports*, XXII (July 1, 1946), 95–96.

82. For the conference, see United Nations, Economic and Social Council, *United Nations Opium Conference: Summary Record*, E/Conf.14/SR. 1–11, 1953 (New York, 1953).

Chapter twelve

Altruism and self-interest in America's narcotics diplomacy

The international movement to suppress the misuse of dangerous drugs arose out of developments in the nineteenth century. Beginning as an effort to rid China of the opium menace, it soon evolved into a campaign to solve what had become an almost universal problem. The initial interest of the United States in the problem stemmed from the participation of its nationals in the China opium trade. These activities were carried on without the countenance of the American government and people, and when their attention was drawn to the situation by the Anglo-Chinese War in 1839, they reacted with almost unanimous denunciation of the trade. Even the American participants in the traffic did not attempt to defend it. On the contrary, they, along with other Americans in China, strongly urged that the trade be brought to a close. But as the traffic was primarily an Anglo-Chinese affair, the power of the United States to alter the situation was limited to insuring that Americans ceased their participation in it.

Steps toward this end were begun, though ineffectually, with the Wanghia Treaty of 1844 and culminated in the 1880's with a treaty and enforcement legislation which barred Americans from engaging further in the trade. These measures were taken in response to the complaints by American missionaries and diplomatic officials to the effect that opium consumption was debauching the Chinese people, and that as a result, China was being weakened both politically and economically not only to its own disadvantage but also to the detriment of foreign trade. Thus an appeal was made not only to the moral and humanitarian sense of Americans, but to their economic self-interest as well. These twin approaches were subsequently to become characteristic features of the American appeal to other governments to help China rid itself of the evil.

By the end of the nineteenth century the United States believed that it had cleared itself of all complicity in the Chinese opium traffic, and while continuing to express a humanitarian interest in China's problem, it rejected the requests of missionaries and Chinese officials that it use its influence to persuade Great Britain to end the exportation of Indian opium to China. The United States maintained that this was essentially an Anglo-Chinese affair. But the subject could not be dismissed so easily. During the course of the century humanitarian problems had become increasingly matters of international concern and therefore subjects of diplomatic negotiations. In addition, the voices of missionaries and other reformers sounded ever louder in the councils of governments. The United States was particularly susceptible to such influence and responded to it in the late nineteenth and early twentieth centuries by becoming a party to international conventions on the liquor and white slave traffic and by taking unilateral action on such matters as the sale of opium and arms to so-called unprotected peoples in backward lands. Then, with the acquisition of the Philippine Islands, the United States acquired a concrete interest in the Far Eastern drug situation. Missionaries called the attention of the government to the opium problem in the islands, and in response to their suggestions, the United States, seeking to demonstrate the beneficence of its rule over dependent peoples, prohibited outright the traffic in and use of the drug except for medical and scientific purposes. It thus became the only Western power with Far Eastern possessions to so restrict the use of the drug, a position which it held until near the end of World War II.

The significance of the Philippine opium situation extended far beyond the islands. Its great importance was in furnishing the United States with ample justification for interceding on behalf of China with the other powers having Oriental possessions. Thus, in 1906, again in response to missionary influence, the United States launched an international campaign to help rid China of the opium menace. Although the movement soon broadened to include most of the world, China remained throughout a major factor in American considerations. And as a result of the great part played by missionaries and other reformers in the inauguration of the movement as well as in carrying it out, American participation in the campaign took on the aura of a moral crusade.

From the American viewpoint, the international movement to control the traffic in narcotic drugs, as covered by this study, may be divided into three periods corresponding to some extent to the influence which various other aspects of American foreign policy had upon American participation in the movement. The first phase covered the decade preceding the outbreak of World War I and was characterized by concentration on the drug traffic in the Far East. During this period the American approach to that traffic fell within the compass of the Open Door Policy in regard to China, although that approach was never officially stated as being a part of this policy. As is well known, the object of American policy with reference to China was the establishment and preservation of a strong, stable, and prosperous nation which would be able to resist the encroachments of foreign powers and at the same time provide opportunities for mutually profitable commercial relations with the West. As the opium habit was believed to be largely responsible for the political, social, and economic degeneration of China, its suppression was considered indispensable to China's revivification and to the development of her commercial potential. The Chinese shared this view, and an antiopium campaign was an important and the most successful part of the reform movement undertaken in China in the first decade of the twentieth century. By the end of the first phase of the international movement, China had made progress in suppressing opium production and consumption, though often through measures which some people regarded as inhumane, and Great Britain had virtually ended exportation of the drug from India to China. In the Hague Opium Convention provisions were made for the powers to assume the obligation of helping China as well as each other to eliminate the drug problem. The most conspicuous feature of that instrument was the requirement that countries prevent the export of opium products to countries prohibiting their entry, a principle first put forward by the United States at the Shanghai Commission.

The second phase of the antiopium movement covered the decade of the 1920's. During this period the United States gave priority to its own internal drug situation. As a result of the investigations in the preceding period, the United States, like other Western nations, had discovered that the drug traffic was not confined to the Far East, but was a growing menace in the West. During the second phase, therefore, the United States perfected its domestic legislation, the foundation of which had already been laid in the preceding period. The international efforts of the United States during this period were severely complicated, however, by the overriding political issue of the degree to which the United States should cooperate with the League of Nations. Effective collaboration with that organization ended in disillusionment with the Geneva Conferences in 1924–1925. For the remainder of the decade, the United States, confused as to what steps to take, adopted a passive role. Its coolness toward the League on the drug question was based not only on political considerations but reflected the long-held American view that most of the member states of the organization which were directly interested in the drug traffic did not really desire to see that traffic restricted because of the financial and other economic benefits which they derived from it. As most of these nations were represented on the Opium Advisory Committee, the United States viewed the League's drug policy as reflecting the interests of the so-called opium bloc.

Despite the unhappy results, the American participation in the deliberations of the League on the narcotics problem cannot be regarded as totally unproductive. By explicitly restating the American position, the American representatives helped to clarify the nature of the narcotics problem and the measures necessary to deal with it. In so doing they gave an impetus to effective action to solve the problem. The American position consisted of three main principles.

(1) The United States regarded the use of opium and other narcotic substances for other than strictly medical and scientific purposes as a moral and social evil.

(2) As a corollary, the United States concluded that the only legitimate transactions in these drugs, from production to consumption, were those designed to meet medical and scientific needs.

(3) The United States maintained that the basic solution to the drug problem lay in limiting the production of raw materials to the quantities necessary to fill the world's legitimate requirements.

Although the United States failed to get the international community to put these principles into effect during the 1920's, the vigorous insistence on their adoption set the stage for serious international efforts in the 1930's in this regard.

The third phase of the international movement falls conveniently within the decade of the 1930's. During this period the three aspects of the drug problem—smoking, smuggling, and surplus production—which had been considered but inadequately dealt with in the Geneva Opium Conferences were tackled anew in separate deliberations. The

United States modified its attitude toward the League, and by collaborating more closely with that body, was able to regain its place of leadership in the international campaign. The most important achievement during this period was the limitation of the manufacture of narcotic drugs to medical and scientific requirements. Less satisfactory, from the American viewpoint, were the measures adopted to deal with illicit traffic. The conference on opium smoking failed, as had previous conferences, to attack effectively the traffic in and use of this type of opium, but out of this failure came the impetus for a concerted effort to deal with the drug problem at what the United States regarded as its source, that is, by limiting production of raw materials. Much progress on a draft convention along this line had been made by the League and the interested states by the time the whole international movement was interrupted by the outbreak of World War II.

Having initiated the international movement, the United States supplied throughout its guiding spirit. Only briefly, when it discovered that its leadership role and its animosity toward the League of Nations were incompatible, did the United States relinquish its position of pre-eminence. On this occasion, individual Americans, either in their private capacities or with some official connection with the League, stepped into the breach. Their action was indicative of the considerable influence which Americans lacking official status with the government exercised throughout the course of the international campaign. The reforming zeal which many of them brought to the movement came even to characterize, to some extent, the official American approach. This was largely responsible for the holier-than-thou attitude often displayed by American representatives in the international discussions, which was so irritating to the other powers. This attitude also stemmed from the failure of the United States to give sympathetic consideration to a dilemma which many of the governments of other states had to face. Many of these states had to take into account the matter of conflicting interests, and the moral approach was not sufficient to pacify the various political, social, and economic groups which had a vested interest in the drug traffic. The United States was not plagued by a similar difficulty. Respectable elements in America were virtually all in accord on the problem. This enabled the American government to speak with a firm voice and to pursue a consistent policy without fear of antagonizing important segments of its population.

Moreover, many countries were genuinely skeptical, on both humanitarian and practical grounds, of the efficacy of the prohibition approach to the drug problem; and there was no convincing evidence from the experience of areas in which the system was in effect to allay this doubt. In the Philippines, opium smuggling remained a problem. China's prohibition of opium smoking was followed by a huge illicit traffic in manufactured drugs. And even in the United States, various claims, official and unofficial, of a reduction in narcotic drug consumption following the introduction of prohibition could not be conclusively substantiated. On the contrary, many persons have contended that from the initiation of the policy of prohibition to the end of the period covered by this study, the consumption of opiates, fed by a growing illicit traffic, not only failed to decline but was exacerbated by the addict's resort to criminal behavior in his efforts to acquire money to purchase the high-priced illicit product.[1] America's prohibition policy was also embarrassed by the failure of her experiment in liquor prohibition, a fact which the foreign press was fond of pointing out.[2]

Though often a source of exasperation to the other powers, the American attitude was beneficial to the movement as a whole. By directing the glare of publicity and moral condemnation on nations which were slow to cooperate in the efforts to suppress the misuse of dangerous drugs, the United States was successful in persuading many of them to take more vigorous action. In the case of certain nations, however, notably China and Japan, where either political instability or official and public indifference prevailed, such actions were of little effect. This is why the Far Eastern drug situation had become, once again during the 1930's the most crucial element in the whole drug-control problem.

The drug-control movement illustrates the fact that even in diplomatic negotiations on primarily humanitarian matters, political considerations are seldom absent. Prominent in the approach of the United States toward the drug problem were its political attitudes and objectives in regard to China, Japan, the Soviet Union, and the League of

---

1. See, for example, "Opium," *The Outlook*, CVIII (Dec. 23, 1914), 896–897; and a draft memorandum in the Far Eastern Division of the State Department entitled, *Experience in the United States with the Plan of Selling Drugs to Addicts at Low Prices*, July 25, 1935, SDR 500C.1197/886. For an extended refutation of the claim of the United States Bureau of Narcotics that there has been a substantial decrease in drug addiction since 1914, see Lindesmith, *op. cit.*, pp. 104–114.

2. See above, p. 204.

Nations. Only in the case of the League did the American views have a detrimental effect, and then only temporarily. Yet, despite the political and economic factors involved, as well as the difficulty involved in controlling such highly desired and easily concealable products as narcotic drugs, considerable progress had been made on the international level by the end of the 1930's in dealing with the drug problem. Several multilateral treaties were in operation and another was in the draft stage which were based largely on principles advocated by the United States. A highly complex control machinery had been fashioned to deal with manufacture and with the international traffic. This control machinery had already been considered as a possible model on which the regulation of other matters of international import, such as the trade in and manufacture of arms, might be based. These international measures were supplemented by strict systems of national control in many countries.

On the other hand, after three decades of national and international effort, the abuse of narcotic drugs was still a pressing problem, and especially so in the United States, to which the illicit traffic naturally gravitated because of the demand and the high prices obtainable for the drugs. One of the reasons for this situation was the fact that owing to the lack of cooperation of certain nations or insufficient time to put into force the control measures called for, the full effects of the international conventions had not been felt. In addition, glaring loopholes in the system of control remained, due to the lack of control over the production of raw materials and the absence of effective provisions for the suppression of opium smoking. Furthermore, despite the emphasis on the limitation of the supplies available, the real solution to the drug problem—the elimination of the demand for drugs for illicit purposes through preventive measures and the care and treatment of addicts—had yet to be given adequate consideration by the international community. The remedy for all of these deficiencies had to await the conclusion of the Second World War when, under the auspices of the United Nations, the fourth phase of the drug control movement began.

Epilogue

A sketch of the international
movement since 1939

As indicated in the body of this study, the war years did not completely interrupt the international efforts at narcotic drug control.[1] The United States took special pains to insure that the momentum that had built up over the previous decades would not be dissipated. Therefore, the Permanent Central Board and the Supervisory Body were invited to carry on their work from the United States, and branches of these agencies were established in Washington, D.C., for the duration of the war. The United States also made representations, already mentioned, to the nations involved in the traffic in prepared opium and the production of raw materials. By 1945 several of the Western nations with Far Eastern possessions had abolished or had promised to abolish the smoking opium monopolies in those of their territories which had been liberated from the Japanese, and some of the producing states had indicated a willingness to continue the discussions on the limitation of the production of raw products.

In 1946 the United Nations took over the functions of the League of Nations in the narcotics field. At its first session in 1946 the Economic and Social Council created the Commission on Narcotic Drugs as a replacement for the Opium Advisory Committee. By the Protocol of 1946 all the functions exercised by the League under the existing narcotics conventions were transferred to the United Nations, and in 1948 the first of the international agreements under United Nations auspices dealing with substantial aspects of the drug problem was con-

1. Convenient summaries of the international efforts since 1939 are contained in Norman Ansley, "International Efforts to Control Narcotics," *Journal of Criminal Law, Criminology and Police Science,* I (July, Aug. 1959), 105–112; Robert W. Cox, "The Suppression of Illicit Narcotic Drug Traffic Through International Cooperation," *Notre Dame Lawyer,* XXXVII, No. 1 (1961), 106–116; Helen H. Moorhead, "International Narcotics Control: 1939–1946"; *United Nations Review,* VIII (Feb., 1961), 3; (May, 1961), 28–29; (Sept., 1961), 26–27; and United Nations, Office of Public Information, *International Control of Narcotic Drugs,* 65–18122–15M–Oct., 1965.

cluded. The Paris Protocol of 1948 supplemented the Narcotics Limitation Convention of 1931 by placing under the control provisions of the latter convention, on the recommendation of the World Health Organization, any new drug found to be capable of producing addiction.

The Paris Protocol was followed in 1953 by the Protocol for Limiting and Regulating the Cultivation of the Poppy Plant, the Production of, International and Wholesale Trade in, and Use of Opium. The Protocol covered raw opium, medicinal opium, and prepared opium, and specifically provided for the restriction of the use of the drug to medical and scientific needs. To this end the use of opium for quasi-medical purposes was to be suppressed within fifteen years after the Protocol came into effect. The inability of the manufacturing and producing states to agree on prices—one of the matters left unresolved in the Advisory Committee's draft of 1939—prevented the adoption of a direct system of limitation on a quota basis. Therefore, curtailment of production was to be achieved indirectly by limiting the stocks of opium to be maintained by the individual producing, manufacturing, and consuming states, a system similar to that of the Narcotics Limitation Convention. Producing states were obligated to establish special government agencies to control production, use, and trade in opium and to limit the area cultivated. Countries producing poppy straw were to prohibit the production of opium from such poppies. Only seven states—Bulgaria, Greece, India, Iran, Turkey, the Soviet Union, and Yugoslavia—were to be permitted to export opium, and imports by manufacturing and consuming countries were to be restricted to opium produced in these seven states. Estimates of needs and statistics on production, consumption, trade, and other opium transactions were to be submitted to the Permanent Central Board. The board would have authority to impose an import and export embargo on a state that was considered to be a center of illicit traffic. For the Protocol to go into effect, ratification by twenty-five countries, including at least three of the producing and three of the manufacturing states listed in the document was necessary. The United States was among the early ratifiers of the instrument, but as ratification by the requisite number of producing countries proceeded at a slow pace, the Protocol did not go into force until March 1963, and then among only forty-five countries. Five states have since become parties to it.

Throughout most of the 1950's the United Nations Commission on

Narcotic Drugs was engaged in efforts to draft a convention which would consolidate the existing multilateral treaties in a single instrument and thereby simplify the law and the international machinery of control. These efforts culminated in a United Nations conference in early 1961, and the Single Convention on Narcotic Drugs was opened for signature from March 30 to August 1 of that year. During that period sixty-four countries signed the Convention, and it came into force on December 13, 1964, after forty countries ratified or acceded to it. In addition to consolidating the existing instruments, the Convention attempted to cover all narcotic substances and to restrict their production and use to strictly medical and scientific purposes. Furthermore, provisions calling for international technical assistance and measures for the treatment of addicts were illustrative of the increasing attention on an international level which has been given over the past thirteen years to the problem of addiction itself—its prevention and treatment, and rehabilitation and aftercare of addicts—in contradistinction to the emphasis on suppressing illicit drug supplies. Thus a new phase of the international drug-control movement appears to be in progress in which efforts are being focused increasingly on reducing the demand for drugs (and thereby limiting the quantities produced) by helping the addict to give up the habit as well as by preventing new recruits to the vice.

The United States did not sign the Single Convention, fearing that as the production of opium for export was not confined to the seven countries listed in the 1953 Protocol, other countries might engage in such production and thereby increase the amount of opium available for the illicit traffic. A secondary fear was that as the Convention was specifically open to reservations, its provisions might not be fully and universally applied. By early 1967, however, the State Department concluded that these fears had been proved groundless, and in view of the acceptance of the Convention by a growing number of countries and the desirability of having a role in its control machinery, recommended adhesion by the United States.[2] Without opposition from any source, the Senate approved the Convention on May 8, and it came into force for the United States on June 24, 1967.

As in other matters, the Cold War has served to complicate efforts at international collaboration in the suppression of the drug menace. Most

2. *Department of State Bulletin*, LVI (April 24, 1967), 672–673.

communist states have cooperated in the drug-control movement. However, since 1951 the United States has complained in the United Nations Commission on Narcotic Drugs about the exportation of heroin from Communist China to feed the illicit traffic to the United States and other areas. The United States charges that the Chinese are promoting this traffic in order to obtain foreign exchange to buy strategic materials and at the same time weaken Western countries by poisoning their inhabitants,[3] thus again making the opium traffic a national weapon.

China is not, of course, the chief source of the drugs found in the illicit traffic in the United States. In 1961, North Korea, South Korea, Mexico, and France were the principal sources in addition to China of the heroin seized in the illicit traffic in the United States, while India and Mexico were the main sources of raw and prepared opium. Cocaine seized in the illicit traffic came from Bolivia, Peru, Panama, and Colombia.[4] With the addition of the Middle East, the sources and routes of illicit drug trafficking to the United States in 1966 were essentially the same as they were in 1961.[5]

Despite the comprehensive and complex international control measures as well as America's own strict system of control, the United States continues to have a serious narcotics problem. Statistics on the extent of the problem are unreliable. The Federal Bureau of Narcotics reported 59,720 narcotics addicts as of the end of 1966,[6] an increase of 12,922 over the number reported in 1961. The Bureau's listings, however, suffer from an inadequate information-gathering system. As conceded in the report of a Presidential task force on narcotics in 1967,

most of the names in the file are of persons arrested by state and local police agencies and reported voluntarily to the Bureau on a form the Bureau provides for this purpose. Thus the inclusion of a person's name in the file depends in large measure on his coming to the attention of the

3. Harry Anslinger and William F. Tomkins, *Traffic in Narcotics* (New York; 1953) chap. iv. See also U.S. Cong., Senate, Committee on the Judiciary, *Communist China and Illicit Narcotic Traffic, Hearing Before the Subcommittee to Investigate the Administration of the Internal Security Act and Other Internal Security Laws,* 84th Cong., 1st Sess., 1955 (Washington: Government Printing Office, 1955).

4. U.S. Treasury Department, Bureau of Narcotics, *Traffic in Opium and Other Dangerous Drugs for the Year Ended December 31, 1961* (Washington: Government Printing Office, 1962), pp. 24, 26.

5. U.S. Treasury Department, Bureau of Narcotics, *Traffic in Opium and Other Dangerous Drugs for the Year Ended December 31, 1966* (Washington: Government Printing Office, 1967), p. 31.

6. *Ibid.,* p. 26.

police, being recognized and classified as an addict, and being reported. Moreover, some police agencies and many health and medical agencies do not participate in the voluntary reporting system. There is also no place in the system for persons who use opiates without becoming addicted. For these reasons many people feel that the Bureau's file does not present a complete statistical picture of opiate use in this country.[7]

The task force went on to note, however, that "other estimates of the present addict population, some of which cite figures as high as 200,000, are without solid statistical foundation."[8]

Another dimension to the current drug situation in the United States is the increasing use of marihuana, a nonaddicting drug having little in common with the opiates but under similar legal controls, state and federal. Controversy rages over the degree to which it can be classified, comparatively, as a dangerous drug.[9] Similar concern is manifested over rising consumption of hallucinogens, amphetamines, and barbiturates. Much of the present anxiety over nonmedical use of the various classes of drugs arises from the fact that whereas once such use was regarded as a vice of depressed social and economic groups, with certain exceptions, it is clear today that large segments of the respectable middle class, especially college students and young professional people, are also using these substances.

There is also much controversy today over the proper approach that should be taken toward reducing the drug problem. Many contend that the problem should be considered primarily a medical matter to be handled by the medical profession rather than a criminal issue to be attacked by law-enforcement agencies. Reflecting the sustained concern with the problem have been the numerous studies and discussions carried on over the past seven years by the federal and several state governments, and by medical and legal societies. On only one point does there seem to be agreement, and that is that before a solution to the problem will be forthcoming, extensive research is needed on all phases of the problem.

---

7. The President's Commission on Enforcement and Administration of Justice, Task Force on Narcotics and Drug Abuse, *Task Force Report: Narcotics and Drug Abuse* (Washington: Government Printing Office, 1967), p. 2. A critical analysis of the Bureau's statistics on drug addiction is given by Lindesmith, *op. cit.*, pp. 99–134.

8. *Task Force Report: Narcotics and Drug Abuse*, p. 2.

9. David Solomon (ed.), *The Marihuana Papers* (Indianapolis, Ind.: Bobbs-Merrill Company, Inc., 1966).

Bibliography

The chief unpublished primary sources consulted for this study were the records of the Department of State for the years 1906 to 1939, the records of the Bureau of Insular Affairs for the years 1899 to 1939, both in the National Archives, Washington, D.C., and the Papers of Bishop Charles H. Brent in the Manuscript Division of the Library of Congress. The State Department material covers primarily American participation in international conferences on narcotics, the collaboration between the United States and the League on the problem, and correspondence with individual nations relative to the illicit traffic and the drug problem as a whole. A wide range of records was consulted, including especially index file 774 and decimal files 500.C1197, 500.C3, 511.4A1, 511.4A2, 511.4A2A, 511.4A5, 511.4A6, 511.4A6A, 511.4Q1, 511.4R1, 511.4T1, 800.114, 867.114, 891.114, and 893.114. Much of the conference material through the year 1914 is duplicated in Record Group 43, Entries 33 through 51, in the National Archives. The records of the Bureau of Insular Affairs constitute the best source on the opium situation in the Philippines.

The Brent Papers are valuable not only for showing the substantial influence of Bishop Brent on the antidrug campaign but also for revealing the story behind the governmental correspondence and the official records of the international conferences. Other papers in the Manuscript Division of the Library of Congress which deal almost exclusively with the narcotics question are those of Ellen N. La Motte and Richmond Pearson Hobson. The former's consist mainly of the mimeographed minutes of the League of Nations Opium Advisory Committee. The latter's, which were of little value for this study, deal with the activities of the International Narcotic Education Association, the World Narcotic Defense Association, and the World Conference on Narcotic Education, all private organizations founded and headed by Hobson for the purpose of conducting an education and propaganda campaign against the misuse of drugs. Additional papers consulted but yielding little of value for this study were those of John Hay, Theodore Roosevelt, Elihu Root, William H. Taft, Philander C. Knox, Leonard Wood, and Admiral Mark Bristol.

Public Documents

Great Britain: Parliamentary Papers

Foreign Office. *Correspondence Respecting the Cultivation of Opium in*

China. China No. 1 (1921), Cmd. 1531. London: H.M. Stationery Office, 1921.

———. *Correspondence Respecting the Opium Question in China.* China No. 1 (1908), Cd. 3881. London: H.M. Stationery Office, 1908.

———. *Correspondence Respecting the Second International Conference, Held at the Hague, July, 1913.* Miscellaneous No. 2 (1914), Cd. 7276. London: H.M. Stationery Office, 1914.

———. *Correspondence Respecting the Third International Opium Conference, Held at the Hague, June, 1914.* Miscellaneous No. 4 (1915), Cd. 7813. London: H.M. Stationery Office, 1915.

———. *Instructions to the British Delegates to the International Opium Conference, Held at the Hague, December, 1911–January, 1912.* Miscellaneous No. 3 (1913), Cd. 6605. London: H.M. Stationery Office, 1913.

———. *Report of the British Delegates to the International Opium Conference, Held at the Hague, December, 1911–January, 1912.* Miscellaneous No. 11 (1912), Cd. 6448. London: H.M. Stationery Office, 1912.

———. *Report of the British Delegation on the International Conferences on Opium and Dangerous Drugs, Held at Geneva, November, 1924, to February, 1925.* Miscellaneous No. 8 (1925), Cmd. 2461. London: H.M. Stationery Office, 1927.

League of Nations

Advisory Committee on Traffic in Opium and Other Dangerous Drugs. *Minutes of the [First through the Twenty-fifth] Sessions.* Geneva, 1921–1940.

———. *Report to the Council Concerning the Preparatory Work for a Conference to Consider the Possibility of Limiting and Controlling the Cultivation of the Opium Poppy and the Production of Raw Opium and Controlling Other Raw Materials for the Manufacture of Opium Alkaloids, Drawn Up by the Advisory Committee at Its Twenty-third Session (May–June, 1938).* C.221.M.123.1938, XI. Geneva, 1938.

———. *Report to the Council Concerning the Preparatory Work for a Conference to Consider the Possibility of Limiting and Controlling the Cultivation of the Opium Poppy and the Production of Raw Opium and Controlling Other Raw Materials for the Manufacture of Opium Alkaloids, Drawn Up by the Advisory Committee at Its Twenty-third Session (May–June, 1939).* C.175.M.104.1939.XI. Geneva, 1939.

———. *Report to the Council on the Work of the Twelfth Session (January 17–February 2, 1929).* C.33.1929.XI, OC.943 (1). Geneva, 1929.

———. *Report to the Council on the Work of the Thirteenth Session.* C.138.M.51.1930. XI. Geneva, 1930.

Assembly. Fifth Committee. *Traffic in Opium and Other Dangerous Drugs. Report of the Fifth Committee to the Assembly.* A.65.1931.V. Geneva, 1931.

————. *Traffic in Opium and Other Dangerous Drugs. Report of the Fifth Committee to the Assembly.* A.86.1929.XI. Geneva, 1929.

Commission of Enquiry into the Control of Opium-Smoking in the Far East. *Report to the Council.* Vol. I: *Report with Comparative Tables, Maps and Illustrations.* Vol. II: *Detailed Memoranda on Each Territory Visited by the Commission.* Vol. III: *Collection of Laws and Regulations Governing the Control of Opium-Smoking in the Territories Visited by the Commission.* C.635.M.254.1930.XI, Vols. I, II, III. Geneva, 1930.

Commission of Enquiry into the Production of Opium in Persia. *Letter from the Chairman of the Commission.* A.16.1927.XI. Geneva, 1927.

————. *Observation of the Persian Government.* A.8.1927.XI. Geneva, 1926.

————. *Report to the Council.* C.580.M.219.1926.XI. Geneva, 1926.

Conference on the Limitation of the Manufacture of Narcotic Drugs, *Control of Narcotic Drugs in Turkey, Memorandum Forwarded by the Minister for Foreign Affairs of the Turkish Republic.* C.382.M.157. 1931.VI. Geneva, 1931.

Conference on the Suppression of Opium Smoking Convened Under Article XII of the Geneva Opium Agreement, 1925, Bangkok, November 9th–27th, 1931. *Minutes of the Meetings and Documents Submitted to the Conference.* C.577.M.284.1932.XI. Geneva, 1932.

First Opium Conference, Geneva, November 3rd, 1924–February 11th, 1925, Minutes and Annexes. C.684.M.244.1924.XI. Geneva, 1924.

Official Journal. February 1934.

Records of the Conference for the Limitation of the Manufacture of Narcotic Drugs, Geneva, May 27th to July 13th, 1931. Vol. I: *Plenary Meetings, Text of the Debates.* Vol. II: *Meetings of the Committees and the Sub-Committee on Control.* C.509.M.214.1931.XI. Geneva, 1931.

Records of the Conference for the Suppression of the Illicit Traffic in Dangerous Drugs (Geneva, June 8th to 26th, 1936). Text of the Debates. C.341.M.216.1936.XI. Geneva, 1936.

Records of the Second Opium Conference, Geneva, November 17th, 1924–February 19th, 1925. Vol. I: *Plenary Meetings, Text of the Debates.* Vol. II: *Meetings of the Committees and Sub-Committees.* C.760.M.-260.1924.XI. Geneva, 1925.

Report of the Opium Preparatory Committee. C.348.M.119.1924.XI. Geneva, 1924.

Secretariat. Opium Section. *Coca Leaf Questionnaire.* C.641.M.303.1933.-XI. Geneva, 1933.

————. *Raw Opium Questionnaire.* C.640.M.302.1933.XI. Geneva, 1933.

United States

Congressional Record. Vols. XXXIII, XXXIV, XXXV, XLIII, LI–LV, LVII, LVIII, LXV, LXVI, LXXII, LXXV.

Federal Narcotics Control Board. *Traffic in Opium and Other Dangerous*

Drugs . . . Report by the Government of the United States of America, 1925/26–1929. Washington: Government Printing Office, 1926–1930.

House of Representatives, Committee on Foreign Affairs. *Hearings on H.J. Res. 195. . . . The Traffic in Habit-Forming Narcotic Drugs.* House Doc. 380. 68th Cong., 1st Sess., 1924. Washington: Government Printing Office, 1924.

———, Committee on Interstate and Foreign Commerce. *To Prohibit the Importation of Opium for Other than Medicinal Purposes . . . Report.* H.R. 1878. 60th Cong., 2nd Sess., Washington: Government Printing Office, 1909.

———, Committee on Ways and Means. *Hearings . . . on H.R. 25240, H.R. 25241, and H.R. 25242, Importation and Use of Opium.* 61st Cong., 2nd Sess., 1910. Washington: Government Printing Office, 1910.

———, ———. *Hearings . . . on H.R. 25240, H.R. 25241, H.R. 25242, and H.R. 28911, Importation and Use of Opium.* 61st Cong., 3rd Sess., 1911.

———, Subcommittee of the Committee on Ways and Means. *Exportation of Opium, Hearings . . . on H.R. 14500, A Bill to Amend Section 6 of an Act Approved January 17, 1914, Entitled "An Act to Prohibit the Importation and Use of Opium for Other Than Medicinal Purposes," Approved February 9, 1909.* 66th Cong., 3rd Sess., 1920–1921. Washington: Government Printing Office, 1921.

———, ———. *Traffic in, and Control of Narcotics, Barbiturates and Amphetamines. Hearings Before a Subcommittee of the Committee on Ways and Means.* 84th Cong., 2nd Sess., 1955. Washington: Government Printing Office, 1956.

Lewis, Elmer A. (compiler). *Opium and Narcotic Laws.* Washington: Government Printing Office, 1955.

Malloy, William M., C. R. Redmond, and Edward J. Trenwith (compilers). *Treaties, Conventions, International Acts, Protocols and Agreements Between the United States of America and Other Powers, 1776–1937.* 4 vols. Washington: Government Printing Office, 1910–1938.

Miller, David Hunter (ed.). *Treaties and Other International Acts of the United States of America.* 7 vols. Washington: Government Printing Office, 1931–1941.

Philippine Commission, Opium Investigation Committee. *Use of Opium and Traffic Therein. Message from the President of the United States, Transmitting the Report of the Committee Appointed by the Philippine Commission to Investigate the Use of Opium and the Traffic Therein.* . . . 59th Cong., 1st Sess., Senate Doc. 265. Washington: Government Printing Office, 1906.

President's Commission on Enforcement and Administration of Justice, Task Force on Narcotics and Drug Abuse. *Task Force Report: Narcotics and Drug Abuse.* Washington: Government Printing Office, 1967.

Senate, Committee on Finance. *Exportation of Opium Hearings on S. 4553. A Bill to Amend Section 6 of an Act Approved January 17th, 1914,*

Entitled "An Act to Prohibit the Importation and Use of Opium for Other Than Medicinal Purposes," Approved February 9, 1909. 66th Cong., 3rd Sess., 1920–1921. Washington: Government Printing Office, 1920–1921.

————, ————. *Manufacture of Smoking Opium.* Report No. 130. 63rd Cong., 1st Sess., 1913. Washington: Government Printing Office, 1913.

————, ————. *Registration of Persons Dealing in Opium.* Report No. 258. 63rd Cong., 2nd Sess., 1914. Washington: Government Printing Office, 1914.

————, Committee on Foreign Relations. *Sale of Poisons in Consular Districts of the United States in China.* Report No. 1267. 62nd Cong., 3rd Sess., 1913. Washington: Government Printing Office, 1913.

————, Committee on the Judiciary. *Communist China and Illicit Narcotic Traffic, Hearings Before the Subcommittee to Investigate the Administration of the Internal Security Act and Other Internal Security Laws.* 84th Cong., 1st Sess., 1955. Washington: Government Printing Office, 1955.

————. *Compilation of Treaties and Laws for the Protection of Native Races Against Intoxicants.* Document No. 200. 56th Cong., 2nd Sess., 1901.

————. *Report of the Hearing at the American State Department on Petitions to the President to Use His Good Offices for the Release of China from Treaty Compulsion to Tolerate the Opium Traffic, with Additional Papers.* Document No. 135. 58th Cong., 3rd Sess., 1905.

————. *Resolution, Adopted by the Senate January 4, 1901, Relative to the Protection of Uncivilized Peoples Against the Destructive Traffic in Intoxicants.* Document No. 159. 56th Cong., 2nd Sess., 1901.

State, Department of. *Bulletin.* Vol. LVI, 1967.

————. *Conference on the Limitation of the Manufacture of Narcotic Drugs, Geneva, May 27–July 13, 1931. Report of the Delegation of the United States to the Secretary of State.* Washington: Government Printing Office, 1932.

————. *The Opium Evil. Message from the President of the United States Transmitting Communication of the Secretary of State Covering the Report of the American Delegation to the International Opium Conference Held at the Hague from December 1, 1911 to January 23, 1912.* Senate Doc. 733. 62nd Cong., 2nd Sess., 1912. Washington: Government Printing Office, 1912.

————. *The Opium, Morphine and Other Drug Evils. Letter from the Secretary of the Treasury, Transmitting Copy of a Communication from the Secretary of State Submitting an Estimate of Appropriations to Continue its Efforts to Mitigate the Opium, Morphine, and Other Allied Drug Evils.* House Doc. 1043. 62nd Cong., 3rd Sess., 1912. Washington: Government Printing Office, 1912.

————. *The Opium Problem. Message from the President of the United States Transmitting . . . A Report on the International Opium Problem*

... *Prepared by Mr. Hamilton Wright....* Senate Doc. 377. 61st Cong., 2nd Sess., 1910. Washington: Government Printing Office, 1910.

———. *The Opium Traffic. Message from the President of the United States Transmitting Report of the Secretary of State Relative to the Control of the Opium Traffic.* Senate Doc. 736. 61st Cong., 3rd Sess., 1911. Washington: Government Printing Office, 1911.

———. *Papers Relating to the Foreign Relations of the United States,* 1869, I; 1871; 1876; 1880; 1881; 1883; 1887; 1906, I; 1918; 1919, *Paris Peace Conference,* IV, V, XI; 1923, I; 1929, I; 1931, I; 1932, I, *General;* 1933, IV, *The Far East;* 1938, IV, *The Far East.* Washington: Government Printing Office, 1869–1939.

———. *Second International Opium Conference. Message from the President of the United States Transmitting a Communication from the Secretary of State, Accompanied by a Report Prepared by Hamilton Wright, on Behalf of the American Delegates to the Second International Opium Conference, Which Met at the Hague ... July [1–9], 1913. ...* Senate Doc. 157. 63rd Cong., 1st Sess., 1913. Washington: Government Printing Office, 1913.

Treasury, Department of, Bureau of Narcotics. *Traffic in Opium and Other Dangerous Drugs ... Report by the Government of the United States of America.* Washington: Government Printing Office, 1931.

———. Special Narcotic Committee. *Traffic in Narcotic Drugs Report of Special Committee of Investigation Appointed March 25, 1918 by the Secretary of the Treasury, June, 1919.* Washington: Government Printing Office, 1919.

Miscellaneous

Conference on the Limitation of the Manufacture of Dangerous Drugs. Preliminary Meeting of Manufacturing Countries, London, October, 1930, Verbatim Report. M. C. (Lond.) PV. 1–20. London, 1930. Mimeographed.)

Hawaiian Islands, Legislature, Special Committee on Opium. *Report of Special Committee on Opium to the Legislature of 1892, Acting Under Resolution of Honorable J. H. Waipulani.* Honolulu, 1892.

Hudson, Manley O. (ed.). *International Legislation: A Collection of the Texts of Multipartite Instruments of General Interest,* Vol. III. Washington, D.C.: Carnegie Endowment for International Peace, 1931.

International Opium Conference, The Hague, December 1st, 1911–January 23rd, 1912. *Summary of the Minutes (Unofficial).* The Hague: National Printing Office, 1912.

MacMurray, John V. A. (compiler and editor). *Treaties and Agreements With and Concerning China, 1894–1919.* 2 vols. New York: Oxford University Press, 1921.

Report of the International Opium Commission, Shanghai, China, February 1 to February 26, 1909. Vol. I: *Report of the Proceedings.* Vol. II: *Re-*

port of the Delegations. Shanghai: North China Daily News and Herald, Ltd., 1909.

Second International Opium Conference. The Hague, 1–9 July 1913. *Summary of the Minutes (Unofficial).* The Hague: National Printing Office, 1913.

United Nations, Economic and Social Council, Commission on Narcotic Drugs. *Illicit Traffic in Narcotic Drugs, Review of World Traffic from 1 January 1940 to 30 June 1946.* E/CN.7/68. New York, 1947.

———, Office of Public Information. *International Control of Narcotic Drugs.* 65–18122–15M–October, 1965. New York, 1965.

———. *United Nations Opium Conference, Summary Record.* E/Conf.; 14/SR. 1–11, 1953. New York, 1953.

United Nations Review, Vols. VIII and IX, 1961–62.

Books

Anslinger, Harry, and Will Oursler. *The Murderers: The Story of the Narcotic Gangs.* New York: Farrar, Straus and Cudahy, 1961.

Anslinger, Harry, and William F. Tompkins. *The Traffic in Narcotics.* New York: Funk and Wagnalls, 1953.

Anti-Opium League. *The Greater Year of Anti-Opium: Annual Report of the Anti-Opium League. . . .* Shanghai: North Chinese Daily News and Herald, Ltd., 1909.

Bemis, Samuel Flagg. *A Diplomatic History of the United States.* 3rd ed. revised. New York: Henry Holt and Company, 1950.

Berdahl, Clarence A. *The Policy of the United States with Respect to the League of Nations.* Graduate Institute of International Studies. Geneva: Libraire Kundig, 1932.

Bishop, Ernest S. *The Narcotic Drug Problem.* New York: The Macmillan Co., 1920.

Bland, John O. P. *Li Hung Chang.* London: Constable and Company, Ltd., 1917.

Buel, Raymond L. *The International Opium Conferences, with Relevant Documents.* World Peace Foundation Pamphlets, VIII, Nos. 2–3. Boston: World Peace Foundation, 1925.

Cameron, Meribeth E. *The Reform Movement in China, 1898–1912.* Stanford University, Calif.: Stanford University Press, 1931.

Campbell, Charles S. *Special Business Interests and the Open Door Policy.* New Haven, Conn.: Yale University Press, 1951.

Chahkar, Mohammed. *Le Problème de l'opium en Iran.* Paris: Libraire Orientale et Américaine, G. P. Maisonneuve, 1936.

China Centenary Missionary Conference Records. Report of the Great Conference Held at Shanghai, April 5th to May 8, 1907. New York: American Tract Society, 1907.

Claude, Inis L., Jr. *Swords into Plowshares: The Problems and Progress of International Organization.* New York: Random House, 1956.

Crafts, Wilbur Fisk. *A Primer of Internationalism with Special Reference to University Debates.* 2nd ed. revised. Washington, D.C.: International Reform Bureau, 1908.

Crafts, Wilbur F., Mrs. Wilbur F. Crafts, Mary and Margaret Leitch. *Intoxicants and Opium in All Lands and Times: A Twentieth Century Survey of Intemperance Based on a Symposium of Testimony from One Hundred Missionaries and Travelers.* 10th ed. revised. Washington, D.C.: The International Reform Bureau, 1904.

————. *Intoxicating Drinks and Drugs in All Lands and Times: A Twentieth Century Survey of Intemperance, Based on a Symposium of Testimony from One Hundred Missionaries and Travelers.* 10th ed. revised. Washington, D.C.: The International Reform Bureau, 1909.

Dennett, Tyler. *Americans in Eastern Asia: A Critical Study of the Policy of the United States with Reference to China, Japan and Korea in the 19th Century.* New York: Barnes and Noble, Inc., 1941.

Dennis, James S. *Christian Missions and Social Progress: A Sociological Study of Foreign Missions.* 3 vols. New York: Fleming H. Revell Co., 1898–1906.

Dulles, Foster Rhea. *China and America: The Story of Their Relations Since 1784.* Princeton, N.J.: Princeton University Press, 1946.

Dunn, Wie Tsain. *The Opium Traffic in Its International Aspects.* New York: Columbia University Press, 1920.

Eisenlohr, Louise E. S. *International Narcotics Control.* London: George Allen Unwin, Ltd., 1934.

Eldridge, William B. *Narcotics and the Law: A Critique of the American Experiment in Narcotic Drug Control.* New York: American Bar Foundation, 1962.

Fleming, Denna Frank. *The United States and World Organization, 1920–1933.* New York: Columbia University Press, 1938.

Foreign Policy Association, Committee on Traffic in Opium. *International Control of the Traffic in Opium: Summary of the Opium Conferences Held at Geneva, November, 1924, to February, 1925.* Pamphlet No. 33, series of 1924–1925. New York: Foreign Policy Association, 1925.

Gavit, John P. *Opium.* London: G. Routledge and Sons, Ltd., 1925.

International Anti-Opium Association. *The War Against Opium.* Tientsin: Tientsin Press, Ltd., 1922.

International Reform Bureau. *Patriotic Studies.* Washington, D.C.: International Reform Bureau, 1905.

Kolb, Lawrence, and A. G. Du Mez. *The Prevalence and Trends of Drug Addiction in the United States and the Factors Influencing It.* Treasury Department, U.S. Public Health Service. Washington, D.C.: Government Printing Office, 1924.

La Motte, Ellen N. *The Opium Monopoly.* New York: The Macmillan Co., 1920.

Latourette, Kenneth S. *A History of Christian Missions in China.* New York: The Macmillan Co., 1929.

————. *The History of Early Relations Between the United States and China, 1784–1844.* New Haven, Conn.: Yale University Press, 1917.

Lindesmith, Alfred R. *The Addict and the Law.* Bloomington, Ind.: Indiana University Press, 1965.

MacCallum, Elizabeth. *Twenty Years of Persian Opium (1908–1928).* New York: Foreign Policy Association, 1928.

MacHair, Harley F., and Donald F. Lach. *Modern Far Eastern International Relations.* New York: D. Van Nostrand Co., Inc., 1925.

Malone, Dumas (ed.). *Dictionary of American Biography.* Vols. XVIII–XX. New York: Charles Scribner's Sons, 1935–1936.

May, Herbert L. *Survey of Smoking Opium Conditions in the Far East: A Report to the Executive Board of the Foreign Policy Association (March, 1927).* New York: Foreign Policy Association, 1927.

Merrill, Frederick T. *Japan and the Opium Menace.* New York: International Secretariat, Institute of Pacific Relations and the Foreign Policy Association, 1942.

Millspaugh, Arthur C. *Americans in Persia.* Washington, D.C.: Brookings Institution, 1946.

————. *The American Task in Persia.* New York and London: Century Co., 1925.

Moore, John Bassett. *The Collected Papers of John Bassett Moore.* 7 vols. New Haven, Conn.: Yale University Press, 1944.

Morse, H. M., and J. F. MacNair. *Far Eastern International Relations.* New York: Houghton Mifflin Company, 1931.

Mudhall, Sara G. *Opium, The Demon Flower.* New York: Montrose Publishing Co., 1928.

National Library of Medicine, Reference Division. *Narcotic Addiction: A Selected List of References in English.* Pamphlet in Library of Congress, July 1959.

Neligan, A. R. *The Opium Question, with Special Reference to Persia.* London: John Bale, Sons and Danielsson, Ltd., 1927.

Owen, David E. *British Opium Policy in China and India.* New Haven, Conn.: Yale University Press, 1934.

Reinsch, Paul S. *An American Diplomat in China.* New York: Doubleday, Page and Company, 1922.

Renborg, Bertil A. *International Drug Control: A Study of International Administration By and Through the League of Nations.* Washington, D.C.: Carnegie Endowment for International Peace, 1947.

Schur, Edwin M. *Narcotic Addiction in Britain and America: The Impact of Public Policy.* Bloomington, Ind.: Indiana University Press, 1962.

Solomon, David (ed.). *The Marihuana Papers.* Indianapolis, Ind.: Bobbs-Merrill, 1966.

Stelle, Charles C. *American Trade in Opium to China in the Nineteenth Century.* Chicago: University of Chicago Libraries, 1941.

Varg, Paul A. *Missionaries, Chinese, and Diplomats: The American Protestant *Missionary Movement in China, 1890–1952.* Princeton, N.J.: Princeton University Press, 1958.

Willoughby, Westel W. *Opium as an International Problem: The Geneva Conferences.* Baltimore: The Johns Hopkins Press, 1925.

Wu, Wen-tsao. *The Chinese Opium Question in British Opinion and Action.* New York: Academy Press, 1928.

Zabriskie, Alexander C. *Bishop Brent: Crusader for Christian Unity.* Philadelphia: Westminster Press, 1948.

Articles and periodicals

American Journal of International Law. Supplement, III (July, Oct., 1909), 253–275, 328–336.

Ansley, Norman. "International Efforts to Control Narcotics," *Journal of Criminal Law, Criminology and Police Science,* I (July, Aug., 1959), 105–112.

Baldwin, Elbert F. "The Background of the Opium Conference at the Hague," *American Review of Reviews,* XLV (Feb., 1912), 214–218.

Bent, Silas. "American Beer in China," *Asia,* XIX (June, 1919), 597–598.

Berdahl, Clarence A. "The Relations of the United States with the Assembly of the League of Nations," *American Political Science Review,* XXVI (Feb., 1932), 99–112.

Chiles, Rosa P. "The Passing of the Opium Traffic," *The Forum,* XLVI (July, 1911), 22–39.

"A Chinese Charge Against Japan," *Literary Digest,* LXI (April 12, 1919), 20.

Collins, William J. "Work of the International Opium Conference at the Hague," *Contemporary Review,* CI (March, 1912), 317–327.

"A Conference of Poisons," *The Outlook,* XCII (June 26, 1909), 422, 430.

Cox, Robert W. "The Suppression of Illicit Narcotic Drug Traffic Through International Cooperation," *Notre Dame Lawyer,* XXXVII, No. 1 (1961), 106–116.

Dewey, John. "Our Share in Drugging China," *New Republic,* XXI (December 24, 1919), 114–117.

Drexel, Constance. "Are We Our Brothers' Keepers? How Our Country is Fighting the Drug Evil," *Harper's Magazine,* CXLIX (Nov., 1924), 740.

"The Fight Against Opium," *The Nation,* LXXXIX (July 29, 1909), 92–93.

"Great Britain, America and the China Opium Problem," *Millard's Review of the Far East,* XII (April 17, 1920), 320.

Hodges, Charles. "Legal Aspects of the Far Eastern Drug Trade," *Far Eastern Fortnightly* (Aug. 2, 1920), 1–6.

Hubbard, Ursula P. "The Cooperation of the United States with the League of Nations, 1931–1936," *International Conciliation,* No. 329 (April, 1937).

"The International Opium Commission," *Missionary Review of the World,* XXII (May, 1909), 323.

La Motte, Ellen. "The Americans Wouldn't Compromise," *The Nation,* CXX (May 6, 1925), 511–512.

——. "Limiting Drug Manufacture," *The Nation,* CXXXIV (April 13, 1932), 418–419.

Lee, Paul. "Drug Addiction in America and China," *Zion's Herald* (Feb. 15, 1922), 202–203.

MacFarlane, Peter C. "The White Hope of Drug Victims: An Everyday American Fighter," *Colliers Magazine,* LII (Nov. 29, 1913), 16–17, 29–30.

Masland, John W. "Missionary Influence upon American Far Eastern Policy," *Pacific Historical Review,* X (Sept., 1941), 279–296.

Mathews, Shailer. "Shall We Make the Chinese Drunkards?" *The Independent,* CIV (Nov. 6, 1920), 186.

Merrill, Frederick T. "The Opium Menace in the Far East," *Foreign Policy Reports,* XII (March 1, 1937), 294–304.

Moorhead, Helen H. "International Narcotics Control: 1939–1946," *Foreign Policy Reports,* XXII (July 1, 1946), 94–103.

——. "Iran's Opium Policy," *Foreign Policy Reports,* XXI (May 1, 1945), 40.

——. "The Opium Problem and the League of Nations: An Address . . . Before the Democratic Women's Luncheon Club, Philadelphia, April 27, 1925," *Addresses* 1–48, No. 22, Philadelphia: Democratic Women's Luncheon Club, 1922–1930.

"Opium," *The Outlook,* CVIII (Dec. 23, 1914), 896–897.

"Opium Traffic in the Philippines," *The Outlook,* LXXIV (June 20, 1903), 440–441; (July 25, 1903), 731–732.

"Opium, War on the Traffic," *Missionary Review of the World,* XXVI (Aug., 1903), 620.

"Poisoning the Chinese," *Literary Digest,* LXVIII (Feb. 26, 1921), 30.

"Shall the Opium Traffic Be Revived in China?" *American Review of Reviews,* LVIII (Dec., 1918), 658.

Starks, J. G. "The Convention of 1936 for the Suppression of the Illicit Traffic in Dangerous Drugs," *American Journal of International Law,* XXXI (Jan., 1937), 31–43.

Stelle, Charles C. "American Trade in Opium to China, 1821–1839," *Pacific Historical Review,* X (March, 1941), 57–74.

Stelzle, Charles. "Uprooted in the United States the Brewery Interests Turn to China," *World Outlook,* V (Nov., 1919), 16–17.

Wilder, Amos P. "The Danger of Strong Drink in China," *Missionary Review of the World,* XLII, (July, 1919), 530–531.

Wright, Elizabeth Washburn. "The Injustice to China," *The Outlook,* CXXII (Aug. 20, 1919), 601–602.

——. "The Passing of the Opium Question," *The Outlook,* CVI (Feb. 14, 1914), 365–368.

Wright, Hamilton. "The End of the Opium Question," *American Review of Reviews*, LI (April, 1915), 464–466.

———. "The International Opium Commission," *American Journal of International Law*, III (July, 1909), 649–673; (Oct., 1909), 828–868.

———. "A Recent Deployment of the Latin Americas in Support of a Diplomatic and Humanitarian Policy Initiated by the American Government," *American Journal of International Law*, X (Jan., 1916), 126–130.

———. "Report on the Opium Conference at Shanghai," *Proceedings of the American Society of International Law* (April, 1909), pp. 89–94.

Wright, Quincy. "The Opium Conferences," *American Journal of International Law*, XIX (July, 1925), 348–355.

Newspapers

New York *American*, Feb. 16, 1925.
New York *Herald Tribune*, Oct. 24, 1929.
New York Times, Jan. 19, 23, Feb. 7, 8, 9, 12, 21, Sept. 25, 1925; Feb. 12, 1928; July 9, 10, 11, 12, 1933; Feb. 14, 1952.

Unpublished material

Fernitz, Henrietta Harriet. "American Participation in International Narcotic Drug Control." Unpublished Ph.D. dissertation, Northwestern University, 1943.

Stelle, Charles C. "Americans and the China Opium Trade in the Nineteenth Century." Unpublished Ph.D. dissertation, University of Chicago, 1938.

U. S. Library of Congress. "List of References on the Drug Habit and Traffic." Mimeographed pamphlet in Library of Congress, May 1, 1926.

Index

71
72
74
75
76
77
79
81
83
85
88